RACHEL CARSON

SUNY series in Environmental Philosophy and Ethics
J. Baird Callicott and John van Buren, editors

Rachel Carson

Legacy and Challenge

Edited by
Lisa H. Sideris
and
Kathleen Dean Moore

STATE UNIVERSITY OF NEW YORK PRESS

Published by
State University of New York Press, Albany

For information, contact State University of New York Press, Albany, NY
www.sunypress.edu

Production by Marilyn P. Semerad
Marketing by Susan M. Petrie

Library of Congress Cataloging-in-Publication Data

Rachel Carson : legacy and challenge / edited by Lisa H. Sideris and
Kathleen Deen Moore
    p. cm. — (SUNY series in environmental philosophy and ethics)
    Includes bibliographical references and index.
    ISBN 978-0-7914-7471-6 (hardcover : alk. paper)
    ISBN 978-0-7914-7472-3 pbk. : alk. paper)
    1. Carson, Rachel, 1907–1964. 2. Environmental ethics. 3. Pesticides—
Environmental aspects. I. Sideris, Lisa H. II. Moore, Kathleen Dean.

QH31.C33R33 2008
179'.1—dc22

20077037536

10 9 8 7 6 5 4 3 2 1

Contents

Acknowledgments vii

Introduction
 Lisa H. Sideris and Kathleen Dean Moore 1

Part I: A Legacy of Activism and Advocacy

1. One Patriot
 Terry Tempest Williams 16

2. Rachel Carson's Scientific and Ocean Legacies
 Jane Lubchenco 29

3. Rachel Carson and George J. Wallace: Why Public
Environmental Scientists Should Be Advocates for Nature
 Peter C. List 41

Part II: Ethics on Land and at Sea

4. Rachel Carson's Environmental Ethics
 Philip Cafaro 60

5. Thinking Like a Mackerel: Rachel Carson's *Under the Sea-Wind*
as a Source for a Trans-Ecotonal Sea Ethic
 Susan Power Bratton 79

6. The Conceptual Foundations of Rachel Carson's Sea Ethic
 J. Baird Callicott and Elyssa Back 94

7. Rachel Carson's *The Sea Around Us*, Ocean-Centrism, and a
Nascent Ocean Ethic
 Gary Kroll 118

Part III: Reflections on Gender and Science

8. The Ecological Body: Rachel Carson, *Silent Spring*, and Breast Cancer
 Lisa H. Sideris 136

9. Science and Spirit: Struggles of the Early Rachel Carson
 Maril Hazlett 149

10. "Silence, Miss Carson!": Science, Gender, and the
Reception of *Silent Spring*
 Michael Smith 168

Part IV: An Ongoing Toxic Discourse

11. After *Silent Spring*: Ecological Effects of Pesticides
    on Public Health and on Birds and Other Organisms
    David Pimentel   190

12. Contested Icons: Rachel Carson and DDT
    Steve Maguire   194

13. In Her Footsteps
    Christopher Merrill   215

14. Living Downstream of *Silent Spring*
    Sandra Steingraber   220

Part V: A Legacy of Wonder

15. The Secular and Religious Sources of Rachel Carson's
    Sense of Wonder
    Lisa H. Sideris   232

16. How to Value a Flower: Locating Beauty in Toxic Landscapes
    Vera Norwood   251

17. The Truth of the Barnacles: Rachel Carson
    and the Moral Significance of Wonder
    Kathleen Dean Moore   267

Contributors   281

Index   283

Acknowledgments

We are extremely grateful to several individuals and publishers for permission to reprint excerpts from Rachel Carson's writings. The details of these permissions are as follows:

- Excerpts from *Silent Spring* by Rachel Carson. Copyright © 1962 by Rachel L. Carson, renewed 1990 by Roger Christie. Reprinted by permission of Houghton Mifflin Company. All rights reserved. Reprinted by permission of Frances Collin, Trustee.

- Excerpts from *Under the Sea-Wind* by Rachel Carson, illustrated by Bob Hines, copyright 1941 by Rachel L. Carson. Copyright renewed © 1969 by Roger Christie. Illustrations copyright © 1991 by Bob Hines. A Truman Talley Book. Used by permission of Dutton, a division of Penguin Group (USA) Inc. Reprinted by permission of Frances Collin, Trustee.

- Excerpts from *The Sea Around Us* by Rachel Carson. Copyright © 1950 by Rachel L. Carson. Reproduced by permission of Pollinger Limited and the proprietor. Reprinted by permission of Frances Collin, Trustee.

- Excerpts from *The Edge of the Sea* by Rachel Carson. Copyright © 1955 by Rachel L. Carson, renewed 1983 by Roger Christie. Reprinted by permission of Houghton Mifflin Company. All rights reserved. Reprinted by permission of Frances Collin, Trustee.

- Excerpts from *The House of Life: Rachel Carson at Work* by Paul Brooks. Copyright © 1972 by Paul Brooks. Reprinted by permission of Frances Collin, Trustee.

- Excerpts from *Always, Rachel: The Letters of Rachel Carson and Dorothy Freeman, 1952–1964.* Copyright © 1995 by Roger Allen Christie. Reprinted by permission of Frances Collin, Trustee.

- Excerpts from *Rachel Carson: Witness for Nature* by Linda Lear. Copyright © 1997 by Linda Lear. Reprinted by permission of Frances Collin, Trustee.

- Excerpts from *Lost Woods: The Discovered Writing of Rachel Carson*. Copyright © 1998 by Roger Allen Christie. Reprinted by permission of Frances Collin, Trustee.

- Excerpts from *The Sense of Wonder* by Rachel Carson. Copyright © 1956 by Rachel L. Carson. Reprinted by permission of Frances Collin, Trustee.

- Excerpts from the unpublished Rachel Carson material. Copyright © 2007 by Roger A. Christie. Reprinted by permission of Frances Collin, Trustee.

- Excerpts from "The Silent Spring of Rachel Carson," CBS Reports, April 3, 1963, telecast. Used by permission of Frances Collin, Trustee.

We wish to extend our gratitude to the following individuals and publishers to reprint previously published essays in this volume. The essays and copyright holders are as follows:

- "One Patriot," by Terry Tempest Williams, originally appeared in *Patriotism and the American Land* by The Orion Society, 2002. Copyright © 2002 by Terry Tempest Williams. It is reprinted by permission of Brandt and Hochman Literary Agents, Inc.

- "Rachel Carson's Environmental Ethics," by Philip Cafaro, originally appeared in *Worldviews*, volume 6, number 1 (2002): 58–80. It is reproduced here, in slightly edited form, with permission of Brill Academic Publishers.

- "Thinking Like a Mackerel: Rachel Carson's *Under the Sea-Wind* as a Source for a Trans-Ecotonal Sea Ethic," by Susan Power Bratton, originally appeared in *Ethics & the Environment*, volume 9, number 1 (2004): 1-22. It is reproduced here, in slightly edited form, with permission of Indiana University Press.

- "The Ecological Body: Rachel Carson, *Silent Spring*, and Breast Cancer," by Lisa H. Sideris, originally appeared in *Soundings: An Interdisciplinary Journal*, volume 85, numbers 1–2 (2002): 107-20. It is reproduced here with permission of *Soundings*.

- "'Silence, Miss Carson!': Science, Gender, and the Reception of *Silent Spring*," by Michael Smith, was originally published in *Feminist Studies*, volume 27, number 3 (Fall 2001): 733–52. It is reproduced here by permission of the publisher, *Feminist Studies*, Inc.

- "The Truth of the Barnacles: Rachel Carson and the Moral Significance of Wonder," by Kathleen Dean Moore, originally appeared in *Environmental Ethics*, volume 27, number 3 (Fall 2005): 265-77. It is reproduced here with permission of Kathleen Dean Moore.

The present volume owes its existence to the hard work and dedication of many individuals over the course of several years. We are very happy to thank our contributors for their hard work and commitment to this project. Needless to say, without their efforts, this volume would not exist. We both wish to express our gratitude to Jane Bunker at SUNY Press for her willingness to take on this challenging and somewhat cumbersome project, and to J. Baird Callicott for recommending Jane and SUNY to us, at a point when the project seemed in danger of foundering. We are grateful for feedback we received on an earlier draft of the manuscript from reviewers at SUNY, as well as comments and advice from Boyd Zenner and two anonymous reviewers for the University of Virginia Press, at an even earlier stage in this process. We also thank Courtney Campbell at Oregon State University who helped to organize a lecture series on Rachel Carson that was the original inspiration for some of these pieces, and for the idea of a volume on Carson. Lisa and Kathy both owe an enormous debt of gratitude to Lisa's husband, Robert Crouch, for his meticulous editorial skills. It is an understatement to say that without Robert's (impossibly cheerful) assistance in requesting permissions, proofreading and formatting text and notes, and his attention to many other important details, this project would never have been completed.

We dedicate this book to all future generations, but most especially to two very dear little ones whose arrival in this world coincided with the book's completion: Lisa's son Ridley, and Kathy's granddaughter Zoey.

Introduction

Lisa H. Sideris
and Kathleen Dean Moore

LEGACY

Rachel Carson has been credited with founding the modern environmental movement. *Silent Spring*, published in 1962, provoked a public outcry against the dangers of indiscriminate pesticide use and chemical toxins in the environment. The book was a catalyst for the creation of extensive environmental legislation of air and water pollution and endangered species, and led to public interest in environmental issues that culminated in the first Earth Day in 1970. Carson identified and attempted to bridge what she saw as dangerous gaps in communication between scientists and laypeople, corporations and citizens; she cleverly drew on a discourse of citizens' rights and government and corporate responsibility that still resonates strongly with American ideals and sensibilities. She has inspired generations of environmental activists and animal rights and welfare advocates. Her private battle with breast cancer, one she lost less than two years after the publication of *Silent Spring*, has made her an icon of women's health movements and others seeking to draw attention to the links between cancer and the environment.

It is difficult to overestimate the importance of *Silent Spring* in shaping our environmental consciousness. Yet, as profound as that impact was and is, *Silent Spring* is only one part of Rachel Carson's legacy. Carson produced three major and highly acclaimed works of nature writing prior to *Silent Spring*. These three books, *Under the Sea-Wind* (1941), *The Sea Around Us* (1950) and *The Edge of the Sea* (1955), established Carson as one of America's most admired and respected science writers long before she became embroiled in the pesticide controversy. Her final work, *The Sense of Wonder*, was published posthumously, though Carson had considered writing such a book at least a decade earlier. A small, beautifully illustrated work intended to help parents teach their children about the natural world, *The Sense of Wonder* reflected Carson's conviction that instilling knowledge and enchantment of nature in young children is as fundamental as instruction in reading and writing.

In the twenty-first century, as debate still rages over the risks and benefits of DDT as an antimalarial agent; as calls for environmental justice are heard in cities worldwide; as populations of marine organisms decline, fisheries collapse, and toxic wastes wash up on our shores, Rachel Carson's work appears remarkably relevant and even prescient. Yet, Carson did not set out to be an "environmentalist" or an "environmental writer" in the modern sense. *Silent Spring*, with its detailed documentation of the dangers of pesticides and explicit warnings against their indiscriminate use, was in many ways a departure from the genre of writing Carson knew and loved best. Carson was first and foremost a nature writer, someone with an extraordinary gift for translation and an ability to evoke in rich detail the fluid boundaries, the tastes and sounds, the pains and pleasures, of the world as experienced by nonhuman forms of life.

Carson believed that protection of the environment would flow automatically from knowledge and appreciation of nature's ancient rhythms and intricate functioning. She resorted to direct arguments for nature protection somewhat reluctantly, when the signs of an impending environmental crisis made it necessary. As she once remarked, science gave her "something to write about;"[1] and later, the pesticide issue would give her a clear imperative. But her first and most enduring love was literature. As several of the pieces in this volume illustrate, Carson's style as a writer was something she deliberately and painstakingly developed and honed from early childhood. Just as she was deeply influenced by a pantheon of authors and poets whom she admired and often consciously emulated, countless writers today look to Carson's work for clues to perfecting their own craft.

Carson had faith in that often-elusive audience of "general readers," average people with innate curiosity about the things they see every day and the things they will never see. An overarching concern, apparent in much of her writing as a whole, was the danger of fragmentation and compartmentalization of knowledge—the gaps between experts and average citizens, but also those among specialists from different disciplines. Carson envisioned cooperative endeavors among specialists from diverse disciplines "all pouring their knowledge and their creative inspirations" into responses to environmental problems.[2] When the various branches of knowledge are cut off from one another, they lose their vitality and cease to grow. This theme is most explicit in *Silent Spring*, where Carson laments the fragmentation of knowledge that attends life in "an era of specialists,"[3] but it runs through much of her work.

Carson did not oppose specialization per se but only the narrowed vision, the inordinate confidence in one's perceptions that sometimes comes with focusing on a small part of the picture for too long. Throughout her writing, over and over again, she presents us with another option to narrowed or fragmented perception. Attempting to convey an almost ineffable sense of these more wholesome and holistic alternatives, she draws upon a set of recurring phrases and metaphors that are familiar to readers of Rachel Carson—an expanded vision; the real world around us; nature as a vast "web" or "stream" of life; the "other road" that beckons us away from destruction. She offers these in the spirit of an invitation, and always with a promise that if we look at the world and our place in it through a different lens, we will be richly rewarded, deeply humbled, and forever changed.

Carson worried about the damage that occurs to nature, and to the human spirit, when experts from different fields of study fail to communicate with one another or, when they try to communicate, find they have no terms in common. Carson hoped that if humans could first come to terms with nature as the shared reality and source of all life, the discovery of a common language, a shared conversation, would follow. Once fully grasped, nature's interconnectedness and integrity would be reflected in the creative connections forged among different areas of knowledge. Rachel Carson's work remains a wellspring of environmental thought, as well as a source of inspiration for interdisciplinary endeavors more generally.

CHALLENGE

In collecting the chapters for this book, we have been guided in part by Rachel Carson's own decisions as a thinker and writer. Sharing her concerns about the effects of compartmentalized vision on understanding, sharing her enthusiasm for the confluences where various currents of knowledge come together, we have gathered essays about Carson from a variety of genres and disciplines. As Carson was a scientist who wrote like a poet, we have chosen to include material ranging from scientific reports to personal narrative. As Carson drew inspiration from many disciplines and traditions, we have chosen pieces from a poet, an ecologist, a philosopher, an entomologist, a historian, a writer, and many others whose work informs our understanding of the whole person who was Rachel Carson, the whole of her work, the wholeness of her view of the earth.

Rachel Carson played many roles in her too-short life, many of them difficult. She was an activist before there was a concept of environmental activism. She was an ethicist, although it took other ethicists a long time to admit her to the club. She was a woman at a time when science and public affairs were dominated by men. She was a scientist who, as she was dying of cancer, warned against the indiscriminate use of pesticides, one of the great "scientific advancements" of her time. In the end, she was a human being, standing at the edge of the sea in wondering gratitude for the world's beauty and mystery. The chapters in this book have been chosen and arranged to honor the fullness of Carson's life work. Each of Carson's roles is explored in turn in each of the five parts of the book: "A Legacy of Activism and Advocacy," "Ethics on Land and at Sea," "Reflections on Gender and Science," "An Ongoing Toxic Discourse," and "A Legacy of Wonder."

In her work, Rachel Carson issues a practical and moral challenge to her readers to find a way to live on earth with care and respect, acknowledging the complex interconnectedness of all life, and taking responsibility for the well-being of the natural systems that sustain us. Perhaps even more than in Carson's time, our generation faces ecological challenges that require our best thinking and writing and our deepest moral resolve. Part I, "A Legacy of Activism and Advocacy," brings together the voices of Jane Lubchenco, a marine ecologist; Peter List, an environmental philosopher; and Terry Tempest Williams, an activist and essayist. All of these authors probe their discipline and conscience for answers to this critical question: What can we learn from Rachel Carson about the responsibility of citizens, and especially scientists, to speak out to prevent damage to the natural systems upon which our lives depend?

In a democracy, where policies ideally serve the commonweal and rest on shared values, citizen activism and scientific advocacy have a complex role to play. Williams calls Rachel Carson a "true patriot," explaining that her life's work links democratic and ecological principles by holding government and corporations accountable for the well-being of communities, both cultural and wild. Because human well-being depends on thriving ecosystems and ecosystem services, *Silent Spring*'s ecological arguments are also a declaration of human rights.

Inspired by Rachel Carson's chronicle of the connections between environmental changes and human well-being, Lubchenco calls for better stewardship of the oceans through marine reserves managed as a public trust—for the common good and in perpetuity. She calls on scientists to "renew their social contract," by taking responsibility for communicating their findings to the public and to policy makers. Government and agency scientists have a particularly important, though profoundly contested, role in managing resources for the common good. List navigates through the government scientist's competing duties to the profession, the public, and the natural world, pointing out that scientists often have not only the right, but the duty, to speak up. This duty is based on their "implicit contract" with society to use their knowledge for the public good. Rachel Carson is a "towering example within American democracy," Williams writes, "of how one person's voice can make an extraordinary difference."

But what is the relation between scientific facts and social action? How can information create change? Logical positivism has left us a legacy that divides facts from values, List argues—the first supposedly the provenance of scientists, the second the provenance of policy makers. But the relationship is far more complicated: Carson is, he says, a "paradigm case of a scientist who became a compelling champion of environmental conservation." With *Silent*

Spring, Carson moved beyond sharing her love of nature, Lubchenco agrees, and became passionately determined to save what she loved.

But the communication of information doesn't always lead to change, or if it does, the process can be excruciatingly, dangerously, sometimes disastrously slow. As Lubchenco notes, scientists often aren't trained to communicate effectively. And as List points out, the powerful communication machinery of government and industry can create a deafening noise. The genius of Rachel Carson's activism was to tell a scientific story so powerfully, and impart a moral lesson so compellingly, that people felt moved to action. Williams calls attention to "a conscientious and directed soul who believed in the eloquence of facts...Rachel Carson did not turn her back on the ongoing chronicle of the natural history of the dead. She bore witness." And because she loved language as much as landscape, Williams argues, her readers respond with both hearts and minds, with the full power of the human imagination to envision a better way of living on earth.

Yet, for many years, environmental ethicists and philosophers largely ignored Rachel Carson's writing as a source of ethical thought. While reflecting on why this might be so, the authors whose pieces appear in the next section, "Ethics on Land and at Sea," help to correct this mistake. They explore the nature and ramifications of Carson's environmental ethic, especially the beginnings of an ocean ethic that can be found in her work prior to *Silent Spring*. Although they approach her work from a variety of angles, these authors converge on respect for Carson as an environmental ethicist.

The chapter by Philip Cafaro represents one of the first treatments of Carson as an environmental ethicist. Cafaro argues that Carson eschewed sustained treatment of metaethical reflection—use of formal principles or foundations for ethics—in favor of appeals to common sense and common values. Carson saw no tension between a human-centered ethic concerned with public health issues and a nonanthropocentric ethic that granted moral considerability to other life forms regardless of value or utility to humans. Although Carson embraced Albert Schweitzer's reverence for life, there was no overtly religious or spiritual dimension to her environmental ethic, Cafaro argues (a claim challenged by Lisa Sideris' piece in the final section of the volume). Cafaro concludes that Carson's work points the way toward a number of ethical insights and developments, whether or not *Silent Spring* presents us with a formal framework of the sort philosophers often seek.

Susan Power Bratton identifies what she calls a trans-ecotonal or transboundary ethic in Carson's sea writing. Comparing Carson's sea ethic to conservationist Aldo Leopold's land ethic, Bratton concludes that Carson did not understand humans as members of the sea community in the way that Leopold described humans as "citizens" of the biotic (land) community. Rather, Carson allowed her readers to cross the boundary between the familiar human terrestrial world and the world of the sea through the power of imagination. As humans, we are not and cannot be fully integrated with the sea. Nonetheless, Carson's writing presents this world to us from the perspective of the sea creatures themselves, in contrast to Leopold's account of terrestrial communities, which retains a human perspective. By such means, Carson invites readers to extend their perceptions and foster a sense of identity with sea creatures, even without the sense of *place* central to an ethic such as Leopold's. A harsh Darwinian struggle prevails in Carson's ocean world, unlike the relative harmony of the land community, Bratton argues.

J. Baird Callicott and Elyssa Back further pursue the question of whether Carson's sea writing contains an ethic of the sort that philosophers have located in Leopold's *Sand County Almanac*. They agree with Cafaro that Carson is simultaneously concerned with biocentric and human values and that her work has been strangely overlooked by environmental philosophers. Callicott and Back return to the question Cafaro raises of whether there are foundational ethical principles in Carson's work. Like Bratton, they compare and contrast Carson's sea ethic to the land ethic of Leopold. They conclude that while both writers drew on a Darwinian worldview, Carson largely embraced the competitive, predatory Darwinism of the *Origin of Species*, while Leopold constructed his arguments, at least implicitly, upon the more cooperative and community-oriented Darwinism of the *Descent of Man*. Cooperation, they note, is more evident in terrestrial life than in aquatic communities, and the sea organisms in Carson's writing are portrayed as solitary and not "affectionally bonded." They perceive Carson's sea ethic as postmodern in its celebration of otherness and difference, rather than sameness, as the basis for moral considerability. While it is true that this emphasis on difference and diversity also creates a different sense of "place" than Leopold's biotic community, one still finds an emergent, holistic harmony in Carson's sea world.

Gary Kroll acknowledges that it is tempting to read Carson's sea writing, particularly *The Sea Around Us*, "backward" through the lens of *Silent Spring*, but contends that it would be a mistake to assume a similar ethic connects these works. Rather, Kroll identifies a form of "ocean-centrism" in Carson's *The Sea Around Us*, typical in some respects of much of postwar sea writing. Carson portrays the ocean as vast, indomitable, and omnipotent. Humans, by contrast, are depicted as small and somewhat insignificant, as unable to control and master the ocean's power and to harness it for our own ends. This contrasts sharply with Carson's later vision of humans in *Silent Spring* as wielding God-like (albeit arrogant and shortsighted) power over the natural world.

However, Kroll points out, a chapter Carson ultimately deleted from *The Sea Around Us* before it went to print offers some clues to Carson's growing concerns about the ocean's resiliency and the possibility of humans plundering the seas as they have plundered and polluted the land. Kroll speculates that Carson may have chosen to leave out this chapter, which discussed the ways in which a "hungry world" might gain food security by harnessing marine resources, for fear of encouraging overfishing and other destructive uses of the sea. Thus Carson's sea ethic is perhaps most apparent not in what she wrote in *The Sea Around Us* but in what she chose to omit.

Carson's writing must be understood in the context of the Cold War and the positivism toward science and technology it fostered, but it would be naive to overlook the gender politics of the era in which she was writing. The gender-inflected criticism of Rachel Carson after *Silent Spring* (the portrayals of her as a "hysterical woman," usually pictured birdwatching or surrounded by children; the criticisms of "sentimental" appeals and "high-pitched sequences of anxieties") has by now become legendary. What to make of it is still contested.

In broad strokes, the usual story of gender and science in Rachel Carson's work goes like this: Carson introduced readers to an organic view of the world in which all life is deeply interconnected, humans—and particularly human children—sit squarely within that web of natural connections, and science and industry are well advised to adopt an attitude of humility and precaution in the face of humankind's terrible power to disrupt the systems on which their lives depend. This is a feminine view of the world, the usual story goes, and when Carson adopted it, she set herself squarely against the entrenched, masculinist, view of the world: The world is a machine, often a machine arrayed against human interests, and the role of humans is as adversary and conqueror, apart and superior to the natural world, which it has the power, through objective science, to control.

No wonder the chemical industry and scientists regarded her as a danger. Not only did she threaten the freewheeling chemical industry and the scientific establishment allied with it, but she threatened to usher in a paradigm shift that would undermine their very base of political and economic power. Those who believed that nature unrestrained threatened humankind found themselves battling also a woman unrestrained and threatening.

Each of the chapters in the section "Reflections on Gender and Science" complicates this story line and by that means enriches the discussion of the meaning of gender and science in Carson's work and the responses to it. Lisa Sideris argues that Carson found a middle ground between an ecological, organic model of science that views the world as subject rather than object, and the "objectifying, manipulative, and disengaged kind of knowledge" criticized by feminists. For Carson as a scientist, controlling and caring for the environment were not mutually exclusive imperatives, and in fact Carson did not call for abandoning the effort to control insect pests, but for an open, dispassionate, fully informed discussion of the best way to do so. As she was writing *Silent Spring*, Carson's thinking about the natural environment was influenced by her reflections on the inner ecology of the human body—particularly the body as it battles cancer. All the more poignant, then, is the struggle Carson waged against silence—the silence of a spring without birdsong, the attempted silencing by her critics, and the lethal silence of her doctor who did not disclose the progress of cancer in Carson's own body.

Maril Hazlett agrees with Sideris that *Silent Spring* signaled a new synthesis in Carson's understanding of nature and the human body. As Carson incorporated the human body into "ecology," she also began to resolve a long-standing tension between two distinct narrative voices with which she had experimented in her major works on the sea: the "heavily masculine" voice of the scientist who coolly organizes, interprets, and summarizes reams of information, and the more feminine voice of the "appreciative nature writer," the close observer and participant, expressing wonder and enchantment with nature's mysteries. As her writing evolved, Carson struggled to make sense of her own dual perspective, sometimes subordinating the feminine voice to the masculine one. Hazlett argues that Carson eventually found resolution in grounding her writing in a new sense of the environment. The pesticide issue forced Carson to abandon her view of humans as relatively insignificant compared with nature, unable to dominate and control its forces. With *Silent Spring*, Carson understood humans as inextricably part of nature, yet capable of destroying it as no other life form could. As she confronted the new reality of human-induced destruction of the environment, this "shift in content and focus changed her writing voice as well."

That shift in Carson's writing voice—the merging of the scientist and the unapologetic nature devotee—provoked a fierce backlash. The balanced voice of reason and emotion that Carson sought to present in *Silent Spring* was heard by many of her male critics as a hysterical rant. Michael Smith examines how and why critics took such strong measures to silence Rachel Carson, including the "extraordinary" use of gendered language to discredit her. In contrast to Sideris, Smith more closely allies Carson with the "organic" view of nature, later articulated by Carolyn Merchant and championed by ecofeminists, as a "living, feminine organism requiring a special kind of stewardship." He places this view in contrast to male scientists' views of nature as "an unpredictable harridan in need of constraint and mastery." The contest between Carson and her detractors took on all the color and urgency of the contest between the ideas of the balance of nature and the dominance of nature, and the struggle for who would control the power to shape society through scientific authority. Just as her work augured a different relationship between men and women, it pointed toward a radically different relationship between humankind and the natural world.

How are we to construe that relationship today, nearly half a century after Carson wrote? Like other well-known conservationists such as Aldo Leopold, Carson came to see humans as part of an interdependent community. We are not isolated and alone. Our lives, like the lives of all animals, are braided into the complex interactions of water, chemicals, and time. The poisons we scatter on suburban lawns, soak onto fruit, spray over neighborhoods and fields are not isolated to a particular place, particular effect, particular time. They reach through the natural ecosystem, affecting not just the "target species," but humans and the animals in which we rejoice and the habitats on which our lives depend. Their effects reach not only across the land, but through time into future generations; toxins flow into eggs, through amniotic fluid and breast milk, into the tissues of developing children and the young of other species. The interdependence of life links us inextricably to the death-dealing effects of toxins.

What are the moral and policy consequences of these facts? Do humans and other animals have the right to be protected from commercial poisons introduced into the landscape for economic gain? How are those rights weighed against the putative rights of corporations to maximize profits, or the rights of children to be safe from diseases like malaria that could be prevented by insecticide spraying? What of the well-being of future generations—how does that count against current needs? Should we design policies that take precautions against possible harms or provide recompense once the harms have occurred?

This is the legacy of Rachel Carson: an understanding, in the heart and the mind, that pesticides are at the center of a web of entangling consequences that affect entire ecosystems, now and in the future. This is her challenge: Can humans find ways to contain "the devils of their own creation?"[4] Can we find the practical solutions, the reverence for life, and the moral and political resolve that will prevent us from making the world toxic to our children? In the fourth part, "An Ongoing Toxic Discourse," authors from very different backgrounds address Carson's responses to these questions.

David Pimentel begins with a deeply discouraging statistic: Since the publication of *Silent Spring*, "pesticide use has increased ten-fold to about one billion pounds annually," and "the toxicity of pesticides has increased ten to twenty times." More than 99 percent of pesticides miss their target, with unintended, sometimes unknown, and often harmful or deadly consequences to ecological (including human) systems. If Carson were today to write a sequel to *Silent Spring*, it could begin with the same grim story and end with the same urgent warning to use pesticides sparingly and with concern for "the integrity of the natural world that supports all life."[5]

One of the factors that complicates our efforts to follow Carson's advice is that DDT has become a highly charged and strongly contested icon, as has Rachel Carson herself. DDT, a war hero that saved American soldiers from malaria, leads the charge in the war of man against nature, protecting children from disease-carrying insects. Or DDT, the invisible agent of silence and death, insinuates itself into the aeries of spring and the wombs of women from the ice fields to the jungles. Steve Maguire tracks the contest to create the meaning of DDT and to revise the meaning of Rachel Carson, contests that may be seen as skirmishes in a larger battle to control the meaning of humanity vis-à-vis nature.

One of the factors that makes DDT such a potent icon, Maguire argues, is that it impacts the very symbols of ongoing life—the fragile egg, the child in the womb, milk in a mother's breast. These symbols become real and meaningful to Christopher Merrill, who writes of walking the beaches of Rachel Carson's island, carrying his newborn child on his chest while his daughter dances along beside him. It is a parent's love for his children, his felt obligations for their well-being, that is so deeply at odds with the barrel of toxic waste that washes up on the shore. The image of a man on a poisoned shore, watching his wife nurse their baby, the mother's body curved around his child, brings urgency to Carson's challenge to find a way to reduce pesticide use.

Sandra Steingraber, an ecologist, mother, and author of environmental literature, took up Carson's challenge in her own books, *Living Downstream* and *Having Faith*. There, she relates stories of her own diagnosis with cancer, her pregnancy, and her daughter's birth, even as she tracks the invasion of pesticides and other industrial toxins into the human body and chronicles the possible effects. Here Steingraber reflects on the parallels between her life and Rachel Carson's, as a cancer patient and biologist investigating the links between chemical toxins in the environment and human health. As a kind of postscript to her two books, Steingraber concedes in her piece that knowledge of our current, decades-old pesticide problems does not necessarily generate outrage and action among all readers; many respond with depression and despair. Her piece ends with a deeply hopeful challenge to readers, detailing "exactly how we are going to divorce our economy from its current dependency on cancer-causing chemicals."

Carson understood the importance of maintaining hope for the future, even while facing squarely the present threats to humans and other life forms. Her own sense of hope and happiness was sustained by exploration and celebration of the natural world, habits engrained in her as a child. But she knew that physical and biological descriptions of nature did not tell the whole story. As she stood at the edge of the dark mystery of the sea or at the dark limits of her own life, as she felt the comfort of the repeated seasons and rejoiced at returning life each spring, Carson felt also that the natural world held a deep spiritual significance. "Underlying the beauty of the spectacle there is meaning and significance," she wrote. "It is the elusiveness of that meaning that haunts us, that sends us again and again into the natural world where the key to the riddle is hidden."[6]

What religious, aesthetic, or moral meanings did Carson find in nature? What are the sources of Rachel Carson's sense of spiritual connection to the natural world? How is a scientist's spirituality expressed in her sense of wonder? What is the moral significance of a sense of wonder? In the final part, "A Legacy of Wonder," Lisa Sideris, Vera Norwood, and Kathleen Dean Moore explore the sense of wonder that was so central to Carson's own spirituality and so much a part of the legacy she wished to impart to future generations.

Carson's story, Sideris argues, provides clues to the theological, literary, and moral influences that shaped her spirituality. Carson was raised in the Presbyterian church, which was steeped in a Calvinism that had mixed views about natural science. Calvinism held that the scientific study of nature could lead to arrogance and pride, a reckless narrowing of vision that hides both reality and mystery. But science could also be a means of glorifying divine creation, a study that promotes reverence, humility, and an expansive vision of a world that was made neither by us nor entirely for us. Although Carson did not often attend church as an adult, her last works evoke her theological legacy: *Silent Spring* decries narrow, prideful, arrogant science; *The Sense of Wonder* celebrates the joy of understanding what can be known and reverence in the face of ultimate mystery.

As a child, Carson was well versed in literature of the nature-study movement. These stories were designed, Sideris points out, to nurture a love of the common things in direct experience of the natural world—not dry facts, but sea anemones blooming underwater and crickets singing at night. As children smell, see, touch, even taste the living world, a sense of wonder will grow in them, as will the moral imagination that allows them to experience the world from the point of view of an organism other than themselves. How exquisitely Carson developed this ethos in the close, loving observation in her sea books and the moral fire in *Silent Spring*. No wonder then, that Carson embraced Albert Schweitzer's ethic of "a true reverence for life" and the "impulse to action" that true reverence requires.

If a true reverence for life—awe, wonder, and indeed love for the natural world—creates the impulse to act in its protection, then what is sometimes called a sentimental or romantic relation to the natural world is significantly related to the hard political work of achieving environmental justice. In fact, Vera Norwood tracks Carson's love for flowers in order to make this argument. It is not an accident that the person who wrote of her deep happiness in the "loveliness that is in nature,"[7] who explored tide pools to find hydroids blooming like flowers in the bitter sea, is the same person who began the environmental movement, launching a powerful blast against the "progress of science and industry" and empowering all people to defend their right to healthy air and water.

Carson's life demonstrated that a deep emotional, aesthetic, and moral appreciation of nature is essentially connected to the fight for social and environmental justice. She wrote, "a world that is no longer fit for wild plants, that is no longer graced by the flight of birds, a world whose streams and forests are empty and lifeless is not likely to be a fit habitat for man himself, for these things are symptoms of an ailing world."[8]

For just this reason, Moore argues, a sense of wonder has profound moral significance. Rachel Carson's essay version of *The Sense of Wonder* ("Help Your Child to Wonder") appeared between the publication of *The Edge of the Sea*, a scientific exploration of the intricately interdependent lives in the land and sea, and the publication of *Silent Spring*, a moral plea for their protection. Moore argues that a sense of wonder bridges the world of fact and the world of value, closing the distance between "this is wonderful" and "this must remain." A sense of wonder is an antidote to the view that the elements of the natural world are commodities to be disdained or destroyed. Rachel Carson's life work shows us how a sense of wonder can be a virtue, perhaps a keystone virtue in our time of reckless destruction, a source of decency, hope, and restraint.

Our hope is that the chapters in this volume testify to the enormous influence of Rachel Carson's work and the many facets of Rachel Carson as a person. We honor and affirm Carson's belief that science and poetry, facts and values, academics and advocacy can, and in some cases must, go hand in hand. And just as Carson wrote for the general reader and found that her words drew the attention of specialists as well, our hope is that this volume will inspire and inform a variety of individuals—students and scholars, activists and ethicists, women and men, cancer patients and chemists, creative writers and all among us who wonder at nature. In a world changed by human hands in ways more dramatic than Carson could have fully imagined, where—despite Carson's warnings—humans are unsettling and may be destroying the habitats upon which their lives depend, Carson's vision and her example call us to reflect on our own vision of how humans might live on earth with appreciation and good care.

NOTES

1. Rachel Carson, "The Real World Around Us," in Rachel Carson, *Lost Woods: The Discovered Writing of Rachel Carson*, ed. Linda Lear (Boston: Beacon Press, 1998), 149.

2. Rachel Carson, *Silent Spring* (Boston: Houghton Mifflin, 1994 [1962]), 278.

3. Ibid., 13.

4. Albert Schweitzer as quoted in ibid., 6.

5. Ibid., 13.

6. Rachel Carson, *The Edge of the Sea* (Boston: Mariner Books, 1998 [1955]), 7.

7. Rachel Carson to Dorothy Freeman, Letter, Jan. 23, 1962, in Rachel Carson, *Always, Rachel: The Letters of Rachel Carson and Dorothy Freeman, 1952–1964*, ed. Martha Freeman (Boston: Beacon Press, 1995), 394.

8. Rachel Carson, "A Sense of Values in Today's World," Speech, New England Wildflower Preservation Society, Jan. 17, 1963, Rachel Carson Papers, Beinecke Library, Yale University. As quoted in Linda Lear, *Rachel Carson: Witness for Nature* (New York: Henry Holt, 1997), 440–41.

Part I

A Legacy of Activism
and Advocacy

1

One Patriot

Terry Tempest Williams

Not long ago, my father, a friend, and I were having tea around our kitchen table. We were discussing politics. The conversation circled back to September 11, 2001.

"I hesitate to say this," our friend said. "But when I watched the Twin Towers collapse and realized thousands of lives were collapsing with them—" She paused to find the right words. "It just didn't seem real. I couldn't believe it. And then seeing the hole in the side of the Pentagon and hearing about more lives lost in Pennsylvania, well, it all felt like I was watching some horrific movie. But afterwards in the privacy of my own fears, I realized, living here in the West, what would truly shatter my world would be if the terrorists bombed the Tetons or the Grand Canyon...."

"Nobody could bomb the Tetons," my father said, interrupting her. "That's ridiculous."

"No, let me finish," she said. "What I mean to say is that for me, the worst thing terrorists could do would be to destroy these wild places—like the Tetons, Yellowstone, all this redrock country...."

"They are," I said.

My father looked at me and said nothing. We drank our tea.

Kenneth Rexroth writes, "The art of being civilized is the art of learning to read between the lies."[1]

There have been many lies delivered in the name of national security since September 11, 2001. Fear has opened the door to fanaticism. The fabric of our civil liberties has been raveled. Those who raise questions are told to raise American flags instead. A hollow patriotism has emerged. We might as well be blowing "My Country 'Tis of Thee" through plastic kazoos.

Meanwhile, corporate America is imploding through its own greed, the stock market has become a trampoline leaving many investors suspended in midair as Bush II makes plans to attack Iraq and we bomb wedding parties in Afghanistan. The American West is being ravaged by oil and gas companies and federal regulations that have kept our air, water, and wildlife safe are now being erased.

Indeed, we are engaged in a war of terrorism.

Here in Castle Valley, Utah, with temperatures hovering around 110 degrees this summer and the valley filled with smoke from fires burning in Colorado and Arizona, it's easy to become apocalyptic about our future. The sun burns blood red through the haze. My Mormon neighbor reminds me of Proverbs 29:18: "Where there is no vision, the people perish."

But America is still a democracy and a strong one. We do have people with vision. That is our history. And, at this moment, no one looms larger in my mind than Rachel Carson. Here was a wildlife biologist, a government employee who worked for the U.S. Fish and Wildlife Service, who with her pen exposed the dangers of the entire chemical industry. It is her spirit I wish to recall and remember now. She is my model for a true patriot, one who not only dared to define democratic principles as ecological ones, but demanded through her grace and fierce intelligence that we hold corporations and our government accountable for the health of our communities, cultured and wild.

Rachel Carson. I first heard her name from my grandmother. I must have been seven or eight years old. We were feeding birds—song sparrows, goldfinches, and towhees—in my grandparents' yard in Salt Lake City.

"Imagine a world without birds," my grandmother said as she scattered seed and filled the feeders. "Imagine waking up to no birdsong."

I couldn't.

"Rachel Carson," I remember her saying.

Later, around the dinner table, she and my grandfather were engaged in an intense discussion of the book they were reading, *Silent Spring*, as my mind tried to grasp what my grandmother had just said about a muted world.

Decades later, I found myself in a used bookstore in Salt Lake City. The green spine of *Silent Spring* caught my eye. I pulled the classic off the shelf and opened it. First edition, 1962. As I read various passages, I was struck by how little had changed. Each page was still a shock and a revelation.

One of the most tragic examples of our unthinking bludgeoning of the landscape is to be seen in the sagebrush lands of the West, where a vast campaign is on to destroy the sage and to substitute grasslands. If ever an enterprise needed to be illuminated with a sense of history and meaning of the landscape, it is this.... It is spread before us like the pages of an open book in which we can read why the land is what it is, and why we should preserve its integrity. But the pages lie unread.[2]

The pages of abuse on the American landscape still lie unread.

Rachel Carson is a towering example within American democracy of how one person's voice can make an extraordinary difference both in public policy and in the minds of the populace. Her name and her vision of a world intact and interrelated entered mainstream culture in the 1960s, heralding the beginning of the modern conservation movement. Even so, forty-five years after *Silent Spring*, I wonder how many of us really know much about Carson's life or have ever read this crucial book?

We can all rattle off a glib two-sentence summation of its text: "All life is connected. Pesticides enter the food chain and not only threaten the environment but destroy it." And yet, I fear that *Silent Spring*'s status as "an American classic" allows us to nod to its power, but to miss the subtleties and richness of the book as both a scientific treatise and a piece of distinguished literary nonfiction.

Rachel Carson presents her discoveries of destruction in the form of storytelling. In example after example, grounded in the natural world, she weaves together facts and fictions into an environmental tale of life, love, and loss. Her voice is forceful and dignified, but sentence by sentence she delivers right-hand blows and counterpunches to the status quo ruled by chemical companies within the Kingdom of Agriculture.

The "control of nature" is a phrase conceived in arrogance, born of the Neanderthal age of biology and philosophy, when it was supposed that nature exists for the convenience of man.... It is our alarming misfortune that so primitive a science has armed itself with the most modern and terrible weapons, and that in turning them against the insects it has also turned them against the earth.[3]

The facts she presents create the case against "biocide": We are killing the very fabric of nature in our attempt to rid the world of pests through these "elixirs of death." She indicts the insecticides by name: DDT, chlordane, heptachlor, dieldrin, aldrin, and endrin. And then she adds parathion and malathion, organic phosphates that are among the most poisonous chemicals in the world.

The fictions she exposes are the myths we have chosen to adopt in our obsession to control nature. She reminds us of the story of Medea, the Greek sorceress who, overwrought with jealousy over her husband's love of another woman, presents the new bride with a gift, a robe that will immediately kill whoever wears it. It becomes a garment of death. Carson calls our use of pesticides "death-by-indirection."[4] We are killing insects and in turn, killing ourselves, as these toxins slowly and violently enter the waters and eventually our own bloodstreams.

Rachel Carson did not turn her back on the ongoing chronicle of the natural history of the dead. She bore witness. It was time, Carson said, "that human beings admit their kinship with other forms of life. If we cannot accept this moral ethic, then we too are complicit in the killing."[5]

With each chapter, she adds to our understanding of the horrors of herbicides and hydrocarbons, the web of life unraveling. It is impossible for us not to be inspired by Rachel Carson's emotional and intellectual stamina, her ability to endure the pain of the story she was telling.

Carson had a vision.

"Sometimes, I lose sight of my goal," she wrote in an essay in her first year of college, "then again it flashes into view, filling me with a new determination to keep the 'vision splendid' before my eyes."[6] Hers was a conscientious and directed soul who believed in the eloquence of facts. She loved both language and landscape. "I can remember no time when I wasn't interested in the out-of-doors and the whole world of nature," Carson said.[7]

Writing became the expression for her passion toward nature. She published her first story when she was ten years old, winning the Silver Badge from the prestigious children's magazine St. Nicholas. "Perhaps the early experience of seeing my work in print played its part in fostering my childhood dream of becoming a writer."[8]

Here was a young woman pulled by her destiny. In 1928, she graduated magna cum laude from Pennsylvania College for Women, now Chatham College, with a major in biology. The strength of her course work in both science and literature supports the evidence of her dual nature as both a scientist and a poet.

"I thought I had to be one or the other," she said. "It never occurred to me...that I could combine the two careers."[9]

Paul Brooks, Rachel Carson's editor, writes, "The merging of these two powerful currents—the imagination and insight of a creative writer with a scientist's passion for fact—goes far to explain the blend of beauty and authority that was to make her books unique."[10]

Rachel Carson's gift to us is seeing the world whole.

Carson continued her education as a biologist, receiving a master's degree in zoology at Johns Hopkins University, where she studied genetics and wrote her thesis, "The Development of the Pronephros During the Embryonic and Early Larval Life of the Catfish (Ictalurus punctatus)."

In 1936, she accepted a position with the United States Bureau of Fisheries, which later became the U.S. Fish and Wildlife Service, as an aquatic biologist. Here she was able to effectively fuse her talents as a scientist and a writer, eventually becoming chief of publications for the bureau. Early in her tenure at Fish and Wildlife, she continued teaching courses at the University of Maryland and Johns Hopkins.

Under the Sea-Wind was published in 1941. *The Sea Around Us* was published in 1951 to great popular and critical acclaim, receiving the National Book Award in nonfiction. It remained on the *New York Times* bestseller list for months. "If there is poetry in my book about the sea," she said, "it is not because I deliberately put it there, but because no one could truthfully write about the sea and leave out the poetry."[11]

In 1955, four years after the success of *The Sea Around Us*, Carson published *The Edge of the Sea*, extending her readers' knowledge of the ocean to the ocean's interface with land. She focused her naturalist's eye on tidepools, writing about the extraordinary nature of adaptation in a littoral world, while at the same time illuminating the magic and intricacies of the sandy beach and rocky shore. Her words not only speak of a natural history but a natural philosophy:

> Now I hear the sea sounds about me; the night high tide is rising, swirling with a confused rush of waters against the rocks below my study window... these coastal forms merge and blend in a shifting, kaleidoscopic pattern in which there is no finality, no ultimate and fixed reality—earth becoming fluid as the sea itself.... Contemplating the teeming life of the shore, we have an uneasy sense of the communication of some universal truth that lies just beyond our grasp. What is the message signaled by the hordes of diatoms, flashing their microscopic lights in the night sea?... The meaning haunts and ever eludes us, and in its very pursuit we approach the ultimate mystery of Life itself.[12]

And then came *Silent Spring*.

Rachel Carson received a letter from her friend Olga Owens Huckins, a journalist, who asked her for help in finding people who could elucidate and speak to the dangers of pesticides. The Huckinses had a small place in Duxbury, Massachusetts, just north of Cape Cod, which they had made into a bird sanctuary. Without any thought of the effects on birds and wildlife, the state had sprayed the entire area for mosquito control. Huckins sent a letter of outrage to the *Boston Herald* in January, 1958. Here is an excerpt:

> The mosquito control plane flew over our small town last summer. Since we live close to the marshes, we were treated to several lethal doses as the pilot crisscrossed our place. And we consider the spraying of active poison over private land to be a serious aerial intrusion.
>
> The "harmless" shower bath killed seven of our lovely songbirds outright. We picked up three dead bodies the next morning right by the door. They were birds that had lived close to us, trusted us, and built their nests in our trees year after year. The next day three were scattered around the bird bath. (I had emptied it and scrubbed it after the spraying but YOU CAN NEVER KILL DDT).

...All of these birds died horribly and in the same way. Their bills were gaping open, and their splayed claws were drawn up to their breasts in agony.[13]

Olga Owens Huckins bore witness. Rachel Carson responded. Four and a half years later, in 1962, *Silent Spring* was published. Carson wrote to Huckins that it was her letter that had "started it all" and had led her to realize that "I must write the book."[14]

This was a correspondence between friends, two women standing their ground in the places they loved, each one engaging the gifts they possessed to make a difference in the world. We can never forget the power of impassioned, informed individuals sharing their stories of place, bearing witness, speaking out on behalf of the land they call home.

Rachel Carson told the truth as she understood it. The natural world was dying, poisoned by the hands of power tied to corporate greed. Her words became an open wound in immediate need of attention. A debate had begun: a reverence for life versus a reverence for industry. Through the strength and vitality of her voice, Carson altered the political landscape of America forever.

Loren Eiseley wrote that *Silent Spring* "is a devastating, heavily documented, relentless attack upon human carelessness, greed, and responsibility."[15]

Not everyone saw it that way.

The Monsanto Chemical Company, anticipating the publication of *Silent Spring*, urgently commissioned a parody entitled "The Desolate Year" to counteract Carson's attack on the industry. Its intent was to show the pestilence and famine that Monsanto claimed would occur in a world without pesticides.

Robert White-Stevens, a biochemist who was assistant director of the Agricultural Research Division of American Cyanamid, became the chemical industry's spokesman. He made over twenty-eight speeches against *Silent Spring*. He was outraged by the evidence waged against DDT, charging that Carson was "a fanatic defender of the cult of the balance of nature."[16]

In its weekly newsletter, the American Medical Association told the public how to obtain an "information kit," compiled by the National Agriculture Chemicals Association, to answer questions provoked by *Silent Spring*.

Time magazine called *Silent Spring* "unfair, one-sided, and hysterically over-emphatic," and accused Carson of frightening the public with "emotion-fanning words," claiming her text was filled with "oversimplifications and downright errors."[17]

Former Secretary of Agriculture Ezra Taft Benson (who later became Prophet of the Mormon Church) wrote to Dwight D. Eisenhower regarding Rachel Carson, asking simply, "Why a spinster with no children was so concerned about genetics?"[18] His own conjecture was that she was "probably a Communist."

Spinster. Communist. A member of a nature cult. An amateur naturalist who should stick to poetry not politics. These were just some of the labels used to discredit her. Rachel Carson had, in fact, lit a fire on America's chemical landscape.

In speeches before the Garden Club of America and the New England Wildflower Preservation Society, Carson fought back against her detractors and addressed her audiences with great passion. "I recommend you ask yourself—Who speaks?—And Why?"[19] And then again, "Are we being sentimental when we care whether the robin returns to our dooryard and the veery sings in the twilight woods? A world that is no longer fit for wild plants, that is no longer graced by the flight of birds, a world whose streams and forests are empty and lifeless is not likely to be a fit habitat for man himself, for these things are symptoms of an ailing world."[20]

President John F. Kennedy became aware of Silent Spring when it was first serialized in the pages of The New Yorker. At a press conference on August 29, 1962, a reporter asked Kennedy about the growing concern among scientists regarding dangerous long-term side effects from the use of DDT and other pesticides and whether or not the U.S. Department of Agriculture or the U.S. Public Health Service was planning to launch an investigation into the matter.

"Yes," the president replied. "I think particularly, of course, since Miss Carson's book."[21]

The Life Science Panel of the President's Science Advisory Committee was charged with reviewing pesticide use. In 1962, the committee issued a call for legislative measures to safeguard the health of the land and its people against pesticides and industrial toxins. The President's report had vindicated Carson. Her poetics were transformed into public policy.

Rachel Carson testified for over forty minutes during the Hearings before the United States Senate Subcommittee on Reorganization and International Organizations of the Committee on Government Operations, "Interagency Coordination in Environmental Hazards (Pesticides)," on June 4, 1963.

According to Carson's biographer, Linda Lear, "Those who heard Rachel Carson that morning did not see a reserved or reticent woman in the witness chair but an accomplished scientist, an expert on chemical pesticides, a brilliant writer, and a woman of conscience who made the most of an opportunity few citizens of any rank can have to make their opinions known. Her witness had been equal to her vision."[22]

Senator Gruening from Alaska called Silent Spring equal to Uncle Tom's Cabin in its impact, and predicted it would change the course of history.

In 1967, five years after Silent Spring was published, the Environmental Defense Fund was born, with a mandate to build a body of case law to establish a citizen's right to a clean environment. Three years after that, in 1970, the Environmental Protection Agency was established.

And today, we have a new generation of individuals carrying the torch of vigilance forward in the name of ecological integrity: Lois Gibbs, who exposed the Love Canal to the American public as a dark example of industry's arrogance and disregard for the health of communities; Monica Moore and Sarojeni Rengah of Pesticide Action Network who provide scientific data and policy proposals worldwide to citizens fighting to maintain the biological health of their communities.

And women like Mary O'Brien in Eugene, Oregon, remind us that the risk assessment question, "How much of this pesticide is 'safe' or 'acceptable'?" is the wrong question to be asking. The better question is, "How little pesticide use is essential?"

These are green patriots who have taken the banner that Rachel Carson raised and have kept it flying high in a world that still refuses to believe in the dangers of biocide.

Tyrone Hayes, the lead researcher on a study concluding that atrazine, the most popular herbicide in the United States, causes a wide range of sexual abnormalities in frogs, was quoted in the New York Times on April 17, 2002, as saying, "I'm not saying it's safe for humans. I'm not saying it's unsafe for humans. All I'm saying is that it makes hermaphrodites of frogs."[23]

As Rachel Carson noted, "if...we have concluded that we are being asked to take senseless and frightening risks, then we should no longer accept the counsel of those who tell us that we must fill our world with poisonous chemicals; we should look about and see what other course is open to us."[24]

Pam Zahoran of Protect Environment and Children Everywhere is showing us an alternative course. She, along with twenty-two thousand other citizens, signed a petition against a major hazardous-waste incinerator to be built by Waste Technologies Industries in East Liverpool, Ohio.

Bill Hedden, former county commissioner in Grand County, Utah, has never given up the hope of seeing 10.5 million tons of radioactive waste removed from the banks of the Colorado River, left from the uranium boom in the 1950s. For almost two decades, he has delivered devastating facts and figures to the United States Congress showing the toxic risks to the entire Colorado River basin, including the Los Angeles water supply.

And Robert Boone, president of the Anacostia Watershed Society, is working with the children of this poverty-stricken community just outside Washington, D.C., to clean up the Anacostia River, one of the most toxic waterways in America. He is restoring hope in this forgotten landscape. So far, they have removed 327 tons of debris, 7,218 tires, and mobilized 25,666 volunteers in their vision of a clean river. They are holding the Environmental Protection Agency accountable to the Clean Water Act.

These are Rachel's sons and daughters who are taking the facts and fueling them with passionate resistance to protect the integrity of their hometowns and communities. This is the bedrock of democracy—"the greatest good for the greatest number for the longest time." By protecting the health of America's open spaces we preserve America's open heart.

Recently, I visited the Rachel Carson National Wildlife Refuge, a rich salt marsh that encompasses approximately 4,500 acres along forty-five miles of coastline in southern Maine. Carson knew this country well and worked toward its protection. It was the place she loved most, the place where she kept summers at her cottage near Boothbay Harbor with her nephew Roger and her dear soulmate, Dorothy Freeman, who lived nearby.

As I walked through the sanctuary and listened to the water songs of red-winged blackbirds and watched the deliberate flight of great blue herons, I wondered, if Carson were alive today, would she find this estuary a bit quieter? Would she find the tide pools less vibrant, vacant of certain creatures? I wondered what accommodations we have made through time without even noticing what we have lost. I would have loved to ask her what price she paid, personally, for her warriorship surrounding *Silent Spring?*

I imagined her looking directly into my eyes, a bit stunned over such a presumptuous question, shaking her head, and then looking out toward her beloved sea.

Sandra Steingraber, author of *Living Downstream: An Ecologist Looks at Cancer and the Environment*, writes, "Carson laid out five lines of evidence linking cancer to environmental causes.... [She] predicted that the full maturation of 'whatever seeds of malignancy have been sown' by the new lethal agents of the chemical age would occur in the years to come."[25]

The irony is a painful one. Rachel Carson died of breast cancer on April 14, 1964, at the age of fifty-six. Diagnosed in 1960, she wrote *Silent Spring* through her illness and faced her powerful detractors with limited physical strength, often having to be hospitalized after strenuous professional obligations. But the public never knew. She proceeded with great presence and resolve, even completing a rigorous television interview on CBS months before her death, where she was paired with a spokesperson from the chemical industry. Carson's "grace under fire" with compelling facts to back her sentiments finally won public opinion over to her side. Brooks Atkinson in his column in the *New York Times* proclaimed her the winner. He wrote, "Evidence continues to accumulate that she is right and that *Silent Spring* is the 'rights of man' of this generation."[26]

In spite of her cancer, Rachel Carson never lost "the vision splendid" before her eyes. Her love of the natural world, especially all she held dear in the coastal landscape of Maine, sustained and supported her tenacious and elegant spirit.

Before her death, she wrote to her friend Dorothy Freeman, "It is good to know that I shall live on even in the minds of many who do not know me, and largely through association with things that are beautiful and lovely."[27]

And she does.

Consider these examples: *Rachel's Daughters*, a film investigating the environmental causes of breast cancer; Rachel's Network, a political organization committed to seeing women in positions of power and leadership within the conservation community; the Rachel Carson Institute at Chatham College, dedicated to the awareness and understanding of current environmental issues inspired by their distinguished alumna. And there are thousands of references to Rachel Carson within American culture, including one by a puzzled Richard A. Posner, who wondered in his book, *Public Intellectuals* why Rachel Carson had more citations in Lexus Nexus than the French deconstructionist Jacques Derrida. What a perfect metaphor for Rachel Carson's impact. After all, didn't she deconstruct the entire chemical industry until we were able to see, collectively, the essence of what it does—destroy natural systems—the dark toxic roots of pesticides exposed?

Rachel Carson writes that "there is also an ecology of the world within our bodies."[28]

Recently, an open letter was signed and sent to the U.S. Senate to ban reproductive cloning and to place a moratorium on therapeutic cloning by a broad coalition of scientists, environmentalists, feminists, health care workers, religious leaders, political leaders, philosophers, and writers. If Rachel Carson were alive, her name would have appeared on that list.

Similar political actions have been taken to elucidate the dangers of genetic engineering, from the possibility of infecting wild salmon populations to the perils of genetically modified foods. Rachel Carson understood that tampering with nature is tampering with health in the broadest, ecological sense.

Rachel Carson's spirit is among us. Like her, we can be both fierce and compassionate at once. We can remember that our character has been shaped by the diversity of America's landscape and it is precisely that character that will protect it. We can carry a healthy sense of indignation within us that will shatter the complacency that has seeped into our society in the name of all we have lost, knowing there is still so much to be saved.

Call it sacred rage, a rage grounded in the understanding that all life is intertwined. And we can come to know and continue to learn from the grace of wild things as they hold an organic wisdom that sustains peace.

Do we have the moral courage to step forward and openly question every law, person, and practice that denies justice toward nature?

Do we have the strength and will to continue in this American tradition of bearing witness to beauty and terror which is its own form of advocacy?

And do we have the imagination to rediscover an authentic patriotism that inspires empathy and reflection over pride and nationalism?

Rachel Carson's name is synonymous with courage. She dared to expose the underbelly of the chemical industry and show how it was disrupting the balance of nature. In *Silent Spring* we see her signature strength on the page, and witness how a confluence of poetry and politics with sound science can create an ethical stance toward life.

But perhaps Rachel Carson's true courage lies in her willingness to align science with the sacred, to admit that her bond toward nature is a spiritual one.

I am not afraid of being thought a sentimentalist when I say that I believe natural beauty has a necessary place in the spiritual development of any individual or any society. I believe that whenever we destroy beauty, or whenever we substitute something man-made and artificial for a natural feature of the earth, we have retarded some part of man's spiritual growth.

Rachel Carson has called us to action. *Silent Spring* is a social critique of our modern way of life, as essential to the evolving American ideals of freedom and democracy as anything ever written by our founding fathers.

"If the Bill of Rights contains no guarantee that a citizen shall be secure against lethal poisons distributed either by private individuals or by public officials," Carson wrote, "it is surely only because our forefathers, despite their considerable wisdom and foresight, could conceive of no such problem."[29]

There are many forms of terrorism. Environmental degradation is one of them. We have an opportunity to shift the emphasis on American independence to American interdependence and redefine what acts of responsibility count as heroism. Protecting the lands we love and working on behalf of the safety of our communities from the poisoned residue of corporate and governmental neglect must surely be chief among them. Perhaps this is what the idea of "homeland security" is meant to be in times of terror.

After my father and his friend left, I walked outside and sat on our back porch. The blinking bodies of fireflies were rising and falling above the grasses. They appeared as a company of code-talkers flashing S.O.S. on a very dark night.

NOTES

1. Kenneth Rexroth, "Greek Tragedy in Translation," in his *With Eye and Ear* (New York: Herder & Herder, 1970), 143.

2. Rachel Carson, *Silent Spring* (Boston: Houghton Mifflin, 1994 [1962]), 64.

3. Ibid., 297.

4. Ibid., 32.

5. Rachel Carson, Speech, Kaiser Foundation Symposium, "The Pollution of Our Environment," Oct. 18, 1963; Rachel Carson Papers, Beinecke Library, Yale University. As quoted in Linda Lear, *Rachel Carson: Witness for Nature* (New York: Henry Holt, 1997), 464. Portions of this speech are

reprinted in Rachel Carson, *Lost Woods: The Discovered Writing of Rachel Carson*, ed. Linda Lear (Boston: Beacon Press, 1998), 227–45.

6. Rachel Carson, "Who I Am and Why I Came to P.C.W.," 1925; Rachel Carson Papers, Beinecke Library, Yale University. As quoted in Lear, *Witness for Nature*, 32.

7. Rachel Carson, "The Real World Around Us," in *Lost Woods*, 148.

8. Paul Brooks, *The House of Life: Rachel Carson at Work* (Boston: Houghton Mifflin, 1972), 16.

9. Ibid., 17.

10. Ibid., 18.

11. Rachel Carson, "Remarks at the Acceptance of the National Book Award for Nonfiction," in *Lost Woods*, 91.

12. Rachel Carson, *The Edge of the Sea* (New York: Mariner Books, 1998 [1955]), 249–50.

13. Olga Owens Huckins, "Evidence of Havoc by DDT Air Spraying," *Boston Herald*, Jan. 29, 1958, sec. 3, 14.

14. Rachel Carson to Olga Owens Huckins, Letter, Oct. 3, 1962, Rachel Carson Papers, Beinecke Library, Yale University. As quoted in Lear, *Witness for Nature*, 422.

15. Loren Eiseley, "Using a Plague to Fight a Plague: Review of *Silent Spring*, by Rachel Carson," *Saturday Review*, Sept. 29, 1962, 18–19, 24.

16. Robert H. White-Stevens as quoted in Lear, *Witness for Nature*, 434.

17. "Pesticides: The Price for Progress," *Time*, Sept. 28, 1962, 45–48.

18. Ezra Taft Benson as quoted in Lear, *Witness for Nature*, 429.

19. Rachel Carson, Speech, Garden Club of America, Jan. 8, 1963. Reprinted as "A New Chapter to *Silent Spring*," in *Lost Woods*, 222.

20. Rachel Carson, "A Sense of Values in Today's World," Speech, New England Wildflower Preservation Society, Jan. 17, 1963; Rachel Carson Papers, Beinecke Library, Yale University. As quoted in Lear, *Witness for Nature*, 440–41.

21. John F. Kennedy, Presidential News Conference, Aug. 29, 1962. As quoted in Lear, *Witness for Nature*, 419.

22. Lear, *Witness for Nature*, 454.

23. Associated Press, "Weed Killer Deforms Frogs in Sex Organs, Study Finds," *New York Times*, Apr. 17, 2002, sec. A, col. 6, 19.

24. Carson, *Silent Spring*, 278.

25. Sandra Steingraber, *Living Downstream: An Ecologist Looks at Cancer and the Environment* (New York: Addison-Wesley, 1997), 27–28.

26. Brooks Atkinson, "Critic at Large; Rachel Carson's 'Silent Spring' Is Called 'The Rights of Man' of Our Time," *New York Times*, Apr. 2, 1963.

27. Rachel Carson to Dorothy Freeman, Letter, Mar. 27, 1963, in *Always, Rachel: The Letters of Rachel Carson and Dorothy Freeman, 1952–1964*, ed. Martha Freeman (Boston: Beacon Press, 1995), 446.

28. Carson, *Silent Spring*, 189.

29. Ibid., 12–13.

2

Rachel Carson's Scientific and Ocean Legacies

Jane Lubchenco

The lights are dim, the crowd expectant. They have viewed films and read about her for years and now finally have a chance to see her in person. Does she really deserve her reputation? Will she do something unpredictable and exciting today? What will it feel like to watch her in action?

Sharp eyes spy her first. Soon, everyone is tracking her movement as she comes closer. Decked out in power colors of white, grey, and black, she is dressed to kill. She is stunning and powerful, sleek and graceful, but surprisingly diminutive. Despite her size, she is indisputably in charge. As she glides by, those around her give way, maintaining a safe distance, recognizing her status, deferring to her strength. She moves with a languid, mesmerizing, rhythmic motion that looks deceptively lazy, but she is quite capable of lightning speed and aggressive behavior. Her rows of razor-sharp, serrated teeth are captivating, menacing. She is the consummate predator.

She is a little girl white shark. Months old, approximately five feet long and around a hundred pounds, she is the new apex predator of the million-gallon Outer Bay exhibit at the Monterey Bay Aquarium in Monterey, California. Since her arrival on September 14, 2004, millions of visitors have flocked to the aquarium to observe her. Months later, she is clearly growing and thriving, and very much in charge of her new, albeit temporary, home.

Caught accidentally in a commercial halibut gill net off southern California, she almost died in the net, the fate of fifty million other sharks around the world who are victims of fishing gear intended to catch other species. (An additional fifty million sharks are slaughtered deliberately every year for their fins, jaws, skin, and cartilage, or simply out of fear or ignorance.) Instead, however, she was rescued by fishermen and a team of white shark research scientists from the aquarium who in 2002 launched a project to learn as much as possible about white sharks.

The knowledge they gained has enabled their stunning success in keeping this white shark so healthy. She is the first white shark ever to feed in captivity, and thus be held long enough for millions of visitors to see her.

I'm surprised at my fascination with her. As a trustee of the Monterey Bay Aquarium, I've visited this exhibit dozens of times to marvel at the incredible assemblage of species that is typical of the coastal ecosystem in the outer portion of Monterey Bay. As a marine biologist, I never tire of watching the immense three hundred-pound bluefin tunas cruising the tank like torpedoes, the more compact but still impressive yellowfin tunas, the bizarre scalloped hammerhead sharks swimming sinuously—their eyes so far apart that it's hard to imagine a brain integrating their disparate signals. I am fascinated by the school of Pacific bonito and cloud of flashing sardines, turning in unison with their neighbors—how *do* they communicate and coordinate so precisely? I'm amused by the nasty-looking California barracuda cruising menacingly, the comical black sea turtles, and sleek Galapagos sharks. But this new creature is different. Aloof. Magnificent. Mesmerizing. She definitely belongs in this ecosystem and is integral to it, yet her presence has altered the dynamics within the tank and in the adjacent room where we watch in awe.

I find myself reflecting on the key role she plays in her ecosystem, the threatened status of all large ocean predators, and the extraordinarily rapid decline in coastal and ocean ecosystems around the world. I feel an urgent need for ocean champions and greater public awareness of both problems and solutions. I muse about how lucky we would be if Rachel Carson were alive today to write eloquently about the wondrous beauty of the creatures and systems at risk and how our own lives depend on theirs. As a marine biologist, she would likely be horrified by the transformation of the ocean ecosystems she so lovingly and knowledgeably described in *Under the Sea-Wind, The Sea Around Us,* and *The Edge of the Sea.*[1] Her powerful ability to communicate complex scientific knowledge in an appealing, compelling, and eloquent fashion is much needed today. This may be one of her most important legacies: to have shown by her example that scientists have important roles as advocates, particularly in the development of an ocean ethic.

The scientific evidence for the dysfunctional state of marine ecosystems is compelling.[2] Two recent U.S. commissions on oceans have summarized the evidence and proposed solutions,[3] but meaningful changes will not occur until more people know and care about what they are losing and clamor for solutions.

This little shark is providing scientists a much-needed opportunity to gain invaluable information about her kind. And she is changing people's minds about sharks and drawing attention to the plight of the oceans. The mission of the Monterey Bay Aquarium is "to inspire conservation of the oceans." The little star is doing just that. Visitors come because of her reputation as a man-eating monster, but leave impressed by her grandeur, though still wary of meeting her in the ocean, and aware of the global threats to sharks and their ocean home.

The aquarium intends to keep her healthy, learn from her, and let her go before she gets too big to release safely and easily.[4] Equipped with high-tech tags, she will continue to provide invaluable information once she is back in the Pacific Ocean. In the meantime, visitors from around the world will have a chance to admire and learn about one of the planet's most magnificent and ancient of creatures.

White sharks, or *Carcharodon carcharias*, have swum in the oceans for over eleven million years. Called "great white sharks" by the public, adults can grow to 21.5 feet and weigh up to seven thousand pounds. They are the indisputable top predators of ocean food webs, with a diet that includes fishes, other sharks, seals, sea lions, porpoises, dolphins, skates, rays, sea turtles, mollusks, crustaceans, and seabirds.[5] As apex predators, they control the size, abundance, and behavior of innumerable other species in their ecosystem. There's good evidence from removal of apex predators in other systems that their loss usually disrupts the entire ecosystem, often resulting in a switch to a completely different and depauperate set of players.

One very obvious reason why we are so taken with white sharks is simply that they *can* eat people, though the myths far surpass the reality. Fewer than thirty people a year are attacked by sharks of all species worldwide. In striking contrast, more than one hundred million sharks are killed each year by people. Nonetheless, the very fact that they can and do occasionally eat people puts them in an elite group of so-called man-eaters. They are one of the ten or so "alpha predators" that David Quammen explores in his book *Monster of God: The Man-Eating Predator in the Jungles of History and the Mind*. Like the tiger, brown bear, Nile crocodile, lion, leopard, polar bear, and a few others, the white shark is "big enough, fierce enough, voracious and indiscriminant enough to—occasionally—kill and eat a human," Quammen writes.[6] That sets them apart. Quammen suggests that these alpha predators are so feared and revered because they "remind us of where we have stood for tens of thousands of years, on the food chain of power and glory. That is, not always and indisputably at the top."[7]

But as Peter Benchley, the noted author of *Jaws* and now ardent shark conservationist, points out, "It's not what we have to fear *from* white sharks, but rather what we have to fear *for* them."[8] All ocean creatures are increasingly at risk, but sharks are in triple jeopardy: their ecosystems are being disrupted by pollution, overfishing, climate change, and coastal development; they are often killed as accidental "by-catch" by the far too numerous and immense commercial fishing nets and hooks; and they are specifically targeted because of their reputation. Among all sharks, whites are the most feared and sought after. According to the World Wildlife Fund, a conservation organization that tracks markets for endangered species around the world, white sharks are one of the ten most wanted species in the international market.[9]

For many people, white sharks are *the* symbol of life in the oceans—encompassing the power, the majesty, and the mystery. The surge in visitors to the Monterey Bay Aquarium provides compelling evidence of the shark's power to fascinate us. Unfortunately, white sharks are also emblematic of the sorry state of the oceans today.

As a marine biologist who has studied coastal ocean ecosystems and marine life around the world, I'm all too aware of the problems and the urgency of addressing them effectively. I feel a kinship with Rachel Carson, both in our paths to and love of marine biology and in our awareness of the threats to the integrity of ocean ecosystems and the consequences to human well-being. Like Rachel Carson, I grew up inland, enthralled with natural history; like Carson, I was seduced by oceans and marine critters during a summer at the Marine Biological Laboratory in Woods Hole, Massachusetts, in my early twenties; like Carson, I studied the spectacular intertidal communities of invertebrates and seaweeds along the rocky shores of Maine; and like Carson, I've been intimately involved in a number of controversial environmental topics where new scientific information has prompted new awareness and strong backlash.

Carson is the ultimate example of a courageous, eloquent scientist who first and foremost was a superb scientist, and who also understood the importance of sharing her knowledge with the broader world. She did it well. I am inspired by her ability to take complex scientific phenomena and communicate them in an engaging, lyrical, and relevant fashion. I greatly admire her courage in making scientific information publicly available, despite nasty criticism. In her biography, Linda Lear highlights a number of Carson's key contributions: She "transformed colorless government research into three brilliant popular books about the sea...and...[became] the most respected science writer in America;"[10] she alerted the world to the hazards of environmental toxins; "she wrote a revolutionary book in terms that were acceptable to a middle class emerging from the lethargy of postwar affluence and woke them to their neglected responsibilities;"[11] she "challenged the culture of her time and, in the process, shaped a powerful social movement that altered the course of American history;"[12] and she transformed the way we understand ourselves and the living world.[13] Her courage, eloquence, and wisdom were keys to her impact.

Carson's influence was predicated upon both her scientific reputation and the public reputation Carson had built with her three best-selling books about the oceans. As Ann Zwinger notes in her introduction to the 1989 special edition of *The Sea Around Us*, "Six years after Carson died we celebrated Earth Day. The controversy and publicity that surrounded *Silent Spring* had served to prod a newly sensitized public. But it was *The Sea Around Us* that started people thinking, that laid the groundwork for stronger medicine to come. *The Sea Around Us* was the book that set the stage and made *Silent Spring* understandable."[14] And Lear notes that by the time *Silent Spring* was published in 1962, Rachel Carson was well established as "the most respected science writer in America."[15]

Silent Spring, however, was a significant departure from her earlier books. In it, Carson went far beyond sharing her love of nature; the book reveals a passionate "determination to save what she loved" from the as-yet unappreciated dangers of DDT and other environmental toxins.[16] Not even her reputation or popularity or her credibility as a scientist could protect her from the barrage of criticism, arrogant dismissal of facts, and insulting and nasty comments triggered by *Silent Spring* and the public testimony she offered. In the end, however, she was vindicated and is now widely admired for her courage. She was vilified because she dared to speak out; but she was exonerated because she was right.

Scientists today take courage from Carson's experiences, and most of them also understand the importance of "getting it right." Increasing numbers of scientists are willing to share their knowledge in public venues, not just in the peer-reviewed scientific literature. Most academic scientists have little training in how to do this effectively, however. Carson was naturally gifted and she also learned by trial and error. Today, the Aldo Leopold Leadership Program teaches other environmental scientists with strong scientific credentials how to share their scientific knowledge more effectively.[17] The program trains tenured, academic environmental scientists in North America to be better communicators of their science to the public, policy makers, the media, and the business. Carson is an inspiration and strong role model for the program.

Carson understood that among the many roles that science plays, one of the most important is to inform people's understanding of their world and themselves. Personal and political decisions will of course be based on a wide variety of factors, including values, economics, social pressures, politics, and more, but those decisions will be better if they are informed by the most current and credible scientific understanding. This role of "informing" is often omitted when governments and people articulate why public funding of science is important. The roles of science that are commonly expressed include science to improve our lives (health, labor-saving devices, communications, education, and intellectual curiosity are all examples); to assist with national security and defense; to enhance national prestige; and to promote economic growth (for example, advances in technology). "Science to inform" should be added to the list. Carson's life's work was informing people about the natural world and their relationship with it.

This role of "science to inform" entails a number of elements: (1) Scientific knowledge can shed light on the basic workings of natural and social systems. (2) It can provide credible documentation of the ways in which changes have occurred as well as the rates. (3) Science can also look to the future and evaluate the likely consequences of a variety of options, that is, describe possible scenarios based on current trends and an understanding of the dynamics of a system. (4) And scientific information can help develop solutions to existing problems.

I believe, as Carson did, that scientists have an obligation to share their knowledge with the public. As obvious as this statement sounds, the reality within the scientific community has been otherwise, with primary emphasis and rewards put on communicating results to other scientists in the peer-reviewed scientific literature. In my address as president of the American Association for the Advancement of Science, I challenged scientists to renew their social contract and be more responsible in also communicating their findings to the public and policy makers.[18] As the state of the planet becomes ever more precarious, increasing numbers of scientists are breaking the academic mold, working on problems of high social relevance and communicating their findings (once they have been vetted by the peer-review process) directly with the public. They have Carson to thank for blazing the trail.

Increasingly, scientists are working together to conduct scientific assessments (evaluations of the state of knowledge on important issues with social relevance). If conducted by a credible group of scientists with a credible process and if designed to be policy-relevant but not policy-driven, scientific assessments can provide much needed information and guidance to the public and to policy makers. Such assessments are often more useful to decision makers than guidance provided by a single scientist, simply because the process of producing an assessment entails vetting the information through peer review and consensus. The Intergovernmental Panel on Climate Change and the Millennium Ecosystem Assessment (MA) are two examples of recent, credible, useful, salient, policy-relevant but not policy-driven, international scientific assessments that are changing the way the world thinks about climate and ecosystems and their services.[19]

The MA, the newer of the two, was released in early 2005. It includes an evaluation of the conditions and trends within coastal and oceanic ecosystems around the world. It highlights the disastrous state of fisheries globally, but points to the importance of recognizing and dealing more holistically with the collective impacts of fishing, coastal development, climate change, and pollution—especially nutrient pollution from nitrogen and phosphorus.

The MA is the first scientific assessment to follow Carson's lead by focusing on the connections between environmental changes and human well-being. Environmental changes affect the functioning of ecological systems that provide ecosystem services. Ecosystem services are the benefits ecosystems provide to people. These services fall into four categories: (1) provisioning services—the provision of food, fuelwood, medicines, and timber; (2) regulating services—the regulation of climate, floods, outbreaks of pests, disease, and the purification of air and water; (3) cultural services—recreation, inspiration, education, and heritage values; and (4) supporting services—those that underpin all of the other services by providing primary production, fertile soil, recycling of nutrients, and so on. These benefits collectively influence human well-being; they affect people's security, basic materials for a good life, health, good social relations, and the freedom of choice and action.

Ecosystem services are provided by all coastal and ocean ecosystems as well as by terrestrial and freshwater ones. Mangroves, coral reefs, kelp forests, open oceans, and the deep sea all provide different services. The services are produced as a by-product of the interactions of the suite of plants, animals, and microbes that live together in a particular place. Mangrove ecosystems, for example, provide seafood, a nursery habitat for fish and shellfish, and protection of shores from storms and tsunamis. The mangroves also trap sediment, preventing it from spilling downstream and smothering coral reefs. They trap and purify toxins and other pollutants coming from the land. And they provide fuelwood, timber, and weaving materials for many indigenous peoples. When these ecosystems are converted to shrimp farms, agricultural lands, or residential areas, those services are all lost. The MA found that 35 percent of mangrove ecosystems around the world have been lost, usually by conversion to other uses. The understanding provided by the MA of the trade-offs in habitat conversion or other environmental changes can enable more informed decision making about the costs and benefits.

The MA documents that ecosystems around the world, but especially marine ones, have been altered more significantly over the last fifty years than at any other time in human history. The changes made have greatly improved the availability of food, for example from agriculture and fisheries. But those changes have come at a high price and have seriously eroded the capacity of ecosystems to provide other services that, in the end, are required for continued production of more food. Depletion of ocean fisheries is highlighted as one of the most serious of global problems.

The MA was able to assess the status of twenty-four ecosystem services globally. It drew the sobering conclusion that 60 percent of those services are being degraded. The MA also provides scenarios that enable exploration of the critical trade-offs in considering futures other than the one resulting from continuing business as usual. And the MA provides a wide range of options for redirecting the current global path to enable more sustainable use of resources, with suggestions about local, national, regional, and global options.

The MA, as an international scientific report, echoes the findings of the 2003 Pew Oceans Commission and the 2004 U.S. Commission on Ocean Policy, both of which focused on changes within U.S. waters. The national ocean reports highlight the importance of and ways to achieve new, more enlightened management of activities that affect oceans. Both reports emphasize the need for better stewardship, improved fishery management, adoption of ecosystem-based management, more integrated governance, and greater public awareness of changes underway, likely consequences, and options for significant improvement.

The Pew Oceans Commission report calls for a new ocean ethic. It suggests that oceans should be managed as a public trust—managed holistically, for the common good, and in perpetuity. One new and potentially very powerful tool to help restore the bounty and productive capacity of oceans is a network of fully protected marine reserves. A marine reserve is an area of the ocean fully protected from any extractive or destructive activity, except as needed to monitor or evaluate the reserve. Commonly called "no-take areas," marine reserves very effectively protect species and habitats within their boundaries. There is compelling logic and increasing evidence that reserves may also help recharge adjacent waters where fisheries have been depleted. A network of marine reserves is a set of reserves that are connected by the movement of larvae, juveniles, or adults. New scientific information about networks and reserves has aided the search for new tools and solutions to help recover ocean bounty.[20]

Scientific assessments, commission reports, and new scientific information provide an excellent starting point for documenting the changes underway, describing their consequences to people, and providing options for alternate paths. However, real change will require individual citizens caring, mobilizing, demanding, and creating change. Inspired by Carson's *Silent Spring*, citizen action and environmental groups, such as the Environmental Defense Fund, mobilized to ban DDT and other pesticides.[21] Today, a range of diverse and nontraditional partners, including fishermen, business people, conservation organizations, scientists and others, are working together to mutiny for the bounty of oceans. Inspired by the commissions' reports, they are working actively to put the primary emphasis on protecting and restoring ocean ecosystems so that people will be able to continue to enjoy the ecosystem services and because being good stewards is the right thing to do.

One state, California, has responded rapidly to the public demand for changes in the way coastal and ocean areas are managed. The legislature passed and the governor signed the Marine Life Protection Act and the California Ocean Protection Act. The first law will create networks of fully protected marine reserves in state waters; the other creates a mechanism and guidelines for vastly improved management of coastal waters. Public polls consistently indicate that Californians value their coastal and ocean ecosystems greatly and put a high priority on their protection.

The Monterey Bay Aquarium, temporary home of the white shark that inspired these musings, is actively engaged in raising public awareness, inspiring conservation of the oceans, and providing ideas for practical, concrete steps that individuals can take to make a difference. Many visitors to the aquarium are keenly interested in knowing what they can do to begin to address problems in oceans. To help meet this demand, the aquarium publishes a "Seafood Watch Card" that lets consumers know which seafood is sustainably caught or farmed.[22]

Public awareness and action are essential to any meaningful change. It is abundantly clear from observing the many visitors of all ages who eagerly watch the white shark that they are smitten. She has indeed been an effective if accidental ambassador for oceans.

Much remains to be learned about white sharks and most other ocean creatures. Scientists do know that this shark was most likely born along with up to fourteen other live young sharks, each of whom immediately swam off to begin life somewhere along the coast of southern California or Baja. But scientists do not know where young sharks spend their time, where they go, how deep they dive, or who their predators are. The aquarium shark research team and their partners, the Tuna Research and Conservation Center at Stanford University's Hopkins Marine Station and the aquarium, will continue their quest to learn more about sharks and the other top predators of the oceans. By studying this young female, and tagging and following other young sharks in the wild, they will add significantly to our understanding.

It is greatly encouraging that public attention to the plight of sharks is beginning to have an impact on public policy. South Africa and Australia have implemented new policies to protect white sharks. A United Nations treaty organization, the Convention on International Trade in Endangered Species (CITES) made trade in white sharks or their body parts more difficult. Stripping live sharks of their fins and dumping the fatally injured body overboard is now banned in U.S. waters. Thus, although huge challenges remain to restore and protect ocean ecosystems and recover the wealth of benefits provided to people by oceans, some good progress is being made.

The oceans were Rachel Carson's realm. Her evocative, engaging, and enlightened writings reveal a rich understanding of the wealth of life in oceans, the physical, chemical and geological processes interacting with that life, the ecological dynamics of ocean ecosystems, and our dependence upon and influence on oceans. Her example, wisdom, courage, and talent have inspired a wealth of new ocean champions who take courage from her experiences and successes.

Her legacy is rich, but her oceans are depleted. In her honor, we should Seas the Day—not in the usual *carpe diem* sense of abandonment of hope for the future, but rather in the spirit of taking individual responsibility for recovering the lost bounty and saving ourselves in the process.

NOTES

1. Rachel L. Carson, *Under the Sea-Wind* (New York: Penguin Books, 1996 [1941]); ibid., *The Sea Around Us* (New York: Oxford University Press, 1989 [1950]); and, ibid., *The Edge of the Sea* (New York: Mariner Books, 1998 [1955]).

2. See the Millennium Ecosystem Assessment Web site (www.maweb.org). The Millennium Ecosystem Assessment (MA) is an international assessment conducted over five years by more than thirteen hundred scientists from ninety-five countries. It evaluates the consequences of ecosystem changes to human well-being. I was one of many lead authors of the MA.

3. Pew Oceans Commission (Leon E. Panetta, chair), *America's Living Oceans: Charting a Course for Sea Change* (Arlington, Va.: Pew Oceans Commission, 2003). Available online at www.pewtrusts.org/our_work.aspx? category=130. I served on the Pew Oceans Commission. And, U.S. Commission on Ocean Policy, *An Ocean Blueprint for the 21st Century: Final Report of the U.S. Commission on Ocean Policy* (Washington, D.C.: U.S. Commission on Ocean Policy, 2004). Available online at www.oceancommission.gov/ documents/full_color_rpt/welcome.html#full.

4. The white shark was returned to the wild on March 31, 2005. During her 198 days at the aquarium, she grew "from a length of 5 feet and a weight of 62 pounds to a length of 6 feet, 4 ½ inches and a weight of 162 pounds" according to the Monterey Bay Aquarium's press release of the day (www.mbayaq.org/cr/whiteshark.asp). According to the release she was "fitted with an electronic data tag that will track her movements for the next month." The aquarium staff decided it was time to release her "when she began to hunt other sharks in the exhibit. She was also growing to a size where it would soon be more difficult to successfully transport her for release to the wild. Her overall health was excellent, as are her prospects for survival in the wild. We hope to exhibit another young white shark in the months to come." The aquarium's Web site provides current information about all of its exhibits.

5. Richard Ellis, John McCosker, and Al Giddings, *Great White Shark* (Palo Alto: Stanford University Press, 1995); David A. Ebert and Mathew D. Squillante, *Sharks, Rays and Chimaeras of California.* (Berkeley: University of

California Press, 2003); and A. Peter Klimley and David G. Ainley, eds., *Great White Sharks: The Biology of Carcharodon carcharias* (San Diego: Academic Press, 1996).

6. David Quammen, *Monster of God: The Man-Eating Predator in the Jungles of History and the Mind* (New York: Norton, 2003), 6.

7. Ibid. 3.

8. Monterey Bay Aquarium, *Saving White Sharks* (Monterey: Monterey Bay Aquarium Press, 2004), 5.

9. World Wildlife Fund, "10 Most Wanted Species." Available online at www.worldwildlife.org/trade/cites/mostwanted.cfm.

10. Linda Lear, *Rachel Carson: Witness for Nature* (New York: Henry Holt, 1997), inside front jacket.

11. Ibid. 4.

12. Ibid. inside back jacket.

13. Ibid.

14. Ann H. Zwinger, introduction to *The Sea Around Us* by Rachel Carson (New York: Oxford University Press, 1989 [1950]), xxv.

15. Lear, *Witness for Nature*, inside back jacket.

16. Ibid.

17. Information about the Aldo Leopold Leadership Program can be found online at www.leopoldleadership.org. The program is housed at Stanford University's Woods Institute for the Environment and led by professors Pamela Matson, Diana Wall, and me.

18. Jane Lubchenco, "Entering the Century of the Environment: A New Social Contract for Science," *Science* 279 (1998): 491–97.

19. The Intergovernmental Panel on Climate Change produces a scientific assessment of the state of knowledge on climate change approximately every five years. The most recent report is the Third Assessment Report, which is available online at www.ipcc.ch/pub/online.htm. The MA is available at www.maweb.org.

20. Summaries of scientific information about networks of marine reserves can be found in (1) Partnership for Interdisciplinary Studies of Coastal Oceans (Jane Lubchenco, Steven Gaines, Robert Warner, Satie Airamé, and Brooke Simler, senior editors), *The Science of Marine Reserves* (Partnership for Interdisciplinary Studies of Coastal Oceans [PISCO], 2002); available online at www.piscoweb.org/files/booklet_final.pdf; (2) Stephen R. Palumbi, *Marine Reserves: A Tool for Ecosystem Management and Conservation* (Arlington, Va.: Pew Oceans Commission, 2002). Available

online at www.pewtrusts.org/our_work_ektid30047.aspx; and (3) Jane Lubchenco, Stephen R. Palumbi, Steven D. Gaines, and Sandy Andelman, "Plugging a Hole in the Ocean: The Emerging Science of Marine Reserves," *Ecological Applications* 13 Suppl. (2003): S3–S7.

21. The Environmental Defense Fund is now Environmental Defense (www.EnvironmentalDefense.org). Its early success in helping to ban DDT led to a robust environmental advocacy organization now working on a range of critically important issues, including climate change, endangered species, and oceans. I serve as a trustee.

22. Monterey Bay Aquarium, "Seafood Watch Card." Available online at www.mbayaq.org/cr/seafoodwatch.asp.

3

Rachel Carson and George J. Wallace: Why Public Environmental Scientists Should Be Advocates for Nature

Peter C. List

Large numbers of robins were mysteriously dead and dying on campus grounds when I arrived at Michigan State University as an undergraduate in 1959. They were at the center of a controversy that had been stewing for several years. An ornithology professor, George J. Wallace, claimed that DDT spraying of the many trees both on campus and in nearby East Lansing caused the deaths. Local newspapers presented this conclusion as if it could be seriously doubted, and Professor Wallace was roundly criticized by both those who genuinely thought that DDT was relatively harmless and others who had something to gain professionally or financially from use of the sprays. This included some academics in the agriculture departments of the university and others in the chemical industry.

My close friends and I were generally suspicious of claims about most anything that emanated from the authorities in power. We were not inclined to be mollified by official assertions and reassurances, but we did respect most of our teachers and believed in the supremacy of science and the integrity of our science professors. I thus came to view Professor Wallace with considerable sympathy because of the attacks that he had to endure.

I have remembered this situation for years because, at the time, it helped to cement my desire to become more involved in environmental issues both personally and professionally. It was a seminal personal experience that convinced me that our society is too indiscriminate in its use of chemicals and too arrogant and ignorant in its relentless destruction of habitat and species. I

41

came to believe then, as I do now, that a sustained effort is needed to challenge customary ways of thinking about our relationships with nature.

With that aim in mind, I taught environmental ethics at Oregon State University for years. As an inhabitant of the Pacific Northwest, a region in which controversies about the management of forests, fish, and many wild species infuse daily life, and as a longtime employee of a land-grant university in which the applied environmental sciences are prevalent, I eventually turned my focus in environmental ethics toward ethical issues affecting scientists in the applied natural resource sciences.

One of the questions that has fascinated me in the past decade has to do very directly with Wallace's situation and that of other environmental scientists who speak out for nature: is it appropriate for scientists employed by local, state, and national governments and government agencies to make ethical judgments about conservation matters in public contexts and forums, outside of their laboratories, research sites, field stations, and organizational settings?

Some critics believe that it is not right for public scientists to express their "opinions" in public about management practices and policies, such as those that Professor Wallace confronted. In fact, scientists who do so are sometimes rather aggressively chastised by public officials and representatives of private industry and political interest groups, regardless of how well supported their views are scientifically—especially if they threaten the status quo. Lurking behind this criticism is the positivistic idea that it is inappropriate for scientists, especially if they are in public employment, to cross the line between facts and values, or between scientific findings and policy prescriptions. According to this view, it is inappropriate for scientists to become "advocates" of particular environmental choices, no matter how sound their scientific knowledge, how urgent the conservation issue, or how deeply they may believe in the need to conserve natural systems. Their job instead is to provide expertise on the relevant science, including predictions of the likely consequences of various policy choices, for policy makers to digest and evaluate, and to keep their conservation judgments to themselves.

I am skeptical of this separatist model of scientists' responsibilities. So I have spent time investigating the circumstances of scientists who do become advocates and considering some of the arguments that would justify their advocacy. What a pleasure and revelation then it was for me recently to read Linda Lear's magnificent biography of Rachel Carson's life and work. Not only did I discover Professor Wallace's impact on Carson's views about the effects of pesticides on birds and their reproduction, but I was reintroduced to a paradigm case of a scientist who was a compelling champion of environmental conservation and wild species.[1]

Lear tells us that, along with several other academic ornithologists, Wallace was a key scientific authority upon whom Carson relied, in writing

Silent Spring, to formulate her position on the very grave threat that pesticide use posed for birds. Carson corresponded with him on the subject, relied on his scientific documentation, and asked him to review the final revision of her chapter on birds before she shipped it off finally to her editor, Paul Brooks. Professor Wallace had read a paper entitled "The Greatest Threat to Life on Earth" at the 1958 National Audubon Society convention, Lear writes, and had thus "taken up the cause" and become committed, as Carson was, to serious scientific and public consideration of alternatives to DDT spraying.

Given the vicious reaction to *Silent Spring* by the chemical industry and by various applied scientists who were beholden to that industry for research support, it would have been courageous on Wallace's part to take the position he did, just as it was for Carson when she published her book in 1962. However, Carson's situation was more far-reaching and poignant. Not only was she undergoing an extremely debilitating bout with cancer at the time, but she had to steel herself against the many nasty attacks that were made on her ideas, her qualifications to speak out, and even her personal attributes. Lear's biography carefully describes the conscientious research and scientist collaboration that Carson did for *Silent Spring,* her calm and convincing public efforts to subsequently defend the evidence and conclusions in her book, and the private emotional toll that much of the fabricated controversy about the book had on her personally, as she was dying of cancer.

Truly, Carson was an extraordinary person. She was an exceptional example of a scientist deeply committed to both human and ecosystem conservation, and to the idea that public scientists should do what they can to educate the public about the social and ethical implications of scientific matters, and to advocate for public policies that promote the conservation of nature.

VALUES IN THE APPLIED ENVIRONMENTAL SCIENCES

One reason why people question whether an advocacy role such as Carson and Wallace played is proper for public scientists is their belief that values and value judgments are not a legitimate constituent of the sciences and scientific practice. Nevertheless, the applied environmental sciences, such as forestry, fisheries, wildlife science, conservation biology, agriculture, and the like, are not driven by scientific concerns alone. They are obviously value-laden activities, as almost all human activities are; their applications to natural resource management are also deeply affected by values and value judgments. In this regard, they do not differ from other scientific and professional disciplines: they not only generate and utilize scientific data and findings, they also embody ethical norms and standards of professional practice that are articulated, reinforced, and applied in the "culture" of the applied resource disciplines and in the interpersonal relationships of environmental and resource scientists.

The sources of these norms and values are obviously quite varied. They can be located in the nature of these disciplines and professions themselves, in the relationships to society of scientists, their professional groups, and their research programs, and in scientists' personal reflection and interpretation of ethical issues that arise in particular cases and situations. Some of the values have to do with the aims and goals of the applied resource sciences and the context of applied scientific research, and some with the methodology and techniques involved in doing good environmental science. Still others are concerned with the particular responsibilities that scientists collectively impose on each other in order to effectively do what they do, with the responsibilities that scientists have to society, and with their duties to nature. The values may not always be very visible—sometimes they may not even be acknowledged to exist by scientists or thought to be critical in their work. Yet they are present nevertheless and an integral part both of the social aspects of scientific research and of some of the methods whereby scientists conduct their research and involve themselves in resource management.

One important source of such values lies in the ethics codes of scientist groups. These codes typically imply that scientists should engage in ethical conduct with regard to each other as well as society, and in a few cases identify duties toward the natural organisms and ecosystems that they are especially concerned with in their work.

CONTROVERSY ABOUT SCIENTIST ADVOCACY: THE EXAMPLE OF SALMON SURVIVAL AND DAM BREACHING ON THE COLUMBIA RIVER SYSTEM

Carson and Wallace are of course not the first examples of scientists who were vilified for their environmental advocacy. And there have been many examples of such controversies since their day, particularly in my region of the country. Doubts about scientist advocacy have been especially present in debates about endangered and threatened species and their preservation in our forest and river systems. For example, in March 1999, 206 highly regarded public fisheries scientists from throughout the Northwest, many of them employed by the U.S. Fish and Wildlife Service, the Oregon and Idaho departments of fish and wildlife, and Oregon State University, sent a letter to President Clinton urging his executive assistance in recovery efforts for Columbia River basin wild Chinook salmon and steelhead. A 90 percent decline in wild salmon and steelhead runs in the preceding thirty years on the Snake River tributary of the basin was central to their position. This near-extinction of native or "wild" fish stocks was linked by the scientists to the construction of four impassable federal dams on the lower Snake River and to a management approach favoring technological solutions instead of more natural river conditions. This included barging juvenile fish downstream, tinkering with such things as river flows, and modifications of dam structures. Attempts to restore fish populations through heavy reliance on fish transportation on the Columbia-Snake system were a failure, the scientists noted. They expressed their "grave concern" that current measures were falling "far short of what is needed to avert mass extinctions in the near future."[2]

The scientists also pointed out that, due to habitat loss from the construction of dams on the Columbia system, the Snake River sub-basin contained "70 percent of the potential production for spring and summer Chinook salmon and summer steelhead in the entire Columbia basin" and was thus crucial to fish recovery efforts throughout the Pacific Northwest. They asserted that "the weight of scientific evidence clearly shows that wild salmon and steelhead runs in the Snake River basin cannot be recovered under existing river conditions" and referred to "a building scientific consensus that the surest way to restore depleted Snake River fish stocks is to reclaim a 140-mile long reach of their migration corridor by partially removing four dams on the lower Snake River."[3] The plan was dubbed "the natural river option." The Idaho Department of Fish and Game chimed in and also favored this as "the best biological choice for recovering salmon and steelhead in Idaho." The department concluded, "This assessment is logical, biologically sound, has the highest certainty of success and lowest risk of failure, and is consistent with the preponderance of scientific data." State fish and wildlife departments in Oregon and Washington also later agreed that dam breaching was scientifically the best alternative. In short, support for the letter-writers' position was provided by many other scientists and their agencies. The 206 scientists ended their letter by calling for abandonment of current strategies and a return to "the normative river conditions under which these fish evolved."[4]

After the letter was made public, political controversy erupted immediately both as to the advisability of this option and the reliability of the science on which it was based. Spokespeople for several prominent Northwest politicians and key river user groups criticized the scientists for acting improperly, arguing that it was inappropriate for government employees to take a public position on a disputed resource issue. Not only were the scientists wrong about the science, one political spokesman said, but they were wrong about their roles. Their job was strictly to inform the public and leave the decision making to elected leaders. Once scientists go beyond advising policy makers on what is "good science" and take a stand, opponents argued, they go beyond their purview as scientists.[5] A spokesman for U.S. Senator Larry Craig, R-Idaho, asserted that "taking one alleged cause for declining salmon and making that the only focus of debate automatically puts their credibility into question. They are ignoring a majority of scientific data that does not call for breaching dams."[6] A representative of Idaho Governor Dirk Kempthorne on the Northwest Power Planning Council said that the letter-signers had "stepped from the role of being scientists to the role of being politicians," had lost "credibility," and should leave the decision making to elected leaders.[7] Others objected as well, representing industrial power consumers, companies that use the Snake River for barge transportation, and farmers who draw irrigation water from behind one of the four dams. An editorial in the major newspaper in Oregon, *The Oregonian*, called the scientists' letter "an act of desperation" and claimed that "a scientific consensus on dam breaching has not been reached," contrary to the scientists' claim.[8]

At the same time support for the scientists was expressed by other scientists, by various regional and national environmental groups, including several Indian tribes in the basin, and by a few regional politicians. Charlie Petrosky, a fisheries biologist with the Idaho Department of Fish and Game, said that "the region has skipped around this problem for years. We keep re-assessing things and dragging things out. Meanwhile, the fish are continuing to decline."[9] Richard Gross, a fisheries biologist and letter-signer, was quoted as saying that "this letter is simply an attempt to speak our minds as citizens with the knowledge we have as scientists. What's wrong with that?"[10] And the Oregon Chapter of the American Fisheries Society, the most important professional group of fisheries scientists in Oregon, released a statement saying that the four dams are a "significant threat to the continued existence of remaining Snake River salmon and steelhead stocks." They concluded that "if society-at-large wishes to restore these salmonids to a sustainable, fishable level, a significant portion of the lower Snake River must be returned to a free-flowing condition by breaching the four lower Snake River dams, and this action must happen soon."[11] One well-known newspaper columnist who frequently wrote about the outdoors argued that objecting politicians could not handle the "truth" about the scientist consensus on salmon science and that delays would favor the status quo that obviously harms wild salmon.[12] Representative Earl Blumenauer, D-Ore., a well-known Oregon politician, called breaching a "legitimate alternative."[13] Finally, in April 1999 the Lower Snake River was designated the most endangered river in the nation by American Rivers as part of its annual effort to bring river problems to the attention of the country at large.[14]

TWO MODELS OF ENVIRONMENTAL ADVOCACY BY SCIENTISTS

Lurking behind these criticisms of the scientists' public stand is what I have called the "separatist" or "engineering technician model" of the role of public scientists. Underneath this, in turn, is the philosophy of positivism.

Positivism declares that there is a wide gap between science and values, between scientific thinking and value judgments.[15] On some interpretations, it follows that there is a logical chasm between scientists explaining science to society and their advocating for particular conservation policies or for the rights of nature and human communities. On this view, laboratory and experimental scientists who work for a public agency or organization should not cross the line supposedly separating scientific findings and policy prescriptions, to become public policy advocates or advocates of particular environmental choices, no matter how deeply they may personally believe in the need to conserve species and natural systems or how urgent the conservation issue. Instead their job is, as noted above, to present the data and findings for legitimate policy makers to digest and to provide the policy makers with technical expertise on the relevant scientific matters at hand. They are like engineering technicians who must do the technical job for which they are hired and leave the policy issues alone.

On the other side of the coin are those who believe that it is perfectly legitimate for public scientists to be advocates of ethical positions in the public policy process. This alternative view says that while environmental and natural resource scientists should be open about their scientific judgments and their environmental ethics, and should not arrogate to themselves the exclusive right to express and promote their values and make policy judgments, they have as much right to do so as others. In fact, they should think of themselves as involved in a joint or shared valuing process with other scientists, resource managers, politicians, members of interest groups, and the public in which all have important contributions to make.

On this "shared decision-making model," scientists should work cooperatively with these other participants as they formulate and express their own ethical judgments, in order to develop consensual values that support particular land management decisions. Public scientists can legitimately present and advocate environmental ethics in public contexts, though they should also understand that their value judgments are not superior just because they are scientists. This second role, the role so powerfully exemplified by the life of Rachel Carson, is the one I would like to support.

ARGUMENTS IN FAVOR OF ENVIRONMENTAL ADVOCACY
BY PUBLIC SCIENTISTS

What would justify the idea that it is acceptable for a public scientist to take an open stand on a public environmental matter—something that might fly in the face of normal scientist behavior or challenge the bureaucratic or political status quo? There are a number of solid reasons, some of which are well exemplified in the stories of Carson and Wallace. One important reason has to do with the scientifically biased or loaded context in which scientific research and public decision making about local or regional environmental problems is sometimes conducted. A second has to do with the fact that public scientists might have assumed legitimate ethical responsibilities to be conservation advocates as a result of membership in a professional scientist group and a personal commitment to the group's ethics code. At the same time, any general conclusion in favor of an advocacy role must still deal with the very practical circumstances in which advocacy arises for public scientists. Because it is difficult to prejudge those circumstances without knowing what they all are, there will certainly be situations in which advocacy is not advisable and also not a responsibility or duty for public scientists. But let me turn to these two points, and formulate them as arguments.

Biased Decision Procedures that Produce
Environmental Harms

The first argument revolves around the fact that sometimes, if public environmental and resource scientists do not take ethical stands on at least some environmental issues and become advocates, public environmental decisions could be made that would be unfavorable to the maintenance of such goals as ecosystem and human health, ecological and human community sustainability, or the protection of biodiversity and endangered species. This can happen because of the scientifically biased way in which some resource decision-processes may be structured from the outset or because of the scientifically biased way that they may be conducted over time (or both).

Philosophers of science have laid the groundwork for understanding how the choices about what particular scientific problem to study, what data to collect and where, and what methodology to use in scientific research projects all involve value judgments. Not all such choices are biased by these values, but some are biased in particular cases.[16] Natural resource policy processes can be biased at the outset, either subtly or blatantly, by political factors or by bureaucratic decision rules, policies, and procedures that already favor less desirable conservation outcomes, even before scientific research is funded and conducted. Scientific opinion is mined for its relevancy to the decision. This can eliminate some very pertinent research proposals and research that would otherwise be worthy by well-accepted criteria within the relevant scientific disciplines. This initial and biased loading can lead to resource decisions that do not promote desirable environmental policy goals even if the subsequent process of conducting the funded research is methodologically sound.

Kristin Shrader-Frechette, a distinguished contributor to the fields of environmental ethics and philosophy of science, argues that decision making in government, industry, and education that has harmful consequences for such things as ecosystem health is often highly "partisan" environmentally and contrary to environmental goals that the public holds dear.[17] This might involve faulty science or the manipulation of scientific data and findings to fit preset objectives that compromise these goals, or it might reflect misplaced research priorities that fail to fund studies that would reveal all of the relevant scientific data or information. Then the time may be ripe for scientists to speak out in order to help move public decision making in a more balanced and favorable environmental direction by advocating for contrary forms of policy and research.

Shrader-Frechette concludes that environmental advocacy by scientists, researchers, and other scholars is not only "permissible but perhaps ethically mandatory" in these situations.[18] She bases her conclusion partly on a consideration of the consequences of environmental neutrality in a world in which environmental abuses and harms are occurring on a regular basis, and are promoted by government and industry. Shrader-Frechette applies her argument primarily to university scientists and faculty, who are more free of political interference than other publicly employed scientists, but the argument can clearly be extended to the latter as well.

Shrader-Frechette analyzes in detail one excellent example in the case of federal government nuclear waste storage studies at the Yucca Mountain site in Nevada.[19] She argues that, because of initial assumptions about how to study the underground waste problem and about the structure of the subsurface geology in the area, research was done and biased results produced which favored the conclusion that such storage would be safe at the site. To use her language, the playing field was tilted against local human health and in favor of environmental contamination at the outset; this "tilt" infected the process of conducting the research itself.

The point is that it is at least ethically permissible if not obligatory for public scientists to speak out in cases like this because they are in the best position to understand the relevant science and the consequences of damaging environmental policies and decisions. As holders of specialized scientific knowledge that may have been developed in the scientists' capacity as scientists or become known to them in their work, they can find themselves in a unique position to say something useful about what are the preferable policy decisions. Because they also have an implied contract with society and the public to use their knowledge for the public good, they can be justified in speaking out in favor of policies that are supported by their knowledge. Moreover, they can know when government agencies and others involved in decision making are not as forthright or honest in representing that scientific knowledge as they should be.

When public resource agencies attempt to integrate scientific findings with other factors, such as agency rules and standards, legal directives, estimates of economic costs and benefits, the desires of politicians, and public

opinion, ecosystem considerations can be seriously watered down in conservation decisions. Thus scientists working for the agencies can end up being the
only ones left with the knowledge and authority to represent the interests of
the public and the natural systems affected by agency decisions.

In the dam-breaching controversy, it was clear that in 1999 the 206 public
scientists represented the community of Pacific Northwest fisheries scientists
and accurately articulated the "building" consensus in that community about
the biological importance of dam breaching. Of all of the participants in the
controversy, they were in the best position to interpret the ecological consequences of the various alternatives being considered by politicians and the
resource management bureaucracy, and uniquely so, because they were the
ones doing the original biological and ecological research on which those
interpretations were based. They were the most competent to determine that
delays to do more research or conduct more evaluations of the alternatives
would further endanger wild salmon and steelhead stocks on the Snake River
and make restoration more difficult and uncertain.

*Ethics Embodied in the Codes of the Applied
Scientific Professions*

The second argument for public scientist advocacy has to do with the fact that
scientists may have a personal commitment to professionalism, to a professional society, and to a code of professional ethics that makes advocacy
morally permissible, even a moral responsibility in some circumstances.

As one examines codes in such applied environmental sciences as
forestry, fisheries, and wildlife biology, three disciplines deeply involved with
forest and aquatic systems in the Pacific Northwest, it becomes obvious that
they differ with regard to the kinds of ethical responsibilities that resource scientists and professionals are said to have. All professional ethics codes identify responsibilities that scientists have to one another, but a few go further
and mention obligations that they have not only to humans but also to nonhuman species and natural systems, to such creatures as owls and fish and
such systems as forests and rivers.

This difference can be seen in two significant codes in forestry and fisheries science. First is the code of the Society of American Foresters (SAF), the
largest professional group of foresters in the United States.[20] The SAF code
has a long history—it was first adopted in 1948—and was revised several times
in recent years to take advantage of new ideas about forester responsibilities
and public values. Nevertheless, the code contains no specific ethical responsibilities of foresters to the components of forest ecosystems such as wildlife
and endangered species.

In contrast, in the early 1990s the Oregon Chapter of the American
Fisheries Society (AFS) designed a supplement to the code of ethics of its

parent organization that is innovative in spelling out the biocentric obliga-tions of fisheries professionals.[21] In addition to the goals of providing responsible nature stewardship and credible science—goals of the SAF as well—it includes more specific environmental norms such as obligations to maintain the structure, function, and integrity of aquatic, riparian, and upland ecosystems.

Especially relevant is that portion of the Oregon chapter code that identi-fies responsibilities of fisheries scientists to "speak and write honestly and openly about the results of" their work, "neither hiding nor exaggerating their implications." Moreover, fisheries scientists are to recognize that their deeply held convictions may conflict with the interests and convictions of others. They are further obligated to distinguish between the "reports of results from rigorous study and professional opinions based on observations or intuition" and to refrain from putting their professional opinions forward "as fact." They should distinguish as well between recommendations based on science and those based on policy, and, most importantly, be aware that their profes-sional convictions may sometimes conflict with the policies of their employ-ers. When such conflict arises, the code advises, they should (the code is written in the first person) "provide decision makers with full supporting evi-dence and sufficient time for study and action before I publicly disclose my views." Finally, their "commitment to the profession and to ecosystems, including their human components, may compel me on occasion to speak against policies or actions of my employer."[22] So this code makes it quite clear that it is ethically permissible and sometimes obligatory for public fisheries scientists to be advocates for ecosystems and nature's aquatic creatures.

ETHICS CODES AND ENVIRONMENTAL ADVOCACY BY SCIENTISTS

As the preceding examples show, at least some codes of professional ethics in the natural resource disciplines incorporate new, more biocentered or ecocen-tered responsibilities to the natural systems and species that resource scien-tists manage and study. There will be times then when it is ethically permissible and sometimes a duty for scientists to speak out not only for humans but for the nonhuman parts of nature, such as endangered stocks of salmon or invertebrate species in old growth forests. Indeed, the Oregon Chapter of the AFS has taken this obligation seriously and intervened in court cases involving endangered salmon stocks in the Pacific Northwest. Moreover, this chapter supported the action of the 206 scientists to write its letter to the Clinton administration, openly acknowledging its commitment to the fish species and aquatic systems that are the focus of their work.

Of course these responsibilities to species and ecosystems have to be bal-anced with those to humans and human society, this code implies. But no longer would it be unethical or out of their purview for fisheries scientists to speak out publicly on issues of public resource management. Speaking out would be justified regardless of whether politicians and others who support the conservation status quo would agree with their ethical or scientific judgments. In the dam-breaching case, many of the letter-signing scientists were members of professional groups such as the Oregon Chapter of the AFS that directly incorporate responsibilities to wild and endangered fish species into their codes of ethics. In fact, it is mostly noncontroversial in these groups that fisheries scientists have such responsibilities and that they must at least occasionally speak out, as the situation warrants, in favor of wild fish and aquatic system protection.

SOME DRAWBACKS TO SCIENTIST ADVOCACY

Advocacy is not always a "pure duty" and must be balanced, in individual cases, with other obligations and considerations. The circumstances in which it might be advisable for a scientist to be an advocate are not always as clear-cut as in the dam-breaching situation or as they were for Carson and Wallace. And there are certainly some drawbacks that public servants will normally have to weigh in the balance. A National Science Foundation-funded social research project on which I worked indicates that public environmental scientists in the Pacific Northwest are typically well aware of these kinds of limitations, and of how speaking out can sometimes work against their personal and professional interests.[23] In our research we have discovered an interesting twist on this matter, for it is not only politicians who may object to conservation advocacy, or representatives of natural resource industries, the usual suspects. But the "culture" of science itself does not always favor this kind of activism, and scientists are sometimes the most avid defenders of the technician role and the most vocal critics of scientists who advocate for nature.

Part of what is behind this is the fact that even though ecological scientists may be in the best position to interpret scientific findings about ecosystems, their communal scientific norms and interactions also promote cautiousness and conservatism in formulating and interpreting those findings. Ecological scientists recognize the obvious complexities of ecosystems and the difficulties of gathering ecosystem data in their own fields and relating it to data in other scientific fields. They understand that there are problems with designing substantive field experiments that can be generalized to large spatial and temporal scales and to different ecosystem types. Scientists also need and are willing to exercise patience in doing research on ecosystems, and the results of their experiments may not be confirmed or secure in the short run unless considerable further research and interpretation is done over very lengthy time periods, sometimes decades or longer. This too lends itself to interpretive conservatism.

Moreover, regardless of whether certain forms of philosophy of science, such as positivism, may have withered away or been substantially revised in contemporary philosophical circles, scientists sometimes still approach their work by following a positivist methodological principle. They often attempt in research to falsify the latest scientific findings and hypotheses rather than seek to confirm them or generate new ones. Thus if a scientist interprets data in a way that does not conform to the "normal science" of the day because it goes out on a limb in some respect, this may appear to be an extreme or incorrect perspective to other scientists in that specialty, whether it actually is or not.

A related difficulty is that, given scientific uncertainty about the functioning of ecosystems, there may really be no very clear line, in some cases, that separates a reasonable from a questionable interpretation of ecological data. Speaking in a public context can thus sometimes seem to require or encourage scientists to step beyond a safe, narrow interpretation of data and favor an option that other reputable scientists might hesitate to embrace. This can happen in public environmental policy contexts, because nonscientists often expect scientists to provide more definitive answers to scientific questions than the scientists are able to produce. The reasons for this in turn may be that politicians and legislators have been led to believe that science is more authoritative and "objective" than it sometimes is, or that public policy and applicable law may require more scientific certainty than is available. Sometimes, short-term political timetables push participants in the policy process to pressure scientists for their opinions. Presenting one's best conservation judgment in these situations can be risky and can subject a scientist to counterattacks by colleagues, by others in the resource industries, or by environmental groups who advocate different policy options.[24]

The public prestige and status that can result when a publicly employed scientist is viewed as an environmental authority in environmental policy may also be very seductive for some scientists, leading some of them to speak too far beyond the data. Thus speaking publicly as if one knew exactly what is correct scientifically and extrapolating this to advocate for a particular conservation option may be hazardous professionally and may cause one to lose credibility within the scientific community itself.

In interviews that were part of our NSF research, we discovered that ecological scientists in the Pacific Northwest can clearly point to several examples of once quite respected scientists who, they believed, had gone so far over the advocacy line that they had lost credibility in the scientific community. Interestingly, most nonscientists would not have raised an eyebrow about this behavior and would still have viewed these scientists as credible experts. In short, there are some clear dangers for public scientists to serve as advocates, and, in fact, for their serving in a public role at all.

It is best to conceive of the scientist's role in public environmental issues as a shared responsibility and task. Some public scientists may not be temperamentally suited to becoming involved in policy matters outside their own scientific organizations, and one really cannot expect them to do so. On the other hand, if other scientists speak their minds as openly, honestly, and effectively as Carson and Wallace did, there is evidence that few citizens will object to their participating actively in environmental decision making. Our research indicates that the public agrees that scientists should work closely with resource managers and others in the policy process to integrate scientific findings into resource decisions. As to whether scientists should actively advocate for the decisions that they personally and professionally prefer, the public is evenly divided.[25] Perhaps if front-line research and field scientists were more directly engaged in the processes of resource decision making, this kind of activism, even if ethically justified, would be more accepted as well.

CARSON AS AN ADVOCATE AND THINKER

Like many others, I read *Silent Spring* in the 1960s and followed the public debate that resulted. I eventually came to understand the book's very significant influence on the environmental movement of the 1960s and 1970s, and its positive effect on decisions by Congress to develop new environmental laws at that time. But I had not paid much attention to the debate about scientist advocacy nor had I understood some of the arguments for why this can make sense. Doing so has given me new admiration for both Carson and Wallace as individuals who had the integrity and fortitude to stand up for their scientific and moral beliefs.

Reading Lear's biography has also led me to more fully realize that, just as Aldo Leopold developed a philosophy about the land,[26] Carson developed a philosophy in regard to the sea and the marine environment. She thought of ecology and aesthetics as essential bases for understanding our ethical obligations to nature and had deep concerns about the consequences of shortsighted and destructive human behavior for the health and beauty of both the land and the oceans. Underneath her philosophical approach was an explicit commitment to Albert Schweitzer's principle of "reverence for life" and a desire to see a more ecologically and aesthetically sensible form of nature stewardship that is backed up by sound science. The story of Carson's life is essential reading for those who wish to understand why it is crucial for scientists to stand up for their scientific and moral beliefs, and to represent the interests of the public and nature, *publicly*, in the continuing effort to reunite humans with the natural world.

NOTES

1. Linda Lear, *Rachel Carson: Witness for Nature* (New York: Henry Holt, 1997).

2. Snake River Campaign, Letter to President Clinton, Mar. 20, 1999. Available online at www.taxpayer.net/snake/TakeAction/scientistletter.htm.

3. Ibid.

4. Ibid.

5. Jonathan Brunckman, "Leaders Object to Stance on Breaching," *The Oregonian*, Mar. 27, 1999, D1.

6. Ibid.

7. Ibid.

8. "Breaching Good Faith," *The Oregonian*, Mar. 29, 1999, C8.

9. Brunckman, "Leaders Object to Stance on Breaching."

10. Ibid.

11. Excerpted in *Reflections, Newsletter of the Program for Ethics, Science and the Environment*, Special issue no. 4, "Environmental Advocacy by Environmental Scientists," Department of Philosophy, Oregon State University, Corvallis, Ore., April 2000, 17.

12. Scott Stouder, "Leaders Can't Handle the Truth on Salmon, Dams," *Corvallis Gazette-Times*, Apr. 4, 1999, B10.

13. Jim Barnett, "Blumenauer Calls Dam Removal 'Legitimate' Alternative for Fish," *The Oregonian*, Apr. 13, 1999, B5.

14. Jim Barnett, "River Receives Dubious Honor," *The Oregonian*, Apr. 12, 1999, B4.

15. I call this "the engineering technician model" because in some respects it makes the scientist a kind of technician responsible for understanding, explaining, and repairing natural systems but not deciding much of anything else about them. I outline this and other models in "Environmental Scientists as Advocates for Nature: Some Medical Models," a paper read at the annual conference of the Society for Philosophy in a Contemporary World, Estes Park, Colorado, August 1994.

16. Helen Longino, *Science as Social Knowledge* (Princeton, N.J.: Princeton University Press, 1990).

17. Kristin Shrader-Frechette, "Ethics and Environmental Advocacy," in *Environmental Ethics and Forestry: A Reader*, ed. Peter C. List (Philadelphia: Temple University Press, 2000), 209–220.

18. Ibid., 209.

19. Kristin Shrader-Frechette, "Unsafe at Any Depth: Geological Methods, Subjective Judgments, and Nuclear Waste Disposal," in *Artifacts, Representations and Social Practice*, ed. Carol C. Gould and Robert S. Cohen (The Hague, Netherlands: Kluwer Academic Publishers, 1994), 501–524; Kristin Shrader-Frechette, "Science, Environmental Risk Assessment, and the Frame Problem," *Bioscience* 44 (1994): 548–51; and Kristin Shrader-Frechette, "High-Level Waste, Low-Level Logic," *The Bulletin of the Atomic Scientists* 50 (1994): 40–45. The theoretical philosophy of science on which part of Shrader-Frechette's analysis is based can be found in Naomi Oreskes, Kristin Shrader-Frechette, and Kenneth Belitz, "Verification, Validation, and Confirmation of Numerical Models in the Earth Sciences," *Science* 263 (1992): 641–46. She also discusses the processes by which such risk assessments are made in regard to environmental situations in her book *Risk and Rationality* (Berkeley: University of California Press, 1991).

20. Society of American Foresters, SAF Code of Ethics. Adopted by the Society of American Foresters by member referendum, Nov. 3, 2000. Available online at www.safnet.org/who/codeofethics.cfm.

21. American Fisheries Society, "Code of Ethics," Oregon Chapter, in List, *Environmental Ethics and Forestry*, 175–76.

22. Ibid.

23. Brent Steel, Peter C. List, Denise Lach, and Bruce Shindler, "The Role of Scientists in the Environmental Policy Process: A Case Study from the American West," *Environmental Science and Policy* 7 (2004): 1–13.

24. Ibid. It is interesting to note that sometimes, even when environmental scientists present accurate and well-researched scientific data and findings in a public context, and confine themselves to the technician role, they are still criticized for doing what clearly follows from even the most narrow interpretation of their professional responsibilities. This is especially true when this appears to run counter to status quo practices in natural resource management or to standard beliefs among natural resource industries and environmental groups. Our NSF research study surveyed public environmental scientists and others involved in federal natural resource management in the Pacific Northwest, and learned that this phenomenon of scientists reporting publicly on their findings and then being criticized for doing so is not uncommon. Public agency and university scientists, whether state or federal, must be careful about what they say and where they say it, especially if a related resource matter is controversial publicly. One very respected forest scientist told us that he and his colleagues had to learn how to couch their findings in language that would be more unassailable, obscure, and neutral seeming in order to avoid needlessly raising the hackles of industry or environmental

groups, even though what they said would have been uncontroversial in their own scientific circles. We were told that some scientists had become so disenchanted or wary of serving in public roles in forest management in the Pacific Northwest that they had returned to the safety and comforts of their laboratories, field stations, and research projects.

25. Ibid.

26. Aldo Leopold, *A Sand County Almanac: and Sketches Here and There* (New York: Oxford University Press, 1949).

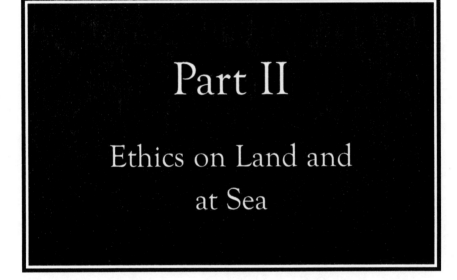

Part II

Ethics on Land and
at Sea

4

Rachel Carson's Environmental Ethics

Philip Cafaro

R achel Carson has been called the founder of the U.S. environmental movement, which some date, plausibly, to the publication of *Silent Spring* in
1962. That best-selling book focused public attention on the problem of pesticide and other chemical pollution, and led to such landmark legislation as the
U.S. Clean Water Act and the banning of DDT in many countries throughout
the world. Whatever Carson's arguments were in *Silent Spring*, they succeeded.
Yet she has received little attention from environmental ethicists.[1]

I believe Rachel Carson was not just a successful polemicist, but an
important environmental thinker. With the publication of a definitive biography, Linda Lear's *Rachel Carson: Witness for Nature*, we can better understand
her environmental philosophy, for Carson lived that philosophy as well as
wrote about it.[2] Meeting Carson the scientist and naturalist clarifies for the
reader Carson's understanding of the role knowledge can play in a larger relationship to nature. Studying her fifteen-year career as a U.S. Fish and Wildlife
Service biologist gives us valuable insight into her views on practical conservation issues. Further, Carson's personal story teaches us much about humility
and courage, as she triumphed over various setbacks and achieved great literary success while faithfully discharging her many responsibilities to family,
friends, and nature. Still, in order to best understand Carson's environmental
ethics, the place to start is with *Silent Spring*.

This chapter originally appeared in *Worldviews*, volume 6, number 1 (2002): 58–80. It
is reproduced here, in slightly edited form, with permission of Brill Academic
Publishers.

SILENT SPRING

Silent Spring constitutes an extended argument for strictly limiting the use of pesticides, herbicides, and other dangerous agricultural and industrial chemicals, and for their careful application and safe disposal when such use is necessary. This argument rests on both factual and evaluative premises. Factually, *Silent Spring*'s case rests on numerous scientific and anecdotal accounts of the abuse of these chemicals. It also rests on such easy-to-establish facts as companies' common failure to test products' effects on humans and nonhumans, users' frequent negligence in following instructions for applying agricultural chemicals, and the weakness and lack of enforcement of government regulations. Carson's clear presentation of such facts, and of the basic science needed to understand the issues, give her book its authority. Carson's scientific credentials had already been firmly established in earlier works that had popularized recent developments in oceanography and marine biology. Without Carson's scientific credibility and impressive presentation of "the facts," *Silent Spring* would not have won such a large hearing.[3]

Nevertheless, evaluative or ethical premises were equally important to Carson's overall position. She avoided complicated ethical argument in *Silent Spring*, perhaps believing that the ethical issues really were quite simple. More likely, Carson reasoned that simple appeals to widely held values would be more convincing. In any case, *Silent Spring* is filled with short, emphatic ethical statements and arguments. Evaluatively (and somewhat schematically) its plea for restraint rests on a triple foundation of human health considerations, the moral considerability of nonhuman beings, and the value to humans of preserving wild nature and a diverse and varied landscape.

Doubtless most important for many readers were Carson's chapters on acute pesticide poisoning, and these chemicals' potential to cause cancer and human birth defects. For these readers Carson states the moral clearly: "Man, however much he may like to pretend the contrary, is part of nature. [He cannot] escape a pollution that is now so thoroughly distributed throughout the world."[4] Examples of human sicknesses and fatalities caused by inappropriate use of chemicals recur throughout the book.

Carson was acutely aware of the importance of good health, having suffered a variety of serious illnesses over the years. In fact, she was dying of cancer as she finished *Silent Spring*. Yet in writing the book, she seems to have been more concerned with the destruction of wild nature and its resultant human loss. Many of her arguments explicitly assert or implicitly rely on the moral considerability of nonhuman beings. For example, she recounts a massive dieldrin spraying program to eradicate Japanese beetles in and around Sheldon, Illinois. Robins, meadowlarks, pheasants, and other birds were virtually wiped out; so were squirrels. Amazingly, 90 percent of area farm cats

were killed during the first season of spraying. "Incidents like the eastern
Illinois spraying," Carson reflected,

> raise a question that is not only scientific but moral. The question is
> whether any civilization can wage relentless war on life without destroying
> itself, and without losing the right to be called civilized.... These creatures
> [wild and domestic] are innocent of any harm to man. Indeed, by their very
> existence they and their fellows make his life more pleasant. Yet he rewards
> them with a death that is not only sudden but horrible.[5]

Carson goes on to describe the ghastly convulsions observed in poisoned birds
at Sheldon, and concludes: "By acquiescing in an act that can cause such suffering to a living creature, who among us is not diminished as a human being?"[6]

This passage clearly implies moral considerability on the animals' part
and moral responsibility on our part. Both inflicting unnecessary suffering
and causing unnecessary loss of nonhuman life are morally wrong. A fully
human being is a humane being, feeling compassion for the suffering of
others. A true civilization does not dominate or destroy the nonhuman world;
it protects and seeks to understand it.

In another section, Carson fights the common prejudice against insects
by explaining to her readers the important role of honeybees, wild bees, and
other pollinators in natural and human economies. "These insects," she concludes, "so essential to our agriculture and indeed to our landscape as we
know it, *deserve something better from us* than the senseless destruction of their
habitat."[7] Here again, the notion of desert clearly implies moral considerability. Similar examples could be multiplied many times. They are not usually
found pure—that is, Carson does not assert nonhuman moral considerability
regardless of, or in contrast to, human self-interest. Instead, as in the examples above, she asserts nonhuman moral considerability and asserts that our
selfish human interests practically harmonize with its recognition.

Our interests and their interests largely coincide—for two reasons. First,
we inhabit the same environment. Hence we cannot poison other animals
without poisoning ourselves. Second, preserving wild nature helps promote
human happiness and flourishing. Carson approvingly quotes ecologist Paul
Shepard and U.S. Supreme Court Justice William O. Douglas on the aesthetic value and intellectual stimulation provided by wildlife, wild places, and
a diverse and varied landscape.[8] She also adds her own arguments:

> To the bird watcher, the suburbanite who derives joy from birds in his
> garden, the hunter, the fisherman or the explorer of wild regions, any-
> thing that destroys the wildlife of an area for even a single year has
> deprived him of pleasure to which he has a legitimate right.[9]

> Over increasingly large areas of the United States, spring now comes
> unheralded by the return of the birds, and the early mornings are

strangely silent where once they were filled with the beauty of bird song....."Can anyone imagine anything so cheerless and dreary as a springtime without a robin's song?"[10]

Who has decided—who has the *right* to decide—for the countless legions of people who were not consulted that the supreme value is a world without insects, even though it be also a sterile world ungraced by the curving wing of a bird in flight? The decision is that of the authoritarian temporarily entrusted with power; he has made it during a moment of inattention by millions to whom beauty and the ordered world of nature still have a meaning that is deep and imperative.[11]

Pleasure, adventure, beauty, grace, even meaning—all these may be driven from our world along with the "target organisms," impoverishing our own lives. A silent spring is a season of loss to us and to them, the losses inseparably linked.

What is the relative importance of these three main evaluative premises—preserve human health; respect the moral considerability of nonhuman beings; promote human happiness and flourishing—in *Silent Spring*? I see no evidence that one is any more important than another to Carson's main argument. They are the three strong legs of an environmental ethics in which a healthy, diverse environment provides the wherewithal for human and nonhuman flourishing.

Carson's critics often tried to drive a wedge between these three ethical premises, forcing her to acknowledge cases where various human interests, and especially human and nonhuman interests, were at odds. As a bit of doggerel in an information packet from the National Pest Control Association had it:

> Hunger, hunger, are you listening,
> To the words from Rachel's pen?
> Words which taken at face value,
> Place lives of birds 'bove those of men.[12]

Many critics argued that DDT was necessary to prevent mosquito-borne diseases and increase harvests in developing nations.[13] Here the question of this necessity became important (were there other ways to accomplish these important goals?) along with a complete reckoning of the actual effects of using these chemicals. Carson generally steered clear of the ethical question of how to balance human and nonhuman interests. She probably believed that she stood a better chance of moving society toward safer, reduced pesticide use by emphasizing the common dangers pesticides posed to humans and nonhumans. In her own life, however, she often went considerably out of her way to avoid harming nonhuman beings, carefully returning microscopic tide pool specimens to the ocean after studying them, for example.[14]

Similarly, Carson criticized the increasing simplification and sterility of modern farm and suburban landscapes, pointing out a *human* cost to such dullness. Her opponents countered that this was the cost of progress and prosperity, in effect arguing that increased wealth and productivity were more important than the merely aesthetic values appreciated by bird-watchers. "We can live without birds and animals," reflected one correspondent, "but, as the current market slump shows, we cannot live without business."[15] Once again, Carson preferred to argue that the choice—birds or business—was a false one, in most cases. But she also stood up strongly for the importance of noneconomic values in a truly human life, particularly the appreciation of beauty, the search for knowledge, and the achievement of wisdom.[16] Such values were important to many of her readers, she believed, and if they weren't, they should be. As for herself, she found birds more essential to her happiness than banknotes.[17]

In general, Carson (and legions of environmentalists to come) emphasized the complementarity in the great majority of cases of the three basic goals of protecting human health, preserving nonhuman life, and promoting human flourishing. She shone a spotlight on the selfishness and shortsightedness which so often undermine all three goals. Meanwhile, in trying to move her society toward greater recognition of nonhuman interests and higher human interests, Carson developed an environmental ethics with both nonanthropocentric and enlightened anthropocentric elements. While *Silent Spring* shows how these two aspects may converge regarding an important public policy issue, Carson's own life, dedicated to knowing and appreciating nature, shows how they converge at the personal level.[18] Recognition of the intrinsic value of nonhuman beings provides benefits that outweigh the restrictions such recognition places upon us. So too, a nobler view of human life—one focused on friendship, the pursuit of knowledge and a rich experience, rather than on getting and spending—should lead to less environmentally destructive lifestyles. The lives of the great naturalists—including Rachel Carson's—suggest that we really will live better lives when we do right by nature.[19]

As philosophers, we are inclined to ask: what are the "foundations" of Rachel Carson's environmental ethics? Otherwise put: how does she justify her three main evaluative premises (or her two controversial ones, concern for human health presumably needing no justification)? Perhaps she believed that people who understood and experienced wild nature would come to accept its moral considerability and its continued importance to human happiness and flourishing, and that philosophical arguments could add little to such understanding and experience. Perhaps she believed that by implying such general ethical principles as "cause no unnecessary suffering" or "preserve opportunities for human knowledge and experience," she was resting on ethical ultimates that were beyond justification.

In *Silent Spring* Carson describes poisoned ground squirrels whose attitudes in death—backs bowed, mouths filled with dirt from biting the ground—suggest they died in agony. She adds the simple reflection that causing such suffering diminishes us as human beings. She pictures a varied and beautiful roadside filled with bright flowers and buzzing insects, then the same after spraying: a dull, sere, silent wasteland. Now, she writes, it is "something to be traversed quickly, a sight to be endured with one's mind closed to thoughts of the sterile and hideous world we are letting our technicians make."[20] Carson could paint such pictures and draw such obvious morals for her readers. In her earlier natural history writings, she helped hundreds of thousands of people to recognize new plants and animals and appreciate what they were seeing. She could create or enhance a mood before nature of wonder, appreciation, or reverence. But more than that she could not do. Without a personal experience of these things, there is no *is* from which to move to the moral *ought*. With such experience, the movement from *is* to *ought* is typically accomplished. Let the philosopher who can better explain this process do so!

Another intriguing question remains at the foundational level: the role that religion or spirituality played in grounding Carson's personal environmental ethic. *Silent Spring* is dedicated to Albert Schweitzer, and Carson's biographer, Linda Lear, reports that a handwritten letter and inscribed portrait from Schweitzer were Carson's most prized possessions in her last years.[21] In her foreword to Ruth Harrison's *Animal Machines*, a pioneering work in the animal welfare movement, Carson wrote of the need for a "Schweitzerian ethic that embraces decent consideration for all living creatures—a true reverence for life."[22] Carson's previous best seller, *The Edge of the Sea*, shows flashes of a genuine if unobtrusive spiritual sensibility, particularly in its final, stirring paean to "the enduring sea" and "the ultimate mystery of life," but also in its appreciation of the "fragile beauty" of small, transient, individual life-forms.[23] Paul Brooks, Carson's friend and longtime editor, wrote that Carson "felt a spiritual as well as physical closeness to the individual creatures about whom she wrote" and asserted that "her attitude toward the natural world was that of a deeply religious person."[24]

Still, I think the importance of religion and spirituality to Carson's environmental ethics can be exaggerated. She clearly had moments of spiritual epiphany, but Carson's more usual posture before nature, in her books and in her life, seems to have been appreciation and interest. Reverence, respect, and appreciation are not three names for the same thing. Appeals to a proper reverence may have strong rhetorical and logical force when addressed to believers, but Carson uses these appeals sparingly in her books. But it could be that for her, the word "reverence" captures an ascription of high value or intrinsic value, rather than an essentially religious view of the world. Too, Carson always puts the emphasis on life rather than on any putative creator. She certainly had little interest in orthodox religious doctrine.

Perhaps it is most accurate to say that Rachel Carson embraced nature in all its manifestations, from the small to the grand and from the scientific to the mystical. These experiences and interactions seem to have motivated her own powerful concern and effective action on behalf of nature. Ultimately, I think, her ethical foundation is experiential. Aesthetic, intellectual, sensual, imaginative, *personal* experience grounds ethical judgments and action. In the main, Carson's writings are concerned to facilitate such experiences, rather than to argue for particular ethical positions. They certainly do not argue for particular religious beliefs.[25]

Three further themes round out the ethical argument of *Silent Spring*: (1) Carson's disapproval of economism—the overvaluation or exclusive focus on economic goals and pursuits; (2) her criticisms of a human "war on nature"; and (3) her warnings concerning the increased artificiality and simplification of the landscape.

Carson criticized the age as one "in which the right to make a dollar at whatever cost is seldom challenged."[26] Corporations and individuals make "insatiable demands"[27] on the land, while commercial advertising lulls the users of dangerous chemicals into a false sense of security. Noneconomic values and interests are routinely sacrificed to economic ones, while the "true costs" of chemical spraying, including costs that cannot be measured in dollars, are left uncounted.[28] Worst of all, people lose the ability to see the land and its natural communities for what they are, to learn their stories and appreciate their beauty and complexity. Instead nature is reduced to natural resources—both in our minds and on the ground—that humans may utterly change, without compunction. Carson believed that conservation had to take economic reality into account, including the need to feed and protect growing numbers of human beings; hence her many suggestions for alternatives to chemical control and safer means of applying chemicals, when necessary. But she also saw the failure to recognize noneconomic realities as a denial of our full humanity. Like the failure to prevent unnecessary suffering, the failure to understand and appreciate nature lessened our stature as human beings.

Carson was equally uncompromising in her criticism of what she saw as a "needless war" on nature. Again and again, she decries the desire for domination behind much of the use of agricultural chemicals.[29] She saw a reveling in power for its own sake and a will to simplify the landscape in order to control it. But "the 'control of nature,'" she concluded in *Silent Spring*,

> is a phrase conceived in arrogance, born of the Neanderthal age of biology and philosophy, when it was supposed that nature exists for the convenience of man....[The] extraordinary capacities of life have been ignored by the practitioners of chemical control who have brought to their task...no humility before the vast forces with which they tamper.[30]

Speaking directly to millions of Americans on the television show "CBS Reports" a few months before her death, she repeated the message: "We still talk in terms of conquest.... I think we're challenged, as mankind has never been challenged before, to prove our maturity and our mastery, not of nature but of ourselves."[31] Carson doubted that human beings would find peace among themselves without first making peace with nature.[32]

Finally, Carson spoke out against artificiality and simplification: on farms, forests, and rangelands, as well as in towns, suburbs, and highway margins. Anticipating our own contemporary concern for the preservation of biodiversity, Carson quotes ecologist Charles Elton that "the key to a healthy plant or animal community lies in...the 'conservation of variety.'"[33] Such conservation of variety, particularly at the local level, is also the key to preserving human opportunities to know and enjoy nature. Carson insists that all native species have a right to persist in their environments—not just the ones human beings find attractive or useful. And while we must manage and change much of the landscape to suit our needs, some areas should be left wild, free from human artifice and control.[34]

Once again, Carson does not provide elaborate arguments to justify the moral considerability of these wild species and natural communities, or the value, to us, of knowing and appreciating them. A true teacher, she knows that she cannot prove the superiority of knowledge over ignorance. But she can make the pursuit of knowledge attractive. Once her readers know and experience that of which she speaks, she is convinced, they will value it. Before we can appreciate ethical arguments for its preservation, we must appreciate wild nature itself, and we cannot appreciate what we have not seen, experienced, or at least imagined. Like a long line of naturalists/conservationists before her, then, Rachel Carson worked to teach us to read in the book of nature. In turning to her earlier natural history writings, we gain a fuller understanding of her environmental ethics.

NONANTHROPOCENTRISM

Today Rachel Carson is primarily known for *Silent Spring*. But that was her fourth book to make the *New York Times* best-seller list. Carson's natural history writings—*Under the Sea-Wind* (1941), the number one best seller, *The Sea Around Us* (1951) and *The Edge of the Sea* (1955)—explore the astounding diversity of littoral and marine ecosystems. In her books Carson takes readers to some of the wildest and hardest to imagine places on earth: Arctic tundra in the grip of winter; the weird, dark depths of the ocean; microscopic planktonic worlds. Just as surely, Carson's writing uncovers the many details of nature close to hand: the fishing techniques of herons and skimmers; the fine structures and hidden beauties of jellyfish. Carson was also a great explainer of relationships and connections. "It is now clear that in the sea nothing lives to itself," she wrote, and what holds true in the sea holds true throughout the biosphere.[35]

We have already seen that Carson's ethics were nonanthropocentric: she recognized the moral considerability of nonhuman beings. But Carson's work reminds us that nonanthropocentrism is both an ethical position and an intellectual task, and the latter demands as much from us as the former. In particular, it demands repeated attention to the nonhuman world: the setting aside of our works and purposes and a concentration on *nature's* stories and realities.[36] Experienced often enough and set within the proper intellectual frameworks, we may, we hope, see ourselves truly as parts of a more-than-human whole. Carson was convinced that such nonanthropocentrism is a part of wisdom.

The attempt to transcend anthropocentrism is found in Carson's earliest book, *Under the Sea-Wind*. In an author's questionnaire submitted to the marketing division of Simon and Schuster, her first publishing house, she wrote:

> I believe that most popular books about the ocean are written from the viewpoint of a human observer... and record his impressions and interpretations of what he saw. I was determined to avoid this human bias as much as possible.... I decided that the author as a person or a human observer should never enter the story, but that it should be told as a simple narrative of the lives of certain animals of the sea. As far as possible, I wanted my readers to feel that they were, for a time, actually living the lives of sea creatures.[37]

Carson goes on to describe her efforts to imagine for herself, and re-create for her audience, the world as experienced by sandpipers, crabs, mackerels, and eels. In this difficult attempt, Carson worked back from what she knew of each animal's natural history, to try to imagine how it might perceive its environment and its varied interactions with other creatures. *Under the Sea-Wind* is a fascinating attempt to marry an imaginative, phenomenological exploration of other consciousnesses with the latest researches in scientific natural history.

Even in this first book, Carson's imagination took her beyond a focus on individual animals to the larger forces that shape their lives. "I very soon realized," she wrote in the questionnaire, "that the central character of the book was the ocean itself. The smell of the sea's edge, the feeling of vast movements of water, the sound of waves, crept into every page, and over all was the ocean as the force dominating all its creatures."[38]

How to make the ocean a character without inappropriate personification thus became a delicate task. Like other serious interpreters of nature, she struggled to avoid bogus personification and the pathetic fallacy, on the one hand, and an unjustified reductionism and simplification of nature's complexity, on the other.[39]

Carson's next book, which gave her fame, also took nonanthropocentrism as a key intellectual goal. *The Sea Around Us* synthesized recent discoveries in oceanography and marine biology, presenting them to a public whose interest in the sea had been aroused by the naval battles and new underwater technologies of World War II.[40] Carson pictures the astonishing variety and strangeness of marine life and instills a sense of the vast, titanic forces that have created it over geologic time scales. She repeatedly invokes the ocean's radical nonhumanity, asking readers to imagine underwater "tides so vast they are invisible and uncomprehended by the senses of man,"[41] or lights traveling over the water "that flash and fade away, lights that come and go for reasons meaningless to man,"[42] though "man, in his vanity, subconsciously attributes a human origin" to them.[43] This ocean wilderness teaches humility and wisdom, she believes, for modern man "in the artificial world of his cities and towns...often forgets the true nature of his planet and the long vistas of its history, in which the existence of the race of men has occupied a mere moment of time."[44]

The wildness and radical otherness of nature should be known, imagined, experienced—on pain of ignorance and arrogance. Achieving such a perspective involves both knowledge and imagination. From such a perspective, nonanthropocentric value judgments will tend to follow, along with a truer sense of the importance of our own problems. Carson's biographer writes: "Carson's fan mail revealed that *The Sea Around Us* had touched a deeper yearning for knowledge about the natural world as well as for a philosophic perspective on contemporary life."[45] The book came out at a time of great anxiety over an escalating Cold War. One reader wrote: "We have been troubled about the world, and had almost lost faith in man; it helps to think about the long history of the earth, and of how life came to be. When we think in terms of millions of years, we are not so impatient that our own problems be solved tomorrow."[46] Such responses were among those most appreciated by Rachel Carson, whose personal ethics placed a premium on the virtues of humility and fortitude.[47]

Nonanthropocentrism is thus a key to Rachel Carson's ethical philosophy, which contains the three complementary and equally challenging injunctions: (1) Respect nature!; (2) Know nature!; and (3) Place yourself in proper perspective! We mistake the nature of ethics, and Carson's ethics in particular, if we separate the intellectual from the ethical challenge here, or fail to acknowledge an ethical force behind all three injunctions. For Carson, arrogance is both an intellectual and a moral failing, while ignorance is as culpable as wrong action.

Because she placed such a strong emphasis on knowing nature and transcending our habitual focus on people, Carson viewed science as a key human activity. "The aim of science is to discover and illuminate truth," she said in a speech accepting the National Book Award.[48] Ideally, that illumination should inform the everyday lives of common people: not by creating more wealth or new consumer products, but by creating people who better know the earth which they inhabit and which has created them. "We live in a scientific age," she continued, "yet we assume that knowledge of science is the prerogative of only a small number of human beings, isolated and priest-like in their laboratories."[49] To believe this is to cut the average person off from self-knowledge, she went on, because "it is impossible to understand man without understanding his environment and the forces that have molded him physically and mentally."[50]

Carson clearly believed in science. She earned a master's degree in marine biology from Johns Hopkins University, worked as a government scientist for the U.S. Fish and Wildlife Service, kept up with the latest developments in a wide variety of fields, and made her name as a science popularizer. Yet she also saw many of science's limitations. In contrast to common scientific practice, Carson emphasized direct appreciation of individual organisms. Personal connections to particular places, such as her beloved Maine coast, were very important to her. She rejected a purely objective outlook; her own writings often sought to create an emotional response to nature, which she believed would help further conservation.[51]

Many of Carson's critics, including some scientists, accused her of "emotionalism" after the publication of *Silent Spring*, usually making more or less explicit reference to her gender.[52] In a typical example, a reviewer for *Time* magazine wrote that Carson's case was "unfair, one-sided, and hysterically overemphatic." "Many scientists sympathize with Miss Carson's love of wildlife," the reviewer continued, "and even with her mystical attachment to the balance of nature. But they fear that her emotional and inaccurate outburst in *Silent Spring* may do harm by alarming the nontechnical public, while doing no good for the things that she loves."[53] In response, Carson suggested that there was something wrong with people who felt no emotion in response to nature or nature's destruction. Emotional attachment, aesthetic appreciation, and a personal connection to particular places should complement the pursuit of rigorous science, she believed, since these all furthered our understanding and appreciation of nature, which in turn improved our lives. "I am not afraid of being thought a sentimentalist," she told a gathering of women journalists,

> when I stand here tonight and tell you that I believe natural beauty has a necessary place in the spiritual development of any individual or any society. I believe that whenever we destroy beauty, or whenever we substitute something man-made and artificial for a natural feature of the earth, we have retarded some part of man's spiritual growth.[54]

Carson reflected long and hard on the proper role of science in human society. Just as it called into question the haphazard, unregulated use of pesticides and herbicides, *Silent Spring* touched off a heated debate, among scientists, on the proper ends of science: whether to control, dominate, and change nature for human purposes, or to preserve, protect, and further our understanding of it, as is. Obviously, this debate continues and has lost none of its urgency, as witnessed by the recent growth of both conservation biology and a massive biotechnology industry. Rachel Carson is properly seen as one of our first and greatest conservation biologists, who popularized the wild worlds of sea and shore and incited people to work to protect all of nature.[55]

Carson valued science and the personal experience of nature because they helped her to understand nature's stories and thus achieve a larger, truer, nonanthropocentric point of view. She was also a self-proclaimed realist, and this seems to have played an important role in her environmental ethics. Science can achieve truth and thus illuminate our lives, she believed. It teaches us, for instance, that we are kin, however distant, to all the life with which we share the earth. As she expressed it in *The Edge of the Sea*, a scientifically informed personal experience gets us in touch with "the realities of existence," with "elemental realities."[56] Carson was aware of the great gulfs of ignorance that surrounded so many scientific questions in her day; her revisions to new editions of her books reminded her of the provisional nature of scientific knowledge. As a natural *historian*, she was also aware of the shifting, evolutionary nature of nature. She wrote in *The Edge of the Sea*'s conclusion of "coastal forms merg[ing] and blend[ing] in a shifting, kaleidoscopic pattern in which there is no finality, no ultimate and fixed reality—earth becoming fluid as the sea itself."[57] What holds for the earth and sea obviously holds for organic nature, as the nature and meaning of life "haunts and ever eludes" the seeker after knowledge.[58] This passage suggests a Peircean limit concept of truth and reality, as the ever elusive goals of an endless process.

Nevertheless, it is a process to which Carson was passionately committed. As a scientist, she needed the concept of reality to make sense of scientific progress. As a naturalist, she valued knowledge over ignorance and personal acquaintance with nature over casual disregard. As a mystic and nature lover, she spoke of "enchanted" experiences when the "realities" of nature "possessed my mind."[59] Only a belief in reality, and in the possibility and sweetness of knowing and connecting to reality, can make sense of the goals Rachel Carson pursued throughout her life. She put it this way in a speech accepting the John Burroughs Award for excellence in nature writing:

> Intoxicated with a sense of his own power, [mankind] seems to be going farther and farther into experiments for the destruction of himself and his world. There is certainly no single remedy for this condition and I am offering no panacea. But it seems reasonable to believe—and I do believe—that the more clearly we can focus our attention on the wonders and realities of the universe about us the less taste we shall have for the destruction of our race.[60]

Carson is surely right here. Environmentalists need to offer some positive alternative to gross economic consumption and the trivial pleasures offered by our destructive modern economy. With Carson, I can think of no alternative superior to a physical and intellectual engagement with the natural world. Away with all epistemological caviling which would deny such realities! Away with all postmodernist literary maunderings which would substitute clever wordplay for knowledge and experience of what Carson elsewhere calls "the great realities"![61] The alternative to such realism is solipsism and the ever more exclusive focus on artificial worlds and virtual realities of our own creation. Reading *Silent Spring* reminds us that it was not sophisticated postmodern deconstructionists but naive realist bird-watchers who provided much of the evidence about the dangers of pesticides that Rachel Carson laid before the public. "In contemplating 'the exceeding beauty of the earth,'" she wrote, "these people have found calmness and courage."[62]

Carson needed such calm fortitude throughout her life: to meet her many family obligations; to stand up to the personal and professional attacks leveled against her after *Silent Spring* was published; to persevere through difficult health problems during her last decade. In fact, she finished *Silent Spring* racing the cancer that she knew would shortly end her life. Half a year before her death, Carson and her best friend spent a morning at the seashore near her cottage in Maine, watching the fall migration of monarch butterflies. "This is a postscript to our morning at Newagen," she wrote later that afternoon:

> ...most of all I shall remember the Monarchs, that unhurried westward drift of one small winged form after another, each drawn by some invisible force. We talked a little about their life history. Did they return? We thought not; for most, at least, this was the closing journey of their lives. But it occurred to me this afternoon, remembering, that it had been a happy spectacle, that we had felt no sadness when we spoke of the fact that there would be no return. And rightly—for when any living thing has come to the end of its cycle we accept that end as natural....That is what those brightly fluttering bits of life taught me this morning. I found a deep happiness in it—so, I hope, may you. Thank you for this morning.[63]

CONCLUSION

I'd like to end by noting several respects in which Rachel Carson's life and work might point the way forward for environmental ethics. First, Carson's frequent criticisms of human attempts to dominate nature suggest important parallels with contemporary ecofeminism. Consider also the roles compassion and caring seem to have played in her environmental ethics; also, her emphasis on the importance of direct experience. Finally, there are her pioneering efforts in the primarily male worlds of science, government service, and conservation—and the misogynistic tone of many of her critics. All this suggests that Carson may be an important resource for ecofeminist reflection.

Second, Carson's philosophy of "reverence for life" seems to support the whole spectrum of environmental activism. During her careers in government conservation work and private advocacy, she tackled many environmental issues, from pollution prevention to natural areas restoration to ending ocean dumping of atomic wastes. A recent collection of Carson's shorter and occasional pieces, titled *Lost Woods*, perhaps gives us a fuller picture of her conservation interests than we have had previously. Several pieces highlight her advocacy for wilderness, including "The Real World Around Us" and "Our Ever-Changing Shore." The latter includes a moving plea for the preservation of wild beachlands:

> Somewhere we should know what was nature's way; we should know what the earth would have been had not man interfered. And so, besides public parks for recreation, we should set aside some wilderness areas of sea-shore where the relations of sea and wind and shore—of living things and their physical world—remain as they have been over the long vistas of time in which man did not exist.[64]

Other articles show a concern for the beauty and health of more developed landscapes.

Lost Woods also contains Carson's prefaces to the U.S. Animal Welfare Institute's educational booklet "Humane Biology Projects" and to Ruth Harrison's *Animal Machines*. These indicate her commitment to the humane treatment of animals. "I am glad to see Mrs. Harrison raise the question of how far man has a moral right to go in his domination of other life."[65]

In her biography, Linda Lear shows that Carson muted her animal welfare advocacy, out of concern that it would undermine her case against the misuse of pesticides. Nevertheless, while writing *Silent Spring*, she wrote in 1959 to a confidante that "I wish I could find time to turn my pen against the Fish and Wildlife Service's [her own former agency's] despicable poisoning activities [of predators and 'vermin' such as prairie dogs]...it is all part of the same black picture."[66]

What are the similarities between sacrificing a wild beach for condominium development and sacrificing the happiness of a veal calf for the pleasure of a gourmand? In both cases, human interests come first, no matter how trivial. In both cases, we dominate or deny nature and create new anthropocentric realities. In both cases, profit trumps a true humanity. This is the "black picture" that commands misery or disappearance for so much that is "not us." Carson's example suggests that a philosophy of love and appreciation for all nature and its creatures can bridge the gaps between environmental

ethics and animal welfare ethics, and between anthropocentric urban environmentalists and biocentric wildlands advocates.

This indicates a final way in which Rachel Carson might point a route
forward for environmental ethics: through her example of personal commitment and activism. Carson was a woman of great character who balanced her
personal, professional, and political responsibilities with utter integrity. She
did not relish controversy, but she did not retreat from it, when controversy
was necessary. No one else, she realized, had the combination of literary skill
and scientific knowledge to write *Silent Spring*. Her struggle to synthesize a
mountain of current scientific work and write one final book that was both
accurate and compelling, in the face of family tragedy and failing health, provides one of the heroic stories in conservation history. One cannot read
about it without being deeply moved. When Carson writes to a friend that it
is "a privilege as well as a duty to have the opportunity to speak out—to many
thousands of people—on something so important," we know she means it and
love her for it.[67]

Here knowledge and respect for nature, and personal humility and commitment to nature, go hand in hand. Such an ethics is certainly demanding.
Yet reading of Carson's life, one learns how much she received in return for
living up to it. Perhaps we too may hope that Nature will repay us for our
attentiveness and efforts on her behalf. As inspiration and provocation,
then, Rachel Carson's life and writings also hold great potential for environmental philosophy.[68]

NOTES

1. Not long ago, a search of the International Society for Environmental
Ethics bibliography turned up zero articles on Rachel Carson's environmental
ethics or environmental philosophy. Popular readers such as Richard Botzler
and Susan Armstrong, eds., *Environmental Ethics: Divergence and
Convergence*, 2nd ed. (Boston: McGraw Hill, 1998); Michael E. Zimmerman,
ed., *Environmental Philosophy: From Animal Rights to Radical Ecology*, 4th ed.
(Upper Saddle River, N.J.: Prentice Hall, 2004); and Lori Gruen and Dale
Jamieson, eds., *Reflecting on Nature: Readings in Environmental Philosophy*
(New York: Oxford University Press, 1994) do not include anything written by
Carson. Louis Pojman's edited volume, *Environmental Ethics: Readings in
Theory and Application* (Boston: Jones and Bartlett, 1994), includes a piece by
Carson, however; and the second edition of Joseph DesJardins' popular intro-
ductory text, *Environmental Philosophy*, 2nd ed. (Belmont, Calif.: Wadsworth,
1997), covers Carson more extensively than the first edition.

2. I have made extensive use of Linda Lear's biography, *Rachel Carson:
Witness for Nature* (New York: Henry Holt, 1997), in preparing this chapter.

Although I have tried to acknowledge that use fully in the notes that follow, I am sure that I have picked up some ideas or information from Linda Lear that remain unacknowledged.

3. Lear, *Witness for Nature*, chapters 17 and 18, 396–456.

4. Rachel Carson, *Silent Spring* (Boston: Houghton Mifflin, 1994 [1962]), 188.

5. Ibid., 99.

6. Ibid., 100.

7. Ibid., 73, emphasis added.

8. Ibid., 12, 72.

9. Ibid., 86.

10. Ibid., 103, 114.

11. Ibid., 127.

12. Quoted in Lear, *Witness for Nature*, 435.

13. Ibid., 433–37.

14. Paul Brooks, *The House of Life: Rachel Carson at Work* (Boston: Houghton Mifflin, 1972), 8. Rachel Carson learned this respectful attitude from her mother, who, according to Carson's brother, "would put spiders and other insects out of the house, rather than kill them" (Carol Gartner, *Rachel Carson* [New York: Frederick Ungar, 1983]), 7).

15. Lear, *Witness for Nature*, 409.

16. Brooks, *House of Life*, 324–26.

17. Gartner, *Rachel Carson*, 8.

18. The "convergence thesis" is the idea that convincing, properly formulated anthropocentric and nonanthropocentric ethics will largely converge in their practical environmental recommendations. See Bryan Norton, *Toward Unity Among Environmentalists* (New York: Oxford University Press, 1991).

19. I discuss this "convergence" and develop the idea of an environmental virtue ethics grounded in our enlightened self-interest in my paper, "Thoreau, Leopold, and Carson: Toward an Environmental Virtue Ethics," *Environmental Ethics* 23 (2001): 3–17.

20. Carson, *Silent Spring*, 71.

21. Lear, *Witness for Nature*, 438.

22. Rachel Carson, foreword to Ruth Harrison, *Animal Machines: The New Factory Farming Industry* (London: Vincent Stuart, 1964), viii; reprinted in

Rachel Carson, *Lost Woods: The Discovered Writing of Rachel Carson*, ed. Linda Lear (Boston: Beacon Press, 1998), 196.

23. Rachel Carson, *The Edge of the Sea* (Boston: Mariner Books, 1998 [1955]), 249, 250, 225.

24. Brooks, *House of Life*, 8, 9.

25. Readers should know that Linda Lear believes that Carson was a more spiritual person than this chapter implies. Lear thinks that the concept of "material immortality," treated in *Under the Sea-Wind* and later writings, is key to Carson's religion, and that her environmental ethics is grounded in this religious sensibility (Linda Lear, personal communication, 2001; see also Rachel Carson, *Always, Rachel: The Letters of Rachel Carson and Dorothy Freeman, 1952–1964*, ed. Martha Freeman [Boston: Beacon Press, 1995], 446–47). See also chapter 15 in this volume by Lisa H. Sideris.

26. Carson, *Silent Spring*, 13.

27. Ibid., 66.

28. Ibid., 69.

29. Recent environmental historiography confirms the importance of an ideology of conquest and domination in the growth of modern industrial agriculture. See Mark Feige, *Irrigated Eden: The Making of an Agricultural Landscape in the American West* (Seattle: University of Washington Press, 1999), 171–81.

30. Carson, *Silent Spring*, 297. Note the close connection between *is* and *ought* implied in the pairing of "biology and philosophy." Post-Darwinian biology has shown us that life on earth was not created for our benefit, that we are evolutionary latecomers, and that we are kin to all life. Philosophical ethics should accommodate this newfound knowledge.

31. Quoted in Lear, *Witness for Nature*, 450. Among others, Thomas E. Hill, Jr., has also suggested that "a proper humility" is an important environmental virtue; see his essay, "Ideals of Human Excellence," *Environmental Ethics* 5 (1983): 211–24, especially 216, 219, 223.

32. See Carson, *Lost Woods*, 196; and Lear, *Witness for Nature*, 407. In a commencement address delivered two years before her death, Carson explicitly linked human domination of nature to "the Jewish-Christian concept of man's relation to nature" (Gartner, *Rachel Carson*, 120).

33. Carson, *Silent Spring*, 117.

34. Ibid., 79. See also Carson, *Lost Woods*, 194.

35. Carson, *The Edge of the Sea*, 39.

36. See Yuriko Saito, "Appreciating Nature on Its Own Terms," *Environmental Ethics* 20 (1998): 135-49.

37. Carson, *Lost Woods*, 55-56.

38. Ibid., 56.

39. Gartner, *Rachel Carson*, 35-36; Lear, *Witness for Nature*, 90-91.

40. Lear, *Witness for Nature*, 203-4.

41. Rachel Carson, *The Sea Around Us* (New York: Oxford University Press, 1989 [1950]), 107.

42. Ibid., 34.

43. Ibid.

44. Ibid., 15.

45. Lear, *Witness for Nature*, 205.

46. As quoted in Lear, *Witness for Nature*, ibid.

47. See *ibid., 219–20*; and, Carson, *Lost Woods*, 62.

48. Rachel Carson, "Remarks at the Acceptance of the National Book Award for Nonfiction," in *Lost Woods*, 91.

49. Ibid.

50. Ibid.

51. Gartner, *Rachel Carson*, 3.

52. Lear, *Witness for Nature*, 430, 461.

53. Quoted in Brooks, *House of Life*, 297.

54. Carson, "The Real World Around Us," in *Lost Woods*, 160.

55. Lear, *Witness for Nature*, 428-40.

56. Carson, *The Edge of the Sea*, 4, 5.

57. Ibid., 249-50.

58. Ibid., 250.

59. Ibid., 4.

60. Carson, "Design for Nature Writing," in *Lost Woods*, 94.

61. Carson, "Remarks at the Acceptance of the National Book Award for Nonfiction," in *Lost Woods*, 92.

62. Carson, "The Real World Around Us," in *Lost Woods*, 163.

63. Carson, "Letter to Dorothy Freeman," in *Lost Woods*, 247.

64. Carson, "Our Ever-Changing Shore," in *Lost Woods*, 124.

65. Carson, "To Understand Biology/Preface to *Animal Machines*," in *Lost Woods*, 196.

66. Rachel Carson to Lois Crisler, Letter, Apr. 16, 1959; as quoted in Lear, *Witness for Nature*, 352. For more on Carson's views and actions on behalf of animal welfare, see Brooks, 314–17, and Gartner, 6–7, 26–27.

67. Rachel Carson to Dorothy Freeman, Letter, June 28, 1958; as quoted in Lear, *Witness for Nature*, 328.

68. Thanks to Kris Cafaro, Clare Palmer, and an anonymous reviewer for detailed comments that significantly improved this piece. Special thanks to Linda Lear, the second "anonymous" reviewer, for detailed comments and for generously answering various questions about Rachel Carson's life and thought.

5

Thinking Like a Mackerel: Rachel Carson's *Under the Sea-Wind* as a Source for a Trans-Ecotonal Sea Ethic

Susan Power Bratton

THE LAND ETHIC AS A FOUNDATION FOR A SEA ETHIC?

Although environmental philosophers have penned extensive commentaries on "the land ethic" based on the writings of Aldo Leopold, the discipline has not generated a parallel ethos for the oceans. A number of commentators have, however, tackled maritime environmental issues by extending widely accepted terrestrial models to oceanic ecosystems. Baird Callicott, for example, applies an unmodified "land ethic" to the problem of establishing moral values for framing American maritime environmental policies and bases his arguments on continental exemplars originating with the "terrestrial" philosophies of Gifford Pinchot, John Muir, and Aldo Leopold. For Callicott, humans are "members of a biotic team" and "citizens of one humming biotic community."[1]

In a later article, Callicott extends the land ethic to a specific marine environmental conflict. He asks if Norwegian defiance of the 1986 International Whaling Commission's moratorium on commercial whaling was consistent with the land ethic if minke whales could be sustainably harvested. Callicott

This chapter originally appeared in *Ethics & the Environment*, volume 9, number 1 (2004): 1–22. It is reproduced here, in slightly edited form, with permission of Indiana University Press.

provides an equivocal response finding that minke harvest fits the holistic criteria of the land ethic, as neither the species nor marine communities were endangered. He reasons whale hunting is inconsistent with respect for intelligent creatures and "fellow members of the biotic community," while worrying that humans, as predators, have not coevolved with whales.[2] But is the land ethic the best model for the seas? Callicott confesses that humans and whales have not long been members of the same ecological community. Until the nineteenth century, we bipeds, in fact, believed the floors of the deep oceans were devoid of life.

AN ETHIC OF TWO REALMS

Callicott's perspective, further explicated in his book, *Beyond the Land Ethic*, captures the preference environmental ethics has shown for authors such as Leopold and Muir, and the paucity of commentary on maritime sources, despite the massive literature describing human encounters with the oceans and the importance of seascapes in the visual arts.[3] An obvious omission is the minimal emphasis on Rachel Carson's voluminous writings focusing on seas and coasts, which are of the same genre as Aldo Leopold's *Sand County Almanac and Sketches Here and There.*[4] We should ask if Carson perceives human relationship with the sea the way Leopold proposes it may be developed with the land. Further, Callicott's question concerning human coevolution, or lack of it, with marine ecosystems and species is a critical one, at least when dealing with the practical issues of maritime environmental management. Although in deepest evolutionary time, all life came from the sea and we primates have many physiological vestiges of our ancient nurturing in saltwater soaked mud, our appearance has become one of the great epics of the Pleistocene. Lucy and her australopithecine kin were probably residents of savannahs or woodlands. *Homo sapiens*, however, have long inhabited coastal regions, and utilized inshore food sources, such as fish and seaweed. Our evolutionary relationship with the oceans has developed around the coastal ecotones. Like giant raccoons, we live on terra firma, but forage at and below the tide line.

In her three masterpieces popularizing scientific marine ecology, Carson recognizes the difficulties humans face in grasping what goes on beneath the waves. Where Leopold might attribute abuse of the fragile soils of the sand counties in Wisconsin to lack of foresight and simple greed, Carson discerns a central feature of human relationship with the oceans—we are *not* fully integrated members of the sea community. Even fishers who spend their entire lives making a living from the sea do not perceive or fully understand what is transpiring underneath their keels. Gill-less, finless organisms are not adapted to existence *in* chaotic salt water. Humans, still largely trapped in the boundary layer at the sea's surface, are clumsy at best when they face the oceans' winds and waves.

In her marine ecology trilogy, Carson attempts to descend through the barrier at the sea's edge and surface, gently pulling her reader along, like a mermaid guiding a bewildered sailor into the magical kingdoms below. Even the titles suggest an inversion of habitats and relationships, and penetration across boundaries. Her first book, *Under the Sea-Wind: A Naturalist's Picture of Ocean Life*, published in 1941, declares Carson's intention to cross between the atmospheric and hydric spheres.[5] Linda Lear notes that this title was inspired by a passage in Richard Jeffries' *The Pageant of Summer*,[6] describing the air passing over the sea and bringing its scent to the shore.[7] Carson's purpose, however, is to take her reader back to the source of these atoms and to plunge them beneath the surface spray. The title also suggests the wind-like movement of the massive submarine currents and the forces that both guide and buffet the long-distance migration routes that so characterize oceanic ecosystems. Her second marine volume, *The Sea Around Us*, transports humans from a position above or next to the sea, to a position in the midst of the oceans, both in time and in space.[8] Her last fully marine book, *The Edge of the Sea*, concentrates on both the beauties and difficulties of living at or near the planet's greatest ecotone, the tide line.[9] She dissolves the usual perceptual boundaries—it is much easier for humans to observe what is happening on the beach—and guides her readers into tide pools, out through shallow water and across coral reefs.

My thesis is that Carson presents us with a trans-boundary or trans-ecotonal ethic of the seas, which is fully expressed in her first book, *Under the Sea-Wind*. In order to acquire knowledge and wisdom concerning the "sea community," and thereby establish a foundation for ethical relationship, we must extend perceptions past the terrestrial plane into the invisible depths. *Under the Sea-Wind* begins with a skimmer's (Rynchops) view of the estuary, and a plover's perspective on the beach. In the first paragraph, Carson merges the boundaries as she describes an island of the Outer Banks: "Both water and sand were the color of steel overlaid with the sheen of silver, so that it was hard to say where water ended and land began."[10]

For Carson, bridging the impenetrable barrier between continents and oceans goes beyond scientific expediency. In *The Edge of the Sea*, Carson begins by seeking out a sea cave, with hydroids and other invertebrates attached to the ceiling. This locale is only open to her at low tide, and will shortly fill to become part of the sea again. She brings the reader into this boundary realm to provide the semi-safety of standing on terra firma, while personally observing the biota of the sea. The entry into the cave is a symbolic transition, through a "magical zone," into a realm not ordinarily accessible to bipeds. The innermost essence of the cave is its "fairy pool," which Carson observes between attacks by unpredictable breakers beating up against a ledge she traversed to reach her secret spot.[11] Carson departs one ecological reality and enters another as she joins them in the first person as she kneels on a carpet of sea moss and observes the roof of the cave mirrored in a tidal pool, where sea creatures contemplate their own image.

Again and again, Carson utilizes human imagination as ballast to sink our earthy souls to benthos, and have us look up at the havoc wreaked by our economic ventures, as an otter trawl drifts over our heads. She recognizes fully how limited terrestrially evolved human perceptions are for seeing and hearing what transpires in marine ecosystems. Carson demonstrates to her readers how we can utilize careful observation of those marine organisms and habitats accessible to us, and our abilities to imagine, synthesize and visualize, to gain a better understanding and appreciation for the hidden realms, across the ecotones, in the open seas.

ILL-ADAPTED FISHERS

Carson's first book, *Under the Sea-Wind*, incorporates portraits of commercial fishermen. Carson does not take a stand against fishing (although she personally tried to return the creatures she observed to their burrows and tide pools). She instead contrasts the "native fishers," such as the great blue heron with their human counterparts. For Carson predation is part of the natural order. She gives nature "red in tooth and claw" great emphasis by including both terrestrial and marine predators such as foxes, ospreys, dogfish, and glass worms. Her description of the heron depicts both the perfection of his patient hunting style and his need for the capture:

> The heron stood motionless, his neck curved back on his shoulders, his bill poised to spear fish as they darted past his legs. As the terrapin moved out into deeper water she startled a young mullet and sent it racing toward the beach in confusion and panic. The sharp-eyed heron saw the movement and with a quick dart seized the fish crosswise in his bill. He tossed it into the air, caught it head first, and swallowed it. It was the first fish other than small fry that he had caught that night.[12]

The heron, graceful, skilled and silent, takes only what he immediately consumes.

The human hunters are less civil. In Carson's account, the gillnetters are in conflict with the pound netters, and due to the placement of fixed gear, "the fishermen who operated movable gear competed bitterly for the few remaining places to set their nets."[13] Carson creates a literary contrast to the silent stalking heron:

> The year before there had been a fight when the fishermen who owned the pound had discovered the gill-netters taking a good catch of shad from

their own net, which they had set directly downstream from the pound, heading off most of the fish. The gill-net fishermen were outnumbered, and for the rest of the season had fished in another part of the estuary, making poor catches and cursing the pound netters. This year they had tried setting the nets at dusk and returning to fish by daybreak. The rival fishermen did not tend the pound till about sunrise, and by that time the gill-netters were always downstream again, nets in their boat, nothing to prove where they had been fishing.[14]

When the gillnetters finally get their nets placed where they snag shad traveling inland on the rising tide, the local eels feast on entangled roe shad, a gourmet treat they would have great difficulty capturing on their own. Carson presents these fascinating creatures as tricksters who eat the shad hollow, thwarting the fishermen's ventures.

Following this disaster with the eels, Carson again presents humans as disruptive and inept, as they raise the anchor on the end of the net and dislodge a clump of widgeon grass, which falls into their boat. She juxtaposes the men to the skimmer, Rynchops, flying skillfully along the tide line. The bird circles easily around the marshes. Rynchops, also a fisher, becomes the expert observer, who watches the gillnetters struggle with their damaged catch and violently toss the damaged fish away as refuse. The watermen are neither fully competent predators, nor can they coordinate with each other the way the skimmers can. The description implies that the Darwinian evolution of a truly marine human remains incomplete and human understanding of the estuary remains imperfect.

Prior to penning *Under the Sea-Wind*, Carson had written a series of articles for the *Baltimore Sun* on the depletion of the shad fishery in the Chesapeake Bay.[15] Rather than composing a direct critique of the situation in *Under the Sea-Wind*, as she was later to do with pesticides in *Silent Spring*,[16] Carson depicts the shad fishermen as separated from the remainder of the estuarine ecosystem by their coarse methods and their insensitivity to ecological processes. Her subtle commentary on human folly is a repeated counterpoint to her descriptions of oceanic food webs as well adapted and efficient. Carson, for example, describes the chaotic wandering of a ghost gill net set adrift by heavy seas. The launch that had been tending it "had been wrecked on a shoal about a mile away." The net "fished on night after night" until dogfish found its trapped cargo and tore holes in the misplaced human contraption.[17] Mullet fishermen are similarly wasteful as they shake the small fish out of their nets on to a beach and "young sea trout and pompano, mullet of the last year's spawning, young ceros and sheepshead and sea bass" die unnecessarily. These ocean residents "—too small to sell, too small to eat—litter the beach above the water line, life oozing from them for want of means to cross a few yards of dry sand and return to the sea."[18] Carson depicts natural process as cleaning up the mess. The rising tide recovers some of the bodies, while tide-line scavengers, such as gulls, fish crows and ghost crabs, feast on the rest.

Carson is realistic about the pervasive impact of predation in ocean ecosystems. For Carson, the oceans are aesthetic, diverse, and full of interest— but never benignly beneficent. In her account of Scomber the mackerel, the young fish dodges both natural and anthropogenic hazards. He has close calls with a long line, an otter trawl, and a seine. Carson describes the otter trawl as a "strange disturbance" when Scomber first detects the trawl as a "heavy, thudding vibration," then: "Something vast and dark, like a fish of monstrous and incredible size, its whole forward end a vast, gaping mouth, loomed in the water." This benthos dragging gear has "scooped up in its cavernous bag thousands of pounds of food fish, as well as quantities of basket starfish, prawns, crabs, clams, cockles, sea cucumbers, and white worm tubes."[19] In an era when invertebrate by-catch was of little concern, Rachel Carson observes the ecosystemic disruption caused by the massive net. As Scomber flees for the surface, the trawl nearly misses a giant old cod, which dodges below it to a ledge. Finally the gear "pitched over the edge of the cliff and went tumbling end over end into the deep water below."[20] Rattling lateral lines as well as eardrums, the net is a "noisy" misfit—too large, too monstrous. The trawl is clumsy, unable to follow the contours of the bottom like the cod, and it ends up bouncing off a submarine cliff. Carson, who died in 1964, would have been saddened to find how prophetic this image was for the fate of western Atlantic bottom fisheries.

THE SEA COMMUNITY

If we compare Carson's descriptions of ecosystem function and structure to those in Leopold's A Sand County Almanac, Carson more frequently describes the harsh Darwinian realities of life as a horseshoe crab or a migratory bird than Leopold does. Leopold's land community behaves almost like an idealized New England town council. The major source of disruption in Leopold's cosmos is the thoughtlessness and indifference of humans. Although he describes predators, the gory details are sparse. His dying wolf is more a responsible mother than a fierce animal capable of ripping the entrails out of a deer or an elk.

Under the Sea-Wind, in contrast, presents a portrait of ocean life from the top of the food chain to the bottom. The process of predators capturing prey is so pervasive that it marks every locale and habitat her book visits. Carson understands the superfluous nature of ocean production. Of the billions of herring or mackerel eggs spawned each year, only a select few produce a mature fish. Conger eels, squid, sharks, and tuna join human fishers in pursuit of Scomber. Deception is normative among the sea's stalkers. The angler fish, Lophius, utilizes seaweed to conceal his intent and waves his bait above the sand, in hopes of tricking other species of fish. Scomber's first encounter with a net or a trap concerns a jellyfish trailing myriad tentacles, not a human in boat. At one point, little Scomber who is still chowing down on "flea-sized crustaceans" as he is not big enough to catch herring, perceives a spreading rusty stain in the water, as the bluefish slash through the terrified aggregation of bait fish. Carson notes: "The taste was disquieting to a small fish that had never tasted blood or experienced the lust of the hunter."[21]

Carson's predators do not feel obligated to fast, clean kills. When caught by a comb jelly's filmy tentacles, miserable Scomber almost becomes a casualty. As the barbed tentacle draws Scomber upward to the ctenophore's mouth, the tiny fish is blinded by the sun and rendered helpless. Only the presence of a previous victim, a herring, prevents his speedy demise. Scomber is not able to free himself, and "in spite of his spasmodic struggles," his efforts to escape grow feeble. A chance attack by a sea trout on the jelly releases Scomber from his agony. "Half dead with pain and exhaustion" the immature mackerel swims away to hide in a drifting clump of seaweed, until he has recovered. This vignette presents a worst possible case for an organism that can experience pain and fear. Scomber is left conscious, hooked and hanging, while the jelly digests another fish. Taking the mackerel's perspective, Carson refers to the ocean layer filled with millions of beautiful comb jellies as "a sea of death" and emphasizes the many young fish hurrying after plankton that have expired in their barbed grasp.[22]

Carson attributes far more will and personality to animals than do many environmental ethicists, such as Paul Taylor, who might take a stand against commercial fishing.[23] For Carson the experienced field naturalist, the structure of the food web is almost certainly extra-moral, as is the day-to-day violence of the environment, which freezes, exhausts, and devours the living at every turn. Carson does not protest the seiners hauling mackerel on the basis that untimely death interferes with the life goals or self-valuation of Scomber. Of millions and millions, not all mackerel will survive to reproduce—in fact, probably only a small percentage will. The sea is the domain of unfulfilled life goals, and even at the top of the food chain the losses are brutal. Carson's ocean churns with fear and struggle. She is concerned, however, that humans do not fully appreciate the realm into which they sink their nets, and that lack of human skill and ecological understanding results in wasteful disregard for the integrity and productivity of ocean ecosystems. For Carson, the ghost gill nets sweeping silently along with the currents, spreading death to dozens of nontarget species, are outside the ethos of the sea, as are the pound nets, which completely block the migration routes of shad returning to the estuaries. The question is not whether all creatures survive to realize their teleological ends, but that enough do. One wonders if the infrequent ethical citation of *Under the Sea-Wind* is partially a response to her less than peaceful, but

biologically accurate, descriptions of food webs, and her emphases on predator-prey relations, the danger of marine environments, and natural mortality.

Toward the end of *Under the Sea-Wind*, Carson begins to close the question of human relationship with the sea by describing the wreck of the *Mary
B*. This fishing boat met her end in a storm that ripped away her hatch cover
and smashed the windows of her deck house as she was driven aground.
Carson does not disclose to her reader the fate of the *Mary B*.'s captain and
crew, but she captures the process of death within the submerged ship: "The
hold was half-full of the crab-cleaned skeletons of the fish that had not
washed out of the hold when the vessel sank."[24] Carson then creates a counterpoint by describing how sea creatures had flourished on and around the
human disaster: "The *Mary B*. was like an oasis of life in miles of sea desert, a
place where myriads of the sea's lesser fry—the small, backboneless animals—
found a place of attachment; and the small fish foragers found living food
encrusting all the planks and spars; and larger predators and prowlers of the
sea found a hiding place."[25] Human mistakes and lack of adaptation too
become part of the ocean's cycles of life.

CYCLES, CORRIDORS, AND LINKAGES

Although she does not fully deploy contemporary scientific terminology such
as the word "ecotone," Carson describes the complex food webs of oceans
and shorelines. She gives the reader a sense of the massive size and complexity
of ocean ecosystems. Carson's zoological heroes are wanderers. Silverbar, the
sanderling, accomplishes an arctic migration and survives the variations of
good and bad weather. Anguilla, the eel, journeys from his birth in the estuary to the stillness of the Sargasso Sea and back.

Carson also takes her reader from the sunlight and storms above the sea
to the shadows and currents of the benthos. Her ocean is three-dimensional,
visible from the depths to the skies above the surface. She demonstrates
repeatedly how these layers are linked. Scomber, for example, is attacked by a
jellyfish near the surface and has a close encounter with a large cod that
resides on a rough bottom with ledges. Lophius begins his feast with some
curious small fish attracted to his lure, then using his sense of smell and taste
discovers waterfowl are resting above. He swims up and reaching the surface,
grabs an eider duck and pulls it down to the depths. Carson astutely captures
the complex interactions between the surface and the benthos, and the
myriad of linkages, corridors, and migratory routes that characterize marine
and coastal ecosystems.

Under the Sea-Wind, which was published prior to Leopold's *Sand County
Almanac*, identifies not just the spatial but also the temporal dynamics of
oceanic ecosystems, and develops this theme in terms of life cycles (mackerels,

eels, shad, plovers). Carson weaves the seasonal changes into her descriptions of marine geography. Her marine organisms move through an ever-changing, sometimes friendly, sometimes hazardous matrix that is chaotic, yet, on the broader scale predictable. Humans cut through the matrix, often misunderstanding its shifts and patterns—underestimating the sea's dangers while severing the critical linkages, such as the shad run, which maintain ocean productivity.

TRANS-BOUNDARY IMAGINATION

Carson is sympathetic to a younger mackerel fisherman who has not been at sea "long enough to forget, if he ever would, the wonder, the unslakable curiosity he had brought to his job—curiosity about what lay under the surface." This fisher wonders: "What had the eyes of the mackerel seen? Things he'd never see; places he'd never go."[26] This human character projects his thoughts to a school of fish milling below him, and tries to visualize their movements. Later:

> He leaned over the gunwales, peering down into dark water, watching the glow fade, seeing in imagination what he could not see in fact—the race and rush and downward whirl of thousands of mackerel. He suddenly wished he could be down there, a hundred feet down, on the lead line of the net. What a splendid sight to see those fish streaking by at top speed in a blaze of meteoric flashes![27]

But even while he is musing about the teeming life below him, the mackerel sound. The men operating the seine thus lose an hour's worth of work as they prepare to haul an empty net.

Carson clearly believed that the youthful curiosity and imagination displayed by the young fisherman should be cultivated, and that thinking like a mackerel could be a very edifying experience. At the time she penned Under the Sea-Wind, the Aqua-Lung had not yet been invented and Carson had not had an opportunity to dive. She deeply desired to "go undersea" herself, and believed that a dive in the cumbersome gear of the time would give her the "feeling of the water as no amount of vicarious experience could do."[28] Yet long before she had an opportunity to don a heavy helmet for the first time in 1949, she wandered a wild section of the Outer Banks observing shorebirds, and spent hours on the docks at Woods Hole, watching predators chase schools of young mackerel and observing the catches of fishermen, in order to accurately portray the lives of marine organisms in Under the Sea-Wind. According to Lear, she saw herself as letting "her imagination go down through the water," and as "piecing 'together bits of scientific fact,' until now she could see the 'whole life of those creatures as they lived them in that strange world.'"[29]

Carson recognizes the range of senses developed by sea creatures. Lophius, for example, "was well aware that birds were somewhere near, for the scent and taste of duck were strong in the water that passed over the taste buds covering his tongue and the sensitive skin within his mouth."[30] After Scomber escapes a school of bluefish, Carson notes: "Scomber's sense cells received once more only the messages of the strong, steady rhythms of the sea."[31] When the trawl rattles across the bottom, fish perceive it as "thudding vibration felt with the lateral-line canals along their sensitive flanks."[32] Carson utilizes her imagination to taste birds and feel the shock waves of a bouncing trawl.

Since Carson was well read in English and nature-oriented literature, and acknowledged the influence of other writers, she may also have been adopting their "vision" of nature. The romantics, such as Wordsworth and Shelley, for example, believed that their imagination allowed nature to reveal itself to them, even to look back at them. Carson *extends* her vision, via imagination, past the science of her era, and begins to use information drawn in fragments from below the ocean's surface to construct a complete portrait of the worlds below. She clearly has entered a special relationship with the sea—so much so that she sympathizes with an angler fish and grasps the global importance of invertebrates. For Carson, it is a tragedy, both for the sea and for humanity, if the young fisherman tending the seine loses his desire to see and contemplate the shimmering dance just a few meters away from his vessel.

More recent writers, such as Sylvia Earle,[33] blessed with deep submersibles and scuba gear, have perhaps given us a more detailed and accurate picture of the ocean's depths than Carson. But Rachel Carson understood our human ability to see without actually sliding through the sediments of the continental shelf, and perhaps more than any other essayist focusing on marine ecosystems, teaches us to think like a mackerel.

LAND ETHICS AND SEA ETHICS

In comparing Aldo Leopold's concept of the land ethic in *A Sand County Almanac* to Rachel Carson's presentation of human relationship to the oceans in *Under the Sea-Wind*, we find the two authors emphasize many of the same themes, including the importance of understanding the structure and function of natural communities and the importance of maintaining ecological processes, such as predation. Both authors believe that humans view the environment through an economic lens and this, in turn, leads to disrespect of nature and thoughtless abuse and destruction of natural resources.

The spatial focus of the works is quite different, however, and suggests a foundational divergence in the relationship of humans to the earth's terrestrial and marine biomes. Leopold and his reader occupy "a place" or an "ecological home" in the sand counties and traverse woodlands and wetlands one can walk across in a few hours. Leopold faults human philosophy and intellectual history for blinding us to our ecosystemic responsibilities. Yet when we read A Sand County Almanac, the vision is essentially human, because people are full participants in the Wisconsin landscape and have been for thousands of years.

Rachel Carson, in contrast, transports her reader into a world where the idea of human "belonging" or "home" is quite foreign. We cannot be full-time residents in the light-depleted depths. Carson gives us a phenomenological account of the individual lives and perceptions of sea creatures from the middle of the food chain. She draws her reader into the animal's perspective in order to give her reader "eyes" to see what transpires below the sea's surface. She recognizes that we devalue creatures such as Scomber and the ecological linkages that sustain them because their adventures and tragedies transpire behind an ecotonal barrier we ourselves are unable to cross. By presenting living organisms at a more personal and relational level than Aldo Leopold, she discourages us from stabbing blindly into the seas with our nets and lines, and wantonly destroying what we cannot fully perceive. "Place" in the currents of the sea does not necessarily mean a topographically static residence, but can be a great web of interconnected paths, each with its own travelers and seasons.

Both Leopold and Carson challenge anthropocentric values. Leopold accomplishes this by allowing us to visualize ourselves as attached to the land as parts of a whole, and by equating our interests with those of other species. Rachel Carson, in contrast, fosters identification with other species, including the unseen, the lower, and the unfamiliar. She senses that in marine realms, where we do not directly share the habitat, we can use our imagination to visit the dark plains of the abyssal benthos or the great gyre of the meandering Gulf Stream. Carson argues we should respect these creatures and systems because of their beauty and complexity and their place in the greater order of the cosmos. She also helps the reader to understand that the life of a mackerel is not too different from her own, and constitutes a journey of discovery in both favorable and hostile environs. We sacrifice our own experience and enrichment when we ignore the darting flashes of silver beneath the boat and content ourselves with lives on the surface, leaving more than half the planet unexplored and unappreciated.

TOWARD A TRANS-ECOTONAL ETHIC FOR THE SEAS

Carson's Under the Sea-Wind suggests four foundational concepts for a transectonal ethic for the seas:

1. *Humans are not fully adapted to life in the oceans, and we do not see or grasp the full extent of our impacts beneath the seas' surface.* In our recent evolutionary history we have foraged in the oceans, but we are not particularly adept predators, and in our clumsiness and blindness can cause massive disruption of ocean ecosystems. Much of the damage we do to the oceans is "out of sight, out of mind." We are in the process of *becoming* members of the sea community. Our technological advances have greatly accelerated our abilities to transverse ocean ecotones, and we can use these newfound powers, like trawl nets and diving gear, for good or ill. In terms of environmental management, this implies we should deploy greater caution in permitting human impacts to disrupt even the simplest or least economically productive of ocean ecosystems. The public would raise an outraged protest if it could personally view the impacts of sewage sludge on parts of the New York Bight or the dead zone at the mouth of the Mississippi River. We need to consciously visualize the extent and intensity of marine degradation we are causing, and give the seas the attention we give the land.

2. *We need to understand the scale and complexity of ocean ecosystems.* Humans, particularly those harvesting marine ecosystems, often ignore or misunderstand the critical linkages between the estuaries and shorelines and the open oceans. These connectors and pathways are fragile and easily disrupted, although we often cannot see the damage we inflict. To respect the sea, we must understand these in terms of appropriate spatial scales, and both seasonal and year-to-year cycles. When managing ocean environments we need to designate special conservation or management zones for these "linkages," such as the mouths of estuaries. Further, we need international regulations that protect the full length of the migration routes for species such as mackerel, salmon, shad, and tuna. Until very recently, our designation of marine sanctuaries or research zones excluded the great banks and "hard bottoms" that provide feeding grounds for species such as cod and lobster. The ledge habitat of Rachel Carson's savvy, old cod, who successfully dodges the otter trawl, is as deserving of conservation and preservation as a coral reef—even if we are not likely to visit it on a scuba diving vacation.

3. *Humans disrupt ocean ecosystems by overharvesting and overestimating their productivity, and by modifying or blocking key ecosystem processes and linkages, such as migrations.* The prob-

lem is not our participation in predation, which is an important process in ocean ecosystems, but our disregard for ecosystem function. The issue is not that we eat shad, which humans have done for millennia, but our stringing pound nets across the estuaries, blocking the migration and completely draining the roe-bearing adults from the reproductive pool. We treat the benthos as if it were mere inorganic mud, rather than a delicate layer of life-giving ooze. We need to be aware of the role different organisms play, in the great web of ecosystem pathways through the oceans and tying the land to the seas. If we fish, we should fish like the heron—leaving little trace of our activities and taking only a small portion of a fish population. Our technology is potentially both disruptive and destructive as we blindly drag massive nets through the oceans' unseen depths. When managing marine environments we should show much greater concern for the adaptive limits of the species we harvest. Our nets should allow adequate escapement, and minimize "collateral damage," such as disturbance of benthic ecosystems and the destruction of juvenile fish and nontarget species.

4. *Human imagination and rational scientific investigation can traverse the ecotones, allowing us to more fully value ocean life and processes.* We can utilize our imaginations and the rational findings of science to grasp how marine ecosystems function and how we change or disturb them. We have the intellectual or mental ability to "see" scenes we cannot literally view. Carson believed we would be better members of the ocean community if we make the effort to fully visualize our activities from below the surface ecotone. Carson demonstrates the value of taking the perspective of a non-charismatic species, such as a mackerel or an eel, who are the "common citizens" of salt water. Today we could add to Scomber's journey a stomachache from consuming plastic pellets, a bath in sewage, and a horrific crossing of an ocean bank crowded with dogfish instead of cod as a result of overfishing. Public education and dedicated marine science, both great loves of Rachel Carson, can aid us in conceptualizing the impact of human disturbance on such mundane organisms as mackerel and sardines. We can imagine what life is like for the occupants of a silt delta or a sandbar, and can award greater consideration to jellyfish and phytoplankton. If we follow Scomber across the sludge-coated New York Bight or around the net-scarred bottoms of near-shore New England, we will

understand how disrespectful we have been of the ocean's great beauty and of its teeming diversity of life. Then the oceans will no longer be "out of sight, out of mind."

NOTES

1. J. Baird Callicott, "Principle Traditions in American Environmental Ethics: A Survey of Moral Values for Framing an American Ocean Policy," *Ocean and Coastal Management* 17 (1992): 299–325.

2. J. Baird Callicott, "Whaling in Sand County: A Dialectical Hunt for Land-ethical Answers to Questions about the Morality of Norwegian Minke-Whale Catching," *Ecology of Industrial Regions* 1 (1995): 83–98.

3. J. Baird Callicott, *Beyond the Land Ethic* (Albany: State University of New York Press, 1999).

4. Aldo Leopold, *Sand County Almanac: and Sketches Here and There* (New York: Oxford University Press, 1949).

5. Rachel Carson, *Under the Sea-Wind* (New York: Penguin Books, 1996 [1941]).

6. Richard Jeffries, *The Pageant of Summer* (Portland, Me.: Thomas B. Mosher, 1905).

7. Linda Lear, *Rachel Carson: Witness for Nature* (New York: Henry Holt, 1997), 104.

8. Rachel Carson, *The Sea Around Us* (New York: Oxford University Press, 1989 [1950]).

9. Rachel Carson, *The Edge of the Sea* (Boston: Mariner Books, 1998 [1955]).

10. Carson, *Under the Sea-Wind*, 3.

11. Carson, *The Edge of Sea*, 3.

12. Carson, *Under the Sea-Wind*, 11–12.

13. Ibid., 19.

14. Ibid., 19–20.

15. Lear, *Witness for Nature*, 79–80.

16. Rachel Carson, *Silent Spring* (Boston: Houghton Mifflin, 1994 [1962]).

17. Carson, *Under the Sea-Wind*, 181.

18. Ibid., 103–104.

19. Ibid., 173–74.

20. Ibid., 175.

21. Ibid., 130, 133.

22. Ibid., 136–37.

23. Paul Taylor, *Respect for Nature: A Theory of Environmental Ethics* (Princeton, N.J.: Princeton University Press, 1986).

24. Carson, *Under the Sea-Wind*, 239.

25. Ibid., 240.

26. Ibid., 200.

27. Ibid., 202–203.

28. Lear, *Witness for Nature*, 91.

29. Ibid., 101.

30. Carson, *Under the Sea-Wind*, 248.

31. Ibid., 133.

32. Ibid., 173.

33. Sylvia Earle, *Sea Change: A Message of the Oceans* (New York: Fawcett Columbine, 1995).

6

The Conceptual Foundations of Rachel Carson's Sea Ethic

J. Baird Callicott and Elyssa Back

THE FOUNDATIONS QUESTION IN CARSON'S
ENVIRONMENTAL ETHICS

Rachel Carson has long been recognized as a key figure—perhaps *the* key figure—around whom popular environmental consciousness and conscience coalesced in the 1960s. Arguably the single most influential text raising environmental consciousness and galvanizing environmental conscience throughout the latter third of the twentieth century and into the twenty-first is *Silent Spring*. Yet Carson has been largely ignored by environmental philosophers seeking seed sources for the cultivation of environmental ethics, as Philip Cafaro notes.[1] By comparison, one can scarcely read a philosophical paper on environmental ethics without finding reference to Aldo Leopold—Carson's older contemporary, twenty years her senior—and his classic *A Sand County Almanac*.[2] One might be tempted to think that the nearly universal neglect of Carson by environmental philosophers can be attributed to the assumption that the concerns of *Silent Spring* are narrowly anthropocentric—how chlorinated hydrocarbons indiscriminately broadcast in the environment adversely affect human health. And because narrow anthropocentrism poses no distinctly philosophical challenge to environmental philosophers, Carson's work little interests them.

However, while one concern of *Silent Spring* is certainly the adverse effects on human health of chlorinated hydrocarbons, that is by no means its only concern, as Cafaro points out. Carson also consistently appeals to what are sometimes called "weak anthropocentric" and even to biocentric values.[3] Such values are evident in much of Carson's earlier work as well.[4] Synthetic chemicals loosed into the environment have even more devastating effects on the well-being of other organisms—to the point of threatening some avifauna with extinction. For Carson, as Cafaro persuasively argues and documents, biocide is a moral issue in its own right.[5] And, in addition to narrow human-health concerns, Carson clearly emphasizes the broader human values that are also at risk from indiscriminate use of pesticides and herbicides. Indeed, her short, arresting title perfectly evokes the weak anthropocentric values at the core of her book.[6] How aesthetically and spiritually depauperate would be a world without the songs of birds and the buzzings of insects! And of course a "silent spring" is only a synechdoche for all the other things of immaterial (or weak anthropocentric) value to human beings that industrial modernity threatens to erase.

If not because her values are narrowly—and thus boringly—anthropocentric, then how can one explain the lamentable fact that Rachel Carson has been largely ignored by environmental philosophers? Perhaps sexism is the cause. But that would hardly explain why ecofeminists have also little drawn on Carson as a source of inspiration and ideas.[7] We are inclined to think that Cafaro gets it right when he notes that, while one can convincingly impute what he calls ethical "premises"—we would call them precepts—to *Silent Spring* ("preserve human health! respect the moral considerability of non-human beings! promote human happiness and flourishing!"), one can there discover no ethical "foundations."[8]

Here we must be careful. Ben A. Minteer, an environmental pragmatist, regards the effort to construct a "foundational justification" for ethics to be cardinal among several "vices" to which environmental philosophers are prone.[9] According to Minteer, philosophers exhibit "a commitment to foundational justification" if "they posit the existence of certain basic or privileged beliefs which are supported non-inferentially" and their "premises are generally claimed to be a priori, self-evident, or directly justified in some manner;" nor do such premises "depend upon any other beliefs for their support."[10] Ironically, this characterization of a commitment to foundational justification applies most unequivocally to Bryan G. Norton, the purportedly vice-free environmental philosopher whose virtues Minteer most commends—because Norton treats belief in (weak) anthropocentrism as privileged and self-evident.[11] It would also seem to apply to Carson in *Silent Spring*. According to Cafaro, one possible reason that Carson provides no foundations for her ethical precepts in *Silent Spring* is "[p]erhaps she believed that by implying such general ethical principles as 'cause no unnecessary suffering' or 'preserve opportunities for human knowledge and experience,' she was resting on ethical ultimates which were beyond justification."[12] If this is indeed why she eschews foundational justification of her (implicit) principles in *Silent Spring*, then, paradoxically, such principles would be a paradigm case, according to Minteer's definition, of foundations!

In contrast to Minteer's idiosyncratic account, what we think Cafaro means by "foundations" and certainly what we would mean by "a commitment to foundational justification," is precisely the attempt to find support for ethical precepts and principles by connecting them (inferentially or otherwise) to other beliefs. We think that Cafaro correctly discerns three basic ethical precepts in *Silent Spring*—one strongly anthropocentric, one weakly anthropocentric, and one biocentic—and that he plausibly suggests two "general ethical principles" lurking there from which these precepts might flow. We also think that Cafaro is correct to observe that Carson provides these precepts and principles with no foundations in *Silent Spring*—justifiably, he suggests, because "meta-ethical reflection would have been out of place in a popular work."[13] And we think that she has (until very recently) been ignored by environmental philosophers of every persuasion—including ecofeminists and, for that matter, pragmatists—precisely because Carson engages in no such explicit reflection.

Aldo Leopold's *A Sand County Almanac*, on the other hand, has, we surmise, attracted such overwhelming attention from environmental philosophers as a source of inspiration and ideas in part because he does engage in a bit of explicit, albeit amateurish, metaethical reflection—just enough to entice philosophers to explore and expand the conceptual foundations of his land ethic. *A Sand County Almanac* is no less a "popular work" than *Silent Spring*—that is, a work written for a broad audience—suggesting that metaethical reflection or foundational justification is not altogether out of place in such books. Leopold himself, however, feared that it might be, as indicated by a caveat in his foreword stating that "[o]nly the very sympathetic reader will wish to wrestle with the philosophical questions of Part III [of *A Sand County Almanac*, which contains "The Land Ethic"]."[14] Albeit equally popular, the scope and goals of *Sand County* and *Silent Spring* are quite disparate. Leopold's goal in *Almanac* is nothing less than to effect a shift in the Western worldview: from an unholy blend of "Abrahamic" beliefs and consumerist values to a more coherent and well-substantiated evolutionary-ecological outlook and its normative implications.[15] His scope is cultural and historical and thus his sorties into metaethics are fitting.

Prior to the publication of *Silent Spring*, Rachel Carson wrote three books about the ocean that also aim, like *A Sand County Almanac*, at reorienting the inherited Western worldview.[16] Can one find a sea ethic in them comparable to the land ethic in *Sand County*? In the most flatfooted sense, the answer is no. The capstone essay of *Sand County* is titled "The Land Ethic" and there is no chapter in Carson's books about the ocean titled "The Sea Ethic" or anything like that. Susan Power Bratton convincingly argues, however, that one can find an implicit and diffuse sea ethic in *Under the Sea-Wind*, just as Cafaro convincingly argues that one can find an implicit and diffuse environmental ethic in *Silent Spring*. If so, can one find in Carson's marine works enough foundational raw material with which academic environmental philosophers might work to construct a Carson sea ethic as well articulated as the Leopold land ethic has become?

Bratton thinks that one can. She enumerates "four foundational concepts for a trans-ecotonal ethic of the seas" implicit in Carson's *Under the Sea-Wind*:

1. Humans are not fully adapted to life in the oceans, and we do not see or grasp the full extent of our impacts beneath the seas' surface....
2. We need to understand the scale and complexity of ocean ecosystems....
3. Humans disrupt ocean ecosystems by over-harvesting and over-estimating their productivity, and by modifying or blocking key ecosystem processes and linkages....
4. Human imagination and rational scientific investigation can traverse the ecotones, allowing us to more fully value ocean life and processes....[17]

These allegedly "foundational concepts" are not, however, the kind of concepts that moral philosophers (setting aside Minteer's idiosyncratic account) would regard as proper foundations for an ethic. The kind of concepts that count philosophically as ethical foundations concern the origin and nature of ethics per se. For example, in the case of the familiar and immensely influential moral philosophy of Immanuel Kant, ethics emanate from the rational law of noncontradiction. And the nature of ethics lies in acting according to self-consistent "maxims" (that is, precepts). To take a case in point, if I insist that others should tell me the truth and keep their promises to me, then I should also tell the truth and keep my promises to them, else I would be acting on contradictory precepts (or maxims): (a) Tell the truth and keep thy promises! and (b) Lie and make false promises when thou deemest it expedient to do so! These, in a nutshell, are the foundations of Kant's cardinal moral principle, his Categorical Imperative: "Act as if the maxim of your action were to become by your will a universal law of nature."[18] In the case of the equally familiar and influential moral philosophy of Hobbes, Locke, Rousseau, and Rawls, ethics originate in a social contract entered into by egoistic parties, each seeking their enlightened self-interest; and the nature of ethics consists in honoring the covenants entered into.

We think that the Carson sea ethic turns out to rest on conceptual foundations that are similar in some respects to the Leopold land ethic, but very different in others. As a consequence of the differences, the Carson sea ethic is not just a watery sibling of the Leopold land ethic; it represents something new to the growing catalogue of environmental ethics. We begin with a review of the now familiar conceptual foundations of the Leopold land ethic as a locus for comparison. That review will provide a more extended example—than these thumbnail sketches of those of Kant and the social contract theorists—of what proper conceptual foundations for an ethic are. It will also provide an example of how such implicit foundations can be identified in an amateur philosopher's popular work.

THE CONCEPTUAL FOUNDATIONS OF THE LEOPOLD LAND ETHIC IN BRIEF

The Leopold land ethic is built on conceptual foundations borrowed from Charles Darwin. Leopold signals his debt to Darwin, not by quotation and citation—as an academic philosopher would—but by allusion. Leopold begins "The Land Ethic" with a vignette from Homer's *Odyssey*, the earliest extant literature in Western culture, intended to dramatize the fact that in the three thousand years between Odysseus' day and our own, ethics have grown in scope (and changed in substance as well, we might add). Then he goes on to write,

> This extension of ethics, so far studied only by philosophers, is actually a process in ecological evolution. Its sequences may be described in ecological as well as in philosophical terms. An ethic, ecologically, is a limitation on freedom of action in the struggle for existence. An ethic, philosophically, is a differentiation of social from antisocial conduct. These are two definitions of one thing. The thing has its origin in the tendency of interdependent individuals or groups to evolve modes of cooperation.[19]

Leopold's discourse in these six sentences—"ecological evolution," "struggle for existence," "origin," "evolve"—seems unmistakably to allude to an evolutionary frame of reference and to Darwin more particularly. Following Leopold's discursive signposts we find in the third chapter of *The Descent of Man* an account of the origin and evolution of the "moral sense...exclusively from the side of natural history"—that is, a foundational account of ethics in biological terms.[20] What Leopold alleges that an ethic is "philosophically"—"a differentiation of social from anti-social conduct"—is actually the central notion of what an ethic is biologically in Darwin's account. For many species, and especially *Homo sapiens*, individual survival and reproductive success depend on living in a cooperative society. And as Darwin succinctly puts it, "No tribe could hold together if murder, robbery, treachery, &c., were common; consequently such crimes within the limits of the same tribe 'are branded with everlasting infamy.'"[21]

Now if the "tribe" cannot hold together, its erstwhile individual members would starve, be preyed upon themselves, or fail to rear their offspring to sexual maturity in the absence of cooperative hunting, mutual defense, and child rearing with other members. Thus, those individuals more inclined to limiting their "freedom of action in the struggle for existence" by resisting impulses to "murder, robbery, treachery, &c." could form cooperative societies and pursue the struggle for existence cooperatively and collectively. Those more inclined to commit "such crimes" would be excluded from the society of their more ethical fellows and be forced to pursue the struggle for existence as solitaries—with poor prospects for success. Thus, for Darwin, ethics is naturally selected as a means of social integration, which in turn is vital for individual survival and reproductive success—that is, for inclusive fitness.

According to Darwin, the preexisting mammalian raw materials from which ethics evolved were the parental and filial affections and the social instincts and sympathy. The parental and filial affections are absolutely necessary for mammalian reproductive success—else offspring would be neglected or abandoned or would wander away at their peril. When such affections chanced to be extended to other relatives—siblings, grandparents, uncles, and aunts—small, extended-family societies emerged. When human beings evolved sufficient intelligence to trace out the destructive affects of certain behaviors on these little societies, sufficient imagination to envision the similar destructive social effects of similar behaviors, and a sufficiently articulate language to encode prohibitions regarding such behaviors, ethics proper came into being. From Darwin's account of the evolutionary origins and nature of ethics we can now formulate a foundational lemma: ethics and society are correlative. And we can formulate a corresponding foundational corollary: as society changes in scope or size and in form or structure, ethics change correlatively.

Competition among primeval human societies (clans or gens—groups of about fifty individuals forming an extended family) drives changes in the scope and form of human ethics. Social integration and cooperative resource-exploitation and defense strategies fostered the further evolution of intelligence and language, and led to increasing success for *Homo sapiens* as a species. As the human population grew, once isolated social groups came into competition with one another. Larger and better-organized societies could outcompete smaller, less well-organized societies and so smaller groups (clans/gens) merged to form larger, stronger ones (multiclan tribes). Because intrasocial ethics is necessary for the society to hold together, as smaller groups merged to form larger ones, ethics were extended from the smaller (clan) to the larger (tribe) membership. Darwin imagined this process of group competition and merger to have repeatedly taken place historically and envisioned its future culmination in a single global human community:

> As man advances in civilisation, and small tribes are united into larger communities, the simplest reason would tell each individual that he ought to extend his social instincts and sympathies to all the members of the same nation, though personally unknown to him. This point being once reached, there is only an artificial barrier to prevent his sympathies extending to the men of all nations and races.[22]

We ourselves are today witnessing the painful birth of the global human community of which Darwin dreamt—for better or worse—as communications and transportation technologies, together with many other forces, are binding humanity into a global village. The human rights ethic—as ratified by the United Nations Universal Declaration of Human Rights in 1948—is the ethic correlative to the emerging global village.

Leopold simply took over Darwin's account of the origin and evolution of ethics and added to those foundations an ecological element. Leopold condenses, as only he can do, Darwin's moral philosophy into a nutshell: "All ethics so far evolved rest on a single premise: that the individual is a member of a community of interdependent parts. His instincts prompt him to compete for his place in that community, but his ethics prompt him also to co-operate (perhaps in order that there may be a place to compete for)."[23] Then Leopold adds the ecological element, "the community concept," vividly articulated by his friend and colleague, Charles Elton, and identified in the foreword as "the basic concept of ecology."[24] Ecology "simply enlarges the boundaries of the community to include soils, waters, plants, and animals, or collectively: the land."[25] Thus, "a land ethic changes the role of Homo sapiens from conqueror of the land-community to plain member and citizen of it. It implies respect for his fellow-members, and also respect for the community as such."[26]

Leopold makes the work of the academic environmental philosopher easy. While Cafaro had to supply the (implicit and unjustified) principles— "cause no unnecessary suffering" and "preserve opportunities for human knowledge and experience"—underlying Carson's (no less implicit) ethical precepts in Silent Spring, Leopold explicitly provides his own ultimate (but well-justified) principle in Sand County and in his own inimitable prose: "A thing is right when it tends to preserve the integrity, stability, and beauty of the biotic community. It is wrong when it tends otherwise."[27]

THE DARWINIAN MARINE COMMUNITY CONCEPT
IN CARSON'S SEA ETHIC

Now with this example of what conceptual foundations for an environmental ethic are and how to look for them in a popular work aimed at transforming environmental consciousness and conscience—and admittedly in A Sand County Almanac they are not hard to find—let's see if one can find any such thing in Carson's sea books. Bratton provides an insightful and enticing clue by calling attention to the way in which the "Darwinian realities of life" pervade Under the Sea-Wind.[28] Here then is a profound similarity between Carson's conceptual orientation and Leopold's: both persistently purvey an evolutionary worldview. And both convey as well an ecological worldview. As

Bratton observes, "Carson never utilizes the term 'sea community' but she paints detailed portraits of how the ocean's inhabitants interact."[29]

However, the differences are equally profound. According to Bratton, "Leopold's land community behaves almost like an idealized New England town council....Although he describes predators, the gory details are sparse. His dying wolf is more a responsible mother than a fierce animal capable of ripping the entrails out of a deer or an elk."[30] Bratton's spin on Leopold is a little exaggerated. In "Thinking Like a Mountain"—in which Leopold shoots the wolf to which Bratton refers—Leopold imagines the meaning of such a wolf's howl from various nonhuman points of view: "To the deer it is a reminder of the way of all flesh, to the pine a forecast of midnight scuffles and of blood upon the snow, to the coyote a promise of gleanings to come."[31] And in "Odyssey," Leopold remarks that in the land community as he conceives it "The only certain truth is that its creatures must suck hard, live fast, and die often, lest its losses exceed its gains."[32]

Nevertheless, Bratton's point is well taken. Darwin's evolutionary coin has two sides and the portrait of the "Darwinian realities of life" on either side is correspondingly dichotomous. In the *Origin of Species* Darwin stresses competition among slightly varying individuals of the same species and survival of the fittest few as the driving force of evolution. In *The Descent of Man* he stresses cooperation among individual members of social groups and the advantage that membership in such groups confers on all cooperating individuals. The Darwinian realities of life that Carson stresses are intraspecies competition and interspecies conflict and predation, while the Darwinian realities of life that Leopold stresses are intraspecies cooperation—reinforced, perhaps, by the pleasant natural history observations, evolutionary speculations, and political ideology of Petr Kropotkin.[33] Of one particularly terrifying moment in the imagined life of one of her main characters, Scomber the mackerel, Carson writes vividly in *Under the Sea-Wind*:

On the tenth morning of his life he had lingered in the upper fathoms of water instead of following down into the soft gloom below. Out of the clear green water a dozen gleaming silver fishes suddenly loomed up. They were anchovies, small and herringlike. The foremost anchovy caught sight of Scomber. Swerving from his path, he came whirling through the yard of water that separated them, open-mouthed, ready to seize the small mackerel. Scomber veered away in sudden alarm, but his powers of motion were new-found and he rolled clumsily in the water. In a fraction of a second he would have been seized and eaten, but a second anchovy, darting in from the opposite side, collided with the first and in the confusion Scomber dashed beneath them.

Now he found himself in the midst of the main school of several thousand anchovies. Their silver scales flashed on all sides of him. They bumped and jostled as he sought in vain to escape. The shoal surged over and beneath and around Scomber, driving furiously onward just under the shining ceiling of the sea. None of the anchovies was now aware of the little mackerel, for the shoal itself was in full flight. A pack of young bluefish had picked up the scent of the anchovies and swung into swift pursuit. In a twinkling they were upon their prey, fierce and ravening as a pack of wolves. The leader of the bluefish lunged. With a snap of razor-toothed jaws he seized two of the anchovies. Two clean-severed heads and two tails floated away. The taste of blood was in the water. As though maddened by it, the bluefish slashed to right and left. They drove through the center of the anchovy school, scattering the ranks of the smaller fish so that they darted in panic and confusion in every direction. Many dashed to the surface and leaped through into the strange element beyond. There they were seized by the hovering gulls, companion fishers of the bluefish.[34]

Why this difference in emphasis? Carson may have simply had a darker outlook on life than Leopold, rendering *Under the Sea-Wind* more of an *oeuvre noire* than *A Sand County Almanac*. However, Linda Lear provides no compelling evidence for any such psychological orientation in *Rachel Carson: Witness for Nature*—indeed, quite the contrary.[35] And, as a matter of fact, Carson regarded Leopold's book *Round River* (an ill-conceived posthumous collection of hunting-journal entries and literary-philosophical essays, edited by Luna B. Leopold) to be a particularly dark work. Of it she wrote,

> The most disturbing thing of all, however, is the glorification of cruelty...but I shall have to express a very deep conviction: that until we have courage to recognize cruelty for what it is—whether its victim is human or animal—we cannot expect things to be much better in the world. There can be no double standard. We cannot have peace among men whose hearts find delight in killing any living creature. By every act that glorifies or even tolerates such moronic delight in killing, we set back the progress of humanity.[36]

Of course the cruelty that Carson here condemns is inflicted by human beings—either on other human beings or on animals. And the kind of ethical judgment that Carson evinces is consistent both with animal welfare ethics and Kant's idea that cruelty to animals is morally wrong because a moral agent's cruelty to animals may inure him or her to cruelty per se and thus lead to acts of cruelty toward other human beings.[37] It is even doubtful that non-human animals can be said to be cruel; and if we can intelligibly say that some kinds of animals are cruel, we cannot say that of many kinds. A cat toying with a mouse until it is dead may—or may not, the question is open—intelligibly be said to be cruel, but one could hardly characterize comb jellyfish that entrap and slowly digest fin fish as cruel or so characterize eels that suck the soft tissues out of fish ensnared in gill nets. Carson's remarks here about cruelty are also consistent with virtue ethics, for by "progress of humanity" Carson almost surely means the collective improvement of human moral character.[38] But—back to the point—the idea that it is possible for humanity to progress ethically is not consistent with a pessimistic or dark view of life.

Why then does Carson stress the competitive side of the coin of Darwinian evolutionary theory, while Leopold stresses the cooperative side? Linda Lear certainly does indicate that Carson herself was a competitive person in an alien environment—a sea of men.[39] Such a psychological etiology is, however, both speculative and demeaning, for it suggests that an intellectual choice is not a coolly cognitive decision at all, but a blind offshoot of temperament. We think, rather, that Carson stresses evolutionary competition, conflict, and predation because of a signal difference between terrestrial biotic communities and marine biotic communities. In short, there is more conscious or deliberate cooperation evident on land than there is under water. In *Under the Sea-Wind*, Carson rather warmly portrays several bonded pairs of animals: Blackfoot and his mate, Silverbar; Ookpik and his (unnamed) mate; and Pandion and his (also unnamed) mate. All, however, are birds—sanderlings, owls, and ospreys, respectively. As the narrative moves from shore to sea, from over land to under water, all the animals we meet pursue life's struggle as solitaries. Except for cetacean societies, one finds few if any affectionally bonded animal communities in marine environments—and cetaceans evolved from land mammals that returned to live in the sea.

To the contrary, one might counter, the most impressive multispecies communities in all of nature lie beneath the waves—coral reefs. Yes, we reply, but coral reefs are not held together by the same "social instincts and sympathy" that Darwin dwells on in *Descent*. Neither are schools of dogfish. Nor, as Bratton notes, have human beings been long a part of any marine biotic communities—plain members and citizens thereof—if it can even be said that we are a part of them now. So, one must conclude that the evolutionary-ecological worldview that Carson shares with Leopold does not warrant the supposition that such a shared worldview is the cornerstone around which foundations of a Carson sea ethic can be constructed simply by following the blueprint that environmental philosophers have already drawn up for the foundations of the Leopold land ethic.

Carson's portrait of marine biotic communities can be aptly summarized by the words of entomologist and naturalist Stephen A. Forbes, words with which Carson was doubtless familiar and which may have influenced her evolutionary and ecological thinking about marine environments. Forbes' famous 1887 paper is titled "The Lake As a Microcosm" and Carson may have taken its meaning to be an ecologist's description of a lacustrine microcosm of the marine macrocosm:

In this lake, ... competitions are fierce and continuous beyond any parallels in the worst periods of human history; ... they take hold, not on goods of life merely, but always upon life itself; ... mercy and charity and sympathy and magnanimity and all the virtues are utterly unknown; ... robbery and murder and the deadly tyranny of strength over weakness are the unvarying rule; what we call wrongdoing is always triumphant, and what we call goodness would be fatal to its possessor.[40]

But, Forbes goes on to emphasize, when we scale up our focus to the level of the aquatic community as a whole, a beautiful order (the literal meaning, incidentally, of the Greek word κοσμος) may be observed:

Out of these hard conditions an order has been evolved which is best conceivable without a total change in the conditions themselves; an equilibrium has been reached and is steadily maintained that actually accomplishes for all the parties involved the greatest good which the circumstances will at all permit. In a system where life is the universal good, but the destruction of life the well-nigh universal occupation, an order has spontaneously arisen which consistently tends to maintain life at the highest limit.[41]

Aquatic biotic communities are doubly—perhaps trebly—alien to human beings. The creatures in them are not familiar and some are strange beyond imagination. Except again for cetaceans, we find no heartwarming interactions among those creatures—no play, no mutual aid, no expressions of affection, no sympathy—such as Darwin relates among terrestrial animals in *The Descent of Man*. And we hold no membership in aquatic biotic communities. We observe them and interact with them strictly as outsiders. What we observe can be foreign and morally repugnant, but we can also recognize, in lakes and seas, ordered worlds that are as beautiful and awesome in their structure as any phenomena on this mysterious planet. And what we do to these κοσμοι can be sickeningly destructive.

THE CONCEPTS OF OTHERNESS AND DIFFERENCE IN CARSON'S SEA ETHIC

Thus we need a sea ethic, but from what elements can it be constructed? How can one provide a sea ethic with solid foundations that will convincingly support its principles and precepts? We suggest a postmodern approach based on otherness and difference.

In mainstream Western philosophy sameness is the conceptual bedrock on which ethics has rested. In the paradigmatic Kantian tradition, persons warrant ethical treatment because we are all the same—we are all equally rational beings. About this Kant is explicit:

Rational nature exists as an end in itself. The human being necessarily represents his own existence in this way; so far it is thus a *subjective* principle of human actions. But every other rational being also represents his existence in this way consequent on *just the same rational ground that also holds for me*; thus it is at the same time an objective principle from which, as a supreme practical ground, it must be possible to derive all laws of the will.[42]

One major theme in the brief but rich history of environmental ethics has been to plausibly substitute some other property for rationality as the shared qualification for moral considerability: being the subject of a life (Tom Regan); being sentient (Peter Singer); being alive (Kenneth Goodpaster); being a teleological center of life (Paul Taylor); being self-valuing (Holmes Rolston, III).[43] In the case of Aldo Leopold and the land ethic, being members of the same biotic community is the tie that binds people, plants, animals, soils, and waters into (an admittedly asymmetrical) moral community. Also in vernacular ethics, such as that of the civil rights movement, the most effective rhetorical appeal has been to sameness. Skin tones, hair color and texture, facial features, and the like among the races may be different, but all people are equally human; beneath such superficial differences, that is, we are all essentially the same.

Extending the standard sameness approach to ethics from the sphere of human to environmental interactions can lead, in extremis, to grotesque conclusions. With few exceptions, animal welfare ethicists shrink from advocating efforts to stop predators from violating the rights of their prey or causing them to suffer, even though that would seem to follow from their premises.[44] Predator-prey dynamics lie at the heart of many fundamental ecological processes—energy flowing through food chains being, perhaps, most fundamental of all—and to conclude that predation per se is bad and should be prevented has ecological repercussions that are too monstrous to entertain. Lisa Sideris, however, finds several environmental theologians envisioning a redeemed world from which predation has been cleansed. Sally McFague, for example, "envisions and urges Christians to work toward a natural world in which 'there is food for all; where neither people nor animals are destroying one another.'"[45] Sideris finds similar ideas lurking in the work of Rosemary Radford Reuther, Jürgen Moltmann, Charles Birch, and John Cobb.[46]

Because of the tremendously large legacy of ethics based on sameness in the Western tradition of moral philosophy, an ethics based on otherness is not only new but still only tentatively theorized. Its wellspring seems to be oppositional politics. Sameness can exert a subtle (or perhaps not-so-subtle) pressure to conform, to assimilate, to measure up to the norm represented by the paradigm case, the reference type of being—or else suffer the fate of self-inflicted exclusion. Thus, as one might expect, ethics of difference appear, among other places, in antiliberal feminism, such as the work of Iris Murdoch, Luce Irigaray, and Julia Kristeva.[47] A few environmental philosophers are attempting to strip away the complex metaphysics from the concept of the Other and its exclusively anthropocentric orientation in the work of Emmanuel Levinas in order to craft a difference-based environmental ethic.[48] A particularly lucid exposition of Levinas' idea of otherness and its relationship to ethics is provided by philosopher Adriaan Peperzak, who endorses the anthropocentric limits that Levinas imposes on ethics:

> In all his works, Levinas has endeavored to show that the (human) other radically differs from all other beings in the world. The other's coming to the fore cannot be seen as a variation of the general appearance by which all other beings are phenomenal.... The way the other imposes its enigmatic irreducibility and nonrelativity or absoluteness is by means of a command and a prohibition: You are not allowed to kill me; you must accord me a place under the sun and everything that is necessary to live a truly human life. This demands not only the omission of criminal behavior but simultaneously a positive dedication: the other's facing me makes me responsible for him/her, and this responsibility has no limits.[49]

Kant's ethic is of course equally militant in its anthropocentric bias: "Beings the existence of which rests not on our will but on nature, if they are beings without reason, still have only a relative worth, as means, and are therefore called *things*, whereas rational beings are called *persons* because their very nature already marks them out as an end in itself."[50] But that has not prevented the Kantian ethic from being coherently transformed, especially by Paul Taylor, into an environmental ethic. Philosopher John Llewelyn has taken the first step toward a difference-based environmental ethic by extending Levinas' concept of radical Otherness from people to animals: "What licenses this extension...is need. It is not only the other human being that can be hungry, thirsty, orphaned, cold or in some other way in need. And if my not giving the other food is tantamount to murder it is not only the other human beings whom I murder or culpably kill. My culpability extends to other animals."[51]

The practical outcome of Llewelyn's extension of Levinas' difference-based ethics to animals would seem to be by now rather familiar and disappointing—animal welfare ethics. Llewelyn faithfully follows Levinas in making his difference-based animal-oriented ethic include positive duties to address needs as well as negative duties to refrain from interference. But that then exposes Llewelyn's ethic of the animal Other to the problem of predation in the wild. It is one thing to feed and water hungry and thirsty domestic animals and to shelter them if they are orphaned or cold—and to protect them from predation. But to respond to the needs of wild animals in the same way is not ecologically appropriate. However, if Llewelyn retained only the negative duties of noninterference and dropped the positive duties of care and protection—at least for wild animals—a difference-based animal-oriented ethic might be quite well aligned with an ecological worldview. Our duty is to let wild animals be. The only positive duty we have toward them—if we have any at all—is the duty to provide them with the kind of habitat they need to carry on, as best they can, with their struggles for existence.

In any case, the foundations, not the indications, are what makes Llewelyn's animal-oriented ethic new and exciting. Whatever duties we do or do not have toward them, wild animals don't have to be measured by human norms to count. They can remain their unassimilated, alien selves and still make a claim—at least a negative claim—on the sense of human moral responsibility. Nor, as Llewelyn makes clear, is that responsibility conditional on a corresponding, reciprocal responsibility on the part of the Other. He devotes considerable effort to highlighting the differences between Levinas' Other-based ethic and the sometimes explicit, sometimes covert, but virtually universal egoism or self-love at the heart of the Western sameness tradition of moral philosophy, previously exposed clearly by Kenneth Goodpaster.[52]

One stylistic peculiarity of *Under the Sea-Wind* is Carson's penchant for individualizing and naming the denizens of the deep and its liminal zones. First the reader meets the avian Rynchops, a black skimmer. Then come Uhvinguk, a lemming mouse; Tullagak, a raven, and White Tip, a bald eagle—in addition to the aforementioned Silverbar and Blackfoot, a pair of sanderlings; Ookpik, an owl; and Pandion, an osprey. The reader is halfway through the book before meeting a fish—face-to-face, as it were—"Mugil, the mullet." As Bratton's title hints, the principal *persona dramatis* of *Under the Sea-Wind* is a mackerel, the also aforementioned Scomber, whose life history fills 100 pages of a 275-page book. After Scomber's adventures are recounted the reader encounters Anguilla, an eel; Lophius, an angler fish, with his "two small, evil eyes;" and Cynosius, a sea trout.[53]

Central to Levinas' difference-based ethic is the immediate apprehension of the face of the Other and, to a lesser extent, the Other's voice. Carson's use of personal names for the animals at first seems hokey, even a bit puerile. But in light of Llewelyn's expansion of a Levinasian difference ethic to animals, it seems an unwitting stroke of genius. For with a name, skimmers and sanderlings, mullets and mackerels, even eels and angler fish have the literary equivalent of a face that demands an ethical response. Actually by comparison with Carson, Levinas and Irigaray seem downright pedestrian and parochial. For the otherness and difference that the latter celebrate comes with a human (and for Irigaray a female) face—thus implicitly reintroducing sameness and, with sameness, exclusion of all other otherness. Carson's Others, by comparison, are radically other—not just other species, but for the most part, species that inhabit a *habitus* utterly foreign to our familiar terrestrial haunts.

Levinas and Irigaray could not have influenced Carson's thinking about a sea ethic because their philosophical works appeared after Carson's ocean books. If there is any anticipation of her difference-based environmental ethic it is to be found in the work of Henry Beston. In *Outermost House*—a *Walden*-like chronicle of a solitary year on the Atlantic coast of Cape Cod—Beston writes:

> We need another and a wiser and perhaps a more mystical concept of animals....We patronize them for their incompleteness, for their tragic fate of having taken form so far below ourselves. And therein we err, and greatly err. For the animal shall not be measured by man. In a world older and more complete than ours they move finished and complete, gifted with extensions of the senses we have lost or never attained, living by voices we shall never hear. They are not bretheren, they are not underlings; they are other nations. Caught with ourselves in the net of life and time, fellow prisoners of the splendour and travail of the earth.[54]

The influence of Beston on Carson was direct. In a letter to Beston, dated May 14, 1954, Carson says that she discovered *The Outermost House* twenty years earlier and reread it "many times" in the intervening years. And while writing *Under the Sea-Wind* in the late 1930s, partly at Woods Hole on Cape Cod, Carson "one day drove to Eastham and walked down the beach to find the little house and the surroundings with which I felt so familiar through your pages."[55] The United States entered World War II in December of 1941, a month after the appearance of *Under the Sea-Wind*—it was not good timing for publishing a book about nonhuman life in the oceans. After selling only two thousand copies, the book went out of print in 1946. Riding the wave of the best-seller success of *The Sea Around Us*, Oxford University Press republished *Under the Sea-Wind* in 1952. In a review of its second coming, Beston emphatically, if only implicitly, affirms our other-grounded interpretation of the Carson sea ethic:

> Here is the glimpse of nature in the full cosmic perspective—nature portrayed in her inexhaustible variety and gigantic ruthlessness. Here is the element of nightmare, here the haunting element of chance, here the splendor and the terror and the beauty of the waters and the air. There is never the slightest humanizing of the creature or its world, for which may Miss Carson be ever blest. Her world of the sea and air is ruled by its own gods and its own values. To make this world, really so alien and remote, a part of the world of the human spirit, is a very great achievement.[56]

Carson told Beston that his review of *Under the Sea-Wind* was "the most beautiful, perceptive, and deeply satisfying one I had read, and because of my feeling for 'The Outermost House,' I was so grateful it was you who had written it."[57] But don't we need in a sea ethic something more than respect for the ocean's denizens severally in all their splendid and complete otherness and difference? Part of the appeal of the land ethic, especially to conservationists and environmentalists, is its provision of respect for "the community as such," in addition to respect for "fellow members." Working in the difference tradition of Levinas, Irigaray, and Llewelyn, philosopher Mick Smith has taken the step from an ethic oriented to animal Others, not to the Leopoldian biotic-community ethic, but to a holistic ethics of place.[58] Reflecting on the distinction between space (which is Euclidean, uniform, and homogeneous) and place (which is unique, particular, and vested with geomorphological, biological, and cultural characteristics), Smith articulates a difference-based ethical holism. In short, space is emblematic of the same, place emblematic of the different. A holistic place ethic would mandate preserving the wide variety of places in all their diverse differences and resisting the homogenizing erasure of places to make spaces for colonizing residential, commercial, and industrial development.

Smith's ethics of place, however, represents an imperfect foundation for the holistic dimension of Carson's sea ethic. To his credit, Smith distances his place ethic from the tradition of bioregionalism begun by Peter Berg and Raymond Dasman and subsequently more systematically articulated by Kirkpatrick Sale.[59] According to Smith classic bioregionalism is reductive and parochial—reductive because the environmental peculiarities of bioregions are alleged to determine their correlative social and cultural characteristics and parochial because bioregional ethics are limited to intrabioregional relationships. On the other hand, Smith warmly endorses the necessary human element in the philosophy of place going back to Yi-Fu Tuan and René Dubos: "Places are particular products of unique combinations of social and environmental relations."[60] The places in Carson's marine world are devoid of any human social nodes in the relationships that constitute them. Carson, rather, more radically makes biotic nodes contribute to the nexus of relations that constitute places in the ocean's spaces.

Can one find an autochthonous holistic dimension to Carson's sea ethic? We think so. As Bratton has perceptively pointed out, the narrative movement of Under the Sea-Wind is guided by the particular place characteristics of the seascape, which may look like featureless space to the terrestrial eye of the surface sailor, but is actually a mosaic of richly textured places—and is so perceived by the senses of aquatic beings. The narrative of Under the Sea-Wind moves from tidal marshes to beaches to the continental shelf with its shallow shoals, to the precipitous slope of the shelf into the abysmal depths of the mid-ocean; from sunlight and warmth to coldness and darkness; from still waters to fast-moving currents. The Sea Around Us is even more explicitly focused on the many and various places that one can find in the world's oceans and near-sea landforms. And, as Cafaro notes, in that book, Carson "repeatedly invokes the ocean's radical non-humanity."[61] In Under the Sea-Wind, Carson also stresses the otherness of the places in the ocean as well as their variety: "There could scarcely be a stranger place in the world in which to begin life than this universe of sky and water, peopled by strange creatures and governed by wind and sun and ocean currents.... It was filled with small hunters, each of which must live at the expense of its neighbors, plant and animal."[62]

Moreover, implicit in Carson's sea ethic is the kind of holism already noted in our discussion of Forbes. When one scales up from the violent and seemingly random and chaotic interactions of the components, one can perceive an emergent harmony of the community as a whole. Beston states it eloquently—and in explicitly ethical terms:

> And what of Nature itself, you say—that callous and cruel engine, red in tooth and fang?...It is true that there are grim arrangements. Beware of judging them by whatever human values are in style. As well expect Nature to answer to your human values as to come into your house and sit in a chair. The economy of nature, its checks and balances, its measurements of competing life—all this is its great marvel and has an ethic of its own.[63]

Carson's style is more circumspect—and more subtle—but if one looks closely, one will find the same point, previously made both by Forbes and Beston, woven seamlessly into her narrative. Here is one example: "Each of the roe fish would shed in a season more than a hundred thousand eggs. From these perhaps only one or two young would survive the perils of river and sea and return to spawn, for by such ruthless selection the species is kept in check."[64] The following example almost suggests a Darwinian mysticism, a literal transubstantiation: "Of the millions of mackerel eggs...thousands went no farther than the first stages of the journey into life until they were seized and eaten by the comb jellies, to be speedily converted into the watery tissue of their foe and in this reincarnation to roam the sea, preying on their own kind."[65] In a single paragraph Carson captures the elegance—and, in this instance, the irony—of a food chain, beginning and ending with the same species:

> The ghost crab, still at his hunting of beach fleas, was alarmed by the turmoil of birds overhead, by the many racing shadows that sped over the sand. By now he was far from his burrow. When he saw the fishermen walking across the beach he dashed into the surf, preferring this refuge to flight. But a large channel bass was lurking near by, and in a twinkling the crab was seized and eaten. Later in the same day, the bass was attacked by sharks and what was left of it was cast up by the tide onto the sand. The beach fleas, scavengers of the shore, swarmed over it and devoured it.[66]

SUMMARY COMPARISON OF THE CARSON SEA ETHIC AND LEOPOLD LAND ETHIC

We return to Cafaro's question, "what are the 'foundations' of Rachel Carson's environmental ethics?"[67] The foundations of her sea ethic, we suggest, are, like the foundations of Leopold's land ethic, traceable first to Charles Darwin. But unlike Leopold, Carson's Darwin is not so much the author of *The Descent of*

Man as of *The Origin of Species*. And just as Leopold added to his Darwin an ecological ingredient borrowed from Charles Elton, Carson added to hers an ecological ingredient borrowed, in all probability, from Stephen Forbes. The ecological idea that Leopold incorporated was that of a cooperative biotic community in which every member fills a niche and performs a role in the economy of nature. The ecological idea that Carson incorporated was also that of a biotic community in which, from the random violence perpetrated by every member in its competitive struggle for existence, a wonderful order and harmony emerges stochastically at the community level of organization.

How—especially in light of Forbes' explicit comments about the conspicuous absence of anything that we would call goodness or virtue in an aquatic community—could one cook up an ethic from these ingredients? One can—and Forbes hints that one might—find a holistic ethic at the community level of organization, for, he thinks, the system "tends to maintain life at the highest limit." Still, at what awful price is a standing crop of biomass maximized? Beston suggests that for one to judge nature's means is presumptive and arrogant; one is in effect making "man the measure of all things" as Protagoras long ago declared—a form of hubris from which geology and evolutionary biology should have by now liberated us all. Beston's recorded metaethical thoughts, however, are occasional and brief. They are completed and elaborated (owing nothing to Beston himself, of course) by Levinas, Llewelyn, and Smith, theorizing an environmental ethic based not on sameness—in which the natural realm is drawn into and trammeled by the human skein of values, duties, and obligations—but on difference and otherness.

Yes, but how much of this can one actually find in Carson? Well, how much of all we set out in our discussion of the Leopold land ethic can one actually find in Leopold? Admittedly, the identification of foundations for a Carson sea ethic is even more speculative than of those for the Leopold land ethic. And, as noted, Carson's approach is more circumspect than that of Leopold and even that of Beston. She proceeds exclusively by a narrative method, never resorting to explicit metaethical reflection. Hers is more a process of accumulation than explicit reflection, a process that has been described by philosopher and nature writer Kathleen Dean Moore through an appropriately aquatic metaphor—a metaphor not drawn from lakes or oceans, however, but from rivers.[68] The Carson sea ethic begins in small narrative watersheds, flows together in streams, which gather finally into a strongly flowing, wide, and deep river of moral import.[69]

NOTES

1. Philip Cafaro, "Rachel Carson's Environmental Ethics," *Worldviews* 6 (2002): 58–80. Cafaro's essay is reprinted in this volume as chapter 4.

2. The first paper on environmental ethics by an academic philosopher mentions and cites Aldo Leopold in the first sentence: Richard Routley, "Is There a Need for a New, an Environmental Ethic," in *Proceedings of the 15th World Congress of Philosophy*, vol. 1, ed. Bulgarian Organizing Committee (Varna, Bulgaria: Sophia Press, 1973), 205-10. The first paper on environmental ethics by an American academic philosopher cites and discusses Aldo Leopold's land ethic: Holmes Rolston, III, "Is There an Ecologic Ethic?" *Ethics* 85 (1975): 93-109. From the mid-1970s on, it would be safe to say that Aldo Leopold is the most frequently cited source of inspiration and ideas for environmental ethics.

3. Cafaro, "Carson's Environmental Ethics," and chapter 4 in this volume. See Bryan G. Norton, "Weak Anthropocentrism and Environmental Ethics," *Environmental Ethics* 6 (1984): 131-48; and Paul W. Taylor, "In Defense of Biocentrism," *Environmental Ethics* 5 (1983): 237-43.

4. See Paul Brooks, *The House of Life: Rachel Carson at Work* (Boston: Houghton Mifflin, 1972); and Rachel Carson, *Lost Woods: The Discovered Writing by Rachel Carson*, ed. Linda Lear (Boston: Beacon Press, 1998).

5. Cafaro, "Carson's Environmental Ethics."

6. We agree with Cafaro ("Carson's Environmental Ethic," 62) that "The book's title suggests, perhaps, that Carson herself was motivated by the latter two [moral precepts—'respect the moral considerability of non-human beings!' and 'promote human happiness and flourishing!'], with human health concerns secondary."

7. Karen Warren has done more than any other scholar to document historically ecofeminist environmental ethics, but one finds no mention of Carson in Warren's "Feminism and Ecology: Making Connections," *Environmental Ethics* 9 (1987): 3-20, or in her "The Power and the Promise of Ecological Feminism," *Environmental Ethics* 12 (1990): 125-46, nor for that matter in the latest iteration of that paper, "The Power and the Promise of Ecofeminism Revisited," in *Environmental Philosophy: From Animal Rights to Radical Ecology*, 4th ed., ed. Michael E. Zimmerman et al. (Upper Saddle River, N.J.: Prentice Hall, 2004), 252-79. The only mention of Carson by ecofeminist philosophers of which we are aware is by Greta Gaard and Lori Gruen, "Ecofeminism: Toward Global Justice and Planetary Health," *Society and Nature* 2 (1993): 1-35, and they provide no discussion. Joni Seager, "Rachel Carson Died of Breast Cancer: The Coming of Age of Feminist Environmentalism," *Signs* 28 (2003): 945-72, distinguishes feminist environmentalism from ecofeminism; and although the name "Rachel Carson" is in Seager's title, she devotes only one paragraph to a discussion of Carson's work and that is confined to a section of the paper under the subhead "Public Health and Feminist Environmentalism."

8. Cafaro, "Carson's Environmental Ethics," 63.

9. Ben A. Minteer, "Intrinsic Value for Pragmatists?" *Environmental Ethics* 23 (2001): 57–75, 65.

10. Ibid., "No Experience Necessary?: Foundationalism and the Retreat from Culture in Environmental Ethics" *Environmental Ethics* 7 (1998): 333–48, 336.

11. Bryan G. Norton, "Why I Am Not a Nonanthropocentrist: Callicott and the Failure of Inherent Monism," *Environmental Ethics* 17 (1995): 341–58.

12. Cafaro, "Carson's *Environmental Ethics*," 64.

13. Ibid., 63.

14. Aldo Leopold, *A Sand County Almanac: and Sketches Here and There* (New York: Oxford University Press, 1949), viii.

15. See Peter Fritzell, "The Conflicts of Ecological Conscience" in *Companion to "A Sand County Almanac": Interpretive and Critical Essays*, ed. J. Baird Callicott (Madison: University of Wisconsin Press, 1987), 128-53.

16. Rachel Carson, *Under the Sea-Wind* (New York: Penguin Books, 1996 [1941]); ibid., *The Sea Around Us* (New York: Oxford University Press, 1989 [1950]); and, ibid., *The Edge of the Sea* (Boston: Mariner Books, 1998 [1955]).

17. Susan Power Bratton, "Thinking Like a Mackerel," *Ethics and the Environment* 9 (2004): 1–22, 19–20. Bratton's essay is reprinted in this volume as chapter 5.

18. Immanuel Kant, *Groundwork of the Metaphysics of Morals*, in *Practical Philosophy, The Cambridge Edition of the Works of Immanuel Kant*, ed. and tr. Mary J. Gregor (New York: Cambridge University Press, 1996 [1785]), 37–108, 73.

19. Leopold, *Sand County Almanac*, 202.

20. Charles R. Darwin, *The Descent of Man and Selection in Relation to Sex* (London: J. Murray, 1871), 71.

21. Darwin, *Descent*, 93.

22. Ibid., 100–101.

23. Leopold, *Sand County Almanac*, 203–204.

24. Ibid., viii; and, Charles Elton, *Animal Ecology* (London: Sidgewick and Jackson, 1927).

25. Leopold, *Sand County Almanac*, 204.

26. Ibid.

27. Ibid., 224–25.

28. Bratton, "Thinking Like a Mackerel," 12.

29. Ibid.

30. Ibid.

31. Leopold, *Sand County Almanac*, 129.

32. Ibid., 107.

33. Petr Kropotkin, *Mutual Aid: A Factor in Evolution* (New York: Knopf, 1925). Kropotkin's influence on Leopold may have been indirect, via the work of P. D. Ouspensky, whom Leopold explicitly mentions in several places. See P. D. Ouspensky, *Tertium Organum: The Third Canon of Thought; A Key to the Enigmas of the World* (New York: Knopf, 1922). See especially Aldo Leopold, "Some Fundamentals of Conservation in the Southwest," in *The River of the Mother of God and Other Essays by Aldo Leopold*, ed. Susan L. Flader and J. Baird Callicott (Madison: University of Wisconsin Press, 1999), 86–97.

34. Carson, *Under the Sea-Wind*, 131–33.

35. Linda Lear, *Rachel Carson: Witness for Nature* (New York: Henry Holt, 1997).

36. Rachel Carson to Fon Boardman, Letter, no date. Rachel Carson Papers, Yale Collection of American Literature, Beinecke Rare Book and Manuscript Library, Yale University. "I suspect," Linda Lear writes (*Witness for Nature*, 521, n. 6), "that Carson never read Leopold's book [*A Sand County Almanac*]." This letter to Boardman documents that she did read *Round River* and found it to be "a truly shocking book." It also confirms Lear's suspicions that Carson did not read *Sand County Almanac*. For Carson tells Boardman that "I too believed in the legend of Aldo Leopold" and adds in penciled marginalia, "without having read anything he had written (for Sand County Almanac came while I was too busy with Sea)"—presumably *The Sea Around Us*. There is no documentary evidence in Leopold's literary remains indicating that he had ever read anything written by Rachel Carson. Although *Under the Sea-Wind* was published in Leopold's lifetime, it had not achieved any notoriety until it was republished in 1952, four years after Leopold's death. There is, however, a striking similarity in literary tropes appearing in *Sea-Wind* and in "Marshland Elegy," first published in *American Forests* 42 (1937): 472–74 and republished in the *Sand County Almanac* in 1949. In the former Carson writes: "As they flew they raised their voices in the weird night chorus of skimmers, a strange medley of notes high-pitched and low, now soft as the cooing of a morning dove, and again harsh as the cawing of a crow; the whole chorus rising and falling, swelling and throbbing, dying away in the still air *like the far off baying of a pack of hounds*" (p. 8, emphasis added). In the latter, Leopold writes, "out of some far recess of the sky a tinkling of little bells falls

soft on the listening land. Then again silence. Now comes *a baying of some sweet-throated hound, soon the clamor of a resounding pack*" (p. 472, emphasis added). Maybe Carson had read a bit of Leopold, after all. And during Leopold's lifetime, Carson published many popular natural history essays in widely circulated periodicals, such as *Atlantic Monthly*, *Collier's*, and even *Field and Stream*. Leopold might well have read some of these.

37. Immanuel Kant, "Duties to Animals and Spirits," in *Lectures on Ethics*, tr. Louis Infield (New York: Harper and Row, 1963).

38. A case for finding a virtue ethics (among other kinds of ethics) in Rachel Carson's work has been made by Philip Cafaro in his "Thoreau, Leopold, and Carson: Toward an Environmental Virtue Ethics," *Environmental Ethics* 23 (2001): 3–17.

39. Lear, *Witness for Nature*.

40. Stephen A. Forbes, "The Lake as a Microcosm," *Bulletin of the Peoria Scientific Association* (1887): 77–87. There is no reference to Forbes in Carson's master's thesis, "The Development of the Pronephros During the Embryonic and Early Larval Life of the Catfish (*Ictalurus punctatus*)." Nor could we find any other document that indicates Carson's knowledge of Forbes or his paper. However, the essay is a classic published at the dawn of aquatic ecology and we assume that Carson was acquainted with it.

41. Ibid.

42. Kant, *Groundwork of the Metaphysics of Morals*, 79–80 (emphasis in middle of quote added).

43. Tom Regan, *The Case for Animal Rights* (Berkeley: University of California Press, 1983); Peter Singer, *Animal Liberation* (New York: New York Review, 1975); Kenneth Goodpaster, "On Being Morally Considerable," *Journal of Philosophy* 75 (1978): 308–325; Paul W. Taylor, *Respect for Nature* (Princeton, N.J.: Princeton University Press, 1986); and Holmes Rolston, III, *Conserving Natural Value* (New York: Columbia University Press, 1994).

44. Tom Regan and Peter Singer do not advocate preventing predation; in his "Predation," *Ethics and Animals* 5 (1984): 27–38, Steve Sapontzis does, but with qualification: "where we can prevent predation without occasioning as much or more suffering than we would prevent, we are obliged to do so by the principle that we are obligated to alleviate avoidable animal suffering."

45. Lisa H. Sideris, *Environmental Ethics, Ecological Theology, and Natural Selection* (New York: Columbia University Press, 2003), 190.

46. Sideris cites Sallie McFague, *Super, Natural Christians* (Minneapolis, Minn.: Fortress Press, 1997), 158; Rosemary Radford Reuther, *Gaia and God: An Ecofeminist Theology of Earth Healing* (San Francisco: HarperCollins,

1994); Charles Birch and John Cobb, *The Liberation of Life: From the Cell to the Community* (Cambridge: Cambridge University Press, 1981); Charles Birch, "Christian Obligation for the Liberation of Nature," in *Liberating Life: Contemporary Approaches to Ecological Theology*, ed. Charles Birch and William Eakin (Maryknoll, N.Y.: Orbis Books, 1990); and Jürgen Moltmann, *God in Creation* (Minneapolis: Fortress Press, 1993).

47. Iris Murdoch, *The Sovereignty of Good* (London: Routledge & Kegan Paul, 1970); Luce Irigaray, *An Ethics of Sexual Difference*, tr. Carolyn Burke and Gillian C. Gill (Ithaca, N.Y.: Cornell University Press, 1993); and Julia Kristeva, *Crisis of the European Subject*, tr. Susan Fairfield (New York: Other Press, 2000). Joni Seager, "Rachel Carson Died of Breast Cancer," notes the critique of ethics based on sameness and a shift to ethics based on otherness and difference in feminist philosophy, but fails to credit Carson with anticipating it.

48. Emmanuel Levinas, *Totality and Infinity* (London: Klewer Academic Publications, 1991); and Adriaan T. Peperzak, Simon Critchly, and Robert Bernasconi, ed., *Emmanuel Levinas: Basic Philosophical Writings* (Bloomington: Indiana University Press, 1996).

49. Adriaan Peperzak, *To the Other: An Introduction to the Philosophy of Emmanuel Levinas* (West Lafayette, Ind.: Purdue University Press, 1993), 21–22.

50. Kant, *Groundwork of the Metaphysics of Morals*, 79.

51. John Llewelyn, *The Middle Voice of Ecological Conscience: A Chiasmic Reading of Responsibility in the Neighborhood of Levinas, Heidegger and Others* (Hong Kong: Macmillan Academic and Professional Ltd., 1991), 245.

52. Kenneth E. Goodpaster, "From Egoism to Environmentalism" in *Ethics and Problems of the 21st Century*, ed. Kenneth E. Goodpaster and Kenneth M. Sayre (South Bend, Ind.: University of Notre Dame Press, 1979), 21–35.

53. Many of these names are derived from the genus name of the animal, but some, obviously, are not.

54. Henry Beston, *Outermost House* (Garden City, N.Y.: Doubleday, 1929), 25.

55. Rachel Carson to Henry Beston, Letter, May 14, 1954. Rachel Carson Papers, Yale Collection of American Literature, Beinecke Rare Book and Manuscript Library, Yale University.

56. Henry Beston, "Miss Carson's First," *The Freeman* 2 (1952): 100.

57. Rachel Carson to Henry Beston, Letter, May 14, 1954, Rachel Carson Papers, Yale Collection of American Literature, Beinecke Rare Book and Manuscript Library, Yale University.

58. Mick Smith, *An Ethics of Place: Radical Ecology, Postmodernity, and Social Theory* (Albany: State University of New York Press, 2001).

59. Peter Berg and Raymond Dasman, "Reinhabiting California," *The Ecologist* 7 (1977): 399–401; and, Kirkpatrick Sale, *Dwellers in the Land: The Bioregional Vision* (Philadelphia: New Society, 1991).

60. Smith, *An Ethics of Place*, 215; Yi-Fu Tuan, *Space and Place: The Perspective of Experience* (Minneapolis: University of Minnesota Press, 1977); and René Dubos, *The Wooing of Earth* (New York: Scribner, 1980).

61. Cafaro, "Thoreau, Leopold, and Carson," 15.

62. Carson, *Under the Sea-Wind*, 117–18.

63. Beston, *Outermost House*, 221.

64. Carson, *Under the Sea-Wind*, 18.

65. Ibid., 119–20.

66. Ibid., 36.

67. Cafaro, "Carson's Environmental Ethic," 63.

68. Kathleen Dean Moore, *Riverwalking: Reflections on Moving Water* (New York: Harvest Books, 1995).

69. We gratefully acknowledge the help of Priscilla Solis Ybarra and Mick Smith for guiding us through the literature and implications of the ethics of difference and otherness.

7
Rachel Carson's *The Sea Around Us,* Ocean-Centrism, and a Nascent Ocean Ethic

Gary Kroll

The final report of the U.S. Commission on Ocean Policy, issued in 2004, calls attention to the deleterious affects of "human ingenuity and ever-improving technologies [that] have enabled us to exploit—and significantly alter—the ocean's bounty."[1] The findings and recommendations of the commission, though somewhat muted in comparison, largely agree with those made by the Pew Oceans Commission in its final report, *America's Living Oceans: Charting a Course for Sea Change.*[2] These ambitious documents echo the concerns of many ocean scientists and environmentalists who have called for a timely embrace of an "ocean ethic." For example, Leon Panetta, chair of the Pew Oceans Commission, borrowed the words of Theodore Roosevelt, IV, who spoke of the "need to extend our conservation ethic to the sea."[3] Carl Safina, an ornithologist and environmentalist, has recently encouraged us to take the dictum of Aldo Leopold's land ethic and launch it into the ocean.[4] The time seems ripe for environmental historians to shed their terrestrial predilections and ask some fundamental questions: what is the history of the ocean's degradation, and what are the historical origins of this nascent "ocean ethic"? Rachel Carson's crucially timed *The Sea Around Us* (1950) is an auspicious place to begin.

The immediate post–World War II years gave way to a dawning realization that the ocean would play a crucial role in the United States' political, economic, and military strength. In realms of fiction, creative nonfiction, war memoirs, international affairs, popular culture, and science, the ocean took on force as a pivotal postwar geography. In 1947, at the leading edge of this profusion of oceanic culture, the septuagenarian fishery biologist Robert Ervin Coker reflected on his life, dedicated as it was to exploring the secrets of the sea. Amidst the glowing embers of postwar cataclysm he looked at both the ocean and his country and noted that "a more widespread 'sea-consciousness' must prevail in the future."[5] What Coker called a "sea-consciousness" can more aptly be termed a sense of ocean-centrism—an understanding that the oceans dominate the earth. Like its more euphonous analogues, biocentrism and ecocentrism, ocean-centrism serves as a check to a terrestrially rooted human-centered consciousness. The earth is largely a water world and our lives are linked and determined by the oceans in illimitable ways. Clearly, the fact had been noted many times before Coker's statement, but it was not until the postwar period that the common phrase, "our earth is comprised of 70 percent ocean," became a matter of vernacular understanding. As an aesthetic, ocean-centrism moved in two directions. It led Americans to revere and love the ocean as a place of beauty, power, and terror; we usually call this the aesthetic of the sublime. But ocean-centrism also pointed to the overwhelmingly puny nature of humans. In this way, the oceans became inviolable, a piece of the earth that would rebuff any human effort of conquest. The latter opened up the doors for humans to try.

It is tempting to read the historical record backward and view Carson's *The Sea Around Us* through the lens of *Silent Spring*. Such a reading may cause us to search for an environmental ethic, an ocean ethic, in the 1950 text. This would be a mistake, for *The Sea Around Us* is a formidable statement on ocean-centrism, a kind of belief that pointed to the inability of humans to cause harm to the oceans. Indeed, ocean-centrism served as an intellectual justification for treating the seas as a trove of illimitable resources and as a sink impervious to the damaging effects of human effluent—a twin fallacy that required fifty years to dismantle. Clearly, Carson held no truck with such justifications; the point is that her text participated, sometimes in unanticipated and ironic ways, in a wider recoding of the ocean in American consciousness. Our task here is to understand the literary and historical narratives that informed Carson's ocean-centrism as manifested in *The Sea Around Us*. Lest I take the argument too far, I would like to suggest that there still remains the possibility of finding a nascent ocean ethic in *The Sea Around Us*; though it is difficult to see an oceanic ethic in what was in the text, it is more apparent in what was left out.

At its heart, the writing and popularity of *The Sea Around Us* has a relatively simple explanation. While working on early drafts of the book, Carson wrote to William Beebe, the ocean and tropical naturalist of bathysphere fame, and told him of her "belief that we will become even more dependent upon the ocean as we destroy the land."[6] The statement reveals Carson's belief in a process that was unfolding before her eyes. The resources of terra firma were showing signs of increasing stress and degradation, despite the hard work of conservationists and preservationists that had advocated a new orientation toward nature for some fifty-odd years. Americans—and perhaps humans in general—would have to turn to the ocean to sustain life. Militarily, economically, and culturally, Americans were poised to demand a great deal of the oceans that surround the North American continent. Carson knew this all too well, and she had some mixed feelings about how the process would unfold.

Carson's sense of ocean-centrism emerged at the intersection of two historical narratives. Perhaps most important, she was a student of a suite of biocentric nature writers who did much to challenge the heroic status of human beings in the first half of the twentieth century. She once called Richard Jeffries her "literary grandfather." She felt a kindred affiliation with Henry Tomlinson, who in his self-effacing writing often turned to nature in an attempt to discover an underlying truth that was somehow out of human beings' grasp. In the late 1930s Carson made a pilgrimage to the setting of Henry Beston's book *The Outermost House* (1924). Henry Williamson's anthropomorphization of the animal kingdom informed the narrative strategy of Carson's *Under the Sea-Wind* (1941). And the self-effacing nature writing of William Beebe echoes through much of Carson's writing, especially her first popular ocean treatise, printed in the *Atlantic Monthly*, "Undersea" (1936). The many references made to these writers in her beautiful correspondence with Dorothy Freeman clearly show that Carson's "sense of wonder" had a distinct literary influence. All speak—in a Thoreauvian vein—to a human insignificance amidst the beauty and majesty of an awe-inspiring nature. Part of Carson's genius lay in extending this biocentric narrative into the *mare incognita*.

But if *The Sea Around Us* is part nature writing, it is an equal participant in the literature of science writing. As an established form of journalism, science writing emerged in the 1920s as an effort to inform the lay public of the many scientific advances of the day.[7] Such writing was less about nature than about the work of science and scientists. Carson came to the field as a result of her editorial work for the Bureau of Fisheries (later the U.S. Fish and Wildlife Service). A large portion of her job consisted of editing the publications of government fisheries biologists, but when Carson was permitted to author her own government publications, she largely dealt with the conservation efforts of government scientists. She was also able to use her acumen for science writing as a freelance writer for the *Baltimore Sun*. Her science writing in the 1930s and 1940s gave her the experience to write about the mushrooming science of oceanography. During World War II federal patronage lavished the oceanographic sciences in return for important data on a large range of ocean statistics that were crucial for the military's execution of the war effort—a new partnership that lasted well into the Cold War.

The Sea Around Us was tentatively titled "Return to the Sea," and Carson wrote late into the night for several years in an attempt to construct an ocean that reflected knowledge obtained by her personal exploration, the government work of bureaucratic marine conservation, the sciences of fishery biology and oceanography, and the self-effacing spirit of nature writing. Two general overviews of the ocean had then recently been published. Carson told Beebe that she wanted her treatment to lie "somewhere between the books by Robert E. Coker and Ferdinand Lane—rather nearer the latter, yet I hope to give it a somewhat deeper significance, while still writing for the nontechnical reader."[8] The remark is revealing. Ferdinand Lane was fast becoming a generalist nature writer with popular books on trees, insects, rivers, and mountains. His *Mysterious Sea* (1947) was a well-written natural history of the ocean that had much in common with Carson's text.[9] Peppering his text with quotes from Shakespeare, Milton, Matthew Arnold, and Coleridge, Lane provided a lucid and comprehensive—perhaps too comprehensive—account of the ocean's geologic, dynamic, and biological history. Robert E. Coker was a respected and long-lived biologist at the Bureau of Fisheries. *This Great and Wide Sea* (1947) was a comprehensive introduction to marine science with sections on the history of oceanography, chemistry and physics of the sea, and life in the sea. In short, the text was a general introduction to oceanography—not exactly a work of science writing, but one that shared in the trade's intent.

Carson wanted to strike a balance between Lane's and Coker's accounts, but the creation of an ocean-centric theme required more than genre-bending. The book emerged at a time when Americans found in the ocean a certain measure of ease from the psychological anxieties of the war, and Carson probably offered some guidance along this line. During the 1940s Carson began corresponding with other nature writers who were in the process of focusing their literature to ameliorate some of the psychic damage done by the war and the bureaucracy of modern life. For instance, she frequently joined Louis Halle, Jr., on bird-watching walks along the C&O Canal towpath with the rest of the local Audubon chapter. Carson thought that Halle's popular *Spring in Washington* (1947) was the quintessential nature guide to Washington D.C.'s environs, a recipe for curing the stifling bureaucracy of capitol life.[10] Another important literary contact was Edwin Teale, a name familiar to readers of *Nature Magazine* and other natural history journals. In late winter of 1949 Teale and his wife started a seventeen-thousand-mile journey in South Florida, heading north with the spring. Attempting to chronicle the flow of spring as it moved northward, Teale's *North with the Spring* (1951) was a truly innovative piece of nature writing. At least for Teale, the journey was something of a balm for the terror of the war. "And while we waited," he explained, "the world changed and our lives changed with it. The spring trip was something we looked forward to during the terrible years of World War II."[11] Carson had the opportunity to lunch with both Teale and Halle, apparently to talk about developing a literary style. The advice they imparted to Carson is unknown, but we may gather from their work that they advised Carson to write of the ocean in a way that might have an ameliorative effect on a populace emerging from the throes of war.[12]

William Beebe continued to serve as another of Carson's frequent correspondents during the years she was engaged in writing *The Sea Around Us*. In the preface of the text, Carson admits that her "absorption in the mystery and meaning of the sea have been stimulated and the writing of this book aided by the friendship and encouragement of William Beebe."[13] Beebe had high admiration for Carson's nature writing. She had received the honor of having a portion of *Under the Sea-Wind* included in Beebe's anthology of natural history writers, which included such notables as Aristotle, William Bartram, Thoreau, Darwin, Wallace, and Muir.[14] In 1949 Beebe wrote a recommendation on Carson's behalf for the Eugene Saxton Memorial Fellowship, which she won in 1950. Apparently, Beebe also made a few personal calls to members of the selection committee. He even credited himself for seeing to it that Carson was awarded the Burroughs Award for nature writing in 1952.[15] It is difficult to trace exactly how Carson's writing was influenced by Beebe's, but she did respond to *Half Mile Down* with "a mixture of awe, envy, and gratitude that one of the two men who ever visited these depths was so exceptionally gifted with the ability to share those experiences with those of us less privileged."[16]

The nature writing of Beebe, Halle, and Teale, as well as that of the biocentric writers mentioned earlier, informed the general theme of *The Sea Around Us*. Through a narrative of the ocean's history, Carson portrays humans as a species that emerged from an ocean to which they will return. She highlighted the fact that the earth was an ocean planet. Over vast periods of geologic time, the ocean had the power to weather down continents, and also the power to create life. Granted, humans have had the power to destroy through war and create through science, but human efforts pale in comparison to the transforming agencies of an omnipotent ocean.[17]

This ocean-centric theme infuses the entire text, but it is the organizing principle of the first chapter. Carson begins the book with a history of the ocean's development. It is rather surprising that she favored the theory of the moon having spun out of the Pacific basin (the moon from Pacific hypothesis was not widely held at this time), but Carson used the point to highlight the connection between the ocean and cosmic history.[18] The first rains, Carson writes, signaled the beginning of the dissolution of the continents: "It is an endless, inexorable process that has never stopped—the dissolving of the rocks, the leaching out of their contained minerals, the carrying of the rock fragments and dissolved minerals to the ocean. And over the eons of time, the sea has grown ever more bitter with the salt of the continents."[19] The destruction of the continents performed a vital function, for it was from those leached elements that the first life would develop. The sea "produced the result that neither the alchemists with their crucibles nor modern scientists in their laboratories have been able to achieve."[20]

Life slowly crept onto the shores of the continents and thus began the slow evolution of terrestrial life, the development of humans being a very small and recent part of a much larger evolutionary history. The earliest oceanic exploration symbolized the return of humans to the sea.

> And yet he has returned to his mother sea only on her own terms. He cannot control or change the ocean as, in his brief tenancy of earth, he has subdued and plundered the continents. In the artificial world of his cities and towns, he often forgets the true nature of his planet and the long vistas of its history, in which the existence of the race of men has occupied a mere moment of time....[When on a long ocean voyage] he feels the loneliness of his earth in space. And then, as never on land, he knows the truth that his world is a water world, a planet dominated by its covering mantle of ocean, in which the continents are but transient intrusions of land above the surface of the all-encircling sea.[21]

Most reviewers took the moral exactly as Carson had intended. An Omaha writer reported that "Rachel Carson, in the *The Sea Around Us*, places terrifying emphasis on man's helplessness against this enormous mass of water."[22] Others, like this Oklahoma reviewer, neglected the ocean altogether and honed in on the text's philosophical implications: "From one point of view, the penalty of such books as Hoyle's *The Nature of the Universe* and Carson's *The Sea Around Us* is their impression of man with his own insignificance."[23] The moral was sometimes interpreted as an anodyne for atomic science. Commenting on Carson's book along with other oceanic natural histories by James Dugan and Jacques Cousteau, a New Haven reporter thought that "the recent rash of books on...the sea are a result of the fact that man has found that there are fields of activity in which he never will emerge as the conqueror. Science has led him to the brink of disaster, and nature offers him a new vehicle for his irrepressible energies."[24] The moral could also be employed to reframe Cold War anxieties. What impressed Bruce Barton the most was

> the age of the world in contrast with man's brief span....It seems to me that we Americans, in our thinking and planning, particularly regarding our so-called "foreign policy," tend too much to ignore the one fundamental that should never be ignored, time....It can and will, with our help, eventually upset Communism. Provided that in our hurry for world salvation, we do not commit national suicide by draining our own land of its resources, and the veins of our sons of their blood.[25]

Yet another reviewer thought that *The Sea Around Us*, along with Maurice Herzog's *Annapurna* and Hemingway's *The Old Man and the Sea*, offered an

enticing retreat from the complexities of civilization: "They offer us also vicarious courage, indomitable perseverance in the face of disheartening odds."[26]
These reviewers found solace in *The Sea Around Us*. Whether they were concerned with nuclear-bomb science, the Cold War, or the complexities of civilization, they all were attracted to the notion that the sea was somehow bigger
than they were, completely out of their control. The ocean put human affairs
into wider perspective.

If we were to look for anything resembling an ocean ethic, it would be in
the chapter entitled "Birth of an Island," for which Carson won the George
Westinghouse Science Writing Award. It was the first chapter that she systematically researched and drafted, and her agent, Marie Rodell, sent the chapter
as a sample to two book publishers. At one point, Carson considered removing the material from the book to write a separate article given the "timely"
nature of the subject—that is, the preservation of fragile island ecosystems in
the war-torn Pacific. The narrative moves from a discussion of underwater
geological formations, to the process of wave denudation, then to colonization by organisms. This seamlessly leads to a treatment of the extraordinary
species that evolve on ocean islands—species that have achieved a delicate balance within isolated environments. The chapter concludes with thoughts on
the recent American colonization of the Pacific and a call to preserve these
fragile islands. The environmental ethos of the chapter is part of a tradition
of island conservation that harks back to seventeenth-century Britain. So
there is an ocean ethic, but only insofar as islands are part of the ocean.

A more direct overtone of an ocean ethic comes through in Carson's general thoughts on the epistemic relationship between science and nature. Her
most clear statement on the matter comes from a speech she gave on receiving
the National Book Award for *The Sea Around Us*:

> We live in a scientific age; yet by a strange paradox we behave as though
> knowledge of science is the prerogative of a small number of men, isolated
> and priestlike in their laboratories. This is not true. It cannot be true. The
> materials of science are the materials of life itself. Science is the what, the
> how, and the why of everything in our experience. It is part of the reality
> of living.[27]

As wartime oceanographers probed the depths of the ocean with the
most technologically savvy equipment, Carson was drawn to a more historical
epistemology that emphasized direct and personal observation of the ocean.
Clearly the invention of the bathythermograph (BT), used to create vertical
temperature profiles, and sonar, used to map seabed topography and to investigate the enigmatic behavior of the deep scattering layer, equipped postwar
oceanographers with unprecedented technologies in their quest to understand the sea. While it is beyond doubt that Carson valued such technologically sophisticated research, she also felt that something of the human quest

for understanding was being sacrificed. She concluded *The Sea Around Us* with a brief look at the modern *Sailing Directions and Coast Pilots* then being issued to all navigators.

The final chapter is as elegant as it is revealing. "Yet in these writings of the sea [*Pilots*]," Carson wrote, "there is a pleasing blend of modernity and antiquity, with unmistakable touches by which we may trace their lineage back to the sailing directions of the [Norwegian] sagas."[28] These *Pilots* direct navigators to carefully examine populations of seafowl for clues on locating specific harbors and islands. They also suggest that mariners traveling through new waters seek out local knowledge. "In phrases like these," Carson wrote, "we get the feel of the unknown and the mysterious that never quite separates itself from the sea."[29] The moral demonstrates Carson's deep sense of humility: humans will never completely divest the ocean of its secrets, and sometimes the old tried and true methods of knowing the ocean—direct experience and observation—serve better than all the equipment of modern oceanography. But Carson also highlights the *Pilots* because they are examples of good literature. At one point she calls one of the guides "Conradian." A *New Republic* reviewer admired Carson's "appreciation of the writing of others; she makes use of many quotations, especially from the Pilot Books of the U.S. Hydrographic Office....It is good to find someone valuing properly the literary merits of these publications."[30] This is not the antireductionism of *Silent Spring*, but it most certainly is a dawning realization that the mechanical onslaught on civilization and the reductionist domination of the sciences both required a dose of humility. This is Aldo Leopold through and through, but still, hardly a full-fledged ocean ethic.

Given the trajectory of Carson's career as an environmentalist, *The Sea Around Us* seems to be something of an aberration. Carson's ocean was indomitable, unconquerable, mysterious. In many ways Carson was continuing Beebe's project of portraying an oceanic sublime that rebuffs all efforts by humans to conquer, control, or destroy. Aside from the important topic of preserving Pacific islands, in *The Sea Around Us* Carson never entertains the possibility of humans altering the state of the ocean, even though she is well aware of dangers of overfishing. Of course, there is a humble biocentrism here that is characteristic of nature writing in general, but there is little of the environmentalism that would emerge from Carson's pen some eleven years later. On the other hand, Carson may have expressed something of an environmental ethic of the ocean not in what she put into *The Sea Around Us*, but rather in what she left out.

It is odd that Carson, long a devoted employee of the Fish and Wildlife Service (FWS), chose to exclude any treatment of ocean fisheries. Indeed, during World War II, Carson had written a number of pamphlets for the FWS that urged Americans to diversify their fish diet so as to alleviate wartime shortages of beef and to also ease the stress on soon-to-be-overexploited fish populations. As early as 1926, William Beebe had suggested that the human race might turn to plankton, "this larder of the ocean," as a food source.[31] But the possibility did not receive any serious attention until after the war when scientists saw in the sea a new frontier of free natural resources. This was a critical time in American history in which the ocean was becoming a literal "new frontier." Walton Smith, founder of the Marine Laboratory at the University of Miami—and also the person responsible for Carson's first and only glimpse under the ocean on a helmet dive—titled a new popular research magazine *Sea Frontiers*. Smith marshaled the energy and resources of South Florida's saltwater angler community to uncover the "secrets of the sea" for the sake of utilization and conservation of marine resources. The idea that the ocean harbors vast useable resources proved extraordinarily resilient, especially with the resurgence of the "population problem" in the late 1960s and early 1970s. As late as 1968, John Bardach was confident enough to title a book *Harvest of the Sea*. "As yet," he noted, "we can do almost nothing to influence the abundance of most marine animals."[32] Beginning roughly in the 1960s, an industrialized fishery joined hands with new laws, policies, and international competition to carry on a heedless onslaught of oceanic life. A recent study has found that today's oceans contain a scant 10 percent of the biomass that it contained in preindustrial times.[33]

Our recent crisis is rooted, at least partially, in a certain enthusiasm that was rampant right after World War II, a time in which marine biologists began devising plans to harvest plankton for world population problems that became such a hot topic after the war. In 1948 William Vogt and Fairfield Osborn published widely read books that raised the specter of environmental decay and its implications for human existence. Among the many topics covered, especially in the case of Vogt, was the alarming exponential growth of human populations and the inability of the earth to sustain its human residents. In Vogt's words, "[b]y excessive breeding and abuse of the land mankind has backed itself into an ecological trap. By a lopsided use of applied science it has been living on promissory notes. Now, all over the world, the notes are falling due."[34] Many scientists mobilized to rectify the situation; others turned to the ocean in a vain search for another promissory note.

Maurice Nelles, a research manager of the Allan Hancock Foundation, organized an expedition aboard the scientific ship *Velero IV* for the purpose of exploring the possibilities of harvesting ocean plankton. Two Carnegie Institution of Washington botanists began an effort in 1949 to harvest fresh- and saltwater algae. A team of Berkeley marine biologists was also looking into marine farming. Yale professor Werner Bergmann was researching the possibility of desalinizing massive quantities of ocean water to turn deserts into productive land.[35] These optimistic projects were doused in the late 1940s when they proved technologically infeasible. Daniel Merriman, whom

Carson interviewed on the subject, and Gordon Riley predicted that ocean fishing could be increased fivefold with more efficient use of fishery technologies. "But to harvest any considerable fraction of the plankton of the world," Riley reported, "seems as fantastic as the old dream of extracting gold from sea water. By and large we must leave the plankton to the fishes."[36] There were dissenters to Riley and Merriman's claims. Columbus Iselin, another of Carson's interviewees, remained sanguine about the potentials of plankton harvesting.

Carson was fully aware of these hopes and drafted a chapter entitled "The Ocean and a Hungry World." Referring to the criticisms of Vogt and Osborn, Carson begins the chapter by outlining the current failings of agriculture to sustain the world's growing population and provides an elegant segue. "But from the plundered land we turn to the sea with many questions." She briefly describes the two schools of thought and comes down squarely on the pessimistic side of the issue. Annual fish catches could be doubled, but only at great expense. And while the earth's plankton amounted to an unfathomable biomass, no reasonable technology was available to retrieve this resource for human use. Scientists and conservationists, in Carson's estimation, should concentrate their efforts on increasing fish yields.[37]

But Carson removed the chapter. Moreover, there is no discussion of the issue whatsoever in the text. It is difficult to imagine the reason for the elimination of such a timely discussion. One historian has suggested that Carson realized that the chapter sounded more like the writing of an agent of the FWS than a "curious scientist or reverent witness."[38] The chapter, she continues, lacks lyricism and is utilitarian in nature. If this was a hard and fast criterion for inclusion, then it is odd that Carson did not remove the chapter on the mineral content of the ocean, both utilitarian and, in my estimation, decidedly non-"lyrical." The excision is troubling because Carson wrote the book to show the connections between humans and the ocean, a relationship that was becoming acute in the postwar period. Carson thought that the entire project was important because "the life that invaded the lands has already so despoiled them it is being driven back more and more to its dependence on the sea."[39] "The Ocean and a Hungry World" fits precisely under this rubric. Carson may have sensed a flagging enthusiasm for plankton processing as the difficulties of the project became apparent.

The removal is also troublesome given Carson's reactions to RKO's documentary adaptation of the book. Though *The Sea Around Us* (1953) won an academy award, Carson was completely dissatisfied with the final product. Irwin Allen, who had much greater success in television with *Voyage to the Bottom of the Sea* and *Lost in Space* and the great disaster dramas *The Towering Inferno* and *Poseidon Adventure*, merely solicited naturalists for stock footage of underwater scenes. Allen edited the footage into a film that Carson thought was "a cross between a believe-it-or-not and a breezy travelogue." In contrast, she had hoped for a film that possessed all the "beauty, the dignity, and the impressiveness of the Pare Lorenz script for *The River*."[40] The allusion to Lorenz is revealing, for *The River*, while certainly providing an environmental critique of land use, was also highly optimistic that science and technology—especially through the example of the Tennessee Valley Authority—could thoughtfully harness nature for social and economic benefit. This utilitarian message was very much at the heart of the missing chapter.

Given Carson's critique of the destruction of land, it is possible that she did not want to entertain the possibility of humans turning to the ocean as a panacea. She was also aware of the key ecological role played by plankton, and as she would later develop in *Silent Spring*, when humans tinkered with the lower levels of the food pyramid, the consequences were often unpredictable, and sometimes devastating. Carson was absolutely right. The ocean-centrism of postwar American culture, coupled with the plundering of terra firma, meant that humans would increasingly turn to the ocean. Whether intentional or not, the missing chapter of *The Sea Around Us* stands as a quiet warning that, if we are not careful, the fate of the world's oceans will resemble that of the land.

Carson would change her opinion on the resiliency of the ocean some ten years later in a new preface to the second edition of *The Sea Around Us* (1961). In the intervening years, the Atomic Energy Commission had made a common practice of disposing of nuclear waste in deep-sea basins. Carson recalled her former attitude regarding the inability of humans to damage the ocean and provided a corrective: "But this belief, unfortunately, has proved to be naïve. In unlocking the secrets of the atom, modern man has found himself confronted with a frightening problem— what to do with the most dangerous materials that have ever existed in all the earth's history, the by-products of atomic fission."[41] Given that she wrote this new preface while frantically engaged in her *Silent Spring* project, it is not surprising that Carson warned her readers that irradiated plankton, even at low levels, would have magnifying effects in organisms higher up the food chain, in organisms that were the fodder for the human race.[42]

Ocean dumping, offshore oil drilling, aggressive industrialized fishing, and a rapid increase in nonpoint source terrestrial runoff would begin to tax the oceans in increasingly visible ways in the 1960s. It was in this context that Wesley Marx published *The Frail Ocean*, a work that may mark the first full blossoming of an ocean ethic. A flurry of environmental activism in the early 1970s elaborated this message in both national and international contexts. Throughout the last quarter of the twentieth century, various groups of committed scientists, naturalists, and environmentalists continued to sound the alarm of the ocean's fragility. Despite a number of successes, their calls largely fell on deaf ears as economic and military policy continued to treat the ocean as the earth's last inviolable frontier. The 1990s witnessed the dramatic collapse of several fisheries, the widespread destruction of coral reefs, and a new concern over global climate change—in which the ocean plays a conspicuous role. Perhaps it is turning out that the oceanic frontier bears some resemblance to its terrestrial analogue. In response, the Pew Oceans Commission and the U.S. Commission on Ocean Policy produced thick reports. While confidence is always fleeting, it is possible that we are poised for a full-scale launching of a sea ethic, an ethic that was made possible and necessary by the understanding of Carson's ocean-centric discourse.

NOTES

1. U.S. Commission on Ocean Policy, *An Ocean Blueprint for the 21st Century: Final Report of the U.S. Commission on Ocean Policy* (Washington, D.C.: U.S. Commission on Ocean Policy, 2004), xxxi. Available online at www.oceancommission.gov/documents/full_color_rpt/welcome.html full.

2. Pew Oceans Commission (Leon E. Panetta, chair), *America's Living Oceans: Charting a Course for Sea Change* (Arlington, Va.: Pew Oceans Commission, 2003). Available online at www.pewtrusts.org/our_work.aspx ?category=130.

3. Leon E. Panetta, "Ocean Dimension of Earth Day," *Washington Times*, April 22, 2002, A17.

4. Carl Safina, "Launching a Sea Ethic," *Wild Earth* 12 (2002–2003), 2–5.

5. Robert E. Coker, *This Great and Wide Sea* (Chapel Hill: The University of North Carolina Press, 1947), v.

6. Rachel Carson to William Beebe, Letter, Sept. 6, 1948. Rachel Carson Papers, Beinecke Library, Yale University, Box 4, Folder 67.

7. Bruce V. Lewenstein, *Public Understanding of Science in America, 1945–1965* (Ph.D. dissertation, University of Pennsylvania, 1987); Dorothy Nelkin, *Selling Science: How the Press Covers Science and Technology* (New York: W. H. Freeman, 1987), 86–91; Ronald C. Tobey, *The American Ideology of National Science, 1919–1930* (Pittsburgh: University of Pittsburgh Press, 1971), 62–95; and Marcel C. Lafollette, *Making Science Our Own: Public Images of Science 1910–1955* (Chicago: University of Chicago Press, 1990), 45–65.

8. Rachel Carson to William Beebe, Letter, Sept. 6, 1948.

9. Lane begins his text with a chapter on the ocean's origins. The first chapter starts, "The origin of the oceans is obscure." Carson begins her first chapter on the origins of the ocean, "Beginnings are apt to be shadowy." Perhaps a

trivial coincidence, but I think it can be reasonably argued that Carson used Lane as something of a model when outlining *The Sea Around Us*.

10. Carson may have been especially attracted to Halle given that his *Spring in Washington* was a missive on the life of a government bureaucrat and the solace that he found observing the district's wildlife. See *Spring in Washington* (New York: William Sloane, 1947), 3–6.

11. Edwin Way Teale, *North with the Spring: A Naturalist's Record of a 17,000-Mile Journey with the North-American Spring* (New York: Dodd, Meade, 1951), 2.

12. Linda Lear, *Rachel Carson: Witness for Nature* (New York: Henry Holt, 1997), 141. One of the clippings in Carson's notes for the project is a *New York Times'* "Topics of the Times," June 5, 1949, E10: "Wars carry men who have spent their lives on land across the seas. Here is an experience with which to reckon. This landlocked man learns from the sea. He learns of his own finiteness.... Here he finds himself a stranger on his own planet. His life until now has been wrapped in the affairs of the land. On the ocean he realizes that ours is a sea world and that land is only the accident of a mountaintop pushing its head above the somber waters.... Man has set fire to the cities of the land. He has made of them rubble and ash. He has pocked the earth and hurt and killed those of his own kind. But the sea is unconquerable. In mockery it echoes back the sound of men's false thunder. Then it swallows his chemical violence. It rolls quietly from the horizon and washes against the prow of the ship. The sea is just as it was before."

13. Carson, *The Sea Around Us* (New York: Oxford University Press, 1989 [1950]), vi.

14. William Beebe, ed., *The Book of Naturalists: An Anthology of the Best Natural History* (New York: Knopf, 1944).

15. Rachel Carson to William Beebe, Letter, Aug. 26, 1949; and Beebe to Carson, Letter, Dec. 11, 1951, both in Rachel Carson Papers, Beinecke Library, Yale University, Box 4, Folder 67.

16. Rachel Carson to William Beebe, Letter, Apr. 5, 1949. Rachel Carson Papers, Beinecke Library, Yale University, Box 4, Folder 67.

17. The point was stated by Tomlinson shortly after the First World War. He wrote that the sea "is the creation of Omnipotence, which is not of human kind and understandable, and so springs of its behaviour are hidden. The sea does not assume its royal blue to please you. Its brute and dark desolation is not raised to overwhelm you; you disappear then because you happen to be there. It carries the lucky foolish to fortune, and drags the calculating wise to the strewn bones" (*Sea and the Jungle* [New York: E. P. Dutton, 1920], 28–29). On another level, it might be said that *The Sea Around Us* was a post–World

War II analogue to Tomlinson's text. This is not to imply that there were no nature writers of the ocean before this time. Le Roy Jeffers, of the New York Public Library and an extraordinary traveler and adventurer, published a book in 1922 entitled *The Call of the Mountains*. The text curiously concludes with a chapter on the "Voice of the Sea." Jeffers states: "The Sea is a symbol of eternity. As we become more deeply acquainted with its spirit we more truly love its mystery and more clearly understand its message to our hearts. There are silent moments upon the mountains when one feels the immensity of nature, and there are storms upon the sea in which one realizes the presence of an immeasurable power.... Both supply an infinite need of the soul. In the solitude of the mountains and in the voice of the storm-driven sea there is companionship with the Eternal" (*The Call of the Mountains: Rambles among the Mountains and Canyons of the United States and Canada* [New York: Dodd, Mead, 1922], 282). The closest analogue to Jeffers' sentiment in the 1950s is Ann Murrow Lindbergh, *Gift from the Sea* (New York: Pantheon, 1955), which strangely elicited little comment from Carson, as far as I know. But to be clear, Carson combined this nature-writing tradition with that of science writing to create *The Sea Around Us*.

18. Carson's information here comes largely from John W. Gregory, "Geological History of the Pacific Ocean," *Proceedings of the Geological Society of London* 86 (1930): 72–136.

19. Carson, *The Sea Around Us*, 7.

20. Ibid.

21. Ibid., 15.

22. Unsigned review, *World Herald* (Omaha, Neb.), Sept. 2, 1951. See also Rachel Carson Papers, Beinecke Library, Yale University, Box 9, Folder 163.

23. "Great Seas Are Our Life," *Daily Oklahoman* (Oklahoma City, Okla.), Sept. 16, 1951, Rachel Carson Papers, Beinecke Library, Yale University, Box 9, Folder 163.

24. "Man's Attempt to Subdue the Sea," *Independent* (Hew Haven, Conn.), Aug. 11, 1956.

25. Bruce Barton, "Bruce Barton Says," *Miami Herald*, Sept. 9, 1951, Rachel Carson Papers, Beinecke Library, Yale University, Box 9, Folder 163.

26. Donald Adams "Speaking of Books," *New York Times Review of Books*, March 2, 1953, Rachel Carson Papers, Beinecke Library, Yale University, Box 9, Folder 163.

27. National Book Award Acceptance Speech for *The Sea Around Us*, January 29, 1951, Rachel Carson Papers, Beinecke Library, Yale University, Box 101, Folder 1883. A slightly different version of this speech is found in

Rachel Carson, *Lost Woods: The Discovered Writing of Rachel Carson*, ed. Linda Lear (Boston: Beacon Press, 1998), 90–92.

28. Carson, *The Sea Around Us*, 210.

29. Ibid., 211.

30. J. S. Colman, "Review of *The Sea Around Us* by Rachel Carson," *New Republic*, Aug. 20, 1951, 20.

31. William Beebe, *The Arcturus Adventure: An Account of the New York Zoological Society's First Oceanographic Expedition* (New York: G. P. Putnam's Sons, 1926), 201.

32. John Bardach, *Harvest of the Sea* (New York: Harper and Row, 1968), 5. Though it is necessary to be fair: Bardach cautioned that "we are clearly embarking on an era when the secondary effect of our activities other than fishing will be felt far out at sea....One such hope is that the next convention of the Law of the Sea will include agreements on all aspects of marine pollution" (p. 233). More will be said about this line of thought later.

33. Michael L. Weber, *From Abundance to Scarcity: A History of U.S. Marine Fisheries Policy* (Washington, D.C.: Island Press, 2002); and Ransom A. Myers and Boris Worm, "Rapid Worldwide Depletion of Predatory Fish Communities," *Nature* 423 (2003): 280–83.

34. William Vogt, *Road to Survival* (New York: William Sloane Associates, 1948), 285; and Fairfield Osborn, *Our Plundered Planet* (New York: Grosset & Dunlap, 1948). On Osborn see Andrew Jamison and Ron Eyerman, *Seeds of the Sixties* (Berkeley: University of California Press, 1994), 64–82; and Gregg Mitman, "When Nature Is the Zoo," *Osiris* (2nd series) *Science in the Field* 11 (1996): 121–33.

35. See notecard "The Allan Hancock Foundation," in Rachel Carson Papers, Beinecke Library, Yale University, Box 4, Folder 79; William Laurence, "Sea Soon May Yield Great Food Stores," *New York Times*, June 21, 1948, 1; "Alga May Avert Famine," *Science News Letter*, Jan. 1, 1949; and Waldemar Kaempffert, "Future Generations from the Sea," *New York Times*, Oct. 23, 1949, sec. IV, 6.

36. Gordon A. Riley, "Food from the Sea," *Scientific American*, October 1949, 16–19; Daniel Merriman, "Food Shortages and the Sea," *Yale Review* 39 (1950): 430–44; and "Topics of the Times," *New York Times*, July 17, 1952, 22, where Dr. K. Starr Chester, of the Battelle Memorial Institute, noted that "The oceans contain enormous tonnages of seaweed and algae that can yield large quantities of highly nutritious food for use directly by humans, or as feed for livestock." In the article, the Chester quotation is followed with a ref-

erence to *Kon Tiki*, where "these scientific adventurers studied plankton—minute ocean life—to make their contribution to knowledge on the subject."

37. Rachel Carson, "The Ocean and a Hungry World," draft of unpublished chapter; Rachel Carson Papers, Beinecke Library, Yale University, Box 7, Folder 134.

38. Mary A. McCay, *Rachel Carson* (New York: Twayne Publishers, 1993), 50–51.

39. From Carson's application to the Eugene F. Saxton Foundation, May 1, 1949; quoted in Lear, *Witness for Nature*, 163.

40. Rachel Carson to Shirley Collier (lawyer at RKO), Letter, Nov. 10, 1952; Rachel Carson Papers, Beinecke Library, Yale University, Box 11, Folder 193.

41. Rachel Carson, "Preface to the 1961 Edition," in *The Sea Around Us*," xi.

42. Ralph H. Lutts, "Chemical Fallout: *Silent Spring*, Radioactive Fallout, and the Environmental Movement," in *And No Birds Sing: Rhetorical Analyses of Rachel Carson's "Silent Spring*," ed. Craig Waddell (Carbondale: Southern Illinois University Press, 2000), 33–37.

Part III

Reflections on Gender and Science

8

The Ecological Body: Rachel Carson, *Silent Spring*, and Breast Cancer

Lisa H. Sideris

Fools, said I, you do not know
Silence like a cancer grows
—Simon and Garfunkel, "The Sounds of Silence"

"THE POISON BOOK"

"Poisoning people is wrong." Thus begins the September 23, 1962, *New York Times* book review of Rachel Carson's *Silent Spring*.[1] "Miss Carson's" newest book, the reviewers go on to say, represents her latest treatment of a theme running through her previous three works, namely, "the relation of life to environment."

Today—more than forty years after the publication of this review—there is something peculiar about these characterizations of *Silent Spring*. In the first place, to distill from this work a warning that people are in peril from chemi-

A version of this chapter was first presented at the First Annual Writers' Conference in Honor of Rachel Carson in Boothbay Harbor Maine, June 2001, sponsored by Nature and Environmental Writers-College and University Educators. I am grateful for insightful comments and criticisms from two anonymous reviewers at *Soundings*. I also wish to thank Kathleen Dean Moore and Carol Burdick for suggestions on an earlier draft. This chapter originally appeared in *Soundings: An Interdisciplinary Journal*, volume 85, numbers 1–2 (2002): 107–120. It is reproduced here with permission of *Soundings*.

cal bombardment does not do justice to Carson's expansive view of life. The ominous hush that Carson prophesied was not, after all, the systematic silencing of humans, but the silencing of the nonhuman world. ("Silent Spring" was originally the title of Carson's chapter dealing with birds.[2]) However, human silence was complicit in the more profound silencing of nature that Carson dreaded. Only by breaking this silence—the reticence of government agencies and chemical companies—could humans avert the silencing of nature, a "spring without voices."[3] No doubt, the chemical companies wished desperately to silence Carson. When a minor ailment prevented her from appearing at a conference on air pollution, a newspaper proclaimed, "Author of *Silent Spring* Silenced by Cold." "What good news in chemical circles!" she laughed to her friend Dorothy Freeman.[4]

The wording of the review of *Silent Spring* also suggests that, in the 1960s, the idea that life existed in "relation" to its environment was still so novel that it sufficed as a "theme" or even an "argument" for a book—or a series of books. During the time that *Silent Spring* was just beginning to germinate in Carson's mind, she employed similar language to describe the topic of her next book: "The theme remains what I have felt for several years it would be: Life and the relation of Life to the physical environment."[5] In the early stages of writing, Carson temporarily settled on pugnacious-sounding titles, including "Man against the Earth" and "The War against Nature." She remarked to Freeman that her basic line of argument could be summarized in a single sentence, one that she was considering as the opening passage for the book: "This is a book about man's war against nature, and because man is part of nature it is also and inevitably a book about man's war against himself."[6] Her own distillation of her ideas differs significantly from that of the *Times* review; the war of "man against man," and the poisoning of people it left in its wake, were somewhat secondary to the poisoning of nature.

Carson continued to experiment with titles. She also equivocated on the issue of whether humans were an integral part of nature or a hostile force acting against it. Dissatisfied with the working title "Man against the Earth," she wrote to a friend, "I still hope to get something better—although, in truth, man *is* against the earth!"[7] At times, in letters to Freeman, she simply alluded to her new project as "the poison book." Freeman shuddered at this phrase, preferring to call it "your Life book."[8] Freeman often worried about the effect that the poison book was having on the health of its creator, and when Carson developed an ulcer, Freeman's fears seemed confirmed.

The title that Carson ultimately settled on, *Silent Spring*, shifts focus away from the dangerous conception that humans are at odds with nature. Carson's literary agent, Marie Rodell, proposed that the title *Silent Spring* fit the content of the entire book, not just the chapter on birds; Paul Brooks at Houghton Mifflin agreed that "metaphorically, *Silent Spring* applied to the book as a whole" (though some at the press considered it a "blind title").[9]

Freeman found it much more to her tastes as well: "I have so often thought what a perfect title *Silent Spring* has been," she wrote to Carson. "And because a woman wrote it I like the feminine quality of the sound of it, as compared with Man against the Earth."[10] In the end, the book was both about poison and about life; it was, and is, about humans and nature. *Silent Spring* demonstrates that we cannot talk about one of these things without talking about the others. But first and foremost, Carson believed, we must talk about them. Her "poison book" prescribed a talking cure, and it is surely a tribute to her efforts that the idea that all life is intimately related to its environment now goes without saying, however that relationship is to be construed.

Carson herself construed this relationship with a subtlety that is often overlooked. In both her ecological writing and her "battle" with cancer, she advocates the reform of scientific technology but not its abandonment, and while she tirelessly documents the destructive effects of the war against nature, she sees some form of struggle to control the natural world as inevitable.

SILENCE, CANDOR, AND "THE RIGHT TO KNOW"

Contemporary environmentalists have carried on Carson's tradition, attempting over and over again to break the silence, to resume the stalled conversation about the environmental—and human—devastation wrought by chemical assaults on life. One notable example is ecologist (and like Carson, cancer patient) Sandra Steingraber who, according to some, has taken up the unenviable task of "shoulder[ing] the legacy of Rachel Carson."[11]

The dust jacket of Steingraber's powerful book *Living Downstream* bears an excerpt from a review by Terry Tempest Williams which reads: "Sandra Steingraber reminds us how the health of the land is inexplicably tied to our own."[12] Inexplicably? Surely the appearance of this word is the result of an editorial lapse, and the reviewer said, or meant to say, inextricably linked. If there is one thing that Carson and Steingraber have demonstrated it is that human and environmental well-being cannot be separated. The patient, painstaking factual documentation on page after page of each of these scientists' works has banished the inexplicability of this connection. Yet writers such as Carson and Steingraber are so necessary precisely because facts do not always speak for themselves.

Silent Spring gave voice to the facts. Professionally as well as personally, Carson valued candor above all else. Fact-facing was a way of life for Carson, a means of redeeming and transforming silence. Silence she associated with paralyzing fear, deception, and death. The inevitable misunderstandings that occurred in the course of her long and intimate relationship with Freeman became most frightening when they trailed off into silence. During one such period, Carson describes reaching for the phone, in happy anticipation of the many thoughts she wished to share with her friend. But then, "I remembered certain things, and I was afraid, and the phone stood silent...I put up the phone feeling sick, and 100 years old."[13] Reconciliation after these painful silences felt as rejuvenating as a springtime thaw: "I do feel so much better about Us," she wrote to Freeman. "One day all was a frozen winter landscape—then, suddenly and as if by magic, there was sunshine and release—and spring!" Spring for Carson was a medium of communication that transcended even the silence of death—communication among all life forms and between human beings. "As between you and me," she wrote in her letter to Freeman, "the one who goes first will always speak to the other through many things—the songs of the veeries and hermits, and a sleepy white throat at midnight."[14]

The association of silence with spring was unthinkable to Carson. She armed herself—and the public—with facts in order to ensure that spring would never be silent. Facts pointed the way to action and provided a basis for choice. "The choice, after all, is ours to make," she reminds her readers in *Silent Spring*. "If, having endured much, we have at last asserted our 'right to know,' and if, knowing, we have concluded that we are being asked to take senseless and frightening risks, then...we should look about and see what other course is open to us."[15] In order to visualize alternative paths, we need only examine the "basic knowledge" we already possess, she argues. But as Carson knew all too well, the flow of information through society can become obstructed, creating distortions of fact and a dangerously narrow vision of what is good. In a discussion of the problem of invasive species, for example, Carson underscores the need for "basic knowledge of animal populations and their relations to their surroundings." Much of this information is already available, she adds, "but we do not use it."[16] Knowledge of nature becomes too compartmentalized and self-contained. Cut off from creative and vital exchange, the various branches of science turn moribund; before long, the deadly effects show up in nature: "We train ecologists in our universities and even employ them in our governmental agencies but we seldom take their advice. We allow the chemical death rain to fall as though there were no alternative, whereas in fact there are many, and our ingenuity could soon discover many more if given opportunity."[17] The ecologist has the necessary knowledge, but the chemical engineer pays no attention to ecology. Average citizens, in turn, assume that knowledge possessed by ecologists is beyond their comprehension; they rely instead on the (mis)information purveyed by chemical specialists who selectively release information to the public, telling the public only what it wishes to hear. The result is a fall "into a mesmerized state that makes us accept as inevitable that which is inferior or detrimental." Thus entranced, the public loses the "will or the vision to demand that which is good."[18]

Carson hoped that familiarizing the public with some basic facts, and the relationship of those facts to one another, might awaken the public from its slumber and rekindle the desire for that which is good. She had little sympathy with the all-too human tendency to ignore unpleasant truths, indicting the "vast majority" of the general public who "rest secure in a childlike faith that 'someone' is looking after things."[19] It is always better to know, Carson believed, than not to know. The *New York Times* review of *Silent Spring* understood this much. Carson's advice was, "Know the facts and do something about the situation," the review notes. "She intends to shock and hopes for action."[20] But Carson, for her own part, did not find facts shocking so much as she found them comforting. Even when the news was bad, she embraced the "comparative peace of mind" that came from having "facts instead of guesses."[21] Facts, once absorbed, could provide insulation against shock.

BODIES OF KNOWLEDGE

Carson was diagnosed with breast cancer in the spring of 1960, during the writing of *Silent Spring*, and she would receive much bad news for the next (and last) four years of her life. As a scientist investigating environmental hazards and as a cancer patient seeking the truth about her disease, she continually struggled with the problem of wresting facts from "specialists." In letters and conversations with her doctors, she implored them to be "direct and detailed" and demanded "no sugar-coating"[22] of her condition. Likewise, in *Silent Spring* she calls for an end to chemical companies "sugar coating unpalatable facts" about pesticides, an end to their "little tranquilizing pills of half truth."[23] She was adamant in asserting her right to know the unalloyed truth about her breast cancer at a time when concepts of informed consent and patients' rights were not well developed. At the time of Carson's diagnosis, it was not unusual for biopsy and mastectomy to be performed as a single procedure, with no inquiry into the patient's wishes regarding her own body.[24] Carson's then surgeon, Fred Sanderson, failed to disclose the truth about Carson's positive biopsy for nine months. Carson knew nothing of her malignancy and likely metastasis. "I was told none of this," she wrote to her editor, "even though I asked directly."[25] From then on, she sought the advice of a surgeon who was willing to match her candor.

While Carson valued truth telling and the measure of comfort and control that facts afforded, she insisted that facts must be situated and interpreted within a larger framework. That framework—the bigger picture of science—ought to be approached with humility and mindfulness of all that is not yet known. Facts, in other words, had their own ecology for Carson, and she embraced this notion of ecology in all aspects of her life. Her respect for the relationships between parts and wholes was apparent in her lifelong habit—instilled in her by her mother—of returning her "specimens" such as sea creatures to the natural environments from which she had removed them for the purposes of scientific study. For Carson, being scientific meant taking seriously the broad contours and the vast unknowns—the parts of the ecology of nature as well as the ecology of the human body that were only dimly understood. "Sometimes we have no choice but to disturb these relationships," she wrote, "but we should do so thoughtfully, with full awareness that what we do may have consequences remote in time and place."[26]

Carson approached her disease much as she approached the environmental crisis her work had brought to light. She combined a profound appreciation for medical technology with an attitude of awe in the face of the mysterious functioning of the disease and the complex interconnections of the body. In her doctor, George Crile (whose wife would succumb to breast cancer a year before Carson's death), Carson at last found an ecological sensibility similar to her own. In her letters to Crile, Carson praises his frankness, his unusually perceptive grasp of the role of humility in science, and his sensitivity to the body's interrelated, systemic functioning. "You smiled when I suggested that medicine could ever be scientific," she wrote to him, "but one of the things I appreciate in you, and one of the things I mean by 'scientific' is your awareness of what is *not* known and your unwillingness to rush in with procedures that may disrupt that unknown but all-important ecology of the body cells."[27]

Carson was forever conscious of the limits of human understanding—as well as the opportunities for wonder that limits entail. Science, she believed, could never exhaust nature's mysteries, for "every mystery solved brings us to the threshold of a greater one."[28] A good scientist never loses sight of all that eludes his or her grasp. In attempting to come to terms with her own death, Carson drew comparisons between the bewildering concept of personal immortality and the startling implications of modern physics. "Because I cannot understand something doesn't mean it doesn't exist," she wrote to Freeman. Certain scientific claims might appear confounding and implausible, she conceded, yet "these concepts deal with proven realities, so it is no more difficult to believe there is some sort of life beyond that 'horizon.'"[29]

Carson and Crile's shared appreciation of the unknowns of bodily ecology led Carson to embark on an experimental treatment with Krebiozen, an anticancer serum derived from living tissue which (it was believed) "really helps the whole body resist," as she explained optimistically to Freeman, "instead of attacking the local manifestations of the disease, as by radiation."[30] Crile cautiously affirmed Carson's optimism about Krebiozen, noting that this sort of treatment might well provide "the type of biological specificity you are looking for in your ecological problems."[31] Carson confessed to having far less confidence in the procedures of another doctor who did not share this ecological understanding of life processes. "Like most specialists," she complained to

Crile, "he is looking chiefly at his own problem without much regard for the whole picture."[32] Ironically, Carson and Crile agreed, the specialist often fails to grasp the importance of specificity. The narrow focus that treats a problem in isolation from its context endangers the broader ecology; only when the whole system is understood can an appropriate, specific response be generated from within the body.

Numerous passages of *Silent Spring* reiterate Carson's general policy of suspicion toward narrow-minded specialists, such as chemical engineers, who would have the world "beat its plowshares into spray guns."[33] Carson decries the ascendancy of the chemical specialist who—like the unenlightened surgeon—generally sees "his own problem and is unaware of or intolerant of the larger frame into which it fits."[34] Carson's remarks to George Crile regarding his cautiously scientific approach to bodily ecology also echo her thoughts on the subject in *Silent Spring*. Here she drew direct parallels between the ecology of the natural world and "an ecology of the world within our bodies." In the "unseen world" of the body, as in nature, "minute causes produce mighty effects; the effect, moreover, is often seemingly unrelated to the cause, appearing in a part of the body remote from the area where the original injury was sustained."[35] Just as chemical radiation and radical mastectomy ignore the ecological integrity of the cancer patient's body, DDT's eradication of an entire spectrum of life forms for the sake of a "beetleless world" reveals a shortsighted, arrogant, and scientifically uninformed methodology.

Despite her criticisms of the narrow focus of many scientists, Carson heartily approved of scientific controls and the attitude of detachment that allows one to stand back from a complex tangle of problems, assess the risks and benefits, and thereby decide which road to take. If the public is to decide whether or not to continue on its present road, she writes in the opening pages of *Silent Spring*, it must do so "in full possession of the facts."[36] In her personal struggle with cancer, she noted that "for the most part" she managed "to be 'matter of fact'" about her disease.[37] Carson's habit of detachment—both from her own "case" and the cases of environmental devastation she documented—undoubtedly permitted her to cope with the depressing burden of information her investigations had unearthed.

Carson maintained a prima facie respect for ecological interrelationships, but she did not counsel scientists to refrain from manipulating or controlling life processes. The leading pioneer of the environmental movement would not feel at home in the current climate of suspicion toward science that is apparent in many environmentalists'—particularly ecofeminists'—condemnation of detached, controlling, and objectifying methodologies. Unlike many contemporary advocates of an "ecological ethic" that endeavors to treat all organic beings as inviolable ends in themselves, Carson did not see human manipulation and even destruction of some parts of nature as inimical to an ecological sensibility. "Controlling" and "caring for" the environment were not mutually exclusive imperatives.

Perhaps because Carson held this view, environmentalists in the ecofeminist camp generally pay scant attention to Carson's work, despite her unique position as a prominent female environmentalist and science writer in a prefeminist era. In keeping with Carolyn Merchant's claim that mechanical philosophy and science induced the "death" of nature, ecofeminists, both religious and secular, have steadily critiqued "masculine" modes of detachment and objectivity embedded in the Western scientific perspective and its controlling gaze.[38] As one ecofeminist asserts, "from the time of René Descartes on, science has advanced on the assumption that what is known is passive and inert, laid out before the subject so it can be reduced to its smallest parts, studied exhaustively, and thereby known."[39] In environmental literature, this model of analysis is repeatedly contrasted with an "ecological" model that jettisons the "objectifying, manipulative, and disengaged kind of knowledge," proposing instead that we relate to all entities on terms of friendship, as "subjects" like ourselves.[40]

Carson might well have been perplexed by such proposals. To be sure, her writing condemns the extreme, heretical claim of some scientists that humans can and ought to direct the course of nature. As articulated by some, she notes, the control of nature "is a phrase conceived in arrogance, born of the Neanderthal age of biology and philosophy, when it was supposed that nature exists for the convenience of man."[41] Carson's critique of controlling, Neanderthal science is one of the most widely quoted of all her remarks in *Silent Spring*, yet the context of this statement deserves closer scrutiny. In fact, she did not object to the control of nature per se. Rather, she endorsed what she called biological or natural control instead of chemical control. As she argued in a speech made shortly after the publication of *Silent Spring*, "I criticize modern chemical control not because it controls harmful insects, but because it controls them badly and inefficiently."[42] She understood, too, that different degrees of control over nature are warranted by different contexts. In the "highly artificial," monocultural farmlands of modern America, she notes, even biological controls will not succeed without the careful planning and direct intervention of scientists, while in relatively wild forests, "with a minimum of help and a maximum of noninterference from man, Nature can have her way."[43] The most important distinction between biological and chemical control is an "awareness" in the former "that we are dealing with *life*."[44] Working together rather than in isolation, she insisted, specialists can create a new definition of control—one that remains conscious of the living nature of organisms. Such methodologies all have one thing in common:

> They are *biological* solutions, based on understanding of the living organisms they seek to control, and of the whole fabric of life to which these

organisms belong. Specialists representing various areas of the vast field of biology are contributing—entomologists, pathologists, geneticists, physiologists, biochemists, ecologists—all pouring their knowledge and their creative inspirations into the formation of a new science of biotic controls.[45]

This form of control from within the "fabric of life" places humans back in nature, even as we manipulate its processes to suit our ends.

THE FINAL BATTLE

Some scholars have noted parallels in Carson's writing between war—especially Cold War—rhetoric and human efforts to eradicate insect "enemies." In his *War and Nature*, Edmund Russell observes that "Carson relied on literal and metaphorical similarities between chemical warfare and pest control" in making her case against DDT and other widely used pesticides.[46] Not surprisingly, military metaphors often shaped her view of her cancer as well. "I still believe," she wrote to Dr. Crile, in "the old Churchillian determination to fight each battle as it comes ('We will fight on the beaches'—etc.) and I think a determination to win may well postpone the final battle."[47] Carson's final battle would come only a few months later on April 14, 1964, but she lived long enough to glimpse the revolutionary impact of her environmental crusade.

In the closing chapter of *Silent Spring*, Carson employs a steady stream of military language in her denunciation of pesticide use. But, again, her objections are lodged specifically against chemical, rather than biological, "warfare." Indeed, she often invokes the metaphor of war in support of natural pest controls, citing a "whole battery of armaments," new "line[s] of attack," and means of "direct destruction" available to those willing to seek the permanence of biological solutions in place of quick-fix chemicals.

One of the "more attractive possibilities" emerging from biological approaches, she notes, involves "what might be termed an experiment in psychological warfare" wherein entomologists use insects' own sexual secretions to confuse and trap males of the species.[48] Compared to such creative methods, she argues, chemical pesticides are an inferior means of warfare, "as crude a weapon as the cave man's club."[49] Better—and more discriminate—weapons were available. Crude chemical controls provide irrefutable evidence of a Darwinian struggle in nature, Carson notes, for spraying results in the weeding out of the "weaker members" of insect populations, leaving the "strong and fit...to defy our efforts to control them."[50] If we are to succeed in this war, she argues, we must learn the art of "forging weapons from the insect's own life processes," thereby turning the "strength of a species against itself."[51] She had dropped the references to warfare from the title of her book, but the motif of combat persists in more subtle forms. In the end, Carson's position on the human war with nature is not so much that of a pacificist as of "a smart general" devising a set of battle plans superior to those of conventional warfare.[52] Biotechnology, if properly applied, is one such plan, an alternative approach that succeeds by "taking account of such life forces...seeking to guide them into channels favorable to ourselves."[53] In other words, biological pest control was to the farmer what—she hoped—Krebiozen would become to the cancer patient.[54]

Overall, Carson's faith in scientific progress was balanced by an abiding skepticism of the sort of scientific idolatry pervading post-Sputnik America and the widespread mentality that "worships the gods of speed and quantity."[55] In 1958, she lamented to Freeman that human history had turned a new and frightening corner with the emergence of technologies capable of altering the very course of life on earth. Before *Sputnik*, it was plausible to believe that "much of Nature was forever beyond the tampering reach of man—he might level the forests and dam the streams, but the clouds and the rain and the wind were God's.... Now the most farfetched schemes seem entirely possible of achievement. And man seems actually to take into his hands—ill-prepared as he was psychologically—many of the functions of 'God.'"[56]

Rachel Carson deified neither humans nor nature. She staked out a middle ground between all-out control of nature and a naive reverence for all that is "natural." Scientists—and indeed citizens—must rely on a firm foundation of facts, combined with an attitude of humility "before the vast forces with which they tamper."[57] Certainly we should proceed into the vast unknowns, she believed, but we should do so with caution. In dealing with the environmental crisis as well as her own health crisis, Carson consistently endeavored to take in this whole, integrated, and interrelated picture, fully aware that neither she nor any human being could completely apprehend that larger framework in which the processes of life—and death—unfold. More than forty years after the publication of *Silent Spring*, the subtleties and the creative tensions in Carson's philosophy of life continue to make her work relevant and compelling.

NOTES

1. Lorus Milne and Margery Milne, "There's Poison All Around Us Now," review of *Silent Spring*, by Rachel Carson, *New York Times Book Review*, Sept. 23, 1962.

2. Carson's editor at Houghton Mifflin, Paul Brooks, suggested this as the title for Carson's bird chapter (Linda Lear, *Rachel Carson: Witness for Nature* [New York: Henry Holt, 1997], 375).

3. Rachel Carson, *Silent Spring* (Boston: Houghton Mifflin, 1994 [1962]), 3.

4. Rachel Carson, *Always, Rachel: The Letters of Rachel Carson and Dorothy Freeman, 1952–1964,* ed. Martha Freeman (Boston: Beacon Press, 1995), 416.

5. Carson, *Always, Rachel,* 248. Carson had originally intended to write a book on evolution and ecology, or life and its environment, as she calls it. Later she decided to fold these ideas into an even more pressing project dealing with pesticide misuse, what would become *Silent Spring.*

6. Ibid., 380.

7. Rachel Carson to Louis Crisler, Letter; quoted in Lear, *Witness for Nature,* 352.

8. Carson, *Always, Rachel,* 254.

9. Paul Brooks, foreword, to *And No Birds Sing: Rhetorical Analyses of Rachel Carson's "Silent Spring,"* ed. Craig Waddell (Carbondale: Southern Illinois University Press, 2000), xvi.

10. Carson, *Always, Rachel,* 461.

11. Dust jacket summary, Sandra Steingraber, *Living Downstream: An Ecologist Looks at Cancer and the Environment* (Reading, Mass.: Addison-Wesley, 1997), back cover.

12. Terry Tempest Williams, comments on dust jacket, Steingraber, *Living Downstream,* front cover.

13. Carson, *Always, Rachel,* 312.

14. Ibid., 266, 446.

15. Carson, *Silent Spring,* 277–78.

16. Ibid., 11.

17. Ibid., 11–12.

18. Ibid., 12.

19. Rachel Carson, foreword, to *Animal Machines,* by Ruth Harrison (New York: Ballantine, 1964), vii; reproduced in Rachel Carson, *Lost Woods: The Discovered Writing of Rachel Carson,* ed. Linda Lear (Boston: Beacon Press, 1998), 194.

20. Lorus Milne and Margery Milne, "There's Poison All Around Us Now."

21. Carson, *Always, Rachel,* 313.

22. Ibid., 430.

23. Carson, *Silent Spring,* 13.

24. Ellen Leopold writes that the "practice of fusing diagnosis with primary surgical treatment, universal at the time of Rachel Carson's surgery, survived

well into the 1980s." In the forty years since Carson's diagnosis, advances in anesthesiology have been "matched by the rise of 'informed consent,' which extended the legal doctrine of self-determination into the medical arena, requiring that patients be informed in advance of the risks and possible benefits of any procedure recommended to them" (A *Darker Ribbon: Breast Cancer, Women, and Their Doctors in the Twentieth Century* [Boston: Beacon Press, 1999], 125).

25. Rachel Carson to Paul Brooks, Letter, Dec. 27, 1960; as quoted in Lear, *Witness for Nature*, 368.

26. Carson, *Silent Spring*, 64.

27. Rachel Carson to George Crile, Letter, Dec. 17, 1960.

28. Rachel Carson, "The Real World Around Us," in *Lost Woods*, 159.

29. Carson, *Always, Rachel*, 447.

30. Ibid., 442.

31. George Crile to Rachel Carson, Letter; quoted in Leopold, A *Darker Ribbon*, 146.

32. Rachel Carson to George Crile, Letter, Mar. 18, 1961.

33. Carson, *Silent Spring*, 69.

34. Ibid., 13.

35. Ibid., 189.

36. Ibid., 13.

37. Carson, *Always, Rachel*, 490.

38. Perhaps it is Carson's "masculine" way of thinking and knowing that makes her unpalatable to environmentalists with ecofeminist sensibilities. Her use of war metaphors for humans and the environment, as I discuss below, are also worth noting.

39. Sallie McFague, *Super, Natural Christians* (Minneapolis: Fortress Press, 1997), 36.

40. Ibid., 38. Such claims are common among eco-theologians who endorse such ecological (and quantum) models and wish to break down the dualism of "subject" and "object" in science.

41. Carson, *Silent Spring*, 297.

42. Carson, Speech to the Women's National Press Club, Dec. 5, 1962. A short excerpt from this speech, containing the passage I have quoted, can be found online at Living on Earth, Apr. 7, 1995, www.loe.org/shows/shows.

htm?programID=95-P13-00014#feature3. The full audio version is available online at Democracy Now, Dec. 29, 1997, www.democracynow.org/article. pl?sid=03/04/07/0331227.

43. Carson, *Silent Spring*, 293.

44. Ibid., 296 (emphasis added).

45. Ibid., 278.

46. Edmund Russell, *War and Nature: Fighting Humans and Insects with Chemicals from World War I to "Silent Spring"* (New York: Cambridge University Press, 2001), 223.

47. Rachel Carson to George Crile, Letter, Feb. 17, 1963; in Carson, *Lost Woods*, 226.

48. Carson, *Silent Spring*, 286.

49. Ibid., 297.

50. Ibid., 263.

51. Ibid., 285, 279.

52. Cheryll Glotfelty, "Cold War, *Silent Spring*: The Trope of War in Modern Environmentalism," in *And No Birds Sing*, ed. Waddell, 160.

53. Carson, *Silent Spring*, 296. She writes, "high hopes now attend tests of another bacterium of this genus—*Bacillus thuringiensis*" (*Silent Spring*, 289). The Bt bacterium has long been used as a "natural" pesticide spray on crops, prior to its direct insertion into genetically altered plants. Recent applications of the Bt bacterium in genetically engineered crops have come under fire when preliminary tests suggested that it may harm insect species other than those specifically targeted, such as the beloved monarch butterfly. Genes from the Bt bacterium have been spliced into hybrid corn crops, among others, in order to control corn borers. Pollen from transgenic corn may land on other nearby plants, such as milkweed, where monarch larvae feed. A primary reason Carson gives for endorsing "natural" controls is that, unlike chemical pesticides, these controls would not (she believed) generate a resistant strain of "super-insects." Carson's belief that natural controls sidestep the problem of resistance appears to have been mistaken.

54. In fact, Carson observed that the American Medical Association's attacks on alternative therapies such as Krebiozen "resemble so closely some of the methods used against those critical of pesticides that the parallel is quite suggestive" (Rachel Carson, letter to George Crile, Apr. 13, 1963).

55. Carson, foreword, to *Animal Machines* by Harrison, vii; reproduced in Carson, *Lost Woods*, 194.

56. Carson, *Always, Rachel*, 248-49.

57. Carson, *Silent Spring*, 297.

9

Science and Spirit: Struggles of the Early Rachel Carson

Maril Hazlett

Scientist, nature writer, Rachel Carson wanted to know nature as fully as she could. Refusing to limit her perspective, throughout her career she remained open to mystery as well as committed to scientific objectivity. Between science and spirit, she never picked sides.

Walking this path, gender bias was among the obstacles Carson encountered. Social groups often use traditional gender stereotypes to hassle each other during conflicts and to haze dissidents into conformity. The role that gender played in the backlash against *Silent Spring* has been well studied. Some sneered at Carson as a spinster over-concerned with the lives of future generations, and *Silent Spring* was called a "marathon tirade with an emotional label." Wrote one angry reader, "as for insects, isn't it just like a woman to be scared to death of a few little bugs...she's probably a peace nut, too." Detractors widely cast her supporters as emotional housewives and crazy organic gardeners who were irrationally opposed to scientific and economic progress.[1]

Carson's struggle against these narrowing forces began long before *Silent Spring*. Her early journey passed through three major stages: her childhood education in nature study, her education and career as a scientist, and her rise as a nature writer. Trying to understand nature in all its complexities, Carson often combined science and spirit. To succeed, however, she had to fight past the predominant idea of her times—that science and spirit were separate—as well as the gender stereotypes that helped to build walls between these realms.

Carson lived before what we know as feminism today, and her understanding of gender and gender biases was not the same as ours. However, in some ways her perspective was richer. She seems to have grasped a complexity to gender that we rarely consider: the larger human connection with nature has the power to blur the boundaries of all cultural maps, including that of gender.

A CHILD IN NATURE

During childhood, Carson's first impressions of nature set the foundation for the rest of her life. As she later wrote in a *Woman's Home Companion* article, posthumously published as the children's book *Sense of Wonder*, knowledge of nature has to be grounded in experience to become meaningful. "I sincerely believe that for the child, and for the parent seeking to guide him, it is not half so important to *know* as to *feel*. If facts are the seeds that later produce knowledge and wisdom, then the emotions and the impressions of the senses are the fertile soil in which the seeds must grow."[2]

Carson's own childhood provided these opportunities. Her mother, Maria, pulled Rachel out of school for long periods of time and educated her at home. The daughter of a Presbyterian minister, Maria believed with an almost evangelical fervor in the nature study movement. In the United States, the nature study movement lasted from the mid-1890s to World War I. At one point, twenty-one states mandated nature study curricula. Among other things, nature study educators believed that such immediate encounters would awaken children's analytical and creative faculties and prepare them for future studies in the sciences.[3]

Rachel Carson, born in 1907—at the height of nature study's influence—watched birds, examined bugs, collected leaves, and generally interacted with any and all aspects of natural history that she and her mother could find in their local environment. In addition to these hands-on experiences, she also absorbed nature study philosophy. The movement, however, contained a conflict. Advocates split over the question of how teachers should interpret nature for their students. Should they teach children to analyze and quantify their surroundings? Or should teachers let children first simply experience nature and develop sympathy with their environment, leaving the analysis for later?[4]

Science or sentiment; chicken or the egg. In this turn-of-the-century context, "sentiment" or sympathy primarily meant the act of connecting to nature through the senses. The word did invoke the presence of emotions, but it did not yet carry connotations of being emotional, as it would during the debate over *Silent Spring*. In 1912, nature writer and nature study advocate John Burroughs wrote of the need to balance science and sentiment:

Science is impersonal and cold, and is not for the heart but for the head. The heart symbolizes so much for us, it stands for the very color and perfume of life, for the whole world of sentiment and emotion—the world that lies outside the sphere of science. ... Without soul and sentiment we cannot have literature, art, music, religion and all that gives charm and meaning to life; and without reason and scientific habit of mind we cannot have exact knowledge and mastery over the physical forces upon which our civilization is based. We must transcend physical science to reach the spiritual and grasp the final mystery of life. To science there is no mystery, there is only the inexplicable; there is no spiritual, there are laws and processes; there is no inner, there is only the outer world.[5]

When Burroughs describes sentiment, distant stars whirl and the wet slick of snail tracks picks up their sparkle. Here sentiment clearly contains a spiritual dimension as well, a sense of nature's mystery. However, Burroughs' perspective eventually lost the battle. As the educational and scientific professions both continued to professionalize, sentiment lost its standing in the sciences. Any sense of spirit simply seemed to disappear. By World War I, nature study was in decline.

In this division between science and "the world that lies outside," gender played a starring role. Gender stereotypes tend to define opposites that exist in rigid hierarchies. In the case of nature study, anything labeled "sentimental" became associated with feminine and thus inferior terrain. "Hard" science came to be identified with a superior, more masculine approach. Western culture has long associated science with masculinity. As historian of science Evelyn Fox Keller has explained, there exists a "deeply rooted popular mythology that casts objectivity, reason, and mind as male, and subjectivity, feeling, and nature as female."[6]

The gender dynamic underpinning nature study remained strong, but by the time Carson entered college in 1925 the movement itself had faltered. Its ethos survived within her, though. The debate over science and sentiment would also become pivotal in her writing. Maria Carson had taught her daughter that science, sentiment, and spirit could coexist. From a very early age, Rachel Carson had learned to look at nature in an integrated way, but she had to struggle to maintain this holistic perspective as a scientist and a writer.

WHEN SCIENCE SPLIT THE WORLD

Just as nature study advocates would have hoped, Carson's childhood experiences with nature helped awaken her interest in a scientific career. As an undergraduate she switched her major from English to biology, and in 1929 she began graduate school in zoology at Johns Hopkins University. At this time, however, the sciences were very inhospitable to women. The predominant belief was that women were not intellectually or physically suited for the rigors of scientific careers. The prospects of a woman finding employment in a research position were very small.[7]

The professional gender barriers Carson faced then intersected with hard economic times and a difficult family situation. The Depression had begun, and at one point during graduate school Carson provided financial support for five partially dependent family members. This burden, as well as unexpected tuition increases, forced her to drop to part-time student status and take various jobs. Eventually accepting that she needed full-time employment, in 1934 Carson gave up her pursuit of a doctorate—and thus any hope of a possible teaching and research career—and left Johns Hopkins University with the master's degree she earned in 1932.

In finding scientific work, though, Carson still faced the same gender barriers that had worked against her in graduate school. Eventually she found a full-time job as a science writer for the U.S. Bureau of Fisheries, based in the Washington, D.C., area. The low-paying position, where she mostly summarized rather than carried out scientific research, bore all the marks of discrimination against women in the sciences. With the lack of fieldwork and research opportunities, it also kept Carson from exploring nature through science as fully as her male colleagues were able to.

However, Carson did leverage her job into benefits. She learned how to synthesize knowledge across many scientific fields and developed a knack for making science relevant to the reading public. Not wedded to any particular research program or perspective, she gained an excellent perspective on critical issues facing the profession. As she eventually moved from government science writer to editor, Carson climbed her particular ladder in the sciences almost as far as any female scientist could go.

Still, certain aspects of scientific inquiry were not completely compatible with Carson's broad yet intimate vision of nature. One problem was the doctrine of scientific objectivity. As historians of science and feminist theorists have explored, objectivity requires the ideal scientist to be a value-free observer of natural phenomena. Yet science, like all other pursuits, is fundamentally shaped by cultural forces.[8] Until recently, for example, many medical studies ignored the often significantly different effects of medications on men versus women. No matter how scientists might presume themselves to be isolated from historical and cultural forces, these values still condition and shape the questions that they do—and do not—investigate.

In contrast, Carson's own perspective was similar to what theorist Donna Haraway has called "situated knowledges." This concept points out that no one, even a scientist holding him- or herself to high standards of fairness, accountability, and empirical analysis, ever sees the world with a completely immune and isolated eye. Thus when drawing scientific conclusions, observers must acknowledge both the limits of their vision and the mysteries that will forever lie beyond their sight.[9] A sense of situated knowledge helps to capture Rachel Carson's position in approaching the natural world. First and foremost she was embedded in experience and observation of the local environment. Science, however, tended to avoid personal accounts of firsthand experiences with natural phenomena. Carson struggled to balance distance on one hand and intimacy on the other.

Throughout her life Carson remained fully committed to the objective practices of scientific inquiry, and she held herself to strict analytical standards. She also believed in nature as a higher order, full of mystery and worthy of respect. Science, though, was not much more hospitable to the latter vision than it was to women. Carson's approach to nature openly incorporated what John Burroughs had called sentiment, and what she came to call emotion. Even today, emotion is not a widely welcomed word in scientific discourse. When Carson mixed science and emotion—or "poetry," as her more positive reviewers came to call it—she stepped into a forbidden zone. Some of the mixed reactions to her early work would foreshadow the negative reactions that followed *Silent Spring*.

FINDING A BALANCE

Between 1937 and approximately 1954, Carson took her first serious steps as a professional writer. Throughout this time she wrote outside articles as well as producing many brochures and scientific summaries during her day job with the U.S. Fish and Wildlife Service. In addition, she took copious field notes during nature walks and birding trips.

In all her writing, Carson remained constant to several major questions. First, how could she represent nature in its own right, instead of as merely a reflection of human needs and judgments? Along these lines, Carson wrestled with how to describe the connections between the vast geophysical forces of the earth and that lighter web known as life, as well as with how to describe the connections between the infinite numbers of life forms. Second, she questioned how to include humans in her stories about natural world. Progressively she became concerned that humans were wreaking radical and damaging changes upon the environment. Last, she investigated the connections between a critique of science and the role of emotion in opening people's eyes to nature's beauty and its importance in sustaining the human spirit. In one way or another, these three major questions all involved the young and evolving field known as ecology: ecology as a scientific practice; ecology as an approach to nature that had the potential to treat humans on equal terms with other organisms; and ecology as a philosophy with the potential to blur scientific and social boundaries and help to understand nature on inclusive, holistic terms.[10]

During this earlier period, most of Carson's bigger writing projects focused on the sea, and she used the topic as a forum for exploring her larger ideas about nature. With *The Sea Around Us* she finally found widespread public success. At this same time, however, her voice as a writer went through some crucial changes. Voice is the tone that writers take to talk to their readers in order to get across the flesh, the passion of their ideas; voice sells or sinks the story.[11] To communicate nature's full story, Carson balanced two voices—the observations of the scientist and the poetry of the nature writer.

FIRST STEPS

By 1937, Carson's household included her two young orphaned nieces, as well as her now widowed mother and herself. In need of extra money to support her family, Carson began writing newspaper and magazine articles at night. Often, she based these writings on the same science articles that she read, wrote, and edited for the government during the day. During this era, she began to experiment with and develop what would become her own unique blend of voices, the scientist and the nature writer. Carson's scientist voice came to characterize her day job: the even, explanatory, professorial tones that she used to make clear the findings and authority of science. Her nature writer voice appeared more often in her outside articles; this voice let loose the poetry and reflected the awe and mystery that Carson experienced in the natural world. Finding the right balance to combine these two voices would become the central project of this first major stage of her career.

Carson's first book, *Under the Sea-Wind* (1941), provides one clear example. Within four years of working for the government, Carson had started working on a story telling how a variety of sea animals interact with each other, mostly in terms of the food chain. *Sea-Wind* also describes the other common forces shaping these animals' lives: migration instincts, weather conditions, the need to reproduce, and above all the sea's mighty power. Carson strove to enter the sea animals' world free of any human bias or anthropomorphism, but humans do appear in her narrative. Mostly, her humans compete with animals for resources; for example, she portrays the fishermen's agendas as little different from those of the voracious sea life feeding all around them. The fishermen's tools for harvesting the sea life (such as enormous nets that indiscriminately scraped the ocean floor), however, are much broader in scale, less selective, and more destructive and wasteful than any of nature's mechanisms. When humans appear in nature, Carson suggests—but does not yet amplify—their role is too often that of destroyers.[12]

Under the Sea-Wind remains Carson's most powerful piece of traditional nature writing. In this book, she speaks out in the nature writer voice that she stifled during her day job. Her voice resonates as an intensely close observer of the organisms and processes she describes. However, the scientist definitely remains present in the book, if all but invisible on its surface. Many of the creatures Carson writes of so movingly, for example, she had researched but never seen.

What is most interesting about Carson's voice in *Under the Sea-Wind* is not just how it describes nature, but how it does not. Compared to Carson's later work, first-person accounts of her deeply felt interactions with nature are missing from the narrative. Only years later did she mention to her best friend Dorothy that the "experience I relate in *Under the Sea-Wind* about the young mullet pouring through that tide race to the sea is one that comes to mind. Of course I guess I didn't tell it as a personal experience, but it was—I stood knee-deep in that racing water and at times could scarcely see those darting, silver bits of life for my tears."[13] Carson knew the mullet firsthand, but she did not yet use the first person to tell that part of the story. Her perspective was grounded, situated in intimate experience of nature, but she did not yet openly put that closeness into words for broad publication. Likewise, in Carson's later works the role of science in the story would change from a voice to a character. With all its intriguing questions and varying interpretations, science would become an entity with agendas and inner conflicts that came to drive the story.

Published on the eve of World War II, *Under the Sea-Wind* was very well reviewed by scientists and naturalists. Sales, however, were poor. When released later in Carson's career, the book rose to the best-sellers lists; however, a country caught up in the tragedy of Pearl Harbor and then entry into war was not much interested in a quiet little nature story. Disappointed in the reception of *Sea-Wind*, Carson still continued to write outside articles. Balancing the scientist and the nature writer, though, always remained an issue. Already, Carson's combination of science and poetry was not to everyone's taste. She often found it hard to market some of her outside writing. Too "poetic," one critic would tell her. Too "unemotional," commented another. More poetry and less science, one friend and advocate requested: "[Y]ou scientists are so impersonal about things and so unemotional. I would like to see more emotion in the piece and that personal touch because you do write a beautiful prose, Rachel."[14]

Despite the mixed messages, Carson persevered. In her own private writings—her field notes—she brought these two perspectives together most fully. As biographer Linda Lear observes, Carson's field notes always combined science and sentiment, ranging "from technically accurate taxonomic descriptions to pure poetry, often in the same entry. At no time was Carson's focus bifurcated; in the field she always saw things in a single vision."[15]

Writing for popular audiences both day and night, Carson continued honing her skill of making science comprehensible to the general reader. Always, she wanted to illuminate the larger mysteries of nature and educate readers about its scientific complexities and details.[16] This path represented a diversion from the one followed by her male colleagues. Most of her male peers wrote only for other scientists, engaging limited audiences in specialized debates. In contrast, Carson wrote for the public, explaining science to a broad popular audience and acknowledging the holes in existing scientific knowledge. If knowledge—especially scientific knowledge—was power, then Carson was interested in spreading that power around.

The debate over *Silent Spring*, however, would reveal that some of her colleagues felt very differently. When she tried to take down the walls between scientists and the public, one reaction would be to accuse her of transgressing other cultural boundaries—not only the lines between science and poetry (or emotion), but also the rules of proper gender roles and behavior.

CROSSING THE SEA

The publication of *Under the Sea-Wind* had disappointed her, and Carson swore off writing books for a while. Still, she had also begun to chafe at the limits of her job. Not only was she interested in more investigative scientific research than the government assignments provided, but she also found herself beginning to question the government's limited, resource-based approach to conservation.[17] Even if she continued progressing in her government career, it would mean an increase in administrative duties that would drain time away from her writing.

Frustrated on many levels and also inspired by the post–World War II advances in oceanography, by 1948 Carson finally began working on another book. The result was a fascinating story of the sea: its evolutionary history, shifting currents, seasons and cycles of its many-layered waters, the vast land masses it covered, even its islands and history in human thought. This second book was an immediate success. Published in 1950, the award-winning success of *The Sea Around Us* eventually made it possible for Carson to quit her job and write books full-time.[18]

The Sea Around Us built on the foundation of *Under the Sea-Wind*. The second book too revolves around the infinite "series of delicately adjusted, interlocking relationships" that compose the forces of life.[19] Carson's fundamentally ecological approach is based on tracing such physical connections and exchanges, but she never loses sight of the fact that the sea ultimately holds the power. Life struggles to adjust to the often hostile sea environment. The sea even establishes the terms of its relationship with man. As Carson writes, "he has returned to his mother sea only on her own terms. He cannot control or change the ocean as, in his brief tenancy of earth, he has subdued and plundered the continents."[20]

Yet on this point, Carson's own narrative belies her. Humans appear in many facets of the *Sea*, as explorers, adventurers, and scientists. She also discusses the various resources that the sea provides for human life: fish, seaweed, petroleum deposits, minerals, and so on. And in her chapter recounting the extinct or fast-disappearing ecologies of islands, she reveals humans in their most dangerous role of all—the destroyers of delicately balanced natural relationships.[21] Perhaps humans could not control the sea, but they could definitely change it. Carson's belief in the power of nature helped her to recognize it as a set of forces that exist beyond human bias or ken. How to reconcile this separate existence of nature, however, with the problematic truth that humans' actions not only blur this boundary but also change the environment for the worse? This tension weaves throughout *The Sea Around Us*.

In Carson's evolution as a writer, *Sea* was most important not for articulating such general concepts, but because it represents a brilliant balance between her scientist and nature writer voices. The scientist, smoothly organizing, interpreting, and summarizing vast reams of oceanic information, dominates the narrative. The nature writer, a close observer and even devotee of nature, expresses a sense of wonder in a respectful, subordinate chorus, bearing witness to nature's mysteries. An interesting change, however: the scientist keeps to the objective third person, while the nature writer now speaks in the first. Still, *Sea* seemingly conforms to the scientific gender politics of the time. The scientist, representing that heavily masculine world, appears to dominate the accordingly more feminine voice of the appreciative nature writer.[22]

By bringing these two voices together Carson openly mixed what many understood as the mutually exclusive worlds of science and emotion. Even Carson's own editor at Oxford University Press strictly patrolled this boundary; Carson had to defend the text of *Sea* against suggested revisions that she thought made her work sound too much like a textbook. Fighting against the proposed changes, she wrote that "my real preoccupation is not with 'pure' or abstract science, but...I am the sort who wants above all to get out and enjoy the beauty and wonder of the natural world, and who resorts only secondarily to the laboratory and library for explanations." Thus, she refused to delete what so many called the "poetry" from her text. "I believe what I have added may suggest—without baldly stating—such emotional as well as intellectual appeal."[23]

In this combination, *The Sea Around Us* was itself a revolutionary book, albeit now dwarfed by the subsequent impact of *Silent Spring*. Carson's unique blend of voices struck a chord with readers and reviewers both, but not always an enthusiastic one. Before the book's publication, several magazines turned down the opportunity to publish chapters from *Sea*, considering Carson's style "too poetic for a work of non-fiction."[24] This criticism—uttered before the work went on to win the National Book Award and sell over

250,000 copies by the end of 1951—echoed the biases that Carson had encountered before in trying to place her freelance work. After *Sea*'s undeniable success, however, many reviewers, scientists, and other readers instead declared themselves "surprised by Carson's ability to master such comprehensive information and to present a balanced picture with such lean yet poetic language."[25]

Sea certainly challenged prevailing ideas about science. In writing the book Carson challenged ideas about women and science as well. Many of her readers—especially male readers—could not believe that a woman had produced such a scientific work. "Among male readers there was a certain reluctance to acknowledge that a woman could have dealt with a scientific subject," she told her audience, "...[one], addressing me properly as *Miss* Rachel Carson, nevertheless began his letter 'Dear Sir.' He explained his salutation by saying that he had always been convinced that the males possess the supreme intellectual powers of the world, and he could not bring himself to reverse his conviction."[26]

Even readers who brought themselves to accept that a woman could do science still perceived Carson as a manly kind of gal. Carson found this stereotype amusing as well. "People often seem to be surprised that a woman should have written a book about the sea. This is especially true, I find, of men. Perhaps they have been accustomed to thinking of the more exciting fields of scientific knowledge as exclusively masculine domains." As a small, slight, soft-voiced woman, Carson knew she further confounded most people's expectations. "Then even if they accept my sex, some people are further surprised to find that I am not a tall, oversize, Amazon-type female."[27]

In their reactions to *The Sea Around Us*, readers expressed some uneasiness at Carson's blurring of gender boundaries. Some of these worries were justified. If gender was one of the anchors of the social order, then Carson did want to challenge certain practices. In the wake of *The Sea Around Us* Carson began voicing the critique of science that she would wield with such force in *Silent Spring*. Her experiences on the margins of science had led her to recognize that not only women were excluded from this masculine domain, but that most people were, regardless of their gender. In one of her post-*Sea* speeches, Carson made this problem clear.

> We live in a scientific age; yet we assume that knowledge of science is the prerogative of only a small number of human beings, isolated and priestlike in their laboratories. This is not true. The materials of science are the materials of life itself. Science is part of the reality of living; it is the what, the how, and the why of everything in our experience.[28]

Carson believed that science was an essential tool for humans to understand not only themselves, but also their natural surroundings. She also believed that the widespread positive public response to *Sea* supported her in challenging the idea that science was "the prerogative of only a small number of human beings." Likewise, she testified to another audience, the "letters that have come to me in the past nine months have taught me never again to underestimate the capacity of the general public to absorb the facts of science."[29] Walls between scientists and the public restricted the public's access to scientific knowledge, and those barriers had to be torn down. While this had the potential to empower the public, some scientists would prove reluctant to let go of the distance—and the power.

Throughout the post-*Sea* publicity binge of speeches and public comments, Carson also challenged science in another way. Her dominant public voice was clearly that of the nature writer, speaking as a firsthand witness to the most intimate of nature's mysteries. The scientist voice took a back seat. Carson believed that by bringing together science and emotion, a mixture of knowledge and reverence, nature writers could help both humans and nature survive the scary new world that scientists had produced. In her 1952 acceptance speech for the John Burroughs medal for nature writing, she described the desperate need to use nature writing to educate the public in science. Carson told nature writers that they needed to stop thinking of nature in isolation from modern civilization, and instead engage the frightening contemporary scientific and technological realities.

> I myself am convinced that there has never been a greater need than there is today for the reporter and interpreter of the natural world. Mankind has gone very far into an artificial world of his own creation. He has sought to insulate himself, in his cities of steel and concrete, from the realities of earth and water and the growing seed. Intoxicated with a sense of his own power, he seems to be going farther and farther into more experiments for the destruction of himself and his world.[30]

In nature writing, Carson saw salvation from scientific inquiry gone awry. Scientists and the public should focus on understanding nature's mysteries, instead of bending its resources to the ruinous priorities of industrialized civilization. "I do believe," Carson maintained, "that the more clearly we can focus our attention on the wonders and the realities of the universe about us the less taste we shall have for the destruction of our race. Wonder and humility are wholesome emotions, and they do not exist side by side with a lust for destruction."[31] By putting science into perspective as just one more limited tool for exploring an infinitely mysterious universe, nature writers could show the way.

On one hand, Carson limited the powers of science to explain nature. On the other, she also explored and expanded the powers of emotion. Mixing science and emotion questioned the traditional definitions and qualities associated with them both. If science was not necessarily infallible or even perfectly objective, then emotion was not necessarily subjective or irrational.

But what did emotion mean, then? Carson's use of the word was nothing if not fluid. Throughout her life she used emotion in a variety of different ways—often interchangeably with poetry, experience, lived experience, feeling, sympathy, wonder, humility, and so on.[32] Consistently, however, she used emotion as a catchall term for qualities that the tightly bound world of science excluded and marked as less important or inferior. In this respect Carson defined emotion as broadly as, a generation or more earlier, John Burroughs had spoken of sentiment. Most often, she used emotion to express an individual connection to nature, a personal, private, even mystic quality. She also used emotion to capture the same sense of "the world outside," the myriad other alternatives of understanding the environment. Mixing science and emotion meant tempering science with respect, even humility before the mystery of nature's unknown powers, and being conscious of the unpredictable consequences of human actions in the environment.[33]

Above all, however—and what is now most lost in discussions or remembrances of Carson's work—her use of "emotion" was both sensory and spiritual. Remaining open to spirit in nature inspired her emotion and led her to pursue science. Spirit—not necessarily religion or even faith but spirit, the essence of humans' conscious connections with the worlds outside of themselves—had always been important to Carson. In her freshman year of college, she wrote an essay on nature writer Dallas Lore Sharp, who was also a prominent advocate of nature study. Carson chose his work because she believed along with him that "religion begins where science ends" and that "good nature writing must have a pre-literary existence as lived reality."[34] Almost thirty years later, she restated her belief in the importance of a spiritual aspect to knowledge of nature. As she told her audience in a 1954 speech:

> The pleasures, the values of contact with the natural world, are not reserved for scientists....I am not afraid of being thought a sentimentalist when I stand here tonight and tell you that I believe natural beauty has a necessary place in the spiritual development of any individual or any society. I believe that whenever we destroy beauty, or whenever we substitute something man-made and artificial for a natural feature of the earth, we have retarded some part of man's spiritual growth.[35]

Throughout her career, Carson had fought to maintain an inclusive, holistic view of nature, one that incorporated the more fluid and personal aspects of human experience with the surrounding environment. As Carson stood poised to produce her next two best sellers, *The Edge of the Sea* and *Silent Spring*, she continued to transcend these barriers and trace back to the source.

WALKING THE EDGE

Before writing *Silent Spring*, Carson still had a long road to travel. It was one thing to start breaking down barriers to knowledge and obstacles to the fullest possible understanding of nature. It was another to start building an alternative vision.

Between publishing *Sea* in 1950 and beginning *Silent Spring* in late 1957, Carson struggled to settle down to new work. She experienced major upheavals in her personal life—such as the death of a beloved niece and the adoption of her great-nephew—but the problem lay at least partially in Carson's writing as well. Her second best seller, *The Edge of the Sea* (1955), never quite hit a rhythm between the scientist and nature writer voices. Despite the exquisite writing (her editor Paul Brooks commented that some passages were even superior to her work in *The Sea Around Us*)[36] the rhythm of *Edge* did not comfortably resolve the two perspectives. Carson was never wholly satisfied with the book.[37] Another project, a proposed book on evolution for Harper, didn't get off the ground. From the writing standpoint, her short article "Help Your Child to Wonder" (1956)—an exploration of feeling and emotion in awakening children's connections to nature—remains Carson's most cohesive, flowing piece of this intermediate period. Another short piece was also successful, an article for *Holiday* titled "Our Ever-Changing Shore."[38]

What was causing this tension? In thinking about nature, Carson was becoming progressively concerned with how humans acted, often drastically, to change the surroundings that sustained them. This problem troubled her, consumed more and more of her thinking, yet she had difficulty confronting it head on. Paradoxically, it turned out that her own integrated connection to nature had always been grounded in one of the biggest divisions of all—the belief that humans were separate from and therefore could never destroy or permanently alter nature. When this assumption turned out not to be true, it shook her, and it shook her writing. Carson slowly came to confront a serious disconnect in her own ideas: the gulf between her longstanding ideas about the purity and permanence of nature, and the cultural reality of chemical contamination and radical change.[39]

This shift in content and focus changed her writing voice as well. Now openly questioning how humans treated their environment, Carson could no longer balance dual roles as scientist and nature writer. The two perspectives and two voices somehow needed to become one. The problem of ecological destruction was forcing Carson to rethink her narrative style. Set up by *Sea*, unresolved in *Edge*, this problem would again become Carson's central struggle in writing *Silent Spring*: how to consider humans as part of nature. As a writer, how could she encompass both the grand sweep of natural cycles and the minute detail of everyday human interactions with the environment? How could she discuss nature from her dual perspective as both objective observer and involved participant? What was the missing link?

Over the years of writing *Silent Spring*, Carson would slowly work out this emerging new voice. First, she had to ground it in a new sense of the environment—a shifting world, full of flux and change. Second, she had to conceive of humans as ecological beings, right down to their cells, yet also acknowledge the human capability to destroy nature on a scale that no other life form could begin to approach. A crucial factor would figure into this new voice: the human body. Carson first worried about the environmental health of her family and friends. Her diagnosis with breast cancer halfway through writing *Silent Spring* then permanently shaped her awareness of how humans were physical, ecological parts of their environment.

With the publication of *The Sea Around Us*, Carson had not only produced a successful best seller. She also finally brought back together science, sentiment, and spirit—paths in her life that, during her formal education and professional employment, had seemed to split apart. To do this, she had to avoid how gender bias limited scientific participation (including her own) and helped scientific inquiry to avoid emotion and shy away from spirit. Gender hazing was one of the tools that helped to limit human exploration of the unknown, and it set up a divided world where science, sentiment, and spirit mixed at their peril, regardless of their shared roots in the common pool of human experience. Carson pushed past such limiting stereotypes and ideologies. When she did the same with a topic as socially, economically, and politically controversial as pesticides, that thread of uneasiness would explode into a powerful backlash.[40]

NOTES

1. Historian Virginia Scharff defines gender as "the bundle of habits and expectations and behaviors that organizes people and things according to the ideas of sexed bodies," (Virginia Scharff, ed., *Seeing Nature through Gender* [Lawrence: University Press of Kansas, 2003], xiii). For a sampling of the gender scholarship on Rachel Carson and *Silent Spring*, see H. Patricia Hynes, *The Recurring Silent Spring* (New York: Pergamon Press, 1989); Linda Lear, *Rachel Carson: Witness for Nature* (New York: Henry Holt, 1997); Vera Norwood, "The Nature of Knowing: Rachel Carson and the American Environment," *Signs* 12 (1987): 740-61; and Michael B. Smith, "'Silence, Miss Carson!' Science, Gender, and the Reception of *Silent Spring*," *Feminist Studies* 27 (2001): 733-52. "Marathon tirade" quote from "The Poison Pen," *Agrichemical West* (August 1962), Rachel Carson Papers, Beinecke Library, Yale University; "Peace nut" quote from H. Davidson to *New Yorker*, June 29, 1962 (San Francisco, Calif.). For an overview of the *Silent Spring* debate, see Maril Hazlett, "The Story of *Silent Spring* and the Ecological Turn" (Ph.D. dissertation, University of Kansas, 2003); ibid., "'Woman vs. Man vs. Bugs': Gender and Popular Ecology in Early Reactions to *Silent Spring*," *Environmental History* 9 (2004): 701-29; ibid., "Voices from the Spring: *Silent*

Tempe Public Library

Checkout receipt

Patron: **JOHNSTON, RACHEL LANIGH**
Date: 10/24/2018 11:11:31 AM

---

1. Rachel Carson : legacy and challenge
Barcode 32953010445239
Due by 11/14/2018

Overdue fine = $0.25 per day per item.
tempe.polarislibrary.com
(480)350-5500

LIBRARY HOURS

Sunday 12:00 pm - 5:00 pm
Monday 9:00 am - 8:00 pm
Tuesday 9:00 am - 8:00 pm
Wednesday 9:00 am - 8:00
Thursday 9:00 am - 8:00 pm
Friday 9:00 am
Saturday 9:00

You just saved $20.99 by using your
public library. You have saved $102.85

Spring and the Ecological Turn in American Health," in *Seeing Nature through Gender*, ed. Scharff, 103-28.

2. Rachel Carson as quoted in Paul Brooks, *The House of Life: Rachel Carson at Work* (Boston: Houghton Mifflin, 1972), 202 (emphasis in original). Carson also repeated similar arguments, but upgraded for the teachers of high school students, in her introduction to the 1956 coursebook *Biological Sciences*. Rachel Carson, "Biological Sciences," in *Good Reading* (New York: New American Library, 1956), reprinted in ibid., *Lost Woods: The Discovered Writing of Rachel Carson*, ed. Linda Lear (Boston: Beacon Press, 1998), 164-67. In this chapter, all biographical detail of Carson's life is taken from Lear's *Witness for Nature*, regardless that I have cited only certain passages. Interpretively, my work also builds on Lear's concept of Carson as witness, a key metaphor that works well on many levels.

3. My discussion of the nature study movement is deeply indebted to Kevin Armitage. His forthcoming book is titled *Knowing Nature: Nature Study, Conservation and American Culture, 1873–1923* (Lawrence: University Press of Kansas, forthcoming 2008).

4. Ibid.

5. John Burroughs, "Science and Sentiment," *The Independent*, Feb. 15, 1912, 360-61. My thanks to Kevin Armitage for bringing this citation to my attention.

6. Evelyn Fox Keller, *Reflections on Gender and Science* (New Haven: Yale University Press, 1985), 6-7. Also see Londa Schiebinger, *Has Feminism Changed Science?* (Cambridge: Harvard University Press, 1999); and Carroll Pursell, "The Construction of Masculinity and Technology," *Polhem* 11 (1993): 206-19.

7. Margaret W. Rossiter, *Women Scientists in America: Before Affirmative Action, 1940–1972*, vol. 2 (Baltimore, Md.: Johns Hopkins University Press, 1995), 304-32; Lear, *Witness for Nature*, 42.

8. Sandra Harding, "'Strong Objectivity' and Socially Situated Knowledge," in her *Whose Science? Whose Knowledge? Thinking from Women's Lives* (Ithaca, N.Y.: Cornell University Press, 1991), 138-63.

9. Donna J. Haraway, "Situated Knowledges: The Science Question in Feminism and the Privilege of Partial Perspective," in her *Simians, Cyborgs, and Women: The Reinvention of Nature* (New York: Routledge, 1991), 183-201.

10. Summary drawn from Hazlett, "The Story of *Silent Spring* and the Ecological Turn." In analyzing Carson's literary evolution, I have also drawn on the following works (in addition to Brooks and Lear): Lawrence Buell, *The Environmental Imagination: Thoreau, Nature Writing, and the Formation of American Culture* (Cambridge: Belknap Press of Harvard University Press,

1995); ibid., *Writing for an Endangered World: Literature, Culture, and Environment in the U.S. and Beyond* (Cambridge: Belknap Press of Harvard University Press, 2001); Carol B. Gartner, *Rachel Carson* (New York: Frederick Ungar, 1983); Cheryll Glotfelty, "Rachel Carson (1907-1964)," in *American Nature Writers, vol. I*, ed. John Elder (New York: Charles Scribner's Sons, 1996), 151-71; and Mary A. McKay, *Rachel Carson* (New York: Twayne Publishers, 1993). When I describe Carson's work as containing two voices, I do not mean that she alternated voices between projects at her day job and her freelance work. She balanced the voices throughout her work—in her science writing, the nature writer sometimes all but disappeared, but quite often the two voices appear together in various combinations.

11. For understanding "voice" in writing, I have drawn on: Helene Cixous, *Three Steps on the Ladder of Writing* (New York: Columbia University Press, 1993); Vivian Gornick, *The Situation and the Story: The Art of Personal Narrative* (New York: Farrar, Straus and Giroux, 2001); Nancy Mairs, *Voice Lessons: On Becoming a (Woman) Writer* (Boston: Beacon Press, 1994); and Virginia Woolf, *A Writer's Diary*, ed. Leonard Woolf (New York: Harcourt Brace Jovanovich, 1953).

12. Rachel Carson, *Under the Sea-Wind* (New York: Penguin Books, 1996 [1941]). Carson's responses to a questionnaire from Simon and Schuster's marketing department are very revealing about her desire to eliminate the human observer—the "human bias"—in her story of the ocean: "its forces are too mighty to be much affected by human activity. So I decided that the author as a person or a human observer should never enter the story, but that it should be told as a simple narrative of the lives of certain animals of the sea....I had to forget a lot of human conceptions." Rachel Carson, Memo to Mrs. Eales on *Under the Sea-Wind* (ca. 1942), reprinted in Carson, *Lost Woods*, 53-62; quote found at 55-56.

13. Rachel Carson to Dorothy Freeman, Letter, Oct. 4, 1959, in *Always, Rachel: The Letters of Rachel Carson and Dorothy Freeman, 1952–1964*, ed. Martha Freeman (Boston: Beacon Press, 1995), 281.

14. Lear, *Witness for Nature*, 105. Lear also observes that Simon and Schuster did not put any special effort into marketing the book. Ibid., 188. "Poetic" and "unemotional" quotes found in ibid., 114-15. For "You scientists..." see Sunnie Bleeker as quoted in ibid., 114.

15. For example, see Carson, "Road of the Hawks," unpublished fragment, Rachel Carson Papers, Beinecke Library, Yale University, 1945; also reprinted in Carson, *Lost Woods*, 31-32; and, Lear, *Witness for Nature*, 231.

16. Lear, *Witness for Nature*, 219.

17. The "Conservation in Action" series expresses some of these tensions in her ideas about government resource conservation. Lear, *Witness for Nature*, 145.

18. Lear, *Witness for Nature*, 178–222.

19. Rachel Carson, *The Sea Around Us* (New York: Oxford University Press, 1989 [1950]), 19.

20. Ibid., 15.

21. Ibid., 93; also see Lear, *Witness for Nature*, 518, n. 35.

22. For example, see Carson, *The Sea Around Us*, 99. In this passage Carson moves easily between a scientific explanation of ancient seas and a first-person account of finding sea fossils on a Pennsylvania mountainside.

23. As quoted in Brooks, *House of Life*, 125.

24. As quoted in Lear, *Witness for Nature*, 174.

25. Ibid., 223, 203. *Newsweek* did not jump on the pro-Carson bandwagon, instead summing up her prose: "A kind of scientific piety pervades such prose, mournful references to endless cycles and astronomical distances which begin by being impressive and end by becoming almost magical incantations" (quoted in Lear, *Witness for Nature*, 205). At this stage, both Carson and her public seem to have most often referred to her writing style as mixing science and poetry, less often than, but interchangeable with, their references to science and emotion. In the controversy over *Silent Spring*, however, her critics' references to emotion would become by far the most prevalent.

26. As quoted in Brooks, *House of Life*, 132. Throughout her government career, Carson had signed her works "R. L. Carson" so readers would assume that she was a man, and thus a credible source. Lear, *Witness for Nature*, 503, n. 69.

27. Rachel Carson, speech given at the *New York Herald-Tribune* Book and Author Luncheon, Oct. 16, 1951, New York, N.Y., Rachel Carson Papers, Beinecke Library, Yale University. Reprinted in Carson, *Lost Woods*, 76–82; quote found at 77.

28. Rachel Carson, "Remarks at the Acceptance of the National Book Award for Nonfiction," in Carson, *Lost Woods*, 91. The quote continues: "[I] wonder if we have not too long been looking through the wrong end of the telescope. We have looked first at man with his vanities and greed, and at his problems of a day or a year; and then only, and from this biased point of view, we have looked outward at the earth and at the universe of which our earth is so minute a part. Yet these are the great realities, and against them we see our human problems in a new perspective. Perhaps if we reversed the telescope and looked at man down these long vistas, we should find less time and inclination to plan for our own destruction" (in Brooks, *House of Life*, 128).

29. Rachel Carson, "Design for Nature Writing," remarks made on the acceptance of the John Burroughs Medal for excellence in nature writing,

Apr. 7, 1952, New York, N.Y., in *The Atlantic Naturalist* (May-August 1952), 232–34, reprinted in Carson, *Lost Woods*, 96.

30. Carson, *Lost Woods*, 94.

31. Ibid. Also see her comments from her National Book Award acceptance speech: Rachel Carson, "Remarks at the Acceptance of the National Book Award for Nonfiction," in *Lost Woods*, 90–92.

32. For example, in the published version of "Help Your Child to Wonder," Carson wrote: "Once the emotions have been aroused—a sense of the beautiful, the excitement of the new and the unknown, a feeling of sympathy, pity, admiration or love—then we wish for knowledge about the object of our emotional response. Once found, it has lasting meaning" (Rachel Carson, "Help Your Child to Wonder," *Women's Home Companion* 83 (July 1956), 24–27, 46–48, 46).

33. While Carson's take was special, it was not exceptional; also, it is crucial not to confuse sex with gender in this discussion. On one hand, it is tempting to generalize that Carson left the world of science—a restricted masculine vision of nature—for nature writing. However, some of the nature writers whose intuitive connections with nature and place most inspired Carson were also men: Richard Jeffries, Henry Beston, Loren Eiseley, Henry Tomlinson. (For example, see Rachel Carson to Dorothy Freeman, Letter, Mar. 4, 1961, in *Always, Rachel*, 354–55.) Carson and these male fellow nature writers were all part of a tradition that had to go outside science to express alternative visions of nature. Certainly the dominant paradigm of the sciences was more welcoming for men. However, just as Carson did, many men also had to somehow escape or go beyond the world of scientific investigation in order to gain emotional access to nature. (The last part of this paragraph comes almost verbatim from an e-mail from Kevin Armitage. Communication on file with author.) Where Carson becomes exceptional in her integrated take on nature is where she went next—considering humans as ecological beings.

34. As quoted in Lear, *Witness for Nature*, 494, n. 18.

35. Rachel Carson, "The Real World Around Us," speech given at the Theta Sigma Phi Matrix Round Table Dinner, Apr. 21, 1954, Columbus, Ohio, Rachel Carson Papers, Beinecke Library, Yale University. Reprinted in Rachel Carson, *Lost Woods*, 147–63; quote found at 160.

36. Lear, *Witness for Nature*, 261.

37. Rachel Carson to Dorothy Freeman, Letter, Feb. 1, 1956, in *Always, Rachel*, 148; see also Lear, *Witness for Nature*, 262.

38. Lear, *Witness for Nature*, 309.

39. Hazlett, "The Story of *Silent Spring* and the Ecological Turn."

40. Thanks to Nancy Jackson, Lisa Sideris, and Donald Worster. Linda Lear has, as always, provided moral support and inspiration. While he might not remember it (the process took a while), this chapter sprang in part from Lawrence Buell's recommendations on two of my dissertation chapters. The original research for this project was carried out thanks to the Linda Hall Library of Science, Technology, and Engineering, Woodrow Wilson Foundation, Society for the History of Technology, University of Kansas and Amherst College.

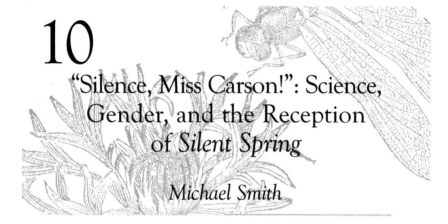

10

"Silence, Miss Carson!": Science, Gender, and the Reception of *Silent Spring*

Michael Smith

The "control of nature" is a phrase conceived in arrogance, born of the Neanderthal age of biology and philosophy, when it was supposed that nature exists for the convenience of man. The concepts and practices of applied entomology for the most part date from that Stone Age of science. It is our alarming misfortune that so primitive a science has armed itself with the most modern and terrible weapons, and that in turning them against the insects it has also turned them against the earth.[1]

Thus did Rachel Carson conclude her most controversial work, a book that has since been compared to Harriet Beecher Stowe's *Uncle Tom's Cabin* for its capacity to awaken Americans out of ethical and moral somnolence and to Darwin's *On the Origin of Species* for its challenge to the dominant scientific paradigm.[2] Despite being largely a synthesis of studies showing the ecological toll pesticides and other agri-chemicals were exacting, *Silent Spring*—which first appeared as an abridged serialization in the *New Yorker* in the summer of 1962—and its conclusions came as a shocking revelation to most Americans. Following on the heels of the thalidomide debacle and recent publicity about the danger of nuclear fallout, *Silent Spring* reached an audience already anxious about the brave new world of chemicals and atomic

This chapter originally appeared in *Feminist Studies*, Volume 27, Number 3 (Fall 2001): 733-52. It is reproduced here with permission of *Feminist Studies*, Inc.

energy.[3] Carson's invocation of Albert Schweitzer's epitaph to humanity in the introduction to her book—"Man has lost the capacity to foresee and to forestall. He will end by destroying the earth"—powerfully primed readers for her account of how illusory humanity's control of nature really is, a most dangerous kind of self-deception. And readers responded. The mailroom at the *New Yorker* received a deluge of letters in support of Carson, as did the mailrooms on Capitol Hill and at the White House.

Carson's broadside against the petrochemical industry, the United States Department of Agriculture, and research universities, and the public support it generated posed a grave and immediate threat to the economic interests and institutional integrity of these entities. Collectively they mounted a frantic public relations campaign to denounce Carson and her collaborators, bringing to bear all the nefarious machinery of the public relations industry.[4]

The history of this effort to discredit Carson is already well-covered scholarly terrain.[5] But although these studies have probed the virulent and ad hominem rhetoric of the attacks against Carson, no one has really scrutinized the gendered nature of these criticisms both of Carson as a person and scientist and of her vision for the praxis of science.[6] The story of how Rachel Carson and her work were received by her mostly male critics is important for both the history of science and the history of women, for this reception illuminates quite starkly the gendered ways in which Western culture has constructed science. Philosophers of science Sandra G. Harding and Evelyn Fox Keller have led the way in identifying and offering correctives to the androcentrism inherent in the evolution of Western science and the effect this has had on women practitioners of science in Western culture. The criticism of Rachel Carson's work as a scientist serves as an important case study for exploring the very cultural dynamics philosophers of science such as Harding and Keller have been urging scholars to address.[7] Moreover, through her use of metaphors about a balance of nature—precisely the language that so incensed many of her critics—Carson crafted a vision of nature that would resonate well with the philosophy of ecofeminism that began to develop a decade after *Silent Spring* was published.

Through an examination of the avalanche of press coverage that followed the publication of *Silent Spring*, I will argue that Carson posed a threat to her detractors not merely because she had marshaled a scientifically sound indictment of the indiscriminate use of chemicals in the United States and the world. Carson was also threatening because she was a woman, an independent scholar whose sex and lack of institutional ties placed her outside the nexus of the production and application of conventional scientific knowledge. In an insightful observation about the plight of women scientists in the Cold War era, historian Margaret Rossiter describes how well-trained women scientists "were, to use some military terms of the period, 'camouflaged' as housewives, mothers, and 'other' and 'stockpiled' in cities and college towns across America...ready but uncalled for the big emergency that never came."[8]

Carson, in a sense, called herself to address a big emergency. Her scientific credentials included a master's degree in marine biology from Johns Hopkins University and considerable work toward a Ph.D. Her family's financial circumstances in the Depression obliged Carson to abandon her doctoral work in favor of a job with the Bureau of Fisheries (later called the Fish and Wildlife Service). Despite her degree, her well-respected research for a government agency, and two best-selling books on ocean biology in the 1950s, she was attacked by critics of *Silent Spring* for both her science and her training.[9]

The gendered language used to discredit Carson was really quite extraordinary, as we shall see. In order to assess why *Silent Spring*—considered apart from its author—proved to be such a provocative book, I will also examine some of the rhetorical flourishes Carson employed. As the quote cited at the beginning of this chapter illustrates, Carson had a vision of the world as an organic system, a living organism. Insofar as humans needed to exploit it, humans had to achieve a delicate balancing act, a tenderness, if you will. As historian Carolyn Merchant and others have pointed out, the scientific revolution of the sixteenth and seventeenth centuries reordered the human perception of the natural world in mechanistic terms. "The world we have lost was organic"—so Merchant begins *The Death of Nature*, her pioneering work on the shift in attitudes toward nature in early modern Europe. Merchant's organic model of relations between humans and nature included the perception of nature as a living, *feminine* organism requiring a special kind of stewardship, one that demanded full reciprocity in human-nature interactions. For Merchant, the most problematic result of the scientific revolution was the fundamental reconstruction of nature as a machine comprised of discrete, comprehensible, controllable bits. Male scientists came to conceive of nature as an unpredictable harridan in need of constraint and mastery, and the notion of nature as a partner eroded. The quest to dominate a female nature paralleled and reinforced the cultural trend toward the increased subordination of women in society.[10]

This, indeed, is the position ecofeminists have staked out in the cultural debates over ecological consciousness: as the "lost world" of a more reciprocal relationship between humans and nature and between men and women has succumbed to various forms of domination by men and male-constructed science, women and nature have suffered together. By positing that women are innately more connected to the natural world (retaining the construction of nature as female) and instinctively conceptualize the world in organic terms, ecofeminists have argued that reestablishing the old notions of reciprocity is a task that should fall predominately to women. While the tacit assumption that women are biologically (rather than merely culturally) ordained to be better stewards of nature remains a controversial tenet of ecofeminism, the ecofeminist critique of culture helps us see that the roots of the oppression of women extend beyond economics.[11] Although the label of ecofeminist would be an anachronistic one for Carson, she clearly evinced a reverence for the natural world that falls under Merchant's rubric of a lost perspective. She also proved to be a catalyst for the then embryonic environmental movement, a movement that has had a disproportionate number of women as its motive force.[12]

SILENCING SPRING

In their profoundly disturbing study of the public relations industry, media critics John Stauber and Sheldon Rampton relate the story of how the public relations men for the chemical industry and the Department of Agriculture got wind of Carson's work even before its appearance in the *New Yorker*. By the end of the summer of 1962, when the book version of Carson's study was being prepared for press, the anti-Carson machinery was already moving in high gear. Monsanto published a parody of *Silent Spring* in its in-house magazine entitled "The Desolate Year" which described a world overrun by insects.[13] The Velsicol Chemical Corporation attempted to convince Houghton Mifflin not to publish the book at all, linking Carson to "food faddists" and other "fringe" groups. They also invoked the imperatives of the Cold War, contending that an overly credulous and uninformed public might call for the elimination of pesticides and that "our supply of food will be reduced to East-curtain parity." Finally, they threatened a libel suit against Carson's "innuendoes."[14] None of these attempts to forestall the publication of *Silent Spring* was successful. So the chemical companies and other entities whose profit margins were threatened by Carson's findings resorted to counterattack through negative book reviews and opinion pieces in major periodicals. These attacks appeared in all forms of periodicals, from trade journals such as *Chemical and Engineering News* to popular news magazines such as *Time* and *U.S. News and World Report* to peer-reviewed science journals such as *Science*. The popularity and appeal of *Silent Spring* developed in spite of this barrage of discrediting assessments. But the rapid disappearance of the issue of pesticides from the national radar screen of public opinion by 1965; the assault on Rachel Carson herself, even in obituaries following her death from breast cancer in 1964; and the cheery "See, there were plenty of birds this spring" rejoinders that appeared in 1963 and 1964 all serve as suggestive, if not conclusive, evidence that the anti-Carson rhetoric did have a chilling effect on the discourse.

For the remainder of this section of the chapter I will examine the dissenting voices that sought to silence *Silent Spring*. These critics fell roughly into two categories. In the first were those who were members of the scientific community. The writers were almost all men. Almost all of them found the research undertaken by Carson for the book to be suspect; many of them questioned Carson's credentials, calling her an "amateur" or a mere "scientific journalist." Many also dismissed her writing as "emotional" and lacking the kind of cold, rational risk assessment required of modern applied science. Reading the reviews today one even senses some reviewers implicitly drawing a line between the "hard" science of chemistry and the "soft" science of biology. The second category of critics was from the popular press, the defenders of Cold War–inflected notions of progress and justified means to ends. These writers also engaged in gendered critiques of what they called Carson's emotionalism and her vision of progress rooted in "sentimentalism" rather than reality. These critiques of *Silent Spring* appeared in magazines whose readership ranged across the spectrum, from *Good Housekeeping* to *Sports Illustrated* to *Life*. To be sure *Silent Spring* received numerous favorable reviews in the popular press. But even some of these reflected the gender biases noted above.

It is not surprising that some of the most vicious attacks on Rachel Carson and *Silent Spring* came from those with the greatest economic stake in the widespread use of chemical pesticides. As noted above, many chemical companies themselves launched anti-Carson campaigns. But the reviews of *Silent Spring* that appeared in some of the trade journals reflected a hysteria that was real, even as they wrongly accused Carson of hysteria herself. The most sexist, most unbalanced review of *Silent Spring* appeared in *Chemical and Engineering News* in October 1962, shortly after the publication of the book. William Darby of the Vanderbilt University School of Medicine attacked Carson from the first paragraph of his review, entitled "Silence, Miss Carson!" The title itself (which the journal later admitted was its own creation, not Darby's) expresses the prevailing attitude among many of Carson's critics that she was an uninformed woman who was speaking of that which she knew not. Worse, she was speaking in a man's world, the inner sanctum of masculine science in which, like the sanctuary of a strict Calvinist sect, female silence was expected.[15] Darby began his review by lumping Carson with groups he considered to be antimodern "freaks." *Silent Spring* would appeal to readers such as "the organic gardeners, the anti-fluoride leaguers, the worshippers of 'natural foods,' and those who cling to the philosophy of a vital principle, and pseudo-scientists and faddists," wrote Darby.[16] He then invoked a series of father figure scientists who supported the use of pesticides and whom Carson supposedly ignored. "It is doubtful that many readers can bear to wade through its high-pitched sequences of anxieties," Darby continued, impugning Carson's critical tone in terms all too reminiscent of sexist critiques of so-called feminine styles of discourse.[17] But, Darby went on, if readers were moved by Carson's pleas and her invocation of Schweitzer and other critics of uncontrolled modernization, their view augured the end of all human progress, reversion to a passive social state devoid of technology, scientific medicine, agriculture, sanitation, or education. It means disease, epidemics, starvation, misery, and suffering incomparable and intolerable to modern man. Indeed, social, educational, and scientific development is prefaced on the conviction that man's lot will be and is being improved by greater understanding of and thereby increased ability to control or mold those forces responsible for man's suffering, misery, and deprivation.[18]

Francis Bacon would have been proud of such a manifesto advocating man's role as conqueror, master, and controller of nature. Here we see not a judicious review of a controversial book but a defense of the ideology of modern science and progress against feminine sentimentality, the frightened growl of cornered dogma. It is worth noting that many readers of *Chemical and Engineering News* objected passionately to Darby's characterization of Carson and *Silent Spring* in his review.[19] But Darby was speaking as someone whose power was being undermined.

Another prominent male physician wrote an only slightly less corrosive review for a trade journal with a slightly different orientation, *Nutrition Reviews*. For Frederick Stare, Carson's "emotional picture" of a possible disaster disqualified her as a scientist and raised questions about her real commitment to humanity for "the broad application of a brilliant technology" has allowed man to "stave off starvation, disease, and social and political unrest." Carson's interrogation of the application of science was, in Stare's mind, naive at best and unpatriotic at worst.[20] Miss Carson, Stare concluded, was no scientist. Her use of phrases such as "never ending stream of chemicals...now pervading the world" and words such as "lurks" and "engulf" in reference to chemical residue consigned her to the role of sentimental essayist. Ignoring Carson's distinguished career as a marine biologist, Stare concluded: "In Miss Carson's case, research limited to selective reading, plus the urging of 'friends' with special interests, is certainly no diploma of equivalency for the academic training and experience required for authority."[21]

Reviews and essays about *Silent Spring* that appeared in scientific journals did not contain such blatant attacks on Carson's character, though most were no less critical of her conclusions. Reviewer after reviewer—in all genres of periodicals—damned Carson's meddling in "progress," condemned her for proposing "unrealistic" alternatives. I will return to the rhetoric Carson used and why it may have so inflamed those who subscribed to conventional notions of progress, but it is worth pointing out here that criticisms of Carson's science often alluded to her "soft" approach to a natural world that was man's adversary. There can be little doubt her belief that the "battle" with nature was not a zero-sum game, that our relationship with the nonhuman part of nature should not be characterized as a battle at all, threatened an entire sector of the economy whose profits were predicated on an adversarial formulation.

One conceit that Carson employed again and again in *Silent Spring* is "the balance of nature." Such a view of the natural world and the place of humanity in it raised the ire of University of Wisconsin agricultural bacteriologist I. L. Baldwin, among others. In his review for *Science* Baldwin wrote: "It is certain that modern agriculture and modern public health, indeed, modern civilization, could not exist without an unrelenting war against the return of a true balance of nature."[22] Like Darby, Baldwin deployed the assertion that from science had sprung modernity, that alternatives to the existing practice of science were antimodern and would inevitably result in humanity being cast back into the cauldron of competition with the rest of the natural world, a nature red in tooth and claw. Besides, Baldwin wrote, "The problem Rachel Carson dramatizes is not a new one"; competent men were working within the dominant scientific paradigm to make necessary corrections: "[Their] reports are not dramatically written, and they were not intended to be best sellers. They are, however, the result of careful study by a wide group of scientists, and they represent balanced judgements in areas in which emotional appeals tend to over-balance sound judgement based on facts."[23] Rachel Carson's science, then, was "unbalanced" and "emotional." Restraint—that is, protecting the status quo—was the most "rational" course. Others criticized Carson in a similar vein. Her use of the image of a "fragile and exquisite songbird dying in paralytic convulsions" was, according to molecular biologist Thomas H. Jukes in *American Scientist*, an unforgivably sentimental tactic for raising awareness about the issue of "possible" pesticide misuse. Jukes condemned those followers of John Muir who wanted to see his vision of pure nature preserved but would not "adopt his diet of tea and bread crusts," those hypocritical idealists who wanted to have both modernity and a balance of nature: not possible, he flatly asserted.[24] (I. L. Baldwin had made a similar claim, stating that the elimination or even significant reduction of pesticides would mean a "back-to-the-farm migration for millions."[25])

These writers and others were trying to preserve the public's credulity in the ability of science and technology to solve both the problems presented by nature and those that developed as unforeseen consequences of applied science. Even one of the more balanced reviews of *Silent Spring* in a scientific magazine had this agenda at its core. "I suspect that the inevitable way to progress for man, as for nature," wrote Cornell University zoologist LaMont C. Cole in *Scientific American*, "is to try new things in an almost haphazard manner, discarding the failures and building upon the successes."[26] It was just this blind faith Carson was trying to shake. The *New York Times* opined even before Carson's book appeared: "she warns of the dangers of misuse and overuse by a public that has become mesmerized by the notion that chemists are the possessors of divine wisdom and that nothing but benefit can emerge from their test tubes."[27]

That a woman should challenge the mesmerists, that she should try to shake Americans from their complacent trust in their own government and most powerful corporations, dismayed not just the chemical companies and their colleagues in research universities. Her *New Yorker* pieces drew overwhelming praise from readers but a vocal minority objected to her and her findings strenuously. One writer wrote:

> Miss Rachel Carson's reference to the selfishness of insecticide manufacturers probably reflects her Communist sympathies, like a lot of our writers these days. We can live without birds and animals, but, as the current market slump shows, we cannot live without business. As for insects, isn't it just like a woman to be scared to death of a few little bugs! As long as we have the H-bomb everything will be O.K.[28]

If letters from cranks had been the extent of the public complaints against Carson in the popular press, one could less confidently assert that gender biases from the culture at large deeply inflected the reception of her work. But when a magazine with the prestige of *Time* called her findings and writing "patently unsound," "hysterically emphatic," and an "emotional outburst," the roots of the criticism, the reason Carson was so threatening, becomes clear: she was a woman and she was challenging a cornerstone of industrial capitalism with a passion considered unbecoming to a scientist. The *Time* piece also trotted out the familiar criticism about the "balance of nature":

> Lovers of wildlife often rhapsodize about the "balance of nature" that keeps all living creatures in harmony, but scientists realistically point out that the balance of nature was upset thousands of years ago when man's invention of weapons made him the king of the beasts. The balance has never recovered its equilibrium; man is the dominant species on his planet, and as his fields, pastures and cities spread across the land, lesser species are extirpated, pushed into refuge areas, or domesticated.[29]

The Catholic periodical of record, *America*, also savaged *Silent Spring*; again Carson's "emotionalism" and lack of balance were noted.[30] The *National Review* called the book "simply a long emotional attack," Carson's approach "emotional and one-sided," an "obscurantist appeal to the emotions." Invoking the need for "rational" and "scientific" (as opposed to emotional or irrational and sentimental), the review concluded by saying that "[the problem of pesticides] is Burkean, and involves a careful weighing of advantages and disadvantages with due regard to our lack of perfect knowledge."[31] *Newsweek* wondered about the critics' view of *Silent Spring* as "innuendo" and having "the quality of gossip."[32] "Her extravagant language..., her unscientific use of innuendo…,her pantheism…,and her disregard for the studies of the problem by her fellow scientists in industry, the university, and government service" (mostly men of course), rendered her study completely unreliable, commented another reviewer.[33] Even a profile of Carson in *Life* purporting to be a balanced assessment of the woman and her work could not overlook the implications of Carson's sex, noting that "for all her gentle mien, Rachel Carson, 55, who is unmarried but not a feminist…is a formidable adversary." The phrasing suggests that were Carson a feminist she would indeed be a subversive force, for (with a wink to the reader) *Life* subscribers all know what *those* women are like. And yet there is also in these words the implication that Carson's unmarried status is itself an expression of some deficiency, that were she married none of this controversy would have developed. Presumably she would have instead been practicing home economics and recognizing the overwhelming benefits of pesticide-enhanced agricultural bounty for the kitchen. There is, in fact, no evidence to suggest Carson openly advocated for women's rights, though her own struggle with the scientific establishment served as a feminist statement. By the second page of the profile, Carson had morphed into a pesky gadfly, a "good indignant crusader." Finally, the article concluded, like troublesome Mother Nature herself, "Hurricane Rachel" must be endured, and becalmed, and then "the real dangers to public health [could] be evaluated, and then controlled by skilled medical men."[34]

Like many of the articles about Carson and *Silent Spring*, the *Life* profile featured photographs of Carson, few of which depicted her in the guise of a professional scientist. There were none of the usual press release–style photographs of a white-coated notable scientist in his lab looking authoritative or the dauntless field researcher above the volcano's mouth. Instead, Carson was almost always photographed with her cat or sitting in the woods surrounded by children, gesturing at the natural wonders of the world. Only occasionally did a photo of her at a microscope appear. By implication, these photos located Carson in the world of the school marm, not the world of science. She was a teacher—to some a subversive, dangerous one—but not someone who was engaged in meaningful scientific research.[35]

Even one year after the publication of the book, even after a commission appointed by President Kennedy had sustained many of Carson's conclusions about pesticides, the assault on Carson in print continued. An early collaborator on *Silent Spring*, Edwin Diamond, described how he simply could not work with a woman who let emotion interfere with accuracy and whose final product relied on the same shock techniques and distortions employed by Joseph McCarthy.[36] The story "Life-Giving Spray" (featuring the obligatory photograph of Carson as sentimental bird-watcher) appeared in the quintessential male magazine, *Sports Illustrated*, and concluded that one year after

Carson's frightening indictment wildlife seemed more abundant than ever, and was, in fact, aided by pesticide use.[37]

Even the airwaves were filled with vilification of Carson, with critiques once again suffused with gendered notions of science and who does "good" science. In a widely distributed speech of January 1963, the president of the Nutrition Foundation, C. G. King, like Frederick Stare and others cited above, condemned Carson as a fellow traveler with all of the fringe elements of society: "Food faddists, health quacks, and special interest groups are promoting her book as if it were scientifically irreproachable and written by a scientist. Neither is true...and [Carson] misses the very essence of science in not being objective either in citing the evidence or in its interpretation."[38] The frequently interviewed biochemist and chemical industry spokesman Robert H. White-Stevens, whose British accent and grandfatherly appearance evidently conferred upon him a trustworthiness unmerited by his intemperate remarks, proved to be the king of anti-Carson critics with variations on the following characterization of *Silent Spring*:

> Her book is littered with crass assumptions and gross misinterpretations, misquotations, and misunderstandings, clearly calculated to mislead the uninformed.... Her book will come to be regarded in time as a gross distortion of the actual facts, essentially unsupported by either scientific experimental evidence or practical experience in the field.[39]

For these men, whose power in shaping society through expert scientific advice hung on their credibility as both protectors of the public interest and exemplars of "true" science, Rachel Carson's conclusions and analysis were terrifying. Carson's critics—mostly men, mostly white, mostly affiliated with some bureaucratic institution—recognized the general public's willingness to accept science as it was being practiced as the ultimate authority. They therefore took two approaches to discrediting Carson, both of which often led the reader to make inferences about how gender inflected her science and both of which sought to shore up the foundations of science that Carson's critique of modernity had shaken. Carson's critics tried to reassure the world that even if some of what Carson alleged was true, the mistakes resulted from misapplication, not misguided science. Science, they argued, was almost solely responsible for the extraordinary standard of living Americans were experiencing by the early 1960s. To heed Carson's warnings would be tantamount to killing the goose that was laying the golden egg. Since the Progressive Era when the federal government had begun regulating American society in earnest for the first time, the burgeoning American middle class had been willing to accept safety regulations only to the extent that such regulations did not incur large increases in the price of consumer goods. As was the case with the meat-packing industry in the first decade of the twentieth century following the publication of Upton Sinclair's *The Jungle*, those who stood to profit directly from the heavy use of pesticides couched their response to *Silent Spring* with the consumer's wallet in mind, thereby striking a putative balance—if it can be called such a thing—between public health safety and affordability. "[Because of pesticides] today's American housewives have the widest choice of fruits and vegetables, and meats and dairy—at prices to fit their budgets," characterizes this rhetoric.[40]

"THE OTHER ROAD"

Something other than just the specter of bad science piqued the ire of Carson's critics. Although Carson's job in *Silent Spring* was largely that of a synthesizer, her conclusions pointed to the practice of a profoundly different relationship between humans and nature than that which obtained in early 1960s America. Carson avoided making prescriptions that amounted to a call for the overthrow of the existing order. Her persistent invocation of "balance" and the rhetoric she employed in advocating a change in the application of science amounted to a subversive act, however. This challenge to the order of things, even when it was not a conscious one, inspired the modern environmental movement and undergirds much of what is now called ecofeminism. For the remainder of this chapter I will examine a few passages from *Silent Spring* that illustrate the radical nature of Carson's critique and briefly outline both her legacy and the legacy of the public relations campaign against her.

In his essay on the politics of nature in *Silent Spring*, Yaakov Garb argues that Carson was not really very radical. She was, he contends, content to practice *realpolitik* to a certain degree; that is, she deliberately avoided connecting the injustices of the social environment that to a certain extent preordained the injustices to the natural environment. To argue that capitalism generally, not merely the corporate greed of chemical manufacturers, was responsible for irresponsible science was not, obviously, Carson's agenda. But, as Garb points out, *Our Synthetic Environment*, a book by the anarchist Murray Bookchin (writing pseudonymously as Lewis Herber) published only months before *Silent Spring* and making the same indictment against pesticides using many of the same sources, received little attention. Why? Because Bookchin's polemic views pesticides merely as a symptom of an economic system that is pathological to its core. Without social justice, he argues, there can be no environmental justice. He hoped to leverage a popular overthrow of the status quo through his exposé of government and corporate complicity in the poisoning of the environment and people. Bookchin's critique of society was simply unpalatable to even many of those "fringe" groups with whom Carson was speciously associated. Garb sees *Silent Spring* as a far less radical critique of society than Bookchin's. Carson, Garb contends, invoked the "balance of nature" because it at once resonated with an antimodern impulse that resides in many denizens of late-twentieth-century society and because it was sufficiently vague not to be threatening to most of society. He writes:

> Terms like "nature," "natural," and the "balance of nature" have great discursive force not in spite of but because of their fuzziness. Their multiple connotations and self-evident (thus unexamined) definition within the community that shares them enable protean versatility. We add great force to any argument by adducing the "natural" to it, so long as no one asks carefully what we mean by the term. If they do, it will often turn out that nature (and its cognates) are not pre-existing, ontologically firm objects or conditions in the natural world, but a reification of human criteria and definitions.[41]

Whatever the wide-ranging resonance of these terms in the popular consciousness, for Carson they had very specific meanings, anchored in a vision of that world Carolyn Merchant called organic.

I agree that Carson did not explicitly make the same sweeping indictments as Bookchin; however, she did offer a vision of science that expressed a reconsideration of the Baconian model that has more or less guided Western science since the seventeenth century. In the first pages of *Silent Spring*—the "Fable for Tomorrow" that so many critics held up as evidence that Carson was a storyteller and nothing more—she evokes a world which, having been treated as a machine more inorganic than vital for so many centuries, has died. "No witchcraft...had silenced the rebirth of new life in this stricken world," Carson wrote. "The people had done it themselves."[42] The scientists, mostly, had done it, with homeowners and farmers abetting, largely unaware of what they were doing. Time and again Carson refers to man's quest for dominion over nature: his "assaults upon the environment," his "[procession] toward his announced goal of the conquest of nature," his tearing of "the earth's green mantle."[43]

Carson's working titles for *Silent Spring* demonstrate that she wanted to bring out the theme of man's relentless struggle to subdue nature more than she did. At various stages of the writing process Carson wanted to call her book "Control of Nature" and "Man against the Earth."[44] And she indicts the dictatorial nature of science and its star chamber of practitioners who make decisions that affect everyone, destroying a part of the world without consent. Someone had appointed himself God. "Who has made the decision that sets in motion these chains of poisonings, this ever-widening wave of death that spreads out, like ripples when a pebble is dropped into a still pond?" She asks:

> Who has decided—who has the *right* to decide—for the countless legions of people who were not consulted that the supreme value is a world without insects, even though it be also a sterile world ungraced by the curving wing

of a bird in flight? The decision is that of the authoritarian . . .; he has made
it during a moment of inattention by millions to whom beauty and the
ordered world of nature still have a meaning that is deep and imperative.[45]

"Man with a spray gun" is a phrase Carson employs to describe the militaris-
tic fervor with which pesticide users have carried out their project to eradicate all pests. This "man with a spray gun" has ignored the balance of nature,
destroying as pests insects that prey on insects even more destructive to the
sculpted environment of humans. There are laws more fundamental than
Bacon's and Newton's. Carson argues that "The balance of nature...is a
complex, precise, and highly integrated system of relationships between
living things which cannot safely be ignored any more than the law of gravity
can be defied with impunity by a man perched on the edge of a cliff....Man,
too, is part of this balance."[46] Carson was not, of course, the first to argue
that humans should attend more carefully to ecological equilibrium. But in a
way more pointed than anyone before her she identified the profoundest
consequence of humanity's tampering with this balance: *humans themselves.*
For Carson, one of the most disturbing aspects of the chemical world of the
postwar era was how it compromised future generations. "[Chemicals] occur
in the mother's milk and probably in the tissues of the unborn child," she
wrote.[47] We had engaged in an experiment with no control group, Carson
worried, a terribly dangerous game. The illusion that human beings, by
virtue of their power to manipulate nature, were immune to the diffusion of
toxins into the environment was no longer tenable after *Silent Spring.*

CODA

The controversy stirred up by *Silent Spring* continues to this day. A presidential commission and congressional investigation into the dangers posed by
pesticides led to stricter guidelines about the testing, labeling, and application
of pesticides. The road from *Silent Spring* led directly to the creation of the
Environmental Protection Agency (EPA). In the years since the publication of
Silent Spring, other scientists have largely corroborated Carson's assertions
about the damage chemical pesticides do to the environment.[48] In spite of
this, the addiction of the industrialized world and, increasingly, the developing world, to powerful poisons for eradicating the "pests" that feast on the
vast acreages of industrial monoculture is as strong as ever. Perhaps even more
troubling has been the ever-growing acceptance of genetically engineered agricultural products, many of which are genetically engineered to resist herbicides. The continued complication of agriculture makes the production of
food increasingly reliant on corporate interests, whose primary interest, of
course, is profit. Though some writers have read Carson as ignoring this ele-

ment of the pesticide problem, they have overlooked several searing indictments of corporate greed. "[This] is...an era dominated by industry," Carson
wrote in the second chapter of Silent Spring, "in which the right to make a
dollar at whatever cost is seldom challenged. When the public protests, confronted with some obvious evidence of damaging results of pesticide applications, it is fed little tranquilizing pills of half truth."[49]

Another kind of opiate for the masses perhaps? Despite the initial uproar
over pesticides there was a marked decline in interest in the issue in the general public by 1965.[50] Environmental activists kept the issue on the table but
attention soon shifted to other social problems: student unrest, the Vietnam
War, racial tensions. Though chemical pollution of the environment
remained (and remains) a very serious problem, the loudest advocates of cur-
tailing the use of pesticides were, ironically, the much disparaged "food faddists," organic gardeners and farmers, and grassroots activists whose own lives
had been directly affected by environmental toxins.[51]

"Have we fallen into a mesmerized state that makes us accept as
inevitable that which is inferior or detrimental, as though having lost the will
or the vision to demand that which is good?" Rachel Carson asked in 1962.[52]
When her predictions of the power of environmental toxins to alter human
germplasm and in some cases disrupt human reproductive capacities have
come true, yet the general public seems largely unconcerned, one has to
wonder about the extent of mesmerism. In Our Stolen Future: Are We
Threatening Our Fertility, Intelligence, and Survival? biologists Theo Colborn
and John Peterson Meyers and science reporter Dianne Dumanoski document just how chlorine-based synthetic chemicals cause serious reproductive
problems in both animals and humans.[53] But the book made much less of a
splash than Silent Spring, in part because the public relations efforts of the
chemical industry worked to undermine the credibility of the book even
before it reached the bookstores. The stakes were even higher for the industry
this time around because Colborn and her collaborators focused on the way
environmental toxins victimized women and children, both already represented by powerful activist organizations. "No definitive proof!" cried the
chemical industry and agribusiness, and that seemed to placate all but the
most determined critics in the booming 1990s economy.[54]

And so it seems we have not learned the moral of Rachel Carson's "Fable
for Tomorrow," her story about a world with no birdsongs, no edible fish, and
poisoned people that opens Silent Spring. The alternative science (with its
view toward maintaining a balanced relationship between humans and their
environment) that she and a minority of others have advocated languishes on
the fringe of the scientific and cultural discourse. Sandra Harding has argued
that a feminist critique of science must have as its agenda the illumination of
both science's progressive and regressive tendencies, of science's inherently
political nature, of science as a social process. Only after such exposure might

it be possible "to use for liberating ends sciences that are apparently so intimately involved in Western, bourgeois, and masculine projects."[55] Rachel Carson would not have assessed Western science in so many words but her indictments in *Silent Spring* most certainly serve to illuminate these dimensions of science. Without discarding science's benefits to humanity Carson shook her finger at the careless, regressive path science had taken with regard to pesticides. With its call to action *Silent Spring* was a politic statement and its very publication expressed the sentiment that science is a social process.

The indignation that has greeted the publication of *Silent Spring* and subsequent critiques of chemical damage to the environment, the campaign that has so successfully painted them as emanations from the radical fringe of society, is not merely about good science versus bad science. The origins of the debate lie with morality, in questions about how to define moral responsibility: moral science versus immoral science. Carson believed that humankind's rigid, impatient attempt to order the natural world constituted an abrogation of moral responsibility to both the human community and the rest of the natural world. "Through all these new, imaginative, and creative approaches to the problem of sharing our earth with other creatures there runs a constant theme," Rachel Carson wrote in *Silent Spring*.[56] And only when we revere all life, and develop a science that embraces accommodation rather than conquest will we evolve beyond that "Neanderthal age of biology," and its attendant equivocating morality.[57]

NOTES

1. Rachel Carson, *Silent Spring* (Boston: Houghton Mifflin, 1994 [1962]), 297.

2. See Linda Lear, "Bombshell in Beltsville: The USDA and the Challenge of *Silent Spring*," *Agricultural History* 66 (1992): 151–71, 152; and Paul Brooks, *The House of Life: Rachel Carson at Work* (Boston: Houghton Mifflin, 1972), 293, for these comparisons.

3. See Ralph Lutts, "Chemical Fallout: Rachel Carson's *Silent Spring*, Radioactive Fallout, and the Environmental Movement," *Environmental Review* 9 (1985): 211–25.

4. See John Stauber and Sheldon Rampton, *Toxic Waste Is Good for You!: Lies, Damn Lies and the Public Relations Industry* (Monroe, Me.: Common Courage Press, 1995), 123–27.

5. See for example, Linda J. Lear, "Bombshell in Beltsville," 151–71; ibid., *Rachel Carson: Witness for Nature* (New York: Henry Holt, 1997), 396-456;

Frank Graham, *Since "Silent Spring"* (Boston: Houghton Mifflin, 1970), 48-81; and Brooks, *House of Life*, 293-307.

6. In this context my use of ad hominem is especially apt. Ad hominem, literally meaning "to the man," is significant because in many instances, as we shall see, Carson was attacked precisely because she was *not* a man, and did not subscribe to a rational "masculine" vision of dominion over nature. Linda Lear's biography of Carson does address the gender issue, but in a less systematic way than this chapter does. See Lear, *Witness for Nature*, 428-41.

7. Feminist philosophers and historians of science have produced much rich scholarship exploring the cultural construction of Western science. The orientation of this chapter was heavily influenced by Sandra G. Harding's *The Science Question in Feminism* (Ithaca, N.Y.: Cornell University Press, 1986) and *Whose Science? Whose Knowledge?: Thinking from Women's Lives* (Ithaca, N.Y.: Cornell University Press, 1991), and by Evelyn Fox Keller's *Reflections on Gender and Science* (New Haven, Conn.: Yale University Press, 1985). See also Eileen M. Byrne, *Women and Science: The Snark Syndrome* (London: Fulmer Press, 1993), esp. 48-87.

8. Although Carson's position as an independent scholar in 1962 was largely voluntary, she, like hundreds of other women, had encountered barriers to advancement in both government service and higher education her entire career. See Lear, *Witness for Nature*, 54-198. On the discrimination against women scientists generally in this period and earlier see Margaret Rossiter, *Women Scientists in America: Before Affirmative Action, 1940–1972* (Baltimore: Johns Hopkins University Press, 1995), xviii.

9. Carson's *The Sea Around Us* (1950) and *The Edge of the Sea* (1955) were viewed as the musings of a nature writer rather than as emanating from the research of a marine biologist, a reaction that reflects the prevailing attitude among many scientists that popularized science equals watered-down science and that natural history is inferior to physical science.

10. See Carolyn Merchant, *The Death of Nature: Women, Ecology, and the Scientific Revolution* (San Francisco: Harper & Row, 1980).

11. Ecofeminism emerged with the publication of Rosemary Radford Ruether's *New Woman/New Earth: Sexist Ideologies and Human Liberation* (New York: Seabury Press, 1975). For the theoretical foundations of ecofeminism see Merchant, "Ecofeminism and Feminist Theory," in *Reweaving the World: The Emergence of Ecofeminism*, ed. Irene Diamond and Gloria F. Orenstein (San Francisco: Sierra Club Books, 1990). Perhaps the best treatise on ecofeminism is Maria Mies and Vandana Shiva, *Ecofeminism* (Halifax: Fernwood, 1993). See also Vera Norwood, *Made from This Earth: American Women and Nature* (Chapel Hill: University of North Carolina Press, 1993), 261-84. The essentialization of women in their stewardship of the environment is hotly debated

even within the feminist community. See, for example, Cecile Jackson, "Radical Environmental Myths: A Gender Perspective," *New Left Review* 210 (1995): 124-40.

12. On Carson's influence on women in the environmental movement, see Carolyn Merchant, *Earthcare: Women and the Environment* (New York: Routledge, 1995). On the role of women in the environmental movement, see Mary Joy Broton, *Women Pioneers for the Environment* (Boston: Northeastern University Press, 1998).

13. Stauber and Rampton, *Toxic Waste*, 123-27.

14. Letter quoted in Graham, *Since "Silent Spring,"* 49.

15. In this context, David F. Noble's analysis of the persistence of the clerical "mantel" of science with its roots in the exclusively masculine world of medieval science is illuminating. See David F. Noble, *A World Without Women: The Christian Clerical Culture of Western Science* (New York: Knopf, 1992).

16. William Darby, "Silence, Miss Carson!" *Chemical and Engineering News* 40 (Oct. 1, 1962): 60-61, 60.

17. Ibid.

18. Ibid., 60-61.

19. See *Chemical and Engineering News* 40 (Oct. 22, 1962): 5, and (Nov. 5, 1962): 4-5. Among the comments in letters to the editor: Ellie A. Shneour wrote, "the most irresponsible review that I have ever seen," (Nov. 5, 1962): 5; Frank A. Meier wrote, "both the title and the review portray an attitude ill becoming a scientist," (Nov. 5, 1962): 4-5; and Robert J. Good wrote, "Instead of [a] positive type of response to Miss Carson, *C&EN* and Dr. Darby have reacted like a cigarette company executive when somebody asks if smoking causes lung cancer," (Nov. 5, 1962): 5. This last remark is an ironic and fascinating comparison in light of the recent demise of corporate tobacco. Another trade journal, *Chemical Week*, published a critical report of *Silent Spring* and also received letters supporting Carson. See *Chemical Week* 91 (Nov. 3, 1962): 7, and 91 (Oct. 27, 1962): 7.

20. Frederick J. Stare, "Some Comments on *Silent Spring*," *Nutrition Reviews* 21 (January 1963): 1,4.

21. Ibid., 4.

22. I. L. Baldwin, "Chemicals and Pests," *Science* 137 (1962): 1043.

23. Ibid.

24. Thomas H. Jukes, "People and Pesticides," *American Scientist* 51 (September 1963): 355-61, 359, 361.

25. Baldwin, "Chemicals and Pests," 1043.

26. LaMont C. Cole, *Scientific American* 207 (Dec. 1962): 173-180, 176.

27. *New York Times*, July 2, 1962, 28.

28. "In the Mail," *The New Yorker* 71 (Feb. 20 & 27, 1995): 18. As part of its seventieth anniversary issue, *The New Yorker* reprinted a number of letters.

29. "Pesticides: The Price for Progress," *Time*, Sept. 28, 1962, 45-48. This article goes on to describe how modern large-scale agriculture was actually part of the problem: the scale and variety of preindustrial agriculture diminished the damage insects could do. Of interest given the context of this chapter: this critique of *Silent Spring* ran in the "science" section of the magazine; immediately following the savaging of the book was a story about the "new heros of the space program," the "handsome men" of the Apollo program.

30. "Rebuttal to Miss Carson," *America* 107 (Oct. 27, 1962): 944.

31. Gordon Tallock, "Of Mites and Men," *National Review*, Nov. 20, 1962, 398-99. This was the only review that honored Carson with a "Dr." before her name. Although Carson, for financial reasons, never did complete her doctorate, she did receive several honorary doctorates. Although reviewers used "Miss" in keeping with contemporary stylistic convention, many seemed to use it as an epithet as they gleefully castigated her for not being scientific enough.

32. "Hiss of Doom?" *Newsweek*, Aug. 6, 1962, 55.

33. "Every Man His Own Borgia?" *The Economist*, Oct. 20, 1962, 248.

34. "The Gentle Storm Center," *Life*, Oct. 12, 1962, 105-110, 105, 106, 110.

35. This connection of Carson to children was not limited to photographs. Even in reviews critical of *Silent Spring* writers praised her earlier books on the sea for their ability to tap into a childlike sense of wonder. Such descriptions of the ocean, even scrupulously scientific ones, were not threatening; they were more like bedtime stories than nightmarish social criticism.

36. Edwin Diamond, "The Myth of the 'Pesticide Menace,'" *Saturday Evening Post*, Sept. 28, 1963, 16-18. Given the theme of this chapter, I was acutely sensitive to the depiction of women as I conducted my research. The cover of this issue of the *Saturday Evening Post* featured a picture of Vietnam's Madame Nhu and the headline "The ruthless beauty who helped provoke the violence." This was the cultural context in which *Silent Spring* was so hotly debated.

37. Virginia Kraft, "Life-Giving Spray," *Sports Illustrated*, Nov. 18, 1963, 22-25.

38. Quoted in Clark C. Van Fleet, "Silent Spring on the Pacific Slope: A Postscript to Rachel Carson," *Atlantic Monthly*, July, 1963, 81-84, 81.

39. Dr. Robert H. White-Stevens, Address to the Synthetic Organic Chemical Manufacturers Association, April 1963, quoted in "Silent Spring on the Pacific Slope," 82. For descriptions of Dr. White-Stevens' behavior during the debates over pesticides and *Silent Spring*, see Lear, *Witness for Nature*, 437–40.

40. "If You Didn't Have Poison Sprays," *U.S. News and World Report*, June 3, 1963, 74–75, 75.

41. See Yaakov Garb, "The Politics of Nature in Rachel Carson's *Silent Spring*," in *Minding Nature: The Philosophers of Ecology*, ed. David Macauley (New York: Guilford Press, 1996), 229-56, 238, and Lewis Herber (Murray Bookchin), *Our Synthetic Environment* (New York: Knopf, 1962). There is nothing particularly original about Garb's assertion that nature is a cultural construction. See, for example, William Cronon, ed., *Uncommon Ground: Rethinking the Human Place in Nature* (New York: Norton, 1995).

42. Carson, *Silent Spring*, 3. Carson's exoneration of "witchcraft" in this passage connects her more closely to Carolyn Merchant and other ecofeminists than a casual reading might reveal. Merchant goes to great lengths to show how so-called witchcraft was really the persistence of premodern relationships with nature. The persecution of "witches" during the fifteenth through seventeenth centuries was part of the attempt to reconstruct nature and eradicate the organic world of before the scientific revolution. See Merchant's *The Death of Nature*, chap. 4.

43. Carson, *Silent Spring*, 6, 85, 63, respectively.

44. Graham, *Since "Silent Spring,"* 21, 25.

45. Carson, *Silent Spring*, 127.

46. Ibid., 246.

47. Ibid., 16.

48. On *Silent Spring*'s regulatory legacy see Graham, *Since "Silent Spring,"* 266–71, and, especially, H. Patricia Hynes, *The Recurring Silent Spring* (New York: Pergamon Press, 1989). See also Kirkpatrick Sale, *The Green Revolution: The American Environmental Movement, 1962–1992* (New York: Hill & Wang, 1997), 3–28, and Samuel P. Hayes, *Beauty, Health, and Permanence: Environmental Politics in the United States, 1955–1985* (New York: Cambridge University Press, 1987), 177–206.

49. Carson, *Silent Spring*, 13.

50. One can get a sense of this by perusing the Reader's Guide to Periodical Literature (RGPL) and newspaper indices from 1962-1968. The entries under the heading "Pesticides" occupied three columns of copy in the RGPL from 1962 to 1963, and half a column by 1965.

51. See H. Patricia Hynes, "Ellen Swallow, Lois Gibbs, and Rachel Carson: Catalysts of the American Environmental Movement," *Women's International Forum* 8 (1985): 291–98, and Merchant, *Earthcare*, 139–66.

52. Carson, *Silent Spring*, 12.

53. Theo Colborn, Dianne Dumanoski, and John Peterson Myers, *Our Stolen Future: Are We Threatening Our Fertility, Intelligence, and Survival?* (New York: Dutton, 1995).

54. See David Helvarg, "Poison Pens," *Sierra*, January/February 1997, 31–37.

55. Harding, *Whose Science? Whose Knowledge?*, 1–15.

56. Carson, *Silent Spring*, 296.

57. The author wishes to thank the participants of Richard Sorrenson's "Science and Gender" seminar at Indiana University, Professor Sorrenson himself, and the two anonymous referees for their many helpful suggestions for the conceptualization and writing of this chapter.

Part IV

An Ongoing Toxic Discourse

11
After *Silent Spring*: Ecological Effects of Pesticides on Public Health and on Birds and Other Organisms

David Pimentel

In 1962, Rachel Carson had the foresight and knowledge to warn against the ecological hazards of pesticides for public health. She warned too about the dangers of pesticides to the well-being of birds and other organisms. With its vivid examples of the interdependence of all living things and their environments, *Silent Spring* gave recognition to the growing field of ecology. For Carson's many contributions, all of us are indebted. But the long-term effects of her warnings remain to be seen.

From 1945, when the use of synthetic pesticides began in the United States, to the time Carson's book was published in 1962, pesticide use increased about sixfold. In the ten years between the publication of *Silent Spring* and the eventual banning of DDT in 1972, pesticide use increased tenfold, to about one billion pounds annually. Since then the total quantity of pesticides in terms of pounds has not increased; however, the actual toxicity of pesticides has increased ten to twenty times.[1]

The primary benefit of the new, highly toxic pesticides that replaced DDT and similar chemicals is that the new toxicants do not persist for long periods of time in the environment. DDT persists in the soil for thirty to fifty years, whereas newer pesticides persist only up to three months. On the other hand, the major problem with the use of pesticides when applied as recommended is that so little actually reaches the target pests. It is estimated that less than 0.01 percent of the pesticides that are applied reach the target pests, which means that 99.99 percent of the pesticide that is applied pollutes the environment. The result is that more than numerous birds, fish, and other nontarget species are killed or affected by the applied pesticides.[2]

In the United States today, more than forty-five years after *Silent Spring*, approximately three pounds of pesticide are applied per acre per year to about four hundred million acres. Incidentally, homeowners apply about eight pounds per acre per year, or nearly three times the level that farmers apply per acre. Worldwide, about five billion pounds of pesticide are applied each year. Some humans, especially those who apply pesticides, are directly exposed to the pesticide sprays. Pesticides also contaminate human food and water resources; about 35 percent of the food that is purchased has measurable levels of pesticide residues, with 1 to 3 percent having residues that are above accepted tolerance levels.[3]

In the United States, about 300,000 humans are poisoned with pesticides annually, with about 25 accidental deaths. Worldwide, the situation is far more serious, with 26 million people poisoned and approximately 220,000 deaths each year. In addition, pesticides can be carcinogenic; estimates indicate over 10,000 cases of cancer resulting from pesticide exposure. Pesticides also disrupt the endocrine, immune, and neurological responses in human and other animals. For example, endocrine disrupters tend to make male animals become female in structure. In addition, sperm production is greatly reduced or is entirely lost.[4]

Like humans, birds are poisoned by pesticides. The image in the title of Rachel Carson's book suggests that if we continue to apply DDT and other pesticides we will have a silent spring, with no birds singing. Like the canary in a coal mine, birds are excellent "indicator species." Birds are poisoned by direct exposure to pesticides and by feeding on contaminated prey. They evidence reduced growth and reproduction due to sub-lethal exposure to pesticides. The full extent of bird kills by pesticides is difficult to determine because birds are secretive, camouflaged, highly mobile, and live in dense grass, shrubs, and trees.

If it is assumed that the pesticide damage inflicted on birds occurs primarily on the four hundred million acres of cropland that receives most of the pesticides, and the bird population is estimated to be 1.8 birds per acre of cropland, then about 720 million birds are directly exposed to pesticides. If it is (conservatively) estimated that only 10 percent of the bird population is killed, then the total number of birds killed is approximately 72 million per year. This 72 million does not include the nestlings lost because one or more parent is killed or because pesticide-contaminated insects and earthworms are fed to the nestlings. The actual number of birds killed might be twice the 72 million estimate.[5]

The American bald eagle and other predatory birds suffered high mortalities due to DDT and other chlorinated insecticides. The bald eagle population declined primarily due to pesticide intoxication and was placed on the endangered species list. After DDT and other chlorinated insecticides were banned in 1972, it took nearly thirty years for the bird population to recover. The bald eagle was recently removed from the endangered species list.[6]

In both natural and agricultural ecosystems, a large number of predators and parasites control and limit the feeding pressure of herbivorous arthropod populations. The biological control organisms help ecosystems remain "green" with foliage on trees, shrubs, and other plants. The beneficial parasites and predator help control pest arthropods in agricultural crops.[7]

While pesticides provide approximately 10 percent of pest control in the United States, natural controls provide an estimated 20 percent. Many cultural controls, such as crop rotation, planting time, crop-plant density, trap crops, mechanical cultivation, polyculture, and soil, water and fertilizer management provide additional protection against pests. Together, these non-chemical controls could be used effectively to reduce U.S. pesticide use by more than 50 percent, without any reduction in crop yields or cosmetic standards. Confirmation that pesticide use in the United States could be cut in half comes from the fact that Sweden has reduced pesticide use by 68 percent from 1992 to date, while at the same time reducing human pesticide poisonings 77 percent.[8]

When pest outbreaks occur because the pests' natural enemies have been destroyed by pesticides, additional and usually more expensive and more toxic pesticide treatments are required to sustain crop yields. It is estimated that the destruction of natural enemies by pesticides, the subsequent crop losses, and additional pesticide applications cost the United States more than $500 million per year.[9]

The widespread use of pesticides has resulted in the development of pesticide resistance in insect pests, plant pathogens, and weeds. The estimate is that more than one thousand species of pests are now resistant to pesticides. As pesticide use increases, the number of pesticide-resistant pests explodes.[10] Increased pesticide resistance in pest populations requires additional applications of pesticides, which tends to compound the problem by increasing selection in the target pests. Despite numerous attempts to deal with this problem, pesticide resistance continues to develop at a rapid rate. In the United States, assuming a 10 percent loss in major crops because of resistance despite heavy pesticide treatments, total losses due to pesticide resistance are estimated to be about $1.4 billion per year.

Pesticides also affect pollinators such as bees.[11] Honeybees and wild bees are vital for pollination of about one-third of the crops in the United States, especially fruits and vegetables. For most agricultural crops, both yield and quality are enhanced by effective pollination. The benefits of bees for pollination are estimated to be about $40 billion per year, if forages and pastures are included in the assessment. Because most insecticides and some fungicides and herbicides are toxic to bees, these pesticides have a major impact on both honeybee and wild bee populations. Based on the analysis of honeybee and pollination losses caused by insecticides, pollination losses attributed to pesticides are about 10 percent of the pollinated crops, at a yearly cost of about $200 million. The combined annual costs of reduced pollination and direct loss of honeybees due to insecticides can be estimated to be at about $320 million each year.[12]

The United States currently spends about $8 billion each year in the use of pesticides, and this use of pesticides returns about $32 billion each year. However, these figures do not account for the environmental and public health costs of using pesticides, which are estimated at about $11 billion annually. It is long past time to reduce the use of pesticides and to apply them in a judicious manner that will benefit farmers, the environment, and the public, as Rachel Carson advised so many years ago.[13]

NOTES

1. David Pimentel, ed., *Insects, Science, and Society* (New York: Academic Press, 1975).

2. David Pimentel and Lois Levitan, "Pesticides: Amounts Applied and Amounts Reaching Pests," *BioScience* 36 (1986): 86–91.

3. David Pimentel, ed., *Techniques for Reducing Pesticide Use: Economic and Environmental Benefits* (Chichester, England: John Wiley, 1997).

4. David Pimentel, "Environmental and Economic Costs of the Application of Pesticides Primarily in the United States," *Environment, Development and Sustainability* 7 (2005): 229–252.

5. Ibid.

6. Ibid.

7. Ibid.

8. Ibid.

9. Ibid.

10. Ibid.

11. Ibid.

12. Ibid.

13. See David Pimentel and Hugh Lehman, eds., *The Pesticide Question: Environment, Economics, and Ethics* (New York: Chapman & Hall, 1993).

12

Contested Icons: Rachel Carson and DDT

Steve Maguire

"DDT killed bald eagles because of its persistence in the environment. 'Silent Spring' is now killing African children because of its persistence in the public mind."[1] This juxtaposition of claims of killing appeared in 2004 in a *New York Times Magazine* article with a title that summarizes its main point: "What the World Needs Now Is DDT." In the article, Tina Rosenberg argues that the unwillingness of aid agencies in developed countries to finance the use of the insecticide DDT was hindering antimalaria campaigns in developing countries, with deadly consequences. This, she charges, is part of Rachel Carson's legacy. In more conservative media, accusations against Carson are more direct, frequent, and hyperbolic. Indeed, her legacy has been characterized as "Rachel Carson's Ecological Genocide": "However, let there be no mistake: Rachel Carson and the worldwide environmentalist movement are responsible for perpetuating an ecological genocide that has claimed the lives of millions of young, poor, striving African men, women and children, killed by preventable diseases."[2]

Whence such killing claims and vitriolic rhetoric? Why are DDT and Rachel Carson so inextricably and emotionally linked? To answer these questions, one must explore the meanings of DDT for different social groups, how these have shifted over time, Carson's role in this shift, and, as a consequence, the meaning of Rachel Carson for these same groups.

Adopting a social constructionist approach to technology and employing discourse analysis, I have explored the rise and fall of DDT from the perspective of product substitution.[3] My research has identified the pivotal role of changes in scientific discourse (fact-making), policy discourse (rule-making), and public discourse (opinion-making) in determining DDT's exit from different markets. From that research, it is clear that struggles over DDT were more than simply struggles over DDT; the stakes were obviously higher for the groups brought together, as if DDT was a particularly meaningful front in a larger and ongoing war. These results prompted me to explore the semiotics of DDT—how its meaning emerges from its associations with other resonant symbols, how different social groups contest its meaning by strategically promoting different associations, and how these are related.

DDT's role as a symbol has been underappreciated in most discussions of that chemical, as well as in those of Rachel Carson's legacy. To understand the rise and fall of DDT—to comprehend the struggles around this chemical—requires an appreciation of DDT's symbolic effects as much as its instrumental insecticidal ones or its undesirable impacts on human health and the environment. I argue that Rachel Carson achieved iconic status herself, in part, because she recognized and exploited DDT's symbolic potential, transforming DDT discourse and the meaning of DDT for the public through her book *Silent Spring*. But in making DDT a negative icon for the general public and environmentalists, Carson set in motion a subsequent process of contested and coevolutionary icon-making: as Rachel Carson became an icon for environmentalism's supporters, she also became a negative icon for its detractors; and just as DDT remains a negative icon for environmentalists, it has also become an icon for their political opponents. Both Carson and DDT are powerful symbols capable of rallying supporters and detractors alike and, simply put, neither would be the contested icon it is today without the other.

THE RISE OF DDT: A WAR HERO COMES HOME

DDT, or dichlorodiphenyltrichlorethane, is an organochlorine insecticide with a very broad spectrum of strong insecticidal activity.[4] First synthesized in 1874 by Othman Zeidler, it was not until 1939 that Paul Muller of Geigy (Switzerland) discovered DDT's incredible insect-killing properties. Much less acutely toxic to humans than the arsenic-based insecticides it replaced, DDT was considered "magic."

Large scale manufacture of DDT began in the United States in 1943; all DDT was allocated to the military, which used it extensively during World War II to protect troops and civilians from typhus, malaria, and other insect-borne diseases. After the war, DDT continued to be used widely in public health programs, especially against mosquitoes carrying the parasites that cause malaria. As a result, DDT was credited with saving millions of lives, and Muller was awarded the 1948 Nobel Prize in medicine.

In 1945 DDT was released into the U.S. civilian economy and in 1946 the U.S. Department of Agriculture (USDA) began to recommend it to farmers. DDT became widely used on many crops, including cotton, tobacco, and foodstuffs such as corn and apples. In addition, DDT had many other applications: on the farm (e.g., against insects attacking livestock); in organized USDA insect "eradication" campaigns (e.g., against gypsy moths); in the home (e.g., against flies, roaches, and bedbugs); in yards and gardens (e.g., against insects attacking ornamental plants); in forestry (e.g., against insects that defoliate trees); and in suburban neighborhoods (e.g., against mosquitoes and bark beetles). As a result, production rose dramatically and DDT quickly became the leading insecticide in terms of quantities applied. Domestic usage peaked in 1959 at 79,000,000 pounds, and DDT maintained its U.S. market dominance until 1964.[5]

Most early scientific discourse about DDT originated in the discipline of economic entomology and the USDA, although medical journals also contributed. These early reports were essentially optimistic, claiming, for example, that "never in the history of entomology has a chemical been discovered that offers such promise to mankind for relief from his insect problems as DDT."[6] But some were cautious, discussing potential risks and warning "DDT, like every other potent insecticide... is really a two-edged sword."[7]

DDT's military accomplishments were widely reported such that, within popular discourse, DDT's reputation was largely positive. Between May 1944 and October 1945, one news service compiled a list of 20,762 items on DDT which were "mostly wildly enthusiastic."[8] DDT's entry into the civilian economy was also accompanied by positive press coverage, as well as aggressive marketing by the chemical industry. Popular discourse, however, was not unanimous, as a construction of DDT as a "two-edged sword" existed as well: *Time* cautioned, "The more entomologists study DDT, the new wonder insecticide, the more convinced they are that it may be a two-edged sword that harms as well as helps"[9]; the *Atlantic Monthly* reported, "It is obvious enough that DDT is a two-edged sword"[10]; the *New Republic* declared, "Unfortunately, DDT and the new and powerful British insecticide, 666 [lindane], are two-edged swords"[11]; while *Fortune* described the "circulation of anti-DDT talk."[12]

As DDT use became ubiquitous and normalized, this "anti-DDT talk" largely disappeared from popular discourse. Yet, within scientific circles and government bureaucracies, DDT discourse was shifting. Within economic entomology, a growing body of literature documented new problems encountered by DDT users—resistance, resurgence, and secondary pests. Toxicologists raised questions about risks posed by DDT's chronic toxicity, especially after it was established that DDT residues were accumulating in the fat of U.S. citizens. And there was a marked increase in government reports produced by departments other than the USDA, especially the Fish and Wildlife Service, that framed insecticides as posing risks for birds, fish, and wildlife. Adding to these concerns, DDT was being found, it seemed, everywhere; its solubility in fat meant that it was accumulating in birds, fish, and wildlife in addition to humans, and its mobility and persistence meant that this could occur far from where DDT had originally been applied. Then, in 1962, Rachel Carson's *Silent Spring* was published, and the risks that DDT and other pesticides posed for human health and the environment received widespread attention. Things would never be the same—not for Carson and not for DDT.

THE FALL OF DDT: A VILLAIN OF *SILENT SPRING*

In 1936, Rachel Carson accepted a job with the U.S. Department of the Interior's Bureau of Fisheries where she wrote, among other things, "seven-minute fish tales"—scripts for a public education radio series.[13] In 1939, the U.S. Fish and Wildlife Service was created, giving Carson access to reports addressing pest control and, in 1945, Carson wrote to *Reader's Digest* with a proposal for a story about DDT:

> Practically at my backdoor here in Maryland, an experiment of more than ordinary interest and importance is going on. We have all heard a lot about what DDT will soon do for us by wiping out insect pests. The experiments at Patuxent have been planned to show what other effects DDT may have when it is applied to wide areas: what it will do to insects that are beneficial or even essential; how it may affect waterfowl, or birds that depend on insect food; whether it may upset the whole delicate balance of nature if unwisely used.[14]

Carson's idea was rejected, however. In 1957 she returned to the topic, reviewing the scientific literature widely for what was known about DDT's and other pesticides' effects on human health and the environment. Her celebrated book, *Silent Spring*, was serialized in the *New Yorker* in June and July of 1962, and appeared in September.

The index of *Silent Spring* reveals the extent to which the book, although addressing pesticides in general, focuses on organochlorine insecticides and, in particular, on DDT. The top six most frequently mentioned chemicals belong to that family of substances and DDT is by far the most prominent. Indeed, DDT is invoked by Carson more than three times as often as the second most frequently mentioned pesticide. Not only is DDT the first pesticide that Carson names specifically, just following her celebrated opening chapter, "A Fable for Tomorrow," but it then reappears in all but three of the book's remaining chapters. In sum, excluding her sources, Carson makes reference to DDT on almost 20 percent of *Silent Spring*'s 297 pages.

Table 12.1. Mentions of Specific Agricultural Chemicals in *Silent Spring*

Substance	Number of pages (calculated from index)
DDT	54
heptachlor	17
dieldrin	15
chlordane	13
BHC	12
aldrin	11
2,4-D	10
parathion	7
endrin	6
malathion	6
toxaphene	6
aminotriazole	4
DDD	4
dinitropheno	4
lead arsenate	4
methoxychlor	3
nicotine sulphate	3
pentachlorophenol	3
rotenone	2

Prior to the publication of *Silent Spring*, the production, dissemination, and consumption of texts addressing risks posed by DDT and other pesticides occurred, for the most part, in closed circles of scientific disciplines and government bureaucracies. But Carson altered DDT discourse forever; discussion of the pesticide risks increased dramatically in the public arena, with implications for actors in policy and scientific arenas as well.

The immediate public reaction to *Silent Spring* was spectacular. Carson's book was widely reviewed and, in April 1963, CBS even produced a documentary film, *The Silent Spring of Rachel Carson*, which brought pesticide issues into the living rooms of U.S. citizens. The public was interested in, attending to, and becoming engaged with the issue of pesticide risks in ways unlike before.

This, of course, had consequences for policy discourse, and *Silent Spring* generated a flurry of activity in the political arena: portions of the *New Yorker* serialization were read into the *Congressional Record*; President Kennedy answered a reporter's question by referring to Carson by name and reassuring the public that his officials were examining the pesticide issue; and when the President's Science Advisory Committee (PSAC) released its 1963 report, it concluded bluntly that "Elimination of the use of persistent toxic pesticides should be the goal,"[15] leading commentators to claim "Rachel Carson Stands Vindicated."[16] Subsequent government reports followed, each reinforcing a framing that highlighted the risks posed by pesticides or "the pesticide problem."[17]

Scientific activity and discourse also changed in the wake of *Silent Spring*. Whereas doctoral dissertations focusing on DDT had once overwhelmingly come from economic entomology, they were now being produced in disciplines concerned with risks to human health and the environment. Ecology, along with newer scientific disciplines such as eco-toxicology and environmental health, flourished and several international conferences addressing the implications of pesticides in the environment were held. The bulk of this new knowledge constructed DDT and other pesticides as problems, and focused on their risks. The fate of meat-eating birds at the top of food chains received special attention, and the hypothesis that DDT caused thinning of eggshells and thus declines in their populations began to emerge as the consensus view. The stage was set for regulatory battles to follow.

OBITUARIES FOR DDT FOLLOWING NATIONAL AND INTERNATIONAL SKIRMISHES

Died, DDT, age 95, a persistent pesticide and onetime humanitarian. Considered to be one of World War II's greatest heroes, DDT saw its reputation fade after it was charged with murder by author Rachel Carson. Death came on June 27 in Michigan after a lingering illness. Survived by dieldrin, aldrin, endrin, chlordane, heptachlor, lindane and toxaphene. Please omit flowers.[18]

This anthropomorphizing "Obituary for DDT (in Michigan)" appeared in the *New York Times Magazine* in 1969 following the state of Michigan's decision to ban DDT from agricultural use. The Michigan ban came closely on the heels of a hearing initiated by the Environmental Defense Fund (EDF) in Madison, Wisconsin, addressing whether DDT constituted a pollutant under the law (it did, concluded hearing examiner Maurice Van Susteren). It also foreshadowed similar suspensions in other states, unprecedented public hearings in Washington, D.C., and, ultimately, a national ban ordered in 1972 by the new (i.e., 1970) Environmental Protection Agency (EPA) and controversial to this day. Though the national hearing examiner, Edmund

Sweeney, did not counsel a ban, the EPA administrator, William D. Ruckelshaus, disagreed. Ruckelshaus based his decision on findings of "persistence, transport, biomagnification, toxicological effects and an absence of benefits of DDT in relation to the availability of effective and less harmful substitutes"; he explicitly credited Carson for stirring public concern and stimulating scientific research.[19] Notably, the EPA ban was not the sole or even most important cause of DDT's exit from the economy; before the 1972 ban, DDT use had already declined 70 percent from peak usage volumes as it had more or less been abandoned in all agricultural uses except cotton.[20]

But reports of DDT's death were premature, to say the least.

Recently, DDT was again at the center of controversy, this time on the global stage, where its regulatory fate was debated during international negotiations leading to the Stockholm Convention on Persistent Organic Pollutants (POPs). This multilateral environmental agreement, which was signed in 2001 and went into effect in 2004, allows for the elimination or restriction of a "dirty dozen" POPs—substances that "are highly toxic"; "are persistent, lasting for years or even decades before degrading into less dangerous forms"; "evaporate and travel long distances through the air and through water"; and "accumulate in fatty tissues" of humans and wildlife—including DDT.[21]

De rigeur in those arenas where policies for addressing toxic chemicals are formed, Rachel Carson and her message were part of the debate. For example, Klaus Topfer, executive director of the United Nations Environment Programme (UNEP), cited Carson in his opening remarks and alluded to the pending treaty as unfinished business flowing from *Silent Spring*. Similarly, the World Wildlife Fund, who had timed the release of their report "Resolving the DDT Dilemma" to coincide with the opening of the POPs negotiations, also invoked Carson: their press briefing, which underlined in its title that "Three Decades after *Silent Spring*, DDT Still Menacing the Environment," called for "a global phase-out and eventual ban on DDT production and use by the year 2007." Against a ban because of DDT's ongoing role against mosquitoes carrying the malaria parasite, a vocal segment of the malaria-fighting community—in conjunction, notably, with conservative think tanks—did not mince words in their opposition: "the insistence to do without DDT is 'ecocolonialism' that can impoverish no less than the imperial colonialism of the past did."[22] Referring to the revival of DDT in a public health role after it had been abandoned, one unit of South Africa's Department of Environmental Affairs and Tourism called DDT the "African Messiah."[23]

Although this debate was bitter, it was for the most part confined to the corridors of the negotiations and to mass and scientific media. Among concerned states, on the other hand, the development of an international consensus on DDT was a cooperative process in which agreement on a policy that balances environmental protection and disease control was reached without the hysteria that one might expect from reading only the popular press.[24]

As a result, DDT yet again stands out: it is the only intentionally produced substance currently covered by the Stockholm Convention and slated for "restriction" rather than "elimination," albeit with an explicitly stated "goal of reducing and ultimately eliminating" its use. Countries can continue to produce and/or use DDT, but only for disease vector control in accordance with the World Health Organization's recommendations and guidelines.

Despite DDT's special status and continued availability, some interpret the Stockholm Convention as heralding the death of DDT on the global stage. One commentator speculated in a *New Yorker* essay just subsequent to the convention's signing, "on the eve of its [DDT's] burial" and as the world was "writing DDT's obituary," "someday, when DDT is dead and buried, and the West wakes up to a world engulfed by malaria, we will think back to Fred Soper [the man whose life project was the focus of the essay—a 'malaria warrior' who 'had a weapon, DDT, that seemed like a gift from God'] and wish we had another to take his place."[25]

It is difficult to imagine any other chemical receiving such extensive, prominent and repeatedly anthropomorphizing journalistic treatment. But no other chemical has such a high-profile public persona. DDT is, in fact, an icon of our modern age; it is a powerful symbol of our "risk society," and Rachel Carson played an important part in making it so.[26]

THE MAKING OF A CONTESTED ICON

In this section, I now turn to the success of DDT as a contested icon—a negative icon for environmentalists and an icon for their opponents. Specifically, I will address the questions of why Rachel Carson focused on DDT, and why this chemical has become such a powerful and enduring symbol for both supporters and detractors of environmentalism.

As suggested above, at the time when Carson was writing, DDT was a logical and likely unavoidable focus for any critique of pesticides. There are several reasons for this, including: DDT's sales volumes and importance in agriculture; its singular reputation and familiarity to most U.S. citizens; its ability to attract media attention; and the sheer volume of research available to be translated by Carson for her target audience.

First, DDT was the top-selling insecticide at the time Rachel Carson wrote *Silent Spring*. Occupying a premier place in farmers' chemical arsenal, DDT was a natural target for Carson. In addition, DDT was also the most widely and well-known pesticide, by far, as it already had a public persona. DDT's status as a war hero whose return home was widely covered by the popular press, not to mention the chemical industry's aggressive marketing of the insecticide, ensured that Carson's audience had heard of the chemical. That DDT had already been called a "double-edged sword," even if this view had disappeared for some time, also helped to set the stage for Carson's critique.

Additionally, DDT's numerous uses meant that Carson's target audience, beyond having simply heard of DDT, would be quite familiar and comfortable with it. Not only were U.S. consumers using DDT in their homes, in their gardens, and on their pets, but many would have seen DDT used in their communities against mosquitoes or against the beetles that spread Dutch elm disease. Although limited in comparison to DDT's primary agricultural markets, these uses greatly increased DDT's familiarity to Carson's audience. Carson acknowledged as much, writing "DDT is now so universally used that in most minds the product takes on the harmless aspect of the familiar" before proceeding to debunk "the myth of the harmlessness of DDT."[27]

DDT's status also increased the likelihood that media would report on issues involving it. This was the case, for instance, when citizens on New York's Long Island contested in the courts the aerial spraying of DDT in 1956 as part of a USDA campaign to eradicate the gypsy moth. Although the court challenge was unsuccessful, "the public airing of the facts resulted in much wider awareness of the hazards, both known and potential, of large-scale chemical control programs."[28] Analysis of the 228 New York Times articles on DDT published prior to Silent Spring confirms that the ratio of articles portraying exclusively or primarily positive claims about DDT to those portraying exclusively or primarily negative/cautionary claims fell from 4.9 to 1 during 1944–1949 to 1.5 to 1 during 1959–1961.[29] The media attention given to DDT not only ensured adequate anecdotal raw materials and a primed audience—Carson describes the Long Island incident as "the height of absurdity" in the tenth chapter of Silent Spring, appropriately titled "Indiscriminately from the Skies"—but it also suggested that any book like the one Carson was writing would not go unnoticed.[30] A savvy publicist of her own work, it is likely that Carson recognized the special relationship between the mass media and DDT. Certainly those on both sides of the DDT issue today do.

In part because of the large volume of DDT sold, its numerous uses, and its high-profile status, DDT was also one of the most widely researched of the pesticides available for Carson to write about. Her many and diverse sources represented a significant volume of raw materials: toxicological studies of DDT; scientific articles and government reports of DDT's impacts on birds, fish, and wildlife; surveys of the occurrence of DDT in human fat and breast milk; and so on. Hidden from the public in obscure scientific journals or government bureaucracies, these texts lay waiting to be uncovered, juxtaposed, synthesized, and—most importantly—interpreted for Carson's target audience.

Thus, important and familiar but with "sinister" secrets, DDT was set to be unmasked by Carson. With DDT, Carson had identified a chemical with much symbolic potential. There are several reasons why DDT was an excellent candidate for negative icon-making among environmentalism's supporters and for environmentalism's detractors to contest this meaning, including: its man-made origins; its incredible success and the magnitude of benefits it conferred on different social groups; the number, variety, and nature of problems and risks it posed to other social groups; several of its biophysical properties which compound these risks; and the distribution of DDT's benefits and risks.

First, DDT and the other pesticides featured in *Silent Spring* are synthetic chemicals, as Carson underlines early, noting that in "being man-made…they differ sharply from the simpler insecticides of prewar days" as they "have immense power not merely to poison but to enter into the most vital processes of the body and change them in sinister and often deadly ways."[31] The product of scientific and technological progress, DDT is a symbol of man's knowledge, ingenuity, and potential for good, if one focuses on its instrumental insecticidal uses, but also of man's ignorance, arrogance, and potential for harm, if one focuses on its undesirable unintended consequences. As has been observed, DDT—"a symbol of the dangers of playing God with nature, an icon of human arrogance,"[32] and "a symbol of all that is dangerous about man's attempts to interfere with nature"[33]—fits well with the Frankenstein myth, and this certainly contributes to ongoing contestation of this chemical's meaning by environmentalists and antienvironmentalists:

> Because the ban on DDT became the midwife to the environmental movement, the debate about it, even today, is bizarrely polarized. Most environmental groups do not object to DDT where it is used appropriately and is necessary to fight malaria. But liberals still tend to consider it a symbol of the Frankenstein effects of unbridled faith in technology. For conservatives, whose Web sites foam at the mouth about the hypocrisy of environmentalists, DDT continues to represent the victory of overzealous regulators and Luddites who misread and distort science.[34]

Others have argued that the central lesson of *Silent Spring*, "the great moral of the twentieth century," is "that even the best-intentioned efforts have perverse consequences, that benefits are inevitably offset by risks."[35] Carson herself invokes the words of Albert Schweitzer immediately following her celebrated dystopian opening chapter, "A Fable for Tomorrow," to remind her readers, "Man can hardly even recognize the devils of his own creation."[36] In other words, a general lesson applicable to all of man's technologies was taught to the world by Rachel Carson using the specific example of man-made chemicals and, in particular, DDT.

Second, the magnitude of the military, public health, agricultural, and thus commercial success of DDT—the benefits it brought to different social groups—also contributed to DDT's iconic status for the environmentalist movement, as well as for that movement's more conservative detractors. DDT's spectacular rise—its appearance as a "magic" tool just when it was needed, during the war; its hero status; Muller's Nobel Prize—set it up for a dramatic fall. Whether DDT's fall was merited, as environmentalists believe, or not, as their opponents believe, there is nonetheless little doubt that the heights it reached gave it dramatic potential. If DDT had been a marginal product for farmers and the chemical industry at the time when Carson wrote *Silent Spring*, a product that they would have abandoned without a fight, then its demise would not have resonated as it did with either environmentalists or their opponents.

In the context of the recent debate over DDT, where the contentious issue is public health rather than agricultural use, the stakes have even more dramatic potential as they involve, arguably, human lives. If a viable substitute for DDT was available at a similar price, the issue would have much less resonance for malariologists and would have deprived their conservative allies, committed detractors of Carson and environmentalism, of a salient front of attack. Indeed, that the claimed magnitude of DDT's benefits (upon which its supporters focus) and risks (upon which its detractors focus) are each so high makes DDT a natural site for contestation and ideological struggle. Carson juxtaposes and underlines this "two-edged sword" or "Dr. Jekyll/Mr. Hyde" essence of DDT and other pesticides—the great benefits *and* risks associated with them—in the third chapter of *Silent Spring*. Titled "Elixers of Death," the chapter introduces pesticides—so-called cure-alls that also kill.[37]

Third, as regards the problems and risks associated with DDT, there were a surprising number upon which Carson could focus. Indeed, among technologies associated with environmental problems, pesticides are perhaps unique in terms of the variety of risks to which they have been linked, including problems for the very social groups for whom they are supposed to be solutions. So, in addition to issues of acute toxicity to humans, chronic toxicity to humans (measured in terms of a long list of clinical endpoints to assess carcinogenicity, teratogenicity, mutagenicity, reproductive effects, immune system impacts, etc.), along with those of acute and chronic toxicity to birds, fish and wildlife, there were also the problems of pesticide resistance, resurgence, and secondary pests. With these, chemical solutions aggravate the very insect problems they are intended to solve. Carson devotes two chapters to these issues—"Nature Fights Back" (chapter fifteen) and "Rumblings of an Avalanche" (chapter sixteen). The title of chapter sixteen refers to the "rumblings" that could be heard about insecticide resistance problems. The images brought to mind are powerful ones; progress is cast as a relentless chemical treadmill or, more sinisterly, as an unending arms race with nature. Indeed, in addition to DDT's association with war, the discourse of economic entomology is riddled with military metaphors.[38] This unavoidable association allowed Carson to introduce early in *Silent Spring* the resonant notion of "man's war against nature."[39]

As regards DDT's various toxicities, here too DDT offers an abundance of symbolic potential. That DDT affects birds is significant because of their special place in our culture. Bird-watching, unlike snake-watching or frog-watching for instance, is a popular activity ensuring that bird populations are attended to; they are watched, monitored, counted, and reported on by enthusiastic amateurs as well as professional experts. If DDT's ecological impacts were primarily on reptiles or amphibians, it's not clear that they would have been discovered as early or that *Silent Spring* would have had the same impact. At a minimum, the book's memorable title and key eighth chapter—"And No Birds Sing"—would have been impossible.

In that chapter, Carson connects DDT to the plight of another icon, itself a national symbol of the United States. Although she does not address the issue of eggshell thinning directly (conclusive studies had not yet been completed), she does devote much space to discussing American bald eagles' and other birds' reproductive problems and therefore to eggs—their laying and hatching or, more ominously, non-hatching. DDT is thus linked, as a defiling or deadly contaminant, with the highly symbolic egg, signifier of intergenerational continuity yet fragility, of new but vulnerable life, of potential. Carson also makes the now iconic connection between DDT and songbirds, drawing upon the public's own experience with bird mortality as a result of spraying to control Dutch elm disease.

The more contested aspects of DDT's toxicity relate to humans. Unfortunately for DDT, any association with cancer, even if inconclusively demonstrated, contributes negatively to a chemical's reputation. Aware of the cancer within herself while writing *Silent Spring,* Carson seems to have grasped the special meaning of this disease, devoting an entire chapter (fourteen) to it and to the carcinogenic risks posed by pesticides. Carson's death from cancer less than two years after the publication of *Silent Spring* renders her message all the more poignant. As regards DDT and cancer, Carson draws readers' attention to this association by writing, "In laboratory tests on animal subjects, DDT has produced suspicious liver tumors" and quotes another scientist who categorized DDT as a "chemical carcinogen."[40] Later, reminding her readers that they are exposed to multiple chemicals in the course of a given day and that the carcinogenic risks posed by interactions among these had not been well addressed by traditional toxicological methods, Carson asks rhetorically, "What then can be a 'safe dose' of DDT?"[41]

As it turns out, the answer to her question is still debated. DDT is currently classified as "possibly carcinogenic to humans" by the International Agency for Research on Cancer, which finds "sufficient evidence in experimental animals" but "inadequate evidence in humans" to establish the carcinogenicity of DDT.[42] Nonetheless, DDT continues to attract research attention and remains the focus of claims and counterclaims. Certainly—it must be underlined—the cancer (and, more generally, the human health) case against DDT is much weaker than one might surmise from its toxic reputation with the public, but it is not nonexistent.[43] And scientific uncertainty does not play in DDT's favor when it comes to this high-profile and dreaded disease. On the other hand, the difficulty of linking DDT conclusively with cancer despite all the research adds to its iconic potential amongst environmentalism's detractors. For them, DDT is an innocent jailed without cause or, worse, an innocent who would otherwise be out in the (developing) world doing good deeds by fighting malaria.

Fourth, several of DDT's properties also contribute to its negative iconic potential. Although DDT is visible when applied, as a residue on food and as a contaminant in the fat of humans and wildlife, it is invisible. It invades with stealth; it hides; it is biochemically active whilst we are unaware. DDT's pervasive yet invisible nature, combined with potential reproductive effects in terms of toxicology, meant that it could be compared metaphorically with radioactive fallout, a concern of the public that Carson recognized and exploited in *Silent Spring*.[44] In 1962, toxic chemicals were not the only artifacts of technological progress emanating from WWII characterized as "two-edged swords"; there was also the atomic bomb. As the most well-known pesticide at the time, DDT became associated through Carson's *Silent Spring* with the resonating notion of chemical fallout.

Other properties of DDT reinforce the chemical fallout metaphor: its persistence and its potential for long-range transport. Together, these mean that DDT's risks are spread across long distances in both time and space. DDT does not respect boundaries; it moves; it travels; it invades. DDT thus reinforces the idea that the natural cannot escape the synthetic. The association of DDT with harmful impacts located far away in time and space makes DDT a natural and highly effective symbol for the environmental movement, with its concern for risks with non-immediate causes as well as those borne by future generations.

In addition, because of DDT's solubility in fat, as DDT residues became ubiquitous soon after the chemical's release into the civilian economy they appeared in the fat and breast milk of U.S. citizens. As a result, DDT is not only linked to the notion of transgression, but of almost sacred sites. Even if it could be conclusively demonstrated that DDT is harmless, it nevertheless contaminates; it defiles; it makes things impure. And the symbolism of contaminating breast milk surely works against the chemical; DDT is associated with the defilement of an almost universal symbol of maternal love and comforting, of nourishment for innocent and helpless babies. Carson made the association quite clear for her readers, underlining in her introduction of synthetic pesticides that "they occur in the mother's milk"[45] and reiterating in her introduction of DDT, "The poison may also be passed on from mother to offspring" and "Insecticide residues have been recovered from human milk in samples tested by Food and Drug Administration scientists."[46] She goes on, in both her introductions of pesticides generally and of DDT in particular, to describe how they also defile yet another emotionally resonant site, itself mysterious and associated with the origins of new life: "the tissues of the unborn child"[47] "while he is still in the womb."[48]

These symbolic connections are inevitably remade whenever DDT is discussed. For example, during the POPs negotiations, the Inuit Circumpolar Conference gave a soapstone carving of a mother and child to UNEP's executive director who, as the chairperson of the POPs negotiations describes, "immediately grasped the significance of the carving with regard to the intergenerational nature of the POPs issue" and requested that "it be displayed during the negotiations as a constant reminder to the delegates" of the significance and importance of their work.[49] The carving thus became a powerful symbol for eliminating POPs. In another instance, at the opening of the POPs negotiations, Greenpeace staged a memorable protest made more effective by its silence. Protestors wore white plastic covers on their abdomens to make them look pregnant, dramatically underlining the intergenerational effects of POPs. These silent symbolic bearers of new life made a powerful backdrop to the interviews the media chose to conduct with them in view.

Related to its solubility in fat, DDT's propensity for bioaccumulation also contributes to its symbolic import and iconic status. As Carson relates to her readers, "One of the most sinister features of DDT and related chemicals is the way they are passed on from one organism to another through all the links of the food chains."[50] In other words, DDT does not merely defile individual organisms, it contaminates entire ecosystems. It is thus a dark symbol of the interconnectedness and oneness of Nature, highlighting the webs of interdependence and networks of vulnerability that connect us all.

Fifth and finally, in addition to the number, diversity, nature, and magnitude of DDT's benefits and risks, there is also the important issue of their distribution. In its unique role in disease vector control, both DDT's benefits and risks are public, not private. With other pesticides, benefits typically accrue privately to chemical manufacturers and farmers while risks are imposed upon and borne by the public as "externalities," resulting in private economic values competing with public environmental ones. This classic environmental trade-off is commonly addressed through the regulation of private property in the public interest, and the balancing of property rights with others, as with the 1972 U.S. ban on DDT. Certainly this is how the argument was framed by Carson, who was addressing a U.S. audience for whom public health uses of insecticides were unimportant as compared to agricultural ones. Describing "an era dominated by industry, in which the right to make a dollar at whatever cost is seldom challenged,"[51] Carson called, in her testimony to a government committee following the publication of *Silent Spring*, for "the right of the citizen to be secure in his own home against the intrusions of poisons applied by other persons. I speak not as a lawyer but as a biologist and as a human being, but I strongly feel that this is or should be one of the basic human rights."[52]

But with DDT, the calculus of benefits and risks is more complicated. Because of DDT's public health benefits, its unintended consequences can be conceptualized as "side effects" and compared with pharmaceutical chemicals that nevertheless deliver therapeutic benefits to those using them. Side effects differ from externalities in that they represent risks borne by the same actor who reaps the benefits—the public, in the case of DDT. With such voluntarily assumed risks there are important issues of informed consent, but the legal and moral calculus is different from that when risks are imposed on others by actors who benefit in so doing. Importantly, however, the side effects analogy only works if one accepts the notion of the public as a single unitary actor making decisions involving homogeneously distributed benefits and risks. A more realistic conceptualization is of different social groups negotiating the distribution of DDT's risks and benefits. The policy developed for DDT in the context of the Stockholm Convention on POPs, for instance, is appropriately different from that for other POPs, because of DDT's important role in the fight against malaria. A global consensus was effectively negotiated as to acceptable levels and distributions of risks and benefits of DDT.

That the risks and benefits associated with DDT use for disease vector control are not homogeneously distributed makes it a preferred point of attack on environmentalism by that movement's detractors. The benefits of DDT accrue to developing countries in the South while, because DDT and other POPs tend to be transported to Arctic regions of developed countries in the North, risks are borne by others. This situation allowed DDT supporters to caricature those environmentalists from developed countries who initially called for a global ban of DDT as putting the lives of birds ahead of the lives of people living in developing countries—children, typically, for dramatic effect and to counterbalance the imagery of intergenerational vulnerability discussed above. Similar accusations were leveled at Carson in the wake of *Silent Spring*, unfairly, as she was quite clear about not abandoning pesticides at any cost:

It is not my contention that chemical insecticides must never be used. I do contend that we have put poisonous and biologically potent chemicals indiscriminately into the hands of persons largely or wholly ignorant of their potentials for harm. We have subjected enormous numbers of people to contact with these poisons, without their consent and often without their knowledge....I contend, furthermore, that we have allowed these chemicals to be used with little or no advance investigation of their effect on soil, water, wildlife and man himself. Future generations are unlikely to condone our lack of prudent concern for the integrity of the natural world that supports all life....It is the public that is being asked to assume the risks that the insect controllers calculate. The public must decide whether it wishes to continue on the present road, and it can do so only in full possession of the facts.[53]

RISK SOCIETY AND THE CONTESTED MEANINGS OF
RACHEL CARSON AND DDT

Carson's words, though more than forty years old, nevertheless get directly at the essence of contestation around DDT and, more generally, risk-generating technologies today. Her words capture why DDT is such an effective stand-in for man's technologies and other interventions into nature because they combine two important themes: "the risks," and "prudent concern," which in today's debates would be termed "precaution."

Sociologist Ulrich Beck has advanced the notion of a "risk society" to describe the most recent phase of modernization which, because it increasingly attends to human-produced risks that are by-products of economic development, is reflexive.[54] Whereas the central focus in governance and study of modern political economies has historically been the production and distribution of wealth, we increasingly are witnessing "the problems and conflicts that arise from the production, definition and distribution of techno-scientifically produced risks."[55] Risks "induce systematic and often *irreversible* harm, generally remain *invisible*, are based on *causal interpretations*, and thus initially only exist in terms of the (scientific or anti-scientific) *knowledge* about them," and, because risks can be constructed and redefined, the mass media and the scientific and legal professions move into key social and political positions in this process of risk construction and definition.[56] Not to mention influential authors, like Rachel Carson.

Carson was a "discursive entrepreneur" who used her own unique discursive position—she was not intimidated by scientific discourse about pesticide harms that provided the raw materials for her text production; she had legitimacy and credibility as a science writer as well as access to important distribution channels that ensured her texts would be widely disseminated; and she had the ability to compose prose capable of moving her readers to action—to alter the social construction of DDT and other pesticides in particular and of (risk-generating) technology more generally. In making DDT into a negative icon for environmentalism, Carson insisted that modernity be reflexive about its risks, advocated a democratic form for this reflexivity (i.e., "the public must decide"), and spoke on behalf of future generations in calling for a precautionary stance towards these risks (i.e., "a prudent concern for the integrity of the natural world that supports all life").

Carson, recognizing that inaction (i.e., the status quo of 1962) towards potential pesticide risks was as political a gesture as taking action (i.e., strengthening regulatory institutions governing pesticides), triggered societal deliberations about acceptable levels of and appropriate responses to these risks. By changing DDT and pesticide discourse and placing the issue of pesticide risks on the agenda of governments, Carson altered the balance of what is termed "nondecision-making power" in society. Whereas narrow conceptions of power focus on overt conflict and decision making, attributing power to whomever prevails in situations of conflicting preferences and interpreting an absence of decisionmaking or participation as signs of consensus, political scientists Peter Bachrach and Morton Baratz drew attention to a "second face of power," the kind exercised when actors devote energy to "creating or reinforcing social and political values and institutional practices that limit the scope of the political process to public consideration of only those issues which are comparatively innocuous."[57] In other words, because the question of what merits societal deliberation is itself a political one, the ability to get specific risks into the public sphere and onto the agenda of governments—to trigger deliberations about acceptable levels of and appropriate responses to these risks—represents a loss of power for those who formerly benefited from and counted on society's absence of reflexivity, inertia, and nondecision making.

Risk management decision—and, importantly, nondecision—making unavoidably has distributional consequences: someone, somewhere, is exposed to residual risk judged acceptable and thus not acted upon; someone, somewhere, pays for actions taken to reduce risks or to mitigate risks to acceptable levels; and sometimes reducing the level of one type of risk for a social group may increase the level of other risks for other groups. As with any political process or negotiation, there may be those who dislike the outcomes of risk management decision making (i.e., the regulatory fate of DDT nationally or internationally); they may be upset by the outcome (e.g., it does not represent a value judgment they would have made) or, not unrelated, by the process (e.g., particular values or interests were represented not at all or not with sufficient power). But blame of those individuals who merely trigger societal deliberations about risks is misplaced unless they are "standing in" as negative icons for frustrated political goals and perceived losses of power relative to opponents. And, of course, the process is symmetrical; Rachel Carson and DDT are symbols of political gains for environmentalism. This is an important aspect of their meaning, and one that underpins their status as contested icons. Power and symbolic politics in our risk society—this is what all the fuss is about.

NOTES

1. Tina Rosenberg, "What the World Needs Now Is DDT," *New York Times Magazine*, Apr. 11, 2004.

2. Lisa Makson, "Rachel Carson's Ecological Genocide," *FrontPageMagazine.com*, July 31, 2003. Available online at www.front pagemag.com/articles/ReadArticle.asp?ID=9169.

3. Steve Maguire, "Sustainable Development, Strategy and Substitution: Lessons from a Study of the Process of Eliminating DDT from the Economy" (Ph.D. dissertation, École des Hautes Études Commerciales, 2000); ibid., "The Coevolution of Technology and Discourse: A Study of Substitution Processes for the Insecticide DDT," *Organization Studies* 25 (2004): 113–34; and Steve Maguire and Jaye Ellis, "The Precautionary Principle and Global Chemical Risk Management: Some Insights from POPs," *Greener Management International: The Journal of Corporate Environmental Strategy and Practice* 41 (2003): 33–46.

4. See Kenneth Mellanby, *The DDT Story* (Farnham Surrey: British Crop Protection Council, 1992); and Thomas R. Dunlap, *DDT: Scientists, Citizens and Public Policy* (Princeton, N.J.: Princeton University Press, 1983).

5. U.S. Environmental Protection Agency, *DDT: A Review of Scientific and Economic Aspects of the Decision to Ban Its Use as a Pesticide*, Report Number EPA-540/1-75-022 (Washington, D.C.: U.S. Environmental Protection Agency, 1975), 149.

6. Sievert A. Rohwer, "Report of the Special Committee on DDT," with S. A. Rohwer as Chairman, *Journal of Economic Entomology* 38 (1945): 144.

7. Clarence Cottam and Elmer Higgins, "DDT and Its Effect on Fish and Wildlife," *Journal of Economic Entomology* 39 (1946): 44–52.

8. Anonymous, "DDT: Just Begun to Fight," *Fortune*, January 1946, 149.

9. Anonymous, "DDT Dangers," *Time*, Apr. 16, 1945, 91.

10. Vincent B. Wigglesworth, "DDT and the Balance of Nature," *Atlantic Monthly* 176 (1945): 107–113.

11. John K. Terres, "Dynamite in DDT," *New Republic*, Mar. 25, 1946, 415–16.

12. Anonymous, "DDT: Just Begun to Fight," 149.

13. Linda Lear, *Rachel Carson: Witness for Nature* (New York: Henry Holt, 1997), 78.

14. Rachel Carson to Harold Lynch, Letter, July 15, 1945, Rachel Carson Papers, Beinecke Library, Yale University. As quoted in Lear, *Witness for Nature*, 118–19.

15. President's Science Advisory Committee, *Use of Pesticides: A Report of the President's Science Advisory Committee* (Washington, D.C.: U.S. Government Printing Office, 1963), 20.

16. Lear, *Witness for Nature*, 451.

17. Abraham Ribicoff, *Pesticides and Public Policy: Report of the Committee on Government Operations, United States Senate* (Washington, D.C.: U.S.

Government Printing Office, 1966); and Emil M. Mrak (Chairman), *Report of the Secretary's Commission on Pesticides and Their Relationship to Environmental Health—Parts 1 and 2*, Report Number EPA/540/9-69/001-HEW (Washington, D.C.: Department of Health, Education and Welfare, and Environmental Protection Agency Office of Pesticide Programs, 1969).

18. Hal Higdon, "Obituary for DDT (in Michigan)," *New York Times Magazine*, July 6, 1969, 6.

19. Environmental Protection Agency, *DDT: A Review of Scientific and Economic Aspects of the Decision to Ban Its Use as a Pesticide*, 255.

20. Ibid., 149.

21. United Nations Environment Programme, *Ridding the World of POPS: A Guide to the Stockholm Convention on Persistent Organic Pollutants* (Geneva: United Nations Environment Programme, 2002), 5. Available online at www.pops.int/documents/guidance/beg_guide.pdf.

22. Amir Attaran, Donald R. Roberts, Chris F. Curtis, and Wenceslaus L. Kilama, "Balancing Risks on the Backs of the Poor," *Nature Medicine* 6 (2000): 729-31, 731.

23. South Africa Department of Environmental Affairs and Tourism, "One Million Deaths under 5...DDT Saves Lives," *Motions@POPs* (third edition: December 6, 2000), 1-3.

24. Kathleen R. Walker, Marie D. Ricciardone, and Janice Jensen, "Developing an International Consensus on DDT: A Balance of Environmental Protection and Disease Control," *International Journal of Hygiene and Environmental Health* 206 (2003): 423-35; and John A. Buccini, "The Long and Winding Road to Stockholm: The View from the Chair," in *Northern Lights against POPs: Combating Toxic Threats in the Arctic*, ed. David Leonard Downie and Terry Fenge (Montreal/Kingston: McGill-Queen's University Press), 224-55.

25. Malcolm Gladwell, "The Mosquito Killer," *The New Yorker*, July 2, 2001, 42-51, 51. Available online at www.gladwell.com/pdf/malaria.pdf.

26. Ulrich Beck, *Risk Society: Towards a New Modernity* (London: Sage Publications, 1992).

27. Rachel Carson, *Silent Spring* (Boston: Houghton Mifflin, 1994 [1962]), 20-21.

28. Robert L. Rudd, "The Irresponsible Poisoners," *The Nation*, May 30, 1959, 496.

29. Valerie J. Gunter and Craig K. Harris, "Noisy Winter: The DDT Controversy in the Years before *Silent Spring*," *Rural Sociology* 63 (1998): 179-98.

30. Carson, *Silent Spring*, 158.

31. Ibid., 16.

32. Rosenberg, "What the World Needs Now Is DDT," 39.

33. Gladwell, "The Mosquito Killer," 44.

34. Rosenberg, "What the World Needs Now Is DDT," 41.

35. Gladwell, "The Mosquito Killer," 51.

36. Carson, *Silent Spring*, 6.

37. Carol B. Gartner, "When Science Writing Becomes Literary Art: The Success of *Silent Spring*," in *And No Birds Sing: Rhetorical Analyses of Rachel Carson's "Silent Spring*," ed. Craig Waddell (Carbondale: Southern Illinois University Press, 2000), 103-125.

38. Edmund P. Russell, *War and Nature: Fighting Humans and Insects with Chemicals from World War I to "Silent Spring"* (New York: Cambridge University Press, 2001).

39. Carson, *Silent Spring*, 7.

40. Ibid., 225.

41. Ibid., 238.

42. International Agency for Research on Cancer, World Health Organization, *Volume 53: Occupational Exposures in Insecticide Application, and Some Pesticides: Summary of Data Reported and Evaluation* (Lyon: IARC, 1999). Available online at monographs.iarc.fr/ENG/Monographs/vol53/volume53.pdf.

43. Andrew G. Smith, "How Toxic Is DDT?," *Lancet* 356 (2000): 267-68.

44. Ralph H. Lutts, "Chemical Fallout: *Silent Spring*, Radioactive Fallout and the Environmental Movement," in *And No Birds Sing*, ed. Waddell, 17-41.

45. Carson, *Silent Spring*, 16.

46. Ibid., 23.

47. Ibid., 16.

48. Ibid., 23.

49. Buccini, "The Long and Winding Road to Stockholm," 241.

50. Carson, *Silent Spring*, 22.

51. Ibid., 13.

52. Carson, quoted in Lear, *Witness for Nature*, 454.

53. Carson, *Silent Spring*, 12-13.

54. Beck, *Risk Society*.

55. Ibid., 19.

56. Ibid., 23.

57. Peter Bachrach and Morton S. Baratz, "The Two Faces of Power," *American Political Science Review* 56 (1962): 947–52, 948.

13

In Her Footsteps

Christopher Merrill

It is my ritual to read Rachel Carson's trilogy of writings on the sea when I visit the Outer Banks of North Carolina, where I take my family every spring for a vacation. This year I had just started *The Edge of the Sea* when I learned that the Carolina Estuarine Reserve Foundation (CERF) would celebrate Carson's birthday, on the eve of our departure, with a hike in her footsteps. It turned out that in 1938 she made the first of several journeys to Beaufort, a port with an illustrious history of whalers and pirates, of shipbuilders and slave owners; her sojourns on the barrier island named after her are recounted in *Under the Sea-Wind* and *The Edge of the Sea*. And it was fortuitous that her birthday fell over the Memorial Day weekend. If she is better known for *Silent Spring*, her writings on the sea—her favorite subject—are no less poignant than her witness to the ravages done by men against nature.

I was struck by the conjunction of events: on Pivers Island, where Duke University's Marine Lab, the National Oceanic and Atmospheric Administration, and CERF share facilities, we would remember a lonely defender of the earth, while across the harbor Beaufort geared up to memorialize the thousands of soldiers who had laid down their lives to protect this country. Indeed the local paper included not only Carson's biography but also Lincoln's "Gettysburg Address," wartime poems by e. e. cummings and Wilfred Owen, and reminiscences of World War Two and Vietnam. The headline about offshore drilling made clear the imperative to end every war, including the one on nature.

Nor could I afford the luxury of imagining I had no stake in this conflict. My parents own beachfront property on Emerald Isle. The first thing I do each spring when we arrive is go to the end of the wooden walkway and measure how much of the shoreline has eroded since our last visit. The evidence of global warming is hard to miss: the sea is rising, and my parents' house is in danger of being swept away in a storm surge. My grandparents lost their house in a hurricane forty years ago. I assume the same will happen to my parents' house, and so I treat each journey to this barrier island with a sense that it may well be my last.

Which means that I may pay more attention than usual to my surroundings. For example, this was the year a humpbacked whale came ashore and died, then was bulldozed deep into the sand; that the regular visits from the dolphins ceased; that cannonball jellyfish washed up on the beach. When my five-year-old daughter, Hannah, stepped on one and realized she had not been stung she cried in glee, I can't wait to tell my teacher I stepped on a jellyfish! The weather was fine, and she took to sea kayaking with a fervor. We paddled through the salt marshes in search of great egrets, drifting as close to the majestic white birds as possible; counted the blue crabs in their cages; debated the merits of living in the solar-paneled house we discovered on an island accessible only by kayak. What Carson called "the intricate design of the fabric of life"[1] was everywhere on display—in the cordgrass and glasswort, in the ospreys and pintails. In the opening chapter of *The Edge of the Sea*, Carson describes the precarious nature of life along the shore, reminding us that margin means edge. But life teems in this place, which should be familiar to poets and writers accustomed to writing on the margins of contemporary discourse. How easily it can fall apart was revealed to us the day a young man wound around and around the estuary on a Jet Ski until his machine finally stalled. Hannah had become obsessed with the idea of jail, and she wondered if he would be arrested for such an offense. I'm afraid not, I said.

This was for our family also a year of mingled bliss and tragedy. My wife was occupied with our infant daughter, who had survived a traumatic birth, while my mother-in-law, who had lately lost her husband to cancer, played imaginary games with Hannah. Meantime my best friend was dying of brain cancer, his vision and memory eaten up by the disease. His sickness accentuated the dread I have lived with since the Bosnian war—dread that became more pronounced with the disputed election of George W. Bush, who wasted no time setting an antienvironmental agenda. And my anxiety was even greater when we set out for Rachel Carson's birthday celebration: I had just received word that a friend who had written extensively about the human dimension of the war in Bosnia had suddenly lost his five-year-old daughter.

A white tent was set up on Pivers Island, where the director of the reserve said that in 1982, when developers tried to build houses on the barrier island across the inlet from Beaufort, the people rose up in arms, partly because they did not want their glorious view obstructed, partly because sound science warned them that developing the marsh would destroy their lucrative fishing industry. Ninety percent of the fish we eat spend part of their lives in estuaries like the one preserved in the National Estuarine Reserve System—the funding for which was about to be cut. A crowd assembled at the dock for the short trip by motorboat across the water to the island bearing Carson's name, and I fell into conversation with a burly, good-natured man who worked at the reserve. Those yachts don't yield to a little boat, he said, gesturing toward what he called a multi-million dollar villa on the sea. He may not even have seen it, I said. He gazed at the yachts in the harbor, many of which had arrived in time for Memorial Day. There's a helluva lot of money floating around the world, he said, and I don't have any of it. Then he guffawed.

Presently the motorboat took us to the island, where we walked through cat grass, bull thistle, and Indian paintbrush over a rise of dredge sprawl and sea oats, until we came to a muddy beach along the inlet. Children caught fiddler crabs running along the shore, and when our tour guide, a plump young woman with a strong accent, said she liked to eat sea lettuce, the children all turned up their noses. She described how the sea oats' root system is four times the size of what we saw stitching together the dunes. She held out a cannonball jellyfish for the children to touch. She said that fiddler crabs smell with their feet, which cheered the little boys. Farther on was needlerush, a taller form of salt grass that grows near fresh water. You can eat the salt that condenses on the blades of the marsh grass, said the guide. Hannah was delighted to sample the briny pickleweed. I can tell my teacher I ate grass, she beamed.

I carried our infant in a front pack, shielding her from the sun. My wife helped her mother to see the white snails clinging to the cordgrass: marsh periwinkles. A great blue heron rose from the rushes; a wild horse grazed in a meadow; a storage tank loomed in the distance. In a tidal flat, among holes dug by blue crabs as they camouflaged themselves to catch unsuspecting prey, our guide picked up a worm egg case and said, Doesn't this look like pantyhose? The mud was deep; oyster shells were piled up in uneven lines. The guide said that an oyster filters two to five gallons of water an hour. And I was thinking of the estuary as a place of healing, of purification, when the old woman near me complained to the little girl by her side, "I'm going to kill your mother." Why? said the girl with a shocked look on her face. Because I'm not a walker, the old woman huffed.

Hannah was tiring, and our infant daughter had awakened, when we came to the sea. There was a sandbar about fifty yards out. The children plunged into the warm water in search of sand dollars and whelks and Venus shells. Hannah put on her purple bathing suit and joined me in the water. Soon we had found two perfect keyhole urchins, their thin apertures radiating from the five-petaled flower. When I looked back my wife was sitting apart from the rest of the group, nursing our daughter: a primal scene. Our stoical infant had become quite agitated in the last days, perhaps because she was teething, but after nursing her, my wife found a way to comfort her: offering her a finger to suck. And on our way back to the boat we picked leaves from the toothache tree to chew. They had a lemony taste, and made our tongues and lips numb. I can't wait to tell my teacher I ate a leaf, said my daughter. More yachts had sailed into the harbor. In the next town a replica of Christopher Columbus's ship the *Nina* had just docked. It occurred to me that the child's vision of the world is always like that of Columbus. This was the New World for my daughter, who had no idea how much of it had already been despoiled.

When we returned to Pivers Island, the burly man was waiting for us. Did you have fun? he asked my daughter. But she was already hurrying to the tent, where birthday cake was being served. He turned to me. Did you learn anything? Yes, I said. Yes, I did.

And that was how I imagined this story ended, until I went to bed that night and fell into a sound sleep only to wake with a start at two in the morning. I lay in the dark listening to the roar of the sea and the steady breathing of my wife and daughters. My anxiety had subsided, but still I could not sleep. And when it grew light I decided to go for a walk on the beach. The tide was out. A large plastic container had washed up in front of our house. I looked for sand dollars and Scotch bonnets and evidence of the buried whale, my mind drifting from one thing to the next. I remembered that besieged Sarajevans most longed for the sea. I prayed for my friend who was dying, and for my friend who had lost his daughter. I thought of how Rachel Carson had intended to write a guidebook about life along the shore in what became *The Edge of the Sea*. Halfway through, she started over. "I decided that I have been trying for a very long time to write the wrong kind of book," she told her editor, Paul Brooks. "I think we could say that the book has become an interpretation of...types of shore."[2] What good luck for her readers that she began again.

Nor did she write quickly, because, as she once explained, "the writer must never attempt to impose himself upon his subject. He must not try to mold it according to what he believes his readers or editors want to read. His initial task is to come to know his subject intimately, to understand its every aspect, to let it fill his mind. Then at some turning point the subject takes command and the true act of creation begins.... The discipline of the writer is to learn to be still and listen to what his subject has to tell him."[3] What Carson heard by the sea and recorded for her readers reverberates to this day.

Fire trucks were on the beach when I walked back; a rescue helicopter flew slowly by, searching not for endangered swimmers but for hazardous materials. It turned out that the plastic container that had come ashore in front of our house was filled with an industrial solvent. And when my family sat down to breakfast Hannah said, Have chemicals ever washed up when I was here before? No, I said. Good, she said. Then I can tell my teacher all about it. She thought for a moment. Will the men who dumped the chemicals go to jail? she asked. I doubt it, I said. Were they too fast for the police? she asked. Maybe, I said. A fireman had told me it was safe to swim. I was not sure. The waves were high. I feared for my children's safety.

NOTES

1. Rachel Carson, *The Edge of the Sea* (Boston: Mariner Books, 1998 [1955]), 14.

2. In Paul Brooks, *The House of Life: Rachel Carson at Work* (Boston: Houghton Mifflin, 1972), 158.

3. Ibid., 1–2.

14

Living Downstream of
Silent Spring

Sandra Steingraber

Two opposing events occurred between the year of my birth and the year I went to kindergarten in 1964. The first was the launching of a manned spacecraft by the Soviet Union and the subsequent scramble on the part of the United States to replicate that feat. The Cold War thus entered the Space Age, and the astronaut became the world's new conquering hero. Command and control were the watchwords of the day. The second event was the publication of *Silent Spring* by biologist and author Rachel Carson. This book, broadly speaking, argued that the command and control style of human decision making, when applied to natural systems here on earth, was doomed to failure. During a 1963 appearance on the television program *CBS Reports*, Carson put it this way: "We still talk in terms of conquest. We still haven't become mature enough to think of ourselves as only a tiny part of a vast and incredible universe. Man's attitude toward nature is today critically important simply because we have now acquired a fateful power to alter and destroy nature."[1]

Silent Spring rocketed to the top of the best-seller list and stayed there, selling a quarter million copies within a few months of publication. Having now sold more than ten million copies, *Silent Spring* is rivaled in its impact only by Charles Darwin's *Origin of Species* one hundred years earlier.

In 1962, when *Silent Spring* was published, I was three. Nevertheless, I knew it was an important book. The city bus driver—who drove my mother and me into town to do laundry and visit friends every Wednesday—had a copy tucked by his windshield. I recognized the cover because my father used the book as a text in the high school economics class he taught; there were copies of *Silent Spring* strewn around our house. More vividly, I remember the bottles used to spray our apple trees disappeared from the garage. Dad built a compost pile. The mailman began delivering airhole-punched boxes full of ladybugs. By age seven, I was put to work selling organic tomatoes at a roadside stand. So even though I didn't actually read *Silent Spring* until I was a college professor—more on this momentarily—the book profoundly shaped my childhood.

Although *Silent Spring* is organized into seventeen interlocking chapters, the book makes four big points. First, Carson contends, we are all being contaminated, without our consent, by inherently poisonous chemicals in the form of pesticides. These chemicals came into being as weapons of war during the 1940s and were subsequently marketed to farmers for use in pest control without any advance testing of their long-term safety or efficacy. Second, the consequent risks to our health and the health of other species are needless because there are so many nontoxic methods of pest control available if we only look about us. Third, in many cases, these alternative methods are more effective than chemical pesticides because the broadcast spraying of poison doesn't really work very well, and more often than not, makes the problem worse rather than better. Fourth, at the very least, we have the right to know about the risks that we are being compelled to endure. And out of that right to know follows the moral obligation to act.

The evidence that Carson gathered to support these arguments came from no one journal or field of study. Rather, she cites hundreds of scientific studies across many disciplines, ranging from pharmacology to wildlife biology. She treats each study like a jigsaw puzzle piece. No single one offers absolute proof but, when assembled together in the right configuration, they create a startling picture, a picture that Carson argues we ignore at our peril.

Because so many of *Silent Spring*'s puzzle pieces were studies published in little-known technical journals, Carson saw her task as one of a trial lawyer. She was going to bring the damning evidence out of the shadows of the arcane and the obscure, translate it into a compelling and simple narrative, and present her case before the public. The description in her private letters about the process of writing *Silent Spring* has pesticides playing the role of a defendant charged with crimes against nature and humanity. Carson is the prosecuting attorney, and the jurors are her readers.[2]

In 1990, when I was a thirty-one-year-old biology professor teaching in Chicago, I received a phone call that changed the course of my life. It was a simple request by a local environmental group asking if I would give a lecture about Rachel Carson for Earth Day. I assumed I was being asked because my dissertation research focuses on the (reckless and unnecessary) use of pesticides in forestry. No, came the reply. What my host wanted me to talk about was Carson's experience with breast cancer and how it shaped her thinking about chemical carcinogens like pesticides. And they wanted me to talk about my own cancer and how being a cancer patient had affected my own research on pesticides.

I was stunned. I had no idea Carson had had breast cancer. I didn't know that she was in treatment for cancer while writing *Silent Spring*, and I certainly didn't know that she had died from it around eighteen months after the book was published. Furthermore, I had no idea how the person on the other end of the line knew that I had had cancer myself.

So I did three things. First, in spite of my flabbergasted state and utter confusion, I said yes to the lecture invitation. Second, I reread *Silent Spring*. Or at least I initially thought I was rereading it. The words in the yellowing copy that I had in my bookshelf—probably bequeathed to me by my father—didn't sound familiar to me at all. I could not, upon further reflection, recall ever having been assigned to read the book by any professor in any of the many ecology and environmental issues classes I had ever taken. So, by chapter four, I was forced to conclude, with head-hanging shame, that I had never before actually read the damn book and that any flashes of recognition I felt were because Carson was forever being quoted by other authors in other books.

Then, once Earth Day was over, I went to Yale. This is where Carson's archives are held. Here, Carson's secret life as a cancer patient was revealed to me in her letters and private writings.[3] I was completely enthralled. While writing publicly about the evidence for the cancer-causing powers of pesticides, Carson privately worried that the revelation of her own diagnosis would cast doubt on her scientific objectivity and, hence, her perceived ability to carry out her appointed task. So she took great pains to make sure that no one, beyond a very few trusted confidants, found out. Carson even encouraged her friends to lie if asked about her health. Meanwhile, her own doctor was misleading her about the evident progression of her malignancy.

This exploration into Carson's personal life in the Yale archives aroused in me the first stirrings of my own book, *Living Downstream: An Ecologist Looks at Cancer and the Environment*.[4] While at Yale, I began reflecting on the various autobiographical details I shared with Carson—graduate research in wildlife biology, a heart-wrenching undergraduate decision to forego creative writing in favor of science, a publicly hidden cancer diagnosis. I began to wonder what it would be like to write an evidence-based book like *Silent Spring* but with a biologist narrator who reveals her cancer diagnosis in the text itself, interweaving the personal story with the scientific data. I hoped that it might be possible now to write such a book: thirty years of feminism lay between Carson's writing life and my own, and the idea that a woman's individual experience was a valid way of knowing the world had long since been affirmed. I hoped that my scientific objectivity would not be doubted simply because I had had a bladder tumor removed at the age of twenty and was willing to talk about that in the same chapter in which I would analyze the evidence for a link between perchloroethylene exposure and bladder cancer incidence among employees of dry-cleaning facilities.

I quit my tenure-track job in 1993 and went off to Harvard on a one-year fellowship to begin the research for *Living Downstream*. It ultimately took me four years to write the book. And because of the decision to disclose my own diagnosis, the book is located in a somewhat different place than *Silent Spring*. Carson's tack was to focus on one class of chemicals (pesticides) and describe their many effects (cancer, infertility, brain damage, extinctions, immunological damage, and so on). By contrast, I chose to examine many chemicals (pesticides, industrial products, solvents, air pollutants, dioxin, and so on) and explore their contribution to only one outcome (cancer). This decision reflects both the power and limitation of autobiography. My own life story was the organizing principle for the science. And my story is that of a cancer survivor who grew up in a small, Midwestern town that was highly industrialized but also situated within an intensely agricultural county. Because this community is the setting for the book, I needed to cast my net widely: the drinking water wells there contain both pesticides and dry-cleaning fluids. Moreover, I also had access to cancer registry data as well as toxics release data made available under right-to-know laws. Cancer registries were started in 1973. Public disclosure about toxic emissions from industrial facilities was mandated in 1986. Carson had neither of these databases at her disposal in the late 1950s when she was assembling the evidence for *Silent Spring*.

So those are some of the deliberate differences between Carson's writing and my own. But there are also many deliberate similarities. My shock at discovering that I, a Ph.D. biologist who makes a living as an environmental writer, had never in fact *read* Rachel Carson led me to immerse myself in her writing. I can now honestly say that I have read all of her books, many times, start to finish, as well as her letters, her collected speeches, magazine articles, books about her, and other miscellaneous work. Some of these readings have been with a writer's eye, I confess. What makes her prose so lyrical anyway? How exactly does she achieve eloquence without emotionalism? And how can I do that, too?

From Carson I learned how to make visible the intercourse between our bodies and the environments these bodies inhabit. There is a kind of exquisite communion between the external biological world that we can see and the hidden one inside our skins that we know as *self* but seldom get to look at. Exploring the permeable boundary between the two is almost always fresh and exciting for readers, and it breaks down the erroneous assumption that the environment is something ELSE, something OUT THERE apart from ourselves. From her first book, *Under the Sea-Wind*, here is Carson's description of a snowstorm in the Arctic:

Little by little, from the ice-strewn sea edge across miles of tundra, even far
south to the fringe of the forests, the undulating hills and the ice-scoured
valleys were flattening out, and a strange world, terrifying in its level white-
ness, was building up. In the purple twilight of the second day the fall slackened, and the night was loud with the crying of the wind, but with no
other voice, for no wild thing dared show itself.[5]

This landscape description is followed by a discussion of the embryological
events taking place inside of an owl's eggs:

As the snow fell on the still warm eggs and the hard, bitter cold of the night
gripped them, the life fires of the tiny embryos burned low. The crimson
streams ran slower in the vessels that carried the racing blood from the food
yolks to the embryos. After a time there slackened and finally ceased the
furious activities of cells that grew and divided, grew again and divided to
make owl bone and muscle and sinew. The pulsating red sacs under the
great oversized heads hesitated, beat spasmodically, and were stilled. The six
little owls-to-be were dead in the snow, and by their death, perhaps, hundreds of unborn lemmings and ptarmigans and Arctic hares had the greater
chance of escaping death from the feathered ones that strike from the sky.[6]

I studied these passages closely while I was working on my own description of embryological events in month four of a human pregnancy.
Specifically, I was looking for a way to make immediate, urgent, and visible
the results from two recent studies that had investigated the presence of pesticides in human amniotic fluid. Influenced by Carson's work, I came up with
the following paragraphs, which describe the first moments after my own
amniocentesis. In this scene, which takes place in Boston's Beth Israel
Hospital, thirty milliliters of amniotic fluid have just been removed from my
uterus. The nurse passes the vials, hot as blood, into my hands.

"That's baby pee," she says, smiling. "We like it yellow. It's a sign of
good kidney functioning."

I look at the vials again. Oh. Right.

The obstetrician is finishing up. She reminds me to drink plenty of
water today.

Drink plenty of water. Before it is baby pee, amniotic fluid is water. I
drink water, and it becomes blood plasma, which suffuses through the
amniotic sac and surrounds the baby—who also drinks it.

And what is it before that? Before it is drinking water, amniotic fluid is
the creeks and rivers that fill reservoirs. It is the underground water that
fills wells. And before it is creeks and rivers and groundwater, amniotic
fluid is rain. When I hold in my hands a tube of my own amniotic fluid, I
am holding a tube full of raindrops. Amniotic fluid is also the juice of
oranges that I had for breakfast, and the milk that I poured over my cereal,
and the honey I stirred into my tea. It is inside the green cells of spinach

leaves and the damp flesh of apples. It is the yolk of an egg. When I look at amniotic fluid, I am looking at rain falling on orange groves. I am looking at melon fields, potatoes in wet earth, frost on pasture grasses. The blood of cows and chickens is in this tube. The nectar gathered by bees and hummingbirds is in this tube. Whatever is inside hummingbird eggs is also inside my womb. Whatever is in the world's water is here in my hands.[7]

That Carson wrote prose like a poet is one of the most common claims made about her writing. I was reassured to learn that the process of her prose writing also resembled the making of poetry. That is, she wrote at a snail's pace and then she rewrote. And rewrote. Carson once said about herself, "I write slowly, often in longhand, with frequent revision. Being sensitive to interruption, I write most freely at night. As a writer, my interest is divided between the presentation of facts and the interpretation of their significance, with emphasis, I think toward the latter."[8]

After the 1997 publication of *Living Downstream*, I traveled with the book for nearly two years and met a lot of my readers. Along the way, I had the chance to talk with sheep farmers in Ireland, professional golfers in West Palm Beach, fashion designers, chefs, farmers, architects, firefighters, midwives, college students, cancer survivors, cancer researchers, garden clubs, church groups, pediatric oncologists, hospital administrators, United Nations delegates, European Union parliamentarians, and Inuit elders in Alaska. I received a lot of feedback.

From these various conversations, I have concluded that I was right about some of my early assumptions and wrong about others. Truly, feminism has opened up a critical space in our culture that allows memoiristic recollections to exist side by side, or even intertwined with, dispassionate, hardheaded analysis. Years of breast cancer activism have also opened spaces for public narratives about formerly private experiences.[9] So, in my own attempt to "make my case," I did not have to engage in the erasure of the self that Carson did. Indeed, most of my readers and reviewers said they appreciated the juxtaposition of the autobiographical with the science. And this was my hope—that the thread of a compelling human story could seduce readers through some fairly complicated toxicology, organic chemistry, and molecular epidemiology that they might otherwise not be willing to read. With a few notable exceptions, no one questioned my scientific objectivity or ability to summarize the state of the evidence.

One negative review—which appeared in the *New England Journal of Medicine*, sadly enough—described me as an emotional cancer patient and never mentioned that I am also a biologist. However, the reviewer was later outed by Physicians for Social Responsibility. It turned out that he was, in fact, a toxicologist employed by Grace Chemical Company, whose environmental crimes I describe in the book itself. The *New England Journal of Medicine* subsequently apologized in the pages of the *Washington Post*.

On the other hand, I underestimated how emotionally overwhelming the book would be for many of my readers. Rather than serve as a call to action—which was my hope—*Living Downstream* made a lot of my readers just feel depressed and helpless. The biggest criticism that I've received is that the book doesn't tell the reader what to do, that it doesn't offer a good clear road map out of the mess. I think this is a good criticism, but it's one that puzzled me for years. I suspect, because I had cancer at such an early age, that my own psychic barometer, if you will, is set differently. To me, knowledge about a problem is a powerful first step—even we don't yet know how to solve the problem. To me, the idea that the environment may play a bigger role in our risk for cancer than the genes we've inherited is good news: we can remove carcinogens from our environment; we can't change our ancestors. But then I am the kind of person who reads cancer registry data in the bathtub and studied birth defect registry data while pregnant. For many folks, as I learned, knowledge of a problem in the absence of a clearly articulated solution induces despair rather than action. This is because the only things they can imagine doing to address the problem—of, say, pesticides in our drinking water supplies—seem puny and insignificant compared to the vast scope of the problem.[10]

So, let me use the rest of this chapter to tell you what to do. Let's write together, right now, the last missing chapter of *Living Downstream* which details exactly how we are going to divorce our economy from its current dependency on cancer-causing chemicals to grow our food and manufacture our goods.

If you are a fashion designer, you need to create markets for organic cotton. Conventionally grown cotton uses more insecticides than any other crop, and these chemicals are traveling in the jet stream and turning up in the breast milk of Inuit mothers in the Arctic Circle. Rachel Carson talked in detail about the special problems created by cotton, and they remain to be solved. You are also going to take on the dry-cleaning industry. You need to pressure dry cleaners to become wet cleaners. Dry-cleaning solvents contaminate 30 percent of U.S. drinking water, while wet cleaning is nontoxic, effective, and equally convenient to the consumer. In this way, fashion designers are going to save our drinking water, protect the health of cotton farmers' children, and clean up breast milk in the Arctic.

If you are an economist, you need to figure out how to capitalize on the transformation of dry cleaners. Dry-cleaning shops are mom-and-pop operations, often owned and operated by immigrant families. What do they need to invest in the new, nontoxic technologies? Tax incentives? Low-interest loans? Grants? Subsidies? Figure it out and get back to us. You, too, can help protect our drinking water and prevent dry-cleaning operators from dying of bladder cancer.

If you are a gerontologist, a nursing home director, or anyone who works with senior citizens, you are going to invest in organic agriculture. Pesticide exposure in rural areas is linked to the risk of developing Parkinson's disease in old age.

If you are an athlete, a coach, or the parent of a budding athlete whom you hope might someday land a sports scholarship, you need to be pushing for the development of more fuel-efficient cars. New research shows that early childhood exposure to air pollutants, such as those that come out of tailpipes, decreases the lung capacity of adolescents. Lung capacity is directly related to athletic performance.

If you are an engineer, you get to design those cars.

If you are a business manager, you are going to become familiar with the new research showing that indoor air pollution in office buildings lowers worker productivity by decreasing reading and typing speeds. And then you are going to call your friend the architect and tell her or him to get busy designing office buildings that are made of nontoxic materials that do not off-gas neurological-impairing fumes. And if you are the architect who receives this call, you are going to get on the phone with your designers and let them know that your first priority is to find cost-effective substitutes for vinyl (PVC). This building material—found in flooring, wallpaper, shower curtains, water pipes, and office furniture—appears to be one of the worst offenders in degrading indoor air and contributing to respiratory distress in employees and children alike.

If you are a Web designer or computer programmer, you need to take a look at some of the Web sites that provide the public with cancer registry data and toxics release information. Many of them are terrible. (Start with www.scorecard.org, which is not terrible but sure could use some jazzing up.) Turn your talents toward making public databases on environmental health more elegant, as well as easier to find, navigate, and link to and from. Additionally, somebody needs to be working on a computer mapping program that would create bridges between health registries (compiled by public health departments on the state level) and toxic inventories (compiled by the Environmental Protection Agency on the federal level). Currently, our government collects mountains of data on environmental releases of cancer-causing chemicals (and where they occur) and mountains of data on who gets cancer each year (and where they live)...but never the twain shall meet.

If you are a teacher, a pediatrician, a child-welfare advocate, or someone who really enjoys fishing, please devote yourself to renewable energy. Why? Because the burning of coal is the leading contributor to atmospheric mercury loading. And when this mercury comes back to us in the form of methylmercury in fish and seafood, it poses a terrible threat to brain development in children. Methylmercury exposure is a known risk factor for learning disabilities and attention deficit disorders, and the leading means by which we are so exposed is through the eating of fish. There is, thus, a relationship between our national energy policy and how many kids need special education services. So, those of you invested in early childhood education, please start talking with advocates of solar and wind power.

Rachel Carson said, in her television appearance on CBS, "Now, I truly believe, that we in this generation must come to terms with nature, and I think we're challenged as mankind has never been challenged before to prove our maturity and our mastery, not of nature, but of ourselves."[11] More than a generation later we are still so challenged. But rather than give in to despair, the answer, I think, is to pick one part of the problem about which you already have expertise and passion and work as hard as you can on that single piece.

If you are a musician, let me put it this way: It is time to play the *Save the World* symphony. It is a vast orchestral piece, and you are but one musician. You are not required to play a solo, but you are required to figure out what your instrument is and play it as well as you can.

NOTES

1. "The Silent Spring of Rachel Carson," *CBS Reports*, Apr. 3, 1963, telecast.

2. Rachel Carson, *Always, Rachel: The Letters of Rachel Carson and Dorothy Freeman, 1952–1964*, ed. Martha Freeman (Boston: Beacon Press, 1995).

3. Much of Carson's private struggle with cancer has since been documented in Linda Lear's biography, *Rachel Carson: Witness for Nature* (New York: Henry Holt, 1997). Carson's letters to her dearest confidante, Dorothy Freeman, have also been published (see *Always, Rachel*) since I visited the Carson archives at Yale.

4. Sandra Steingraber, *Living Downstream: An Ecologist Looks at Cancer and the Environment* (New York: Addison Wesley, 1997).

5. Rachel Carson, *Under the Sea-Wind* (New York: Penguin Books, 1996 [1941]), 50.

6. Ibid., 51–52.

7. Sandra Steingraber, *Having Faith: An Ecologist's Journey to Motherhood* (Cambridge, Mass.: Perseus Book Group, 2001), 65–67.

8. Rachel Carson, as quoted in Jonathan Norton Leonard, "Rachel Carson Dies of Cancer; 'Silent Spring' Author Was 56," *New York Times*, Apr. 15, 1964.

9. The structure of these narratives are the topic of a recent book; Marcy Jane Knopf-Newman, *Beyond Slash, Burn, and Poison: Transforming Breast Cancer Stories into Action* (New Brunswick: Rutgers University Press, 2004).

10. My thoughts on the origins of environmental despair are further elaborated in "The Obligation to Endure...Again," in *What We Do Now*, ed. Dennis Loy Johnson and Valerie Merians (Hoboken: Melville House Books, 2004), 131–39.

11. "The Silent Spring of Rachel Carson," *CBS Reports*, Apr. 3, 1963, telecast.

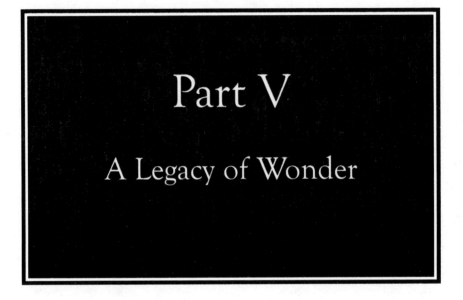

Part V

A Legacy of Wonder

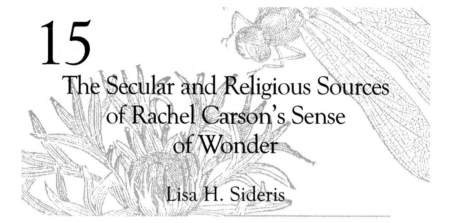

15

The Secular and Religious Sources of Rachel Carson's Sense of Wonder

Lisa H. Sideris

A few years ago, I presented a paper that touched upon Rachel Carson's struggle with breast cancer and her determination to finish *Silent Spring* before she died. The discussion afterward turned to Carson's religious background and beliefs. A member of the audience, familiar with Carson's life and work, characterized Carson as "two parts evolutionist, one part fallen Presbyterian." Perhaps because I am something of a fallen Presbyterian-Darwinian myself, I remembered that phrase and have continued to wonder about these different parts of Rachel Carson. How, if at all, did Carson integrate these aspects of herself? Are there clues to be found in her writing?

Anyone who reads Carson's work immediately recognizes in it a person of very strong convictions, perhaps religious in nature and origin, though not explicitly so. Often the word "spiritual" is applied to her writing and her worldview. While it is not inaccurate to depict Carson as such, this characterization is frustratingly vague to scholars of religion.[1] So, here I wish to delve a bit more deeply into Carson's story—her literary, moral, and theological influences—in search of clues to the *kind* of spirituality she displayed. Carson's familial religious roots, as well as the influence of a certain romantic and religiously moralistic genre of children's literature that she encountered early in life, point to a fairly distinct ethical and spiritual stance, I believe. Carson's affinity with the theology and ethics of humanitarian and theologian Albert Schweitzer—an affinity she maintained throughout her adult life—forms another important dimension of Carson's particular type of religiousness.

232

That, at least, is the argument I intend to make. But first, keeping this characterization of Carson as part evolutionist, part fallen Presbyterian in mind, consider the following passage from a letter she once wrote to a concerned reader of her sea books. Carson's correspondent was a conservative Christian who wished to register his disapproval that her observations as a naturalist seemed to leave God and the Bible entirely out of the picture. Here is Carson's response:

> It is true that I accept the theory of evolution as the most logical one that has ever been put forward to explain the development of living creatures on this earth. As far as I am concerned, however, there is absolutely no conflict between a belief in evolution and a belief in God as the creator....And it is a method so marvelously conceived that to study it in detail is to increase—and certainly never to diminish—one's reverence and awe both for the Creator and the process.[2]

Carson was never one to sidestep controversy, so it is unlikely that she merely told this reader what he wanted to hear. Rather, her two claims here—first that "no conflict" exists between belief in God and evolution, and second, that studying nature enhances reverence—are convictions Carson seems to have held throughout her life. She may have slipped a bit from her religious roots, but all in all, I don't believe she fell very far.

CHILDHOOD RELIGIOUS AND LITERARY INFLUENCES

Growing up, Carson was surrounded by religious influences. Her maternal grandfather was ordained in the Presbyterian Church and became a pastor in Allegheny City, Pennsylvania. Carson's mother, Maria McLean, attended seminary at a United Presbyterian institution and later became a school teacher. Because married women were prohibited from teaching, Maria gave up her position when she wed Robert Carson, a somewhat older man who shared her solid United Presbyterian background. Maria and Robert Carson moved to Springdale, Pennsylvania, and joined the Springdale United Presbyterian Church; their daughter Rachel, born in 1907, was christened there and attended Sunday school regularly.[3]

Presbyterianism is a descendent of the Calvinist branch of Protestantism. Calvinism tends to have a bad reputation among environmentalists, so it is worthwhile to dwell for a moment on some of its key tenets. Calvinist theology is typically portrayed as upholding the radical sovereignty and transcendence of God, and the total depravity and dependence of humans—twin doctrines that seem to leave no vestige of divinity in the natural world. Corrupted and weakened by sin after the Fall, human reason no longer discerns God clearly in nature. Moreover, the belief that one can turn oneself toward God by turning to nature detracts from God's unconditioned sovereignty and undermines the primacy of *scriptural* authority as the source of knowledge of the divine. After the Fall, "the human mind because of its feebleness can in no way attain to God," Calvin writes in the *Institutes of the Christian Religion*, "unless it be aided and assisted by his Sacred Word."[4]

The reform tradition in general, and Calvinism in particular, has always been wary of the danger that natural knowledge of God might make humans—as the knowers—the object of reverence rather than the Creator. In other words, natural theology can quickly turn into idolatry when we search in nature for key indicators of our own importance, or glorify ourselves and our knowledge rather than God. Calvin's writing displays a deep concern with overweening human pride and vanity. Though we dwell our entire lives in a "workshop graced with God's unnumbered works," he writes, we offer no praise to God but are instead "puffed up and swollen with all the more pride."[5]

Yet Calvin also asserted that natural evidence of the Creator is so overwhelming and ubiquitous that we have "no excuse" for failing to see God all around us. Humans have a "natural instinct" of divinity implanted in our minds.[6] Indeed, one finds in Calvin an endorsement of a painstaking study of nature as a means of glorifying God. Calvin considers science "one of God's excellent gifts" that ought to evoke awe and gratitude.[7] In this sense, Calvin's theology contains a subtle and qualified form of natural theology. His qualifications spring from the indisputable fact of human sinfulness: signs of God in nature are compelling and undeniable, but because we have fallen, we can scarcely see them. "It is therefore in vain that so many burning lamps shine for us in the workmanship of the universe to show forth the glory of its Author," Calvin argues. Our turn to nature is often motivated by reckless curiosity, a desire to find clues to our own existence, and particularly affirmations of our importance. We read nature selectively, and discover merely our own narrow view superimposed on God's creation. In modern parlance, we might say that our study of nature becomes anthropocentric. In Calvin's language, the moment we receive a "taste of the divine" we proceed to taint it by glorifying not God but "dreams and specters of our own brains."[8]

Fortunately, sin leaves us with a correctible myopia rather than total blindness. Calvin resolves the apparent tension between a pious investigation of nature and an idolatrous one by arguing that natural signs of God become fully apparent to us when viewed through eyes of faith. Faith is likened to spectacles that restore proper vision: "the invisible divinity is made manifest in such spectacles, but we have not the eyes to see this unless they be illumined by the inner revelation of God through faith."[9] In the absence of faith, natural signs never constitute "proof" of God's existence and the skeptic demanding it will not be granted that clear vision. But for the believer, nature plays a crucial role in evoking a sense of God's overwhelming presence, and a sense of piety and gratitude in response to that presence.

While it would be absurd to suggest that Rachel Carson maintained some strict adherence to Calvinist doctrine and principles, certain quasi-Calvinist themes are evident in her account of nature and *human* nature. Among these is her basic conviction that a properly oriented study of nature promotes reverence, mystery, and humility—an expanded and clarified vision of the world around us. Knowledge, so long as it remains tethered to piety, never dispels wonder. Yet, human nature being what it is, the study of the natural world, and science generally, can also foster idolatrous and arrogant tendencies that warrant constant vigilance. As our pride swells, the world contracts around us. We lose sight of both reality and mystery. These themes, and others related to them, are likewise present and continuously reinforced by many of the influential figures and texts in Carson's life.

Of central importance to Carson was her mother. A devout Presbyterian and outdoors enthusiast, Maria encouraged love and respect for nature. Later in life, when writing *Silent Spring*, Carson would count her mother as a chief ally in her "crusade" (as she termed it) to protect nature from the destructive effects of indiscriminate pesticides. "More than anyone else I know," Carson reflected, "she embodied Albert Schweitzer's, 'reverence for life.'"[10] Religious instruction and love of nature were intimately linked in the particular genre of literature that Carson imbibed as a child. Carson was instructed in the juvenile literature promoted by the nature study movement of the late nineteenth and early twentieth century—often religious, always moralistic, and at times sentimental nature tales replete with woodland fairies, angels, and young, idealistic protagonists. With roots in the Victorian tradition of children's literature, the nature study movement sought to inculcate moral virtue, civic responsibility, aesthetic appreciation, and respect for life through stories, essays, poems, and especially direct encounters with the natural world. "Embracing the ideas of natural theology that by studying nature, the intricate design of the Creator would become visible, the nature-study movement taught that nature was holy" and its protection "'a divine obligation.'"[11]

NATURE STUDY GOALS AND PRINCIPLES

As part of their elementary schooling, the Carson children received nature study readers compiled by advocates such as Anna Botsford Comstock and Liberty Hyde Bailey of Cornell University. As Lear notes, not only was Maria Carson "the perfect nature-study teacher" but the Carson children had access to a "sixty-four acre laboratory."[12]

The nature study movement grew out of concern for the moral and spiritual development of children in urban environments who were cut off from the natural world and agrarian lifestyles. In works such as Comstock's widely used and encyclopedic *Handbook of Nature Study* (1911), the movement emphasized such goals as: involvement of the senses; a criticism of "facts only" approaches to study promoted by "specialists"; instilling sympathy with all living things; and the encouragement of natural preservation through such bonds of sympathy.

In *The Nature-Study Idea*, Bailey defines nature study as a program designed to "open the pupil's mind by direct observation to a knowledge and love of the common things and experiences in the child's life and environment."[13] Proponents of nature study were careful to distinguish it from the mere teaching of biology or natural history. A kind of revolt against formal science, "dry-as-dust science teaching" and "mechanical" memorization, nature study instilled not facts but "spirit."[14] Teachers sought to avoid rigid instruction on the one hand, and a fall into "mere sentimentalism and gush on the other."[15] Comstock, for example, acknowledged the teacher's perennial challenge to "inculcate in the child a reverence for life and yet to keep him from becoming mawkish and morbid."[16] Teachers and parents were advised to find ways of linking nature study to the child's other lessons, such as those in math or history, including biblical history. "The study of the grasshopper," Comstock observes, "brings to the child's attention stories of the locusts' invasion mentioned in the Bible, and the stars which witnessed our creation and of which Job sang and the ancients wrote, shine over our heads every night."[17]

Instilling spirit meant engaging the senses. Children should see, touch, and smell nature prior to reasoning about it. "All the senses should be so trained and adjusted that all our world becomes alive to us," Bailey urged.[18] Once the senses were awakened, a child's natural curiosity would lead to closer, more detailed study of nature. But facts introduced too soon and too emphatically might damage the child's ability to wonder, to sense nature's mystery. From the child's perspective, Bailey wrote, there are "elves whispering in the trees...chariots of fire rolling on the long, low clouds at twilight. Wherever it may look, the young mind is impressed with the mystery of the unknown."[19] Science education should never remove the child's sense of mystery, for the true scientist loves, and is humbled by, the unknowns. "For every fact that they discover they turn up a dozen mysteries," Bailey wrote. Knowledge both begins and ends in wonder, if it can be said to end at all. "The consciousness of ignorance is the first result of wonder, and it leads the pupil on and on: it is the spirit of inquiry."[20] Carson echoes these beliefs in her letter to her Christian critic.

Proponents viewed the development of "nature-sympathy" as progress in civilization. "It is one of the marks of progress of the race," Bailey wrote, "that we are coming more and more into sympathy with the natural world in which we dwell."[21] Scientific progress without ethical progress is dangerous and in fact regressive. This too would become a central theme of Carson's works, particularly in *Silent Spring*.

For some nature study advocates, a pernicious product of modern science was the expert or specialist who isolates the living organism from its natural environment, studies and dissects it in the lab, and never grasps the significance of natural relationships or the relationship of nature study to other kinds of pursuits. The result is a kind of "dead accuracy." By contrast, nature study embraced *living* accuracy: while discouraging a diet of facts alone, it emphasized the need for accurate knowledge about the world—the world as it really is, in a phrase that Carson would later invoke frequently. This entailed exposing the child to what Bailey calls "things in the large and in relation"— that is, understanding the broad relationships between life forms before delving into details and definitions. A child is "by nature a generalist," Bailey insisted. "He should not be forced to be a specialist."[22] Living accuracy discouraged "collecting" of specimens as an end in itself; parents and teachers should be careful about inflaming a passion for hunting and catching organisms.

Nature study also called attention to the difference between "intrinsic" and "extrinsic" knowledge—or what we might today call inherent versus instrumental value. It opposed purely utilitarian knowledge, the search for the extrinsic function or usefulness of all things in nature to humans. The student instead must try to imagine the world from the intrinsic perspective of the organism— an exercise in imagination that Carson would develop into a fine art when writing of the ocean and its strange inhabitants. When the study of nature merely serves to reassure us that nature is designed for our benefit and use, the purpose of nature study is defeated. Bailey writes that the "notion that all things were made for man's special pleasure is colossal self-assurance. It has none of the humility of the psalmist, who exclaimed, 'What is man that Thou art mindful of him?'" The lamentable result is that "much of our interpretation of nature is only an interpretation of ourselves"—a sentiment with which Calvin would have agreed.[23] The intrinsic perspective seeks to correct this conceit.

Intrinsic study is facilitated by blending science and poetry because poetic approaches effectively shift attention from "human interest in natural things to the things themselves."[24] In general, nature study critiqued the split between the two cultures. A true scientist is a kind of poet but, again, good nature writing should not be mere sentimentalism. Even the poet must have his facts straight. "His poetry is misleading if his observations are wrong,"[25] Bailey contends.

OTHER CHILDHOOD INFLUENCES

Besides her exposure to these ideas at home and school, Carson's interests as a child independently led her to other sources of nature study wisdom.

One was the writer Gene Stratton-Porter; another was the children's magazine *St. Nicholas*.

Novelist and naturalist, Gene Stratton-Porter was a childhood favorite of Carson's—an "apostle of the nature-study movement who believed that through nature a child was led to God."[26] Born in Wabash County, Indiana, in 1863, Porter was an avid bird-watcher and outdoorswoman. Her books were popular, romantic, wholesome works, geared largely toward women and girls, and full of "woodlore, birdlife, and salubrious prescriptions for home happiness."[27] She was particularly interested in the domestic habits of birds, their "nest building, diet, and social behavior," but had little taste for dry, academic, or statistical study.[28] Her father was a preacher in the local Methodist church, but she described her own religious affiliation as membership in "the Big Cathedral of the Woods, where God furnishes music and sermons of His own making."[29]

From an early age, Carson shared Stratton-Porter's interest in the "home-life" and habits of birds.[30] Carson may also have read one of Stratton-Porter's most enchanting nonfiction works, *Birds of the Bible* (1909). A religious ornithology of sorts, the book exemplifies well the nature study conviction that the lyrical and the scientifically accurate are inseparable.[31] In *Birds of the Bible*, Stratton-Porter takes readers on a tour of the Bible, illustrating the relevance and accuracy of the biblical authors' eloquent observations about birdlife. At times she interjects a defense of certain birds and a plea for their protection, particularly predatory birds considered to be "abominations" in the Bible (the same bird species that, decades later, would be threatened with extinction by DDT). "Herons are beautiful birds," she insists, "and do no harm in any way that I can think, so they should be protected rigorously."[32]

Birds of the Bible opens with a number of bird photographs, including one of a fossilized archaeopteryx, the beloved bird of evolutionists in search of a "transitional form" with which to refute biblical creationists. Stratton-Porter apparently saw nothing incongruous in featuring archaeopteryx so prominently in a work on biblical birds; the caption beneath the photo bears the words of the Apostle Peter, "One day is with the Lord as a thousand years, and a thousand years as one day." Her mission as a writer and naturalist was fueled by the nature study conviction that science should awaken and increase, never deplete, our capacity for wonder and mystery. Scientific investigation "reaches the hearts of things we want to know, how matter and life originated"; yet at a certain point it invariably reaches "a granite wall...and there science may search, climb, and batter until it is worn out, but the answer never comes."[33] Carson might not have put the point so bluntly, but she embraced the mystery that continually outstrips science and is at the same time the inspiration for further research.

Carson's mother subscribed to a number of children's magazines, and *St. Nicholas* was a favorite with Rachel. Throughout her childhood and early adolescence, Carson was an avid reader and eventually a contributor to this magazine. Published by the St. Nicholas League—St. Nicholas being, of course, a protector of children—the magazine undertook an indirect moral education of the young, not by commanding morality outright but through developing sympathy from within. Literature published in *St. Nicholas* exemplified the romantic-realist perspective of nature study, attempting to inculcate moral teaching and encourage sympathy through stories and poems about the natural world. Facts alone were thought to inhibit the child's natural moral sympathies.

An important goal of the St. Nicholas League was the "protection of the oppressed, whether human or dumb creatures."[34] Authors who published in *St. Nicholas* while young include e. e. cummings, F. Scott Fitzgerald, and E. B. White (author of *Charlotte's Web*). At the age of eleven, White published a story depicting a natural world in which no harm would come to what he called "God's innocent little folk"—a story that Maria Carson might well have read to young Rachel.[35] Carson submitted stories and essays to *St. Nicholas*, as well as other publications associated with nature and humane movements such as *Our Animal Friends*, and soon joined *St. Nicholas*' distinguished group of child authors. In one of these stories, she describes her "favorite recreation" of going "bird-nesting." Carson continued to submit essays to magazines throughout her teen years and eventually determined that she would enroll in college with a major in English.

COLLEGE YEARS: A SPIRITUAL ADVENTURE

In 1925 Carson entered the Pennsylvania College for Women (PCW), a school that met with the approval of both Maria and Rachel Carson as a Christian college with a good reputation.[36] Carson arrived at PCW with high ideals regarding the goals of education and high expectations of herself. Believing that any education worth pursuing should include moral education, she wrote in an early essay that college should give one a "sense of values—the ability to judge the good from the bad, the worthwhile from the unprofitable." In short, she wrote, college should be "a spiritual adventure."[37]

Carson's spiritual adventure at PCW eventually culminated in a switch from a major in English to one in science. Looking back on her college years and her choice of science, Carson later remarked, "I had given up writing forever, I thought. It never occurred to me that I was merely getting something to write about" ("apparently," she adds, "it didn't occur to any of my advisors, either.")[38] It's worth noting that while Carson felt torn between literature and her growing love of science, she apparently sensed no similar conflict between religion and science. The combined teachings of Presbyterianism and the romantic realism of nature study had taken root. Shortly after arriving at

PCW, Carson submitted an English composition entitled "Who I Am and Why I Came to PCW." Her self-portrait expresses her ties both to religion and nature—as well as the sense of confidence and independence that would mark all her endeavors. Carson describes herself as "a Presbyterian, Scotch-Irish by ancestry, and a graduate of a small, but first class high school....I love all the beautiful things of nature," she continues, "and the wild creatures are my friends." She adds that she chose PCW as "a Christian college founded on ideals of service and honor." The only requirement at PCW that consistently received Carson's "approval and compliance," Lear notes, "was to attend church on Sunday."[39] It's not clear that Carson attended religious services with any kind of regularity after leaving college, though she had contact off and on with the Unitarian church.

After PCW, Carson pursued a master's degree in zoology at Johns Hopkins, graduating in 1932; following that she maintained for many years a grueling schedule of working for the Fish and Wildlife Service while supporting and caring for her mother, sister, and nieces, and churning out articles and books in her "spare" time. By the mid-1950s Carson had published three books about the sea—*Under the Sea-Wind*, *The Sea Around Us*, and *The Edge of the Sea*—and along the way, became successful enough as a writer to resign from her government job and devote herself to writing full-time.

As many readers have noted, Carson's three sea books embody perfectly a blending of poetic and scientific writing. She receives consistent praised for her ability to translate scientific data into magic and enchantment. In a statement reminiscent of Bailey's nature study philosophy, Carson once remarked that if there was poetry in her writing about the sea it was not "because I deliberately put it there, but because no one could write truthfully about the sea and leave out the poetry."[40]

Humans, when they appear in Carson's marine narratives, are often a destructive or insignificant presence. For example, in a chapter of *The Sea Around Us*, Carson describes the precariousness of island environments such as the Galapagos, and the dangers posed by introduced species. In an intriguing twist on biblical stories, she depicts an Edenic island setting with tame, docile creatures lacking natural fear of humans being threatened by a perverse Noah's ark that annihilates species rather than saving them from destruction.

> [Man] has destroyed environments by cutting, clearing, and burning; he has brought with him as a chance associate the nefarious rat; and almost invariably he has turned loose upon the islands a whole Noah's Ark of goats, hogs, cattle, dogs, cats, and other non-native animals as well as plants. Upon species after species of island life, the black night of extinction has fallen.[41]

Perhaps this somewhat cryptic allusion is Carson's way of reminding readers of the biblical precedent for preserving rather than destroying species.

On the whole, the insignificance of humans, compared with the vast, timeless forces of nature, was a comforting thought to Carson. One finds a distinctly "Jobian" perspective in some of her writing—a perspective that recalls the biblical story of Job with its decentralization of humans, and expressions of wonder and awe for natural processes that are fully comprehended only by God. Many readers responded favorably to these themes. "I am overwhelmed with a sense of the vastness of the sea, and properly humble about our goings-on," wrote one. Another said that Carson's expansive vision "helps one reduce so many of our man-made problems to their proper proportions."[42]

SPUTNIK, SCHWEITZER, AND *SILENT SPRING*

The belief that knowledge of nature engenders humility and reverence was, for Carson, an article of faith, with roots in the religion of her childhood and the nature literature she loved. But it was a belief that would be challenged by so-called advances in science and technology in the years following World War II. In articulating and defending her shock-worn convictions, Carson often turned to the theology of Albert Schweitzer and his account of reverence for life. She would also dedicate herself to an exposé of human arrogance—namely, *Silent Spring*.

By the late 1950s, Carson had begun to think seriously about writing a book on the misuse of pesticides, particularly DDT. A number of events and people influenced Carson's decision to mount a full-scale critique of human destructiveness toward nature. Among these was the launching of *Sputnik* in 1957.

For Carson, Sputnik changed the world in ways that were immediately and profoundly disturbing. "But what a strange future we all have to face!" she wrote to her friend Dorothy Freeman shortly after the launch. "It seems to me all I have ever said or believed has lost much of its meaning in the light of recent events."[43] Carson had been thinking of writing a book on the broad theme of life in relation to its environment, a book about evolution and ecology, but had been mentally "blocked." Sputnik galvanized and gave direction to her ideas. For Carson, Sputnik represented a kind of technology capable of undermining the Jobian vision of humans, nature, and God that she had long taken for granted. In a remarkable letter to Dorothy in February, 1958, she outlines these views and describes her comfort in the belief—increasingly threatened—that the forces of nature remain vast, mysterious, and beyond the control of humans. She also expresses her fear that the idolatrous and arrogant tendencies of science have triumphed over humility and wonder, with humans now usurping a divine role.

It was pleasant to believe...that much of Nature was forever beyond the tampering reach of man—he might level the forests and dam the streams, but the clouds and the rain and the wind were God's....It was comforting to suppose that the stream of life would flow on through time in whatever course that God had appointed for it....And to suppose that, however the physical environment might mold Life, that Life could never assume the power to change drastically—or even destroy—the physical world. These beliefs have almost been part of me for as long as I have thought about such things....I still feel there is a case to be made for my old belief that as man approaches the "new heaven and the new earth"—or the space-age universe, if you will, he must do so with humility rather than arrogance....Of course, in pre-*Sputnik* days, it was easy to dismiss so much as science-fiction fantasies. Now the most farfetched schemes seem entirely possible of achievement. And man seems actually likely to take into his hands—ill-prepared as he is psychologically—many of the functions of "God."[44]

Rather than devote a book solely to these themes, as she had once intended, Carson folded them into an even more urgent project which would become *Silent Spring*.

As is noted frequently, *Silent Spring* contains a dedication to Schweitzer, "who said 'Man has lost the capacity to foresee and to forestall. He will end by destroying the earth.'"[45] Carson cites him again in her second chapter where she depicts pesticides moving "mysteriously" through groundwater, and mutating, through an "alchemy of air and sunlight," into new, even deadlier poisons. She concludes the passage with a quote from Schweitzer: "Man can hardly even recognize the devils of his own creation."[46]

Several years before *Silent Spring* was published, *Life* magazine sent Carson an advance copy of a feature on Schweitzer for her comment. Schweitzer had recently been awarded a Nobel Prize and Carson was impressed with him. "We must talk about him sometime," she wrote to Dorothy. "I think he is an extremely significant figure—his Reverence-for-Life philosophy is of course somewhat like my own," she added.[47] Later, battling cancer while working to streamline her arguments in *Silent Spring*, Carson would look to Schweitzer for an example of what she hoped to achieve: "I want it to be a much shortened and simplified statement, doing for this subject (if this isn't too presumptuous a comparison) what Schweitzer did...for the allied subject of radiation."[48] She achieved her aims: in 1963, the Animal Welfare Institute awarded Carson their Albert Schweitzer Medal.

Much of Schweitzer's ethic toward life is articulated in a two-volume work called *Philosophy of Civilization* (1923). Schweitzer once said that throughout his life he felt a strong sense of compassion for animals, and as a child, could never understand why bedtime prayers should include only humans.[49] He grew up in Alsatia, the son of a Lutheran minister, and took advanced degrees in philosophy and theology before deciding, at the age of thirty, to study medicine. He eventually earned a degree in tropical medicine and set off to do missionary work in Africa. The inspiration for his lifelong service to others—all kinds of others—grew out of a doctrine he eventually termed reverence for life.[50]

Schweitzer, like L. H. Bailey, feared that progress in civilization was rapidly outstripping progress in sympathy, or moral progress. He argues that the ethical person accepts self-imposed constraints to help all life and avoid causing injury whenever possible.[51] Each living thing is an instance of what he calls "will to live" continually coming into contact with others similarly willing: "I am life which wills to live, in the midst of life which wills to live."[52] A genuine ethic of life does not "ask how far this or that life deserves one's interest as being valuable, nor, beyond that, whether and how far it can appreciate such interest. Life as such is sacred."[53] Schweitzer shared Carson's conviction–and the conviction of nature study advocates such as Stratton-Porter and Bailey—that scientific investigation reinforces sympathy for life, and adds to a sense of mystery. He was likewise suspicious of the specialist who accumulates facts but misses the wonder of life. In Schweitzer's view, science could never fully capture the essence of life—"what life is, no science can tell us." An unlearned person captivated by nature's beauty and wonder "knows more truly than the learned one who studies under the microscope...[one] who, with all his knowledge of the life-course of these manifestations of the will-to-live, is unmoved by the mystery."[54] Such a scientist is "puffed up with vanity" at his ability to describe some mere "fragment of life," Schweitzer argues, but never grasps life with a capital L, the essence of life.[55] Pride in our own power and knowledge will result in our own destruction, he warns; humans are "intoxicated by progress in discovery and invention...we forgot to trouble ourselves about men's progress in spirituality."[56]

The image of humans drunk with knowledge and power is one Carson often evoked in later years. In a speech entitled "The Real World Around Us," Carson similarly describes man as "intoxicated with his own power," and suggests that the remedy may well lie in focusing more attention on the inseparable wonder and reality of our world.[57]

Carson's concern for life extended beyond wild nature to animals in farms and laboratories, and her debt to Schweitzer is perhaps most apparent here. Much of her advocacy for humane treatment of these animals went on behind the scenes but Carson also wrote an introduction to a booklet published by the Animal Welfare Institute, a group wanting to implement changes in high school biology experiments with animals. Echoing Schweitzer, Carson writes there, the "essence of life is lived in freedom" and not something that can be isolated and understood in the artificial environment of the laboratory.[58] Drawing on a theme from the nature study literature of her childhood, Carson also insists that a child should first encounter organisms in the wild, in their true relations, prior to laboratory study, if an "awareness and reverence for the wholeness of life" are to develop.[59]

But perhaps what impressed Carson most was Schweitzer's insistence that ethical orientation must involve a strong *activist* component. Sacrifice to others, Schweitzer wrote, is not merely "intellectual" but carries an "impulse to action"[60] None of us is exempt from acting for life. "While so much ill-treatment of animals goes on," Schweitzer wrote, "we all share the guilt."[61] Carson's lifelong sense of "Calvinistic responsibility and civic obligation," as Lear terms it, prepared her well to receive the message of Schweitzer's life and work.[62] Carson adamantly defends this vision of ethical citizenship—of *vocation*, in the Calvinist sense[63]—in her foreword to Ruth Harrison's *Animal Machines*, a *Silent Spring*-like exposé of the horrors of factory farms. Here, near the end of her life, Carson does not mince words. She delivers a sermon that indicts the twin evils of technological idolatry and citizens' failure to take action on behalf of animal life. "The modern world," she writes, "worships the gods of speed and quantity, and of the quick and easy profit, and out of this idolatry monstrous evils have arisen."[64] The general public is complicit in these horrors, and can no longer "rest secure in a childlike faith that 'someone' is looking after things."[65] She concludes with a warning that human beings will never know real peace until we recognize the "Schweitzerian ethic that embraces decent consideration for all living creatures—a true reverence for life."[66]

A SENSE OF WONDER AS CORRECTED VISION

The specialist is the *bête noire* of *Silent Spring*. Numerous passages castigate the tunnel vision of specialists such as the chemical engineer peddling pesticides and urging the world to "beat its plowshares into spray guns"[67]—a phrase that surely rings a bell for readers with even rudimentary knowledge of scripture! "This is an era of specialists," she writes, "each of whom sees his own problem and is unaware of or intolerant of the larger frame into which it fits."[68]

During her college years, as she first experienced pressures to choose an area of specialization, Carson briefly sensed an incompatibility between her love of literature and her love of science; later she would understand that science gave her something to write about. Her final book, published posthumously, reflects most clearly Carson's convictions that science and poetry, fact and fancy, knowledge and mystery, belong together, reinforce one another, and are crucial for a child's early development as a *generalist*. Originally entitled "Help Your Child to Wonder" and later named *The Sense of Wonder*, this little book is firmly within the nature study tradition of Gene Stratton-Porter, Anna Comstock, and L. H. Bailey. It also sounds a distinctly Schweitzerian note.

Carson's decision to write this book grew out of experiences of sharing her love and knowledge of nature with her grandnephew Roger, whom she adopted after his mother died in 1957. *The Sense of Wonder* is a distillation of many of the nature study themes that undoubtedly shaped her own view of life when she was a child. It brings Carson's life and work full circle. She endorses the sort of indirect method of teaching advocated by nature study: factual information such as the names of organisms should remain subordinate to the goal of creating a deeper response of wonder and curiosity. Once a child's curiosity is sparked, he will want to know more about facts and details. She emphasizes the importance of awakening the senses, rather than memorizing facts, as the most enduring path to understanding and appreciating nature.

> If facts are the seeds that later produce knowledge and wisdom, then the emotions and the impressions of the senses are the fertile soil in which the seeds must grow. The years of early childhood are the time to prepare the soil. Once the emotions have been aroused—a sense of the beautiful, the excitement of the new and the unknown, a feeling of sympathy, pity, admiration or love—then we wish for knowledge about the object of our emotional response.[69]

She likewise discourages collecting and labeling of organisms—what she calls the "game of identification"—as the goal. "If it becomes an end in itself," she writes, "I count it of little use." One could compile an "extensive list of creatures seen" without once glimpsing the mystery and "wonder of life," she notes.[70] Carson laments that most adults have suffered a loss of vision, and have developed an inability to see nature as it really is, to see it through eyes of wonder. "It is our misfortune that for most of us that clear-eyed vision, that true instinct for what is beautiful and awe-inspiring, is dimmed and even lost before we reach adulthood."[71]

The loss of a natural instinct for reverence—this narrowing and dimming of our vision—is reminiscent of Calvin's interpretation of the effects of sin on natural knowledge. Here and elsewhere in Carson's writings, constricted and impaired vision corresponds to, or may lead to, an inflated sense of human importance, a compulsion to value all things in relation to ourselves, an arrogant and idolatrous displacement of God. Openness to the bigger picture of nature offers a correction, encouraging humility and reverence.

To be sure, Carson does not urge us to repent and turn to God, nor does she advocate faith as a means of correction, but her language nevertheless evokes the theology of the tradition in which she was raised. Humans have for "too long been looking through the wrong end of the telescope," Carson writes. "We have looked first at man with his vanities and greed, and at his problems of a day or a year; and then only, and from this biased point of view, we have looked outward at the earth and at the universe of which our earth is so minute a part."[72] Carson simply asks us to reverse the telescope and discover our place in the amazing universe we actually inhabit, the world as it really is. This, in a nutshell, was her religion.

Rachel Carson died of metastatic breast cancer in the spring of 1964. Fact is sometimes stranger than fiction, as Carson certainly knew, and her own story ends in a peculiar religious twist. Her close friends were aware of her wish to be cremated, and for her ashes to be scattered along the Sheepscot River of her adopted coastal Maine. She had requested a simple service at a Unitarian church, suggesting to one Reverend Howlett that he read from the concluding pages of *The Edge of the Sea*. Her final wishes were overridden by her controlling older brother Robert who insisted on a large funeral at Washington National Cathedral with a "traditional burial service according to the *Book of Common Prayer*"; Carson's remains, Robert insisted, would be placed alongside their mother's grave.[73] Eventually a bizarre compromise was struck and half of her ashes were buried next to her mother, the other half scattered over the waters at Sheepscot by Dorothy Freeman, as Carson had wished.

This struggle over Carson's body, and perhaps her soul, may appear sadly symbolic of her tireless efforts to unite those things—knowledge and wonder, fact and poetry, reason and emotion, even evolutionism and Presbyterian-ism—that humans seem determined to drive apart. But Carson might have taken a more reverential, and hopeful, view of this final partitioning of her remains between land and water. After all, as she stressed repeatedly, the dividing line between land and sea is itself an illusion that falls away when we expand our vision. The sea encircles us always; no separation exists in the world as it *really* is. Such was her view, as she expressed it in the final passage of *The Sea Around Us*:

> the sea lies all about us....The continents themselves dissolve and pass to the sea, in grain after grain of eroded land....In its mysterious past it encompasses all the dim origins of life and receives in the end, after, it may be, many transmutations, the dead husks of that same life. For all at last return to the sea—to Oceanus, the ocean river, like the ever-flowing stream of time, the beginning and the end.[74]

NOTES

1. Phil Cafaro suggests, in chapter four of this volume ("Rachel Carson's Environmental Ethics") that the relationship between religion and Carson's environmentalism can be (and perhaps has been) overestimated. I think it has been largely underappreciated. However, I would agree that Carson did not adhere to any form of "organized" religion throughout her life.

2. Quoted in Paul Brooks, *The House of Life: Rachel Carson at Work* (Boston: Houghton Mifflin, 1972), 9.

3. Linda Lear, *Rachel Carson: Witness for Nature* (New York: Henry Holt, 1997). Lear writes that the Carsons left one Presbyterian church to join another, perhaps out of disapproval of the minister, but continued to attend Presbyterian services throughout Rachel's youth.

4. John Calvin, *Institutes of the Christian Religion*, ed. John T. McNeill (Louisville, Ky.: Westminster John Knox Press, 1960), 74.

5. Ibid., 55.

6. Ibid., 43.

7. Ibid., 273.

8. Ibid., 68, 69.

9. Ibid., 68.

10. Rachel Carson to Marjorie Spock, Letter, Dec. 4, 1958, Rachel Carson Papers, Beinecke Library, Yale University; as quoted in Lear, *Witness for Nature*, 338.

11. Ibid., 14.

12. Ibid.

13. Liberty Hyde Bailey, *The Nature-Study Idea*, 4th ed., rev. (New York: Macmillan, 1911 [1903]), 4.

14. Ibid., 18.

15. Ibid., 53.

16. Anna Botsford Comstock, *Handbook of Nature Study* (Ithaca: Comstock Publishing Associates, 1967 [1911]), 12. The book is dedicated to L. H. Bailey.

17. Ibid., 18.

18. Bailey, *Nature-Study*, 47.

19. Ibid., 36. Calvin would no doubt take issue with this somewhat animistic account of nature.

20. Ibid., 44.

21. Ibid., 27.

22. Ibid., 71.

23. Ibid., 128–29.

24. Ibid., 160.

25. Ibid., 37.

26. Lear, *Witness for Nature*, 17.

27. Judith Reick Long, *Gene Stratton-Porter: Novelist and Naturalist* (Indianapolis: Indiana Historical Society, 1990).

28. Ibid., 8.

29. Ibid., 53.

30. A story Carson wrote as a child, "The Little Brown House," anthropo-morphically depicts two wrens searching for a suitable house (Lear, *Witness for Nature*, 17).

31. Lear observes that "since Carson's mother was such a devoted practi-tioner of the nature study movement, and since she was a Presbyterian minis-ter's daughter and a conscientious student of the Bible," it is likely that *Birds of the Bible*, "would have been one of the things Carson read" (personal com-munication).

32. Gene Stratton-Porter, *Birds of the Bible* (Cincinnati: Jennings and Graham, 1909), 169.

33. Ibid., 68.

34. Quoted in Lear, *Witness for Nature*, 17.

35. Ibid., 19. Carson remained a devoted reader of E. B. White all her life and the feeling was reciprocated. Some forty years later, Carson would suggest to White that he write an exposé on the pesticide problem in the United States; White shared her concerns but could not take on the assignment and encouraged Carson to pursue it herself. The result was *Silent Spring*.

36. Ibid., 25.

37. Ibid., 42.

38. Carson, "The Real World Around Us," in Rachel Carson, *Lost Woods: The Discovered Writing of Rachel Carson*, ed. Linda Lear (Boston: Beacon Press, 1998), 149.

39. Rachel Carson, "Who I Am and Why I Came to P.C.W.," 1925; as quoted in Lear, *Witness for Nature*, 32.

40. Rachel Carson, "Remarks at the Acceptance of the National Book Award for Nonfiction," in *Lost Woods*, 91.

41. Rachel Carson, *The Sea Around Us* (New York: Oxford University Press, 1989 [1950]), 93.

42. Quoted in Brooks, *House of Life*, 129.

43. Rachel Carson to Dorothy Freeman, Letter, Nov. 7, 1957, in Rachel Carson, *Always, Rachel: The Letters of Rachel Carson and Dorothy Freeman, 1952–1964*, ed. Martha Freeman (Boston: Beacon Press, 1995), 233.

44. Rachel Carson to Dorothy Freeman, Letter, Feb. 1, 1958, in *Always, Rachel*, 248–49.

45. Carson, *Silent Spring*, v.

46. Ibid., 6.

47. Rachel Carson to Dorothy Freeman, Letter, Nov. 12, 1954, in *Always, Rachel*, 62.

48. Rachel Carson to Dorothy Freeman, Letter, Mar. 4, 1961, in *Always, Rachel*, 357.

49. Albert Schweitzer, *Out of My Life and Thought* (New York: Henry Holt, 1933).

50. From a strict Calvinist standpoint, reverence for "life" might not be reverence for God; however, Schweitzer defines "Life" in such a way that it seems to entail reverence for the source of life itself.

51. Albert Schweitzer, *Civilization and Ethics. Philosophy of Civilization, Part 2* (London: A&C Black, 1929 [1923]), 254.

52. Ibid., 246.

53. Ibid., 247.

54. Ibid., 245.

55. Ibid.

56. Ibid., 277.

57. Carson, "The Real World Around Us," in *Lost Woods*, 163.

58. Carson, "To Understand Biology," in *Lost Woods*, 193.

59. Ibid., 194.

60. Schweitzer, *Civilization*, 243.

61. Ibid., 257.

62. Lear, *Witness for Nature*, 24.

63. Calvin denies that the monastic life is a "higher" calling than active service to God and others in a lawful, secular society of believers. (See *Institutes*, 4.13.11 and following.)

64. Carson, foreword to Ruth Harrison's *Animal Machines* (New York: Ballantine, 1964), in *Lost Woods*, 194.

65. Ibid.

66. Ibid., 196.

67. Carson, *Silent Spring*, 69.

68. Ibid., 13.

69. Rachel Carson, *The Sense of Wonder* (New York: HarperCollins, 1998 [1965]), 56.

70. Ibid., 94.

71. Ibid., 54.

72. Quoted in Brooks, *House of Life*, 129. This is from her National Book Award acceptance speech, reprinted, in part, in *Lost Woods*, 90–92.

73. Lear, *Witness for Nature*, 481–82.

74. Carson, *The Sea Around Us*, 212.

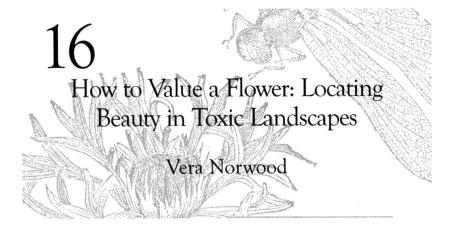

16

How to Value a Flower: Locating Beauty in Toxic Landscapes

Vera Norwood

Rachel Carson stands as a fingerpost pointing toward environmental problems of the early twenty-first century most often because of the continued relevance of her concerns about the impacts of chemical pesticides on the health of humans and other animals. Recently, environmental history has focused on the failures of influential voices in the environmental movement during the mid- and late-twentieth century to pay attention to pollution in our daily lives–particularly among working-class and minority populations. For many scholars, one of the distinguishing characteristics of a new environmentalism has been a shift in emphasis away from aesthetic appreciation of nature's defining place in everyday experience. Critiques of the romantic entrancement with wilderness and pastoral and suburban landscapes, in favor of a hard-edged, often pessimistic, analysis of urban, industrial places and their toxic qualities for women, children, families, and workers predominate. Social justice issues raised by the power of government and corporations to pollute our workplaces, schools, and homes are fundamentally important. Carson would have been deeply moved to know that she was instrumental in bringing Cesar Chavez, Lois Gibbs, and others to the table in the contest over citizen rights to a healthy environment for humans.

Carson's comments about her sense of accomplishment at the release of *Silent Spring,* however, focused not on the threat of chemicals to human health, but on her effort to remind humanity of the debt we owe to the beauties of nature: "last night the thoughts of…all the loveliness that is in nature came to me with such a surge of deep happiness, that now I *had* done what I

could—I had been able to complete it."[1] Key to a fulsome appreciation of
Carson's legacy is to understand that, at heart, her concern about pesticides
was embedded in her conviction of the importance of every citizen's right to
explore natural beauty—across all landscapes/spaces/places/scales. Much has
been written about Carson's concern for wildlife. That emphasis is driven in
large part because of connections to other sentient animals, who share much
the same physiology as humans. What about the rest of the natural world?
Carson located a great deal of her wonder and appreciation for nature among
the flora; her writings never fail to give equal voice to the contributions of the
plant kingdom not only to our understanding of the ecological complexities
of nature, but also to its inspiring beauties.

The focus of this chapter is how to value a flower—an effort that, I think,
Carson would appreciate as critical to her legacy. Valuing a flower is a complex task in twenty-first-century environmentalism, and the difficulty is, perhaps, best explained by an essay Alice Walker wrote about mid-twentieth-
century African-American political agendas. Walker argues that it was difficult in the 1960s and 1970s for politically aware African Americans to write
anything about their love of nature. Discussing her colleagues' assessment of
Sammy Lou, the hero of Walker's poem "Revolutionary Petunias," as "incorrect," she posits that the most incorrect thing about Sammy Lou is her love of
flowers: "I have heard it said by one of our cultural visionaries that whenever
you hear a black person talking about the beauties of nature, that person is
not a black person at all, but a Negro. This is meant as a put-down, and it is.
It puts down all of the black folks in Georgia, Alabama, Mississippi, Texas,
Louisiana—in fact it covers just about everybody's mama."[2]

Walker's comments document just the divide mentioned above between
wilderness advocates, suburban gardeners, city beautification planners and
civil rights activists concerned about workplace pollution, lead poisoning in
inner-city housing, and the siting of incinerators in poor neighborhoods.
While scholarly literature has made an exceptional contribution to understanding how to "unbind" (to use Robert Gottlieb's phrase) the environmental movement from its roots among middle-class, white elites, we have not
been very adept at addressing the extent to which common interests in the
aesthetic values of nature, wherever we find them, deserve attention as well.
Carson is a helpful guide to understanding what really might be revolutionary
in the defense of a petunia.[3]

Rachel Carson struggled a good deal with the title of her new book on
the dangers of pesticides. Her agent, Marie Rodell, found a quote from the
British poet John Keats' "La Belle Dame Sans Merci" that clinched *Silent
Spring* as the final choice: "The sedge is wither'd from the lake / And no
birds sing." These lines encapsulate the heart of Carson's message about
nature in her book—how tightly woven are the lives of local plants and animals (including humans) in any landscape. The Keats selection serves as a

coda to Carson's lyric opening. Her imaginative "Fable for Tomorrow" is set in an unnamed small town "in the heart of America" that experiences a spring with no robins and "roadsides...lined with browned and withered vegetation."[4] Keats' lyric use of the natural closing down of a winter lake forcefully contrasts with this mysterious, unnatural failure of spring. The glorious and uplifting moment of spring bloom is fundamental to Rachel Carson's appreciation of nature, and to get at that, we must pay attention to her love of the green world, of the plants whose lives define the seasons as much as do the habits of robins.

Carson's mother, Maria, early on instilled in her an interest in birding and botany. Both were occupations considered suitable in the education of young women of the early twentieth century. On the family's sixty-five-acre property and the surrounding woods on the outskirts of the small town of Springfield, Pennsylvania, Maria and Rachel enjoyed sightings of local birds and gathered native wildflowers. While attending the Pennsylvania College for Women in Pittsburgh, Carson continued to enjoy the combined pleasures of botanizing and birding with her science teacher/mentor, Mary Scott Skinker, with whom she shared a developing sense of the importance of conservation and preservation of the native plants and animals they discovered on field trips.[5]

Her love of the mixed landscape of suburb and native woods carried throughout her life. For many years she had planned to expand an early essay on teaching children an appreciation of nature into a longer work. The locus of the piece was her property in Southport, Maine—which looked out to the ocean and back to deep woods. Published posthumously, *The Sense of Wonder* describes her "Wildwoods" where "there are lady's-slippers and wood lilies and the slender wands of clintonia with its deep blue berries."[6] Admiring the native plants of the woods, she incorporated many into her gardens surrounding her cabin. A letter to her neighbor and close friend, Dorothy Freeman, described her goals for her garden at Southport: "Planned or orthodox gardens wouldn't interest me...and if I could get anything to 'running wild' at Southport I'd be delighted. And of course I want only things that seem to belong there."[7] She and Freeman deeply loved the remnant wild places between their two properties and they dubbed them "Lost Woods." Carson dedicated much time to an ultimately unsuccessful attempt to buy "Lost Woods" and set up a nature sanctuary; such work led her to help found the Maine chapter of the Nature Conservancy.

Dorothy Freeman became Rachel Carson's closest and most intimate confidante in the 1950s and that relationship was nurtured by their mutual love of birds and flowers. Their correspondence is filled with evocative descriptions of seasonal blooms around their summer homes in Maine and their winter homes in the suburbs of Massachusetts and Maryland. The spring bulb bloom always elicited a letter exchange comparing and suggesting

new gardening endeavors. Flowers provided both material and symbolic evocation of the depth of their feelings for each other. Writing to Dorothy about
how she treasured their friendship, Carson told of hearing of a man who said,
"if he had two pennies he would use one to buy bread and the other to buy a
'white hyacinth for his soul'...You, dearest, are the 'white hyacinth' in which
I invest part of my time."[8] Over the years, they exchanged flowers (often
hyacinths but also freesias, roses, and orchids) when they could not see each
other; they relied on different kinds of flowers to express how they felt about
each other. When apart, they could look out in their gardens and see flower-
ing plants that reminded each of the other. Most poignantly, as Carson's illness made it more difficult for her to return to the Maine coast, Freeman
re-created the place and their love for one another in evocative descriptions of
the wildflowers: "The lovely lavenderish blue asters have been breath-takingly
lovely (emphasis by repetition)....As the light intensified, the color deep-
ened—there they were, as I saw them growing out of a long fissure in the granite exactly marking the spot beneath which is Our Cave."[9]

Carson was raised to appreciate the beauties of the flora, was trained in
the ecological meanings of that beauty, and read deeply in the literary naturalists and romantic poets. She understood well the powerful emotions that
descriptions of a lovely, budding landscape could evoke in many of her con-
temporaries. Although her reputation as a nature writer was established in
her series of sea books, it is the shared appreciation of the moment when
spring arrives that she called upon to draw readers into the strange worlds of
the oceans.

The Sea Around Us, the book that established her as an internationally
acclaimed nature writer, depends on images drawn from land flora to convey
the natural rhythms and cycles of the sea. The third chapter, "The Changing
Year," focuses on seasons in the sea. Carson acknowledges the common sense
experience of the otherness of the oceans—particularly noting ominous poisonous plankton blooms and mysterious phosphorescent displays of "lights
that come and go for reasons meaningless to man."[10] But she embeds the
strange in the familiar. The chapter opens with a reminder of the beauties of
spring blooming on the land and a lesson in how spring advances on the sea
as well. Thus, the "lifeless" winter ocean is only an illusion—as are the dreary
winter colors on land—for every niche contains a future: "Most of all, perhaps, there is assurance in the fine dust of life that remains in the surface
waters, the invisible spores of the diatoms, needing only the touch of warming sun...to repeat the magic of spring."[11.]

The most powerful (and longest) chapter in her other acclaimed sea
book, *The Edge of the Sea*, is based directly on her beloved property in Maine
and draws on her experience of the connections between land and sea. In this
chapter, "The Rocky Shores," Carson takes the reader along with her on a
foggy morning walk through her evergreen forest down to the rugged coast-

line. Key to the aesthetic pleasures of the shore is the interdependency of flora and fauna. The "Rocky Shores" chapter emphasizes the synergies between forest spruce, lichens, moss, and birds and requires that we take such ecological understanding of the relationship of flora and fauna into the undersea world of kelp, urchins, and starfish. Carson describes an ocean plant kingdom due the honor and respect of America's great native forests. Reminiscent of the mysterious forest on her walk to the coast, Carson takes the reader on an underwater stroll through its mirror image—the laminarias of the deep waters—"a dark forest" whose "holdfasts" share with a tree's roots the support of an entire microcosm.[12]

Carson did not initially intend for The Edge of the Sea to deal in such ecological communities. It was first meant to follow the life of representative creatures of a specific coastal area, but over the five years of the book's creation, the emphasis shifted to the ecology of the ocean, necessarily divided by distinctive regions. Ecologists routinely referred to the interrelationships of plants and animals as like the relationships within a household. Carson's readers had to come to think of nature as "home."[13] Carson's version of home had to do with gardens, flowers, nearby woods with loved native plants. Thus, The Edge of the Sea opens not with the great forests of sea kelp but with delicate tide pools and their floral-like creatures. The spring tides bring Carson and her reader to the edge of the sea, to search out the "hydroid Tubularia," "the most delicately beautiful of all the shore's inhabitants—flowers that are not plant but animal, blooming on the threshold of the deeper sea."[14] Perfectly adapted to their difficult environment, "every detail was functionally useful, every stalk and hydranth and petal-like tentacle fashioned for dealing with the realities of existence. I knew that they were merely waiting...for the return of the sea. Then in the rush of water, in the surge of surf and the pressure of the incoming tide, the delicate flower heads would stir with life."[15] Just as she could call upon a familiar experience of a walk through the forest to build appreciation and attachment to kelp forests, she could call upon a search for a rare native flower, remind her readers of its difficult dependence on the confluence of sun, rain and wind in order to bloom along the path, and use that experience to bring home the synchronous interdependence of ocean life.

From the beginning of her professional writing career in the 1930s, Carson was concerned about the loss of habitat resulting from human activities and by the 1950s had written many government and popular pieces documenting the problem. She was a longtime and influential member of state and national Audubon societies and, by 1950, had also joined the Wilderness Society. During the 1950s Carson became actively engaged in efforts to preserve habitat, including her efforts to found the Maine branch of the Nature Conservancy and pursuit of preservation of the Lost Woods with Dorothy Freeman. At work on The Sea Around Us, she wrote an essay on the formation of islands that concluded with an indictment of human impacts on fragile island ecosystems and she was particularly concerned about the need for seashore preservation. *The Sea Around Us* includes a scathing indictment of "man's" "interfering with natural balances"[16] in island ecologies in Hawaii, not only by introducing non-native animals like cattle and hogs but also plants such as lantana which compete with and ultimately wipe out natives. Even though both of the sea books end with a sense that the oceans control their own destiny (and thereby the destiny of all the plants and animals they nurture), by the end of the 1950s Carson was convinced that the world of delicate yet tough beauty that had inspired her and her readers was not as immune to human dominion as she once had imagined.

The point of the fable opening *Silent Spring* is that humans are responsible for the failed spring. Efforts to suppress disease-carrying insects and insects and weeds that competed for the food supply ultimately led to most of the unintended consequences detailed in the fable. The second chapter of *Silent Spring*, "The Obligation to Endure," locates the key to the problem in twentieth-century agricultural monocropping practices: "Nature has introduced great variety into the landscape, but man has displayed a passion for simplifying it."[17] The urge to create a landscape filled only with plants useful to humans extends as well to ornamental gardening—as a single tree such as the elm becomes the national standard for city beautification. Plant importations for agriculture and ornament served as a primary agent in ratcheting up problems with pests and the use of chemicals for control.

Although discussion of the impacts of chemical spraying on the flora are scattered throughout *Silent Spring*, plants receive concentrated attention in the chapter called "Earth's Green Mantle." Here Carson argues that the underpinnings of an ethos that values a simplified landscape rest in a problematic view of plants: "Our attitude toward plants is a singularly narrow one. If we see any immediate utility in a plant we foster it. If for any reason we find its presence undesirable or merely a matter of indifference, we may condemn it to destruction forthwith."[18] Monocropping is an obvious example of fostering only plants directly useful to humans, while importing plants with no thought to the consequences of tag-along pests is another. Broad-spectrum herbicides also simplify the landscape with unintended consequences. Carson outlines how spraying for ragweed creates a "boomerang" effect of more ragweed: the annual seedlings find the open soil created by herbicides fertile ground to sprout the next spring. Isolating and targeting a single plant without thought to its community creates such problems. Another example of such thinking is the impact of "clean cultivation and the chemical destruction of hedgerows and weeds"[19] that eliminates forage for pollinating insects like bees—which benefit both agriculture and wildlife.

Carson is sensitive to the difficulty of defining what we mean by "weed" and shows how the easy acceptance of concepts of "good" and "bad" plants contributes to the simplified landscape. Embedded in managerial concepts of "brush control" is a blanket assignment of many native and naturalized plants in a community to the lowly status of weeds—to be eradicated. Use of chemical spraying for "roadside brush control" in Maine comes under heavy indictment for its impact on native and naturalized shrubs and wildflowers: "Azaleas, mountain laurel, blueberries, huckleberries, viburnums, dogwood, bayberry, sweet fern, low shadbush, winterberry, chokecherry, and wild plum are dying before the chemical barrage. So are the daisies, black-eyed Susans, Queen Anne's lace, goldenrods, and fall asters which lend grace and beauty to the landscape."[20] Even those who make some distinction among the plants are willing to lose "good" plants if they grow in "bad company" among unwanted plants. Again, Carson is pointing to the problems caused when we lose sight of the diverse living communities that make up any green landscape.

Carson's goal for her garden at Southport was that it include "only things that seem to belong here." She was not, however, a purist when it came to native plants, either in the garden or along the roadside. Queen Anne's lace, for example, is a European introduction that has become a naturalized wildflower along the highway. As long as the plant adapted to a diverse community (rather than choking out the natives as the lantana had done in Hawaii) it was a welcome sight. In landscapes closer to home, with long settlement and waves of migration, Carson offered a cosmopolitan aesthetic that also blurred the boundaries of easy conceptions of "good" and "bad" plants.

Some of the most emotionally powerful descriptions of the wages of chemical campaigns on the flora are based in Carson's ecological understanding of the interdependencies of plant/animal communities—of the interrelationships of sedge and bird. Describing a U.S. Forest Service spraying campaign aimed at eradicating sagebrush to support more grassland for cattle in Bridger National Forest in Wyoming, Carson notes that streamside willow thickets were also destroyed. Relying on the thickets were moose and beaver. The beaver built ponds that supported trout and attracted waterfowl, making for good hunting and fishing. With the loss of the willow thickets the moose and beaver left—as did the birds and the trout: "The living world was shattered."[21] The willows were innocent of weediness, the consequences were unintended, but the results were the same as agricultural monocropping—a simplification of the landscape that, ironically, resulted in the loss of a plant/animal community with both utilitarian and aesthetic value for humans.

As she does in each chapter of *Silent Spring* Carson offers an alternative approach to plant management—one with a much wider view of the green world. On the simplest level, landscape managers should keep a close eye on objectives. Roadside spraying, for example, aims to eliminate plants that interfere with a driver's vision or utility rights of way. Selective spraying can take care of trees while leaving shrubs and wildflowers. Control of weeds works best when the conditions of their production are understood. Crabgrass, for example, is a sign of an unhealthy lawn, and grows in empty spaces where there is not competition from healthy grass. Introduced invasives like Klamath weed in California are best controlled by importing their native animal partners— in this case a species of beetle from France that feeds on the weed. Success against weeds comes from working with rather than against the grain of nature, as "Nature herself has met many of the problems that now beset us, and she has usually solved them in her own successful way."[22]

Most importantly, a wider view would recognize that the green world holds a history with much to teach us. Carson makes a strong case for the preservation of remnant native plant communities as laboratories to help us understand the consequences of the changes wrought by chemical spraying. The expansive sagebrush lands of the West provide a deep history of plant/animal coevolution and adaptation where "The bitter upland plains, the purple wastes of sage, the wild, swift antelope, and the grouse"[23] offer a natural landscape "eloquent of the interplay of the forces that have created it."[24] Her lyric evocation here of the intrinsic beauty located in natural history is central to the case she wants to make for preservation. But places close to home can provide similar education with similar aesthetic rewards. Carson tells of a stretch of roadside in Maine that had slipped through the broadside spraying net, where "nature's own landscaping has provided a border of alder, viburnum, sweet fern, and juniper with seasonally changing accents of bright flowers...oases of beauty in the midst of austere and regimented control....In such places my spirit lifted to the sight of...the flaming cup of a wood lily."[25] Thus does *Silent Spring* issue an impassioned call to preserve and protect flora—whether far away in wilderness or close to home along well-traveled highways.

But a call requires a response—to whom is the call issued? Critical to the success of *Silent Spring* was Carson's ability to locate a caring figure in the landscape. There are many such figures in the book. In the chapter on plants the figure serves to empower many of Carson's readers with the "right" to place the beauties of a living plant community against the values of the practitioners of the narrow view. Carson repeats a story from then Supreme Court justice, and avid wilderness advocate, William O. Douglas about a public protest in the 1950s against federal plans for eradicating sagebrush on rangeland in which a woman from the community spoke for the native plants. The Forest Service "men considered it hilariously funny that an old lady had opposed the plan because the wildflowers would be destroyed."[26] Carson agreed with Douglas that the issue was citizens' rights: "was not her right to search out a banded cup or a tiger lily as inalienable as the right of stockmen to search out grass or a lumberman to claim a tree?"[27] Another incarnation of this figure is a protestor against the killing of wildflowers in roadside spraying campaigns, who is castigated in a scientific paper by a weed-control profes-

sional as about as out of touch as the "antivivisectionists." Commenting on
such characterization, Carson places herself squarely in the camp of the mar-
ginalized: "To the author of this paper, many of us would unquestionably be
suspect, convicted of some deep perversion of character because we prefer the
sight of the vetch and the clover and the wood lily in all their delicate and
transient beauty to that of roadsides scorched as by fire."[28]

To espouse beauty—particularly beauty located in something as ephemeral
and seemingly inconsequential as a wildflower—as a reason for questioning
the "progress" of science and industry in pushing nature to ever greater productivity for humankind may have seemed genuinely an eccentric notion in
the middle of the twentieth century. Carson backed up her diverse audience
of concerned citizens with a wealth of professional findings they could use in
efforts to protect and nurture beloved flora in their own communities. Most
of "The Earth's Green Mantle" is a litany of more sensible approaches to
plant management, with successful programs described in detail and clear
trails to more information for her readers to follow. Thus the figure of the
"old lady" gains the power of professional expertise to bring to the table as
she argues for her right to a tiger lily.

Carson is, however, being somewhat coy in her reference to "us" as mar-
ginalized characters "suspected" of suffering a "deep perversion of character"
for our appreciation of the value of a wildflower, since her personal circle of
roused citizens was both influential and expansive. To appreciate the legacy
of her call for the protection of the flora it first is important to remember
who she meant by "us" in her own community at the time. In 1957 Carson
had become interested in and supportive of a lawsuit filed by a group of
Long Islanders to stop pesticide spraying in their homes and gardens.
Although the case was dismissed on a technicality in 1960, she was
impressed by the dissenting opinion of Justice Douglas. Carson found in
Douglas someone with a like appreciation of the beauties of wildflowers, and
he provided her material for the chapter on plants. Douglas' outrage at the
dismissal of the old woman was published in his *My Wilderness* and was
grounded in an emotional response to the flora he encountered in his wildlands tours. The wildflower became a critical component in Douglas' call for
a "bill of rights" for wilderness.[29]

Carson was also involved with a variety of organizations and individuals
interested in promoting remnant wildlands and naturalized landscapes in
cities and suburbs. Frank Egler, at one time on the professional staff of the
American Museum of Natural History and founder of an organization aimed
at preserving native plants along America's roadsides, is cited in *Silent Spring*
as a leader in promoting selective spraying for brush control on roadways. He
had also written a pamphlet that later was published (under the pseudonym
Warren G. Kenfield) as *The Art of Naturalistic Landscaping*, for suburbanites
who desired gardens with a cosmopolitan mixture of native and exotic plants.

Egler in turn encouraged Ruth Scott, a landscape designer in Pittsburgh, to provide Carson with information about her creation of a "roadside vegetation management project," which encouraged locals to work to protect native plants along their community roadways. Scott had national standing as well in the federation of State Garden Clubs, the national and state Audubon societies, and the Nature Conservancy.

Once *Silent Spring* was published, organizations with interests in horticulture and native plant protection invited Carson to speak to their groups. At a speech to the New England Wildflower Preservation Society that was later widely disseminated, Carson argued against the application of labels like "impractical" and "sentimental" to concern for the "substitution of the 'brownout' for the color and beauty of flowers along our roads"[30] and argued that "a world that is no longer fit for wild plants, that is no longer graced by the flight of birds, a world whose streams and forests are empty and lifeless is not likely to be a fit habitat for man himself, for these things are symptoms of an ailing world."[31] In a speech to the national meeting of the Garden Club of America, Carson recognized the audiences' "interest in plant life" and "fostering of beauty" and encouraged the citizens present to use the courts to test the intrusion of chemical spraying into their yards and gardens and nature preserves. For Carson, a critical effect of the publication and reception of *Silent Spring* was "an awakening of strong public interest and concern. People are beginning to ask questions and insist on proper answers."[32]

Carson advocated for the rights of nature across many scales—in the wild, in the garden, in the city, and in our bodies. The questions and the answers citizens from every demographic have desired since *Silent Spring* are located in all such spaces. But, there remains a tendency among her supporters to reduce her legacy to single issues. In recent environmental history, most of the environmental organizations mentioned above have been cast as speaking primarily for the interests of a middle-class elite concerned with wilderness preservation and antiurban, "not in my backyard," protectionism.[33] Until the publication of *Silent Spring*, Carson's voice resonated most strongly among conservation and preservation circles. *Silent Spring* continued to appeal to these groups because of its impassioned concern for a green world with ecological values articulated through an aesthetic lens. One revolutionary aspect of the book is its focus on the rights of plants. Carson's concerns about the limitations of our approaches to the value of plants remain cogent today and have become even more pressing with the increasing loss of habitat for natives.[34]

Carson has also recently been championed in environmental justice literature, and among these circles there is some embarrassment about the "romantic" views of nature espoused in her earlier work. Like Alice Walker's Sammy Lou, to discuss Carson's love of nature is a bit of a "put down" these days. In such a reading, Rachel Carson's critical legacy to the twenty-first cen-

tury is her call for citizens' rights to name and question life in a toxic landscape. Lawrence Buell argues that Carson's inclusive allusions to a populace
threatened by the onslaught of chemical pesticides (the "us" in *Silent Spring*)
crossing race, gender, and class lines (as well as her own martyrdom and
untimely death from cancer) accounts for her "adoption" by the environmental justice movement as "harbinger, prophet, and foremother." *Silent Spring*,
he writes, is "a work of 'universal' scope speaking from as well as to and for
the positions of toxic victims in every place and social niche."[35] Sandra
Steingraber, in *Living Downstream: An Ecologist Looks at Cancer and the
Environment*, agrees and argues that Carson's "final legacy" is the idea "of an
individual's right to know about poisons introduced into one's environment
by others and the right to protection against them."[36] But such a view of
Carson's legacy is (as Carson herself said about our attitude toward plants)
singularly narrow. In fact, Steingraber demonstrates throughout her personal
narrative the complex legacy owed to Rachel Carson—our understanding of
the value of the beauties of nature in coming to grips with the toxic world we
have created.

   Living Downstream is Steingraber's chronicle of her diagnosis of bladder
cancer, and its links to her childhood in Pekin, Illinois, on the Illinois River,
just downstream of Peoria and next to Normandale, "situated on a triangular
wedge of land near Dead Lake, a dumping pond for industrial wastes near the
river's east bank."[37] She uses her own search for knowledge of the polluted
landscape in which she grew up as a call to her readers to take up Carson's
challenge to know about carcinogens "in our environment." Such knowledge
"entails a three-part inquiry": "we must first look back into our past, then
reassess our present situation, and finally summon the courage to imagine an
alternative future."[38] Her search for "ecological roots" takes her to the natural
history of the Illinois River, which becomes a lament for a lost world of native
plants and animals due in large part to "the flow of silt and weed killers from
surrounding fields" into Peoria Lake.[39] This is not simple misplaced nostalgia
for a pastoral landscape, nor is it more complex disenchantment with the illusion of a pristine green world now overwhelmed by pollution. Following
Carson, we experience here a deeply felt understanding that to know one's
environment requires knowing the history of its flora and fauna.[40]

   Steingraber perseveres in her attempt to connect with the ecological
past. Coming to terms with her cancer diagnosis is matched by coming to
terms with the contemporary prairie landscape. While she never loses sight
of the chemical pollution in the "dust, soil, and air" she continues to study
in the scientific papers on pesticides in Illinois, she also looks for what has
survived, in particular what there is of natural beauty. She reports that in the
year following her cancer diagnosis, she took a field ecology class and
"learned to identify plant species in the rarest of rare Illinois habitats: the
black soil prairie."[41] Remnant native plant stands are located in pioneer

gravesites. As she "became ever more enchanted with the Illinois prairie, I found that I was, nevertheless, unable to banish from my heart its remaining enemies—the nonnative invading species. Queen Anne's lace, ox-eye daisy, chicory, foxtail, goat's beard, teasel: all European immigrants, these are the familiar weeds of roadsides and fallow fields. My mother taught me the names of most of them."[42]

The teasel is also valued for its particular history: it was spread by immigrants who took bouquets from their yards to the graves of their families. Thus both teasel and remnant natives mingle—often in uneasy competition—in these historic places. Like Carson, Steingraber takes a cosmopolitan approach to landscape diversity, privileging neither pristine wilds, human-created gardens, nor toxic landscapes. She keeps reminders of both native and introduced plants near her desk—dried teasel and a monograph of the prairie plants together. Her desk looks out the window to the city where she lives. The plants, the articles on pollution, and the view of the city all combine to describe for her the "contours of home."[43]

Home for her, as it was for Carson, is deeply connected to local plants that provide history and beauty to the landscape—without which the fight for protection from a toxic landscape would be much less meaningful. Finally, the most poignant legacy Carson willed to Steingraber is a place: the Rachel Carson National Wildlife Refuge in southern Maine. Surrounded by developed land—burgeoning urban/suburban sprawl as Maine becomes more and more a bedroom community of Boston—the refuge draws hundreds of thousands of visitors a year. Seeking more understanding of Rachel Carson the person, Steingraber makes a trek to the salt marsh refuge with a friend who has also been diagnosed with cancer. The two women follow the trail through the marsh, moving back and forth between conversations about their illness and responses to the place. At first disappointed that the refuge is not farther north among the more romantic "craggy tidal pools and moonlit coves" of Carson's Southport home, Steingraber gradually comes to appreciate the subtle beauties of the salt marsh in November.[44] Particularly entranced by the "luminous oak groves" that seem to trick the season, the walk culminates at one of the salt pans with their specialized, salt-tolerant stands of sea-blight and glasswort—"Life thriving among bitterness."[45]

Like Dorothy Freeman and Rachel Carson, these women find solace and deeper meaning in a natural world that at once takes them outside themselves and resonates with their difficult personal histories. Without purple asters, how would Rachel and Dorothy have understood each other so well and how would Rachel have completed *Silent Spring*? Without the trail through the salt marsh sedge, how would Sandra and her friend have found a common landscape in which to ground their efforts to cope with the toxic world they now find located in their bodies as well as their homes?

Though the marsh contains much that is wild, it functions not simply as romantic refuge from people and history. It is, rather, a place that, through its bittersweet beauty, offers a space for action in the world today. The value of a wildflower along the roadside, the revolutionary virtues of a petunia in a country yard or an inner-city window box, the aesthetic appeal of sea-blight for cancer victims on a winter day, each references a human figure who understands a fundamental ecological truth. Just as sedge and bird require each other, the survival of person and plant are inextricably linked. One of Rachel Carson's most important, and least recognized legacies, was her insistent and path-breaking reminder of our fundamental reliance on the green world—a reliance best expressed by our location of beauty in a flower.

NOTES

1. Rachel Carson to Dorothy Freeman, Letter, Jan. 23, 1962, in Rachel Carson, *Always, Rachel: The Letters of Rachel Carson and Dorothy Freeman, 1952-1964*, ed. Martha Freeman (Boston: Beacon Press, 1995), 394. For considerations of Carson's place in the history of the rise of the confluence of social justice and environmental movements see: Robert Gottlieb, *Forcing the Spring: The Transformation of the American Environmental Movement* (Washington, D.C.: Island Press, 1993), 319; and Vera Norwood, "Rachel Carson," in *The American Radical*, ed. Mari Jo Buhle, Paul Buhle, and Harvey J. Kaye (New York: Routledge, 1994), 313-20.

2. Alice Walker, *In Search of Our Mothers' Gardens: Humanist Prose* (San Diego: Harcourt Brace Jovanovich, 1983), 267.

3. Robert Gottlieb, *Environmentalism Unbound: Exploring New Pathways for Change* (Cambridge: MIT Press, 2001).

4. Rachel Carson, *Silent Spring* (Boston: Houghton Mifflin, 1994 [1962]), 1, 3. Unless otherwise noted, I will be using Linda Lear's biography of Carson for details on her life. Linda Lear, *Rachel Carson: Witness for Nature* (New York: Henry Holt, 1997).

5. For background on women's education in botany and birding see Vera Norwood, *Made from This Earth: American Women and Nature* (Chapel Hill: University of North Carolina Press, 1993).

6. Rachel Carson, *The Sense of Wonder* (New York: HarperCollins, 1998 [1965]), 22.

7. Rachel Carson to Dorothy Freeman, Letter, Mar. 12, 1954, in *Always, Rachel*, 32.

8. Rachel Carson to Dorothy Freeman, Letter, Feb. 6, 1954, in ibid., 20.

9. Rachel Carson to Dorothy Freeman, Letter, Oct. 6, 1963, in ibid., 477.

10. Rachel Carson, *The Sea Around Us* (New York: Oxford University Press, 1989 [1950]), 34.

11. Ibid., 36.

12. Rachel Carson, *The Edge of the Sea* (Boston: Mariner Books, 1998 [1955]), 64.

13. Carson trained in ecology, whose central metaphor for describing nature is as household or home. For background on the history of the idea see Donald Worster, *Nature's Economy: A History of Ecological Ideas* (Cambridge: Cambridge University Press, 1977).

14. Carson, *The Edge of the Sea*, 3.

15. Ibid., 4.

16. Carson, *The Sea Around Us*, 94. For examples of Carson's early writings see her *Lost Woods: The Discovered Writing of Rachel Carson*, ed. Linda Lear (Boston: Beacon Press, 1998).

17. Carson, *Silent Spring*, 10.

18. Ibid., 63.

19. Ibid., 73.

20. Ibid., 70.

21. Ibid., 68.

22. Ibid., 81.

23. Ibid., 66.

24. Ibid., 64.

25. Ibid., 71.

26. Ibid., 72.

27. Douglas quoted by Carson, ibid., 72.

28. Ibid., 72.

29. Some of the material Carson used from Douglas comes from his *My Wilderness: East to Katahdin* (Garden City, N.J.: Doubleday, 1961), 290.

30. Rachel Carson, "A Sense of Values in Today's World," Speech, New England Wildflower Preservation Society, Jan. 17, 1963, Rachel Carson Papers, Beinecke Library, Yale University. As quoted in Lear, *Witness for Nature*, 440.

31. Ibid., in Lear, *Witness for Nature*, 440–41.

32. Rachel Carson, Speech, Garden Club of America, Jan. 8, 1963. Reprinted as "A New Chapter to *Silent Spring*," in *Lost Woods*, 214.

33. The most influential critiques of preservation/conservation-oriented environmental organizations are the essays in William Cronon, ed, *Uncommon Ground: Rethinking the Human Place in Nature* (New York: Norton, 1995). Lawrence Buell summarizes the distinctions most often made between such groups and environmental justice organizations which are "more explicitly anthropocentric, focused more on populated areas than open space and on community betterment rather than alone-with-nature experiences" (*Writing for an Endangered World: Literature, Culture, and Environment in the U.S. and Beyond* [Cambridge: Harvard University Press, 2001], 38).

34. Of Carson's generation, perhaps the most influential contemporary spokesperson for both naturalized and native plants has been Lady Bird Johnson. Through her roadside beautification campaigns, Johnson carried on Carson's call to protect regional distinctiveness along the highways. See Lady Bird Johnson and Carlton B. Lees, *Wildflowers Across America* (New York: Abbeville Press, 1988). Her National Wildflower Center in Austin, Texas, is a member of a national network of botanical gardens involved in research about native plants and working to preserve habitat for endangered and threatened plants. The center is also a member of a consortium organized by the Center for Plant Conservation that is building a collection of the rarest native plants in America.

35. Buell, *Writing for an Endangered World*, 44–45.

36. Sandra Steingraber, *Living Downstream: An Ecologist Looks at Cancer and the Environment* (Reading: Addison-Wesley, 1997), 266.

37. Ibid., 58.

38. Ibid., 266–67.

39. Ibid., 191.

40. Buell, building on Leo Marx, has written most cogently on the various types of pastoral. Carson's early sea books represent, under this matrix, "simple pastoral"—imagining a natural world of secure and "inexhaustible natural beauty." By the 1950s, and most spectacularly with *Silent Spring*, Carson had moved to "complex pastoral" in which the green world is "disrupted" and threatened by pollution of various sorts. But, Buell argues, *Silent Spring* also poses a more totalistic vision—that of "a world without refuge from toxic penetration" (*Writing for an Endangered World*, 37–38). I am not here so much arguing with this matrix, as suggesting that Carson's legacy is not so linear—from simple to complex to toxic—but rather nuanced in a way that centers an ongoing beauty in nature as the reason for and the way to continued action in the face of polluted landscapes.

41. Steingraber, *Living Downstream*, 272.
42. Ibid.
43. Ibid.
44. Ibid, 18.
45. Ibid., 20.

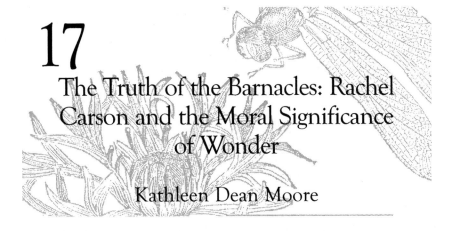

17
The Truth of the Barnacles: Rachel Carson and the Moral Significance of Wonder

Kathleen Dean Moore

> I believe that the more clearly we can focus our atten-
> tion on the wonders and realities of the universe
> about us, the less taste we shall have for destruction.
> —Rachel Carson, "The Real World Around Us"

The wind is ferocious, an April wind butting into the headland, so I've
taken shelter behind a shale bank where a stream fingers into the Pacific.
The tide seethes in, lifting rockweed and tumbling the periwinkles. I'm reading about barnacles in *The Edge of the Sea*, Rachel Carson's third book. So
much I never knew. I never knew that a barnacle larva will float in the sea
until it bumps into a rock touched by chemical traces of other barnacles. In
such a manifestly promising place, it cements the back of its head to the rock
and encloses itself in a little tower of calcified plates, like a rough white volcano among the rocks in the intertidal zone. After it metamorphoses into an
adult, it points its feet to the sky, opens the top of the tower, and waves its
legs in the current, catching morsels of food. It pulls its legs inside when the
tide backs away, and shuts the doors behind them.

This chapter originally appeared in *Environmental Ethics*, Volume 27, Number 3 (Fall
2005): 265–77. It is reproduced here with permission of Kathleen Dean Moore.

I've climbed among barnacles, cut my hands on them, leaned close to smell them, listened to them bubble in the dark, watched crows pick crabs from their shadows. But I never knew—I guess I never asked—about the little crustaceans within the interlocking plates. I never knew that they have eyes, then lose them when they shut themselves inside their shells. I've never seen their feet. It changes everything, to look across the fields of barnacles on the outer rocks and think about the little animals working so hard, in their own odd ways, to live. I shake my head at the wonder of it, the improbable series of events that creates the little animal that gulps and flicks on a rock in the swash.

"Contemplating the teeming life of the shore, we have an uneasy sense of the communication of some universal truth that lies just beyond our grasp," Carson wrote in *The Edge of the Sea*, and I confess I feel this too. "What truth is expressed by the legions of the barnacles, whitening the rocks with their habitations, each small creature within finding the necessities of its existence in the sweep of the surf?"[1]

After she published *The Edge of the Sea*, Rachel Carson wrote an article, "Help Your Child to Wonder," for the *Woman's Home Companion*. The mysteries at the edge of the sea—ghost crabs waiting in the night, the moon setting the waves on fire, the tide edging into bunchberries, and delight and gratitude for the mysteries—these are her topics in this short essay.

Carson intended to turn the "Wonder" essay into a book, and what a book it would have been. "I want very much to do the Wonder book," she wrote. "That would be Heaven to achieve."[2] Judging from the chapter outline she sketched for her agent, the book would have been a celebration of life seen through the eyes of a scientist who loved her subjects:

> The Sky
> The Woods
> The Sea
> The Changing Year
> The World of Tiny Things
> The Miracle of Life
> Beauty in Nature

But before she could celebrate this world, she had to turn her attention to a more pressing task—protecting it. At a stage in her life when she had very little time left, all her time went into *Silent Spring*. Carson died of breast cancer soon after *Silent Spring* was published. We are left with a keen sense of loss and the "Wonder" essay, reissued as a slender, illustrated book called *The Sense of Wonder*.

Wading into Pacific saltwater, I lean over a tide pool, hoping to see an acorn barnacle's hairy legs. But in this wind, I can see only the surging reflections of clouds and skidding gulls. The air carries the iodine smell of *Fucus*, the rockweed. I think it's significant that the "Wonder" essay is positioned between *The Edge of the Sea*, a close observation of the intricate balance of life, and *Silent Spring*, a plea for its protection. A sense of wonder closes the distance between "this is wonderful" and "this must remain," between the "is" and the "ought." It is a bridge of moral resolve that links the physical world and the moral world. And so I believe that a sense of wonder may well be a moral virtue, perhaps the keystone virtue of an environmental ethic.

What are the elements of a sense of wonder? What value does it have? What difference does it make, what *in the world* difference does it make? What, I want to ask here, is the moral significance of wonder?

THE SKY: WONDER AS A WAY OF FEELING AND RESPONDING

The Sense of Wonder begins on the seacoast at night, in the rain, "just at the edge of where-we-couldn't-see."[3] Of the sky, nothing is visible. Of the sea, only dimly seen white shapes. Carson and her little nephew laugh for pure joy, sharing the "spine-tingling response to the vast, roaring ocean and the wild night around us."[4] Carson calls a sense of wonder an emotion, but the full scope of her wonder might be better embraced by the more expansive, old-fashioned word 'passion'—when, moved by some force outside oneself, a person feels and responds. What outside force, what feelings especially, what response? Those are complicated questions.

Wonder begins with surprise. René Descartes defined wonder as a sudden surprise of the soul. "When the first encounter with some object surprises us, and we judge it to be new, or very different from what we knew in the past or what we supposed it was going to be, this makes us wonder and be astonished at it."[5] Astonish, from the Latin *tonus*, thunder, to be struck, as by lightning; the sudden flash that startles us and, just for a moment, lights the world with uncommon clarity. This calls forth a response not mediated by social conditioning, the honest awe that philosopher Crispin Sartwell calls "the shock of the real."[6]

For Carson, it's the natural world that calls forth this response: its sudden beauty, its intricate interrelations, its power, its contingency, the 'ingenuity' of its design, the stunning fact of it, and—most important—its ultimate mystery. One might be surprised by the complexity of an urban design or impressed by the power of a computer, but human creations yield to human understanding in ways the natural world does not, and so it's not wonder they evoke, so much as fascination perhaps, or appreciation.

Sometimes a person is struck by the beauty of nature or the brilliance of its design. Then the response is delight. As Carson observes again and again, and as my own experiences confirm, a wondering encounter can be pure joy. I've watched eagles spiral higher and higher into the sky until they disappear altogether. One night, the sky came alive with meteors that darted and disappeared like a school of silver fish. And now, as I sit at the edge of the sea, the dull sky suddenly cracks apart and light pours through the fissure, flooding over the mussel beds, blue and steaming. I catch my breath, throw back my head, and laugh—it is that astonishing and beautiful.

But what catches a person by surprise can take her into a darker place too, a sudden encounter with the vastness of time and space where she's brushed by the sweeping wing of what cannot be known—the deeply mysterious beyond the boundaries of human experience. I felt this in a kayak at night, when a dark cloud of sardines turned in a slow gyre under my bow, black fish in black water, moving steadily toward a place I couldn't know, flashing unexpectedly when a fish turned its silver side to the moon. I was struck by the profound otherness and indifference, or maybe the mystery, of what was beyond me, and by my own terrifying insignificance. So wonder can be a wash of fear—awe in the ancient sense of dread.

Carson reminded us that there is loneliness in a sense of wonder too, what she called "a sense of lonely distances," as we feel our isolation from what is profoundly apart. Loneliness turns to yearning, a kind of love, an overpowering attraction to something beautiful and mysterious and other, the desire to hold on forever to the object of our wonder, to be part of it, united with it; and mourning, knowing that the object can never be possessed.[7]

THE WOODS: WONDER AS A WAY OF SEEING

Separating out these elements of surprise, delight, dread, and yearning is a mistake, of course, because a sense of wonder involves them all, in powerful combination. Reflecting on the complexity of wonder, one of my students, Eric Grey, tried to put into words his feelings when he stood for the first time at the feet of giant redwood trees. "Shock. Trembling acceptance of a thing so beautiful that I was afraid of it in ways I can't explain. Fear bleeding into love. Face-aching smiles and laughter from the center of my being; tears that came with no warning and no explanation."[8]

While Carson referred to wonder as an emotion, she understood it also as the capacity to see in a particular way. Carson compared wonder to a child's view of the world, where everything is new, and the child is open to—in fact, expects and watches for, even more, runs with open arms toward—a surprise around every corner. A person with a sense of wonder marvels at a redwood's muscled trunk, at a sword fern's fiddlehead, as if he were seeing it for the first time; hears as if he had never heard before the song of the winter wren or smelled the bracken. Wonder is the opposite of boredom, indifference, or exhaustion—the lapse into unseeing familiarity. Standing alone on a headland one star-streaming night, watching the lights of unknowing people in their houses and cars across the bay, Carson thought, "if this were a sight that could be seen only once in a century or even once in a human generation, this little headland would be thronged with spectators…[but] because they could see it almost any night perhaps they will never see it."[9] One way to open oneself to wonder, she said, is to ask, "What if I had never seen this before? What if I knew I would never see it again?"[10]

The late rabbi Abraham Heschel called this new seeing "radical amazement." He wrote,

> Wonder is a state of mind in which…nothing is taken for granted. Each thing is a surprise, *being is unbelieveable*. We are amazed at seeing anything at all; amazed…at the fact that there is being at all.…Amazed beyond words.…Souls that are focused and do not falter at first sight, falling back on words and ready-made notions with which the memory is replete, can behold the mountains as if they were gestures of exaltation. To them, all sight is suddenness.[11]

Understood this way, a sense of wonder is an attitude of openness or receptivity that leads a person from a preoccupation with self into a search for meaning beyond oneself. A person with a sense of wonder will lift a rotten log to see what might burrow in the dampness, will listen to the fall of rain and the subtle rustle of Sitka spruce, so hard to tell apart, will go out early in the morning or late at night, not searching for something, but open to everything, exposed to the raw wind of what we can never understand. The philosopher R. W. Hepburn compared the way he gives himself to wonder to how he gives himself in friendship, "entrusting myself to another in an open and therefore vulnerable way."[12]

If wonder is the capacity to see as if for the first time, then wonder has a moral function, much like the moral function John Dewey found in art: "to do away with the scales that keep the eye from seeing, tear away the veils due to wont and custom, perfect the power to perceive,"[13] and "enter…into other forms of relationship and participation than our own."[14] Citing Dewey, aesthetician Yuriko Saito believes it is a necessary condition for any moral relationship to cultivate the ability to set aside our own stories and recognize and sympathetically lend our ears to the story, however unfamiliar to us, told by the other.[15] Wonder is the open eyes, the sympathetic imagination and respectfully listening ears, seeking out the story told by nature's rough bark and flitting wrens, and by that listening, one enters into a moral relationship with the natural world.

THE SEA: WONDER AS A WAY OF BEING

One of the joys of reading Rachel Carson is to watch this openness, this sense of wonder, at work in the world. Again and again, she sought out the night.

She could tell you the name of whatever she found in the beam of her flash-light, and how it was born, where it hides from the light, and on what its life depends. She was a scientist above all, trained in marine biology. But her sci-ence, as it revealed more of the marvelous workings of the world, revealed more and deeper mysteries. Each new discovery, opening her eyes to new understanding and new questions, allowed her to see the denizens of the tide pools as if she were seeing them for the first time: the intricate interdependen-cies, the beautiful, ineffable patterns of living and dying. Her science, this openhearted knowing, this deep questioning, led her to a contemplation of the meaning of what she saw, the mystery of how such a thing can come to be.

Here, she finds a ghost crab:

> The flats took on a mysterious quality as dusk approached and the last evening light was reflected from the scattered pools and creeks...I sur-prised a small ghost crab...lying in a pit he had dug just above the surf....The blackness of the night possessed water, air, and beach....There was no sound but the all-enveloping, primeval sounds of wind blowing over water and sand, and of waves crashing on the beach. There was no other visible life—just one small crab near the sea....In that moment time was suspended; the world to which I belonged did not exist and I might have been an onlooker from outer space. The little crab alone with the sea became a symbol that stood for life itself—for the delicate, destructive, yet incredibly vital force that somehow holds its place amid the harsh realities of the inorganic world....Underlying the beauty of the spectacle there is meaning and significance. It is the elusiveness of that meaning that haunts us, that sends us again and again into the natural world where the key to the riddle is hidden.[16]

One ghost crab, one haunted woman in the dark by the edge of the sea: in this image, Carson shows us that a sense of wonder is not just a way of feeling or a way of seeing, it is a way of being in the world. To contemplate, and thereby acknowledge the meaningfulness of the other, opens the door to a moral relationship.

A person with a sense of wonder moves quietly and humbly across the sand, recognizing that there is a hidden world there in the night, quite apart from the brightly lit human world behind the dunes, and that this world is marvelous in itself, a fanciful world of tiny legs, sparking brains and wary eyes, sighing, striving, and dying in utter disregard of the vanities of humankind.

A sense of wonder impels us to act respectfully in the world. There is worth in these products of time and rock and water, far beyond their useful-ness to human purposes. The sweep of time, the operations of chance have cre-ated something that leaves us breathless and rejoicing, struggling to understand the very fact of it, its colors, its squeaks and songs. It deserves respect; which is to say that a sense of wonder leads us to celebrate and honor the earth.

And, yes, a sense of wonder shows us our own responsibilities to care for the objects of wonder—to do them no harm, to protect their thriving. But more about this in a moment.

THE CHANGING YEAR: WHAT IS THE VALUE
OF A SENSE OF WONDER?

Carson takes pains to articulate the value of a sense of wonder, urging parents to give their children the gift of the land and the sea. Her words, and her life, teach that a close relationship with the natural world is a source of strength, healing, and renewal. "Those who contemplate the beauty of the earth find reserves of strength that will endure as long as life lasts," she wrote.[17] And in fact, during those terrible times when Carson struggled for the strength to continue her work even as she was dying of cancer, she found comfort at her beloved coast. There, when winter turned to spring, sanderlings stopped to feed on sandy beaches as they migrated through ancient cycles of living and dying and living again that Carson chronicled over and over, the life cycles of the barnacles, the journeys of the eels, the necessity of death to life. "There is something infinitely healing in the repeated refrains of nature," Carson wrote, "—the assurance that dawn comes after night, and spring after the winter."[18]

But the moral significance of wonder goes beyond its instrumental value. Philip Cafaro has argued that Carson's moral views fall into the tradition of virtue ethics.[19] Following Aristotle, he defines virtues as "qualities which allow a person to fulfill his or her proper or characteristic functions, and to flourish as a good of his or her kind."[20] A virtue ethic asks after those qualities: what is a good life for a human being, and what are the personal qualities that allow a person to thrive? So also does *The Sense of Wonder* urge on readers a vision of what qualities might help a child thrive. Here is Carson taking her nephew by the hand and leading him to the places that have brought her so much comfort and fulfillment, crawling on hands and knees after singing insects, showing by her example how he also might live a significant and joyful life in close relation to nature. So I think that a sense of wonder is a virtue in at least this sense, finding what it means to be fully human in a celebration of our place in the more-than-human world.

Wonder deepens lives that might otherwise be shallow, probing depths of meaning and allowing a person fully to experience the rich texture of a life. "If I had influence with the good fairy who is supposed to preside over the christening of all children," she wrote, "I should ask that her gift to each child in the world be a sense of wonder so indestructible that it would last throughout life, as an unfailing antidote against the boredom and disenchantment of later years, the sterile preoccupation with things that are artificial, the alienation from the sources of our strength."[21]

I think of "sterile preoccupations" and marvel that Carson could have so clearly foreseen our own time, fifty years away. The economic forces of our lives are centripetal, tending to spin us in smaller and smaller circles, creating a kind of solipsism that comes from separation from the natural world and our bio-cultural communities. It's not that we aren't natural creatures, it's not that we don't live always in the most intimate contact with the natural world that seeps in our pores and rushes through our blood. It's that we lose track of that fact or deny it, and so shut ourselves off from a large part of our own humanity. We measure our successes and failures against our own mean interests, and so they grow to grotesque proportions. Self-importance, self-absorption bloat and distort our lives and our relationships.

Meanwhile, earth turns, birds fly north or south, fish rise or sink in the currents, the moon spills light on snow or sand, and we—do we think we turn the crank that spins the earth? A good dose of wonder, a night of roaring waves, a faceful of stars, the kick in the pants of an infinite universe, the huge unknowing—these remind us that there is beauty that we didn't create. There is mystery we cannot fathom. There are interests that are not our own. There is time we cannot measure. When we live humbly in full awareness of the astonishing fact that we have any place at all in such a world, we live richer, deeper lives, more fully realizing our humanity.

But Carson has a larger point to make. A sense of wonder is an important element of human thriving, yes. But a sense of wonder offers hope also for the thriving of the more-than-human world. Wonder is an antidote to the view that the elements of the natural world—sanderlings, shale reefs, ancient pines—are merely means to human ends, commodities to be disdained or destroyed. Wonder reminds us of the essential worth of the world we're part of, as it reminds us of how much we love its birdsong and beauty. And so it reminds us of the responsibilities that grow from that regard. Carson: "Wonder and humility are wholesome emotions, and they do not exist side by side with a lust for destruction."[22] If she's right, wonder may be the keystone virtue in our time of reckless destruction, a source of decency and hope and restraint.

THE WORLD OF TINY THINGS: WHAT IS THE MORAL SIGNIFICANCE OF WONDER?

Leaving the beach, I climb into the dim light of the fogbound headland where wind has raked the pines to the ground and reduced the plants to miniature forms of their inland kin. I lie across a rocky outcrop and look down on a dwarf garden, drenched with color. Surf beats a slow pulse, light rises and dims as shreds of fog blow through, a foghorn murmurs in time. Here are blue iris, the Douglas iris, with stems only two inches high. Pink checkerblooms crawl among yarrow in flat rosettes, sessile buttercups, and spreading mats of a flower called goldfields, so bright that I'm tempted to warm my hands over its yellow fire.

Rachel Carson didn't draw explicit moral conclusions in the "Wonder" essay, and if she had lived long enough to write the book on wonder, I'm not sure she would have made explicit the moral sensibility that built so strong a foundation for *Silent Spring*. So let me simply say what I believe is true. We live in the physical world of rocks and checkerblooms, and at the same time, we live in a moral world of hopes and a vision of what ought to be. Some philosophers and scientists would have us believe they are different worlds, the "is" and the "ought." But I believe the worlds come together in a sense of wonder. The same impulse that says, this is wonderful, is the impulse that says, this must continue. A sense of wonder that allows us to see life as a beautiful mystery forces us to see life as something to which we owe respect and care. If this is the way the world is: extraordinary, surprising, beautiful, singular, mysterious, and meaningful; then this is how I ought to act in that world: with respect and celebration, with care, and with full acceptance of the responsibilities that come with my role as a human being privileged to be a part of that community of living things. Wonder is the missing premise that can transform what-is into a moral conviction about how one ought to act in that world.

Carson came close to making this same argument in *Silent Spring*. The "natural landscape is eloquent of the interplay of forces that have created it. It is spread before us like the pages of an open book in which we can read why the land is what it is, and why we should preserve its integrity. But the pages lie unread."[23]

THE MIRACLE OF LIFE: WHAT, THEN, SHALL I DO?

What, then, is a person to do? I think Carson's answer would be, cultivate wonder. If you are a nature writer, cultivate wonder in your readers. If you are a professor and a scientist, cultivate wonder in your students. If you are a parent, cultivate wonder in your children. And since you are a human being, no matter where you are or what you are doing, live openly and deeply and gratefully, wading hip-deep into the dark mysterious sea.

As she accepted the John Burroughs Award for excellence in nature writing, Carson used the opportunity to urge fellow writers to create a new kind of nature writing in response to the urgency of the times. "I myself am convinced," she said, "that there has never been a greater need than there is

today for the reporter and interpreter of the natural world."[24] Human beings
have created an artificial world, insulated by glass and steel, she explained.
Behind their closed doors and locked windows, they have lost track of the
beauty of the natural world and the essential processes of water and land and
living seeds upon which their lives depend. Worse, "intoxicated with a sense
of [their] own power, [they seem] to be going farther and farther into more
experiments for the destruction of [themselves and their] world."[25] Nature
writers—almost by definition people who have been moved by their awareness
of the natural world—have a unique and urgent opportunity to convey their
sense of wonder to the public, which is hungry for connection to something
meaningful and astonishing. "We have been far too ready to assume that
these people [who have very little knowledge of natural science] are indifferent to the world we know to be full of wonder. If they are indifferent it is only
because they have not been properly introduced to it—and perhaps that is in
some measure our fault."[26]

And what of scientists? According to biographer Linda Lear, Carson told
her friend Dorothy Freeman "that she considered her contributions to scientific
fact less important than her attempts to awaken an emotional response to the
world of nature."[27] Once the emotions have been aroused and a person senses
the beauty and excitement of something new and unknown, Carson said, the
person will want more knowledge about the object of that emotional response.
In that context, the knowledge will become important and meaningful.

Carson made the point again in *The Sense of Wonder*. You don't have to
know the names of the plants and animals to nurture a sense of wonder in a
child. "It is not half so important to *know* as to *feel*."[28] And then she offered a
beautiful analogy that goes like this: Think of the emotions and the sense
impressions as the soil. Prepare that soil, make it rich and nourishing.
Scientific facts are the seeds. Planted in that fertile soil, the facts will grow
into knowledge and wisdom.[29] I would go further: if those seeds land on
barren stone, or on the sticky floor of a video arcade or the shag carpet of the
TV room, they will never sprout. Scientific facts are essential. But a scientist
who has lost a sense of wonder, or scientists who try to teach facts without
feeling, will not find their work transformed into the wisdom and knowledge
that the times so urgently require.

As for parents, they should nurture the sense of wonder with which a
child is born. And how is that to be done? "If a child is to keep alive his
inborn sense of wonder…he needs the companionship of at least one adult
who can share it, rediscovering with him the joy, excitement and mystery of
the world we live in."[30] Take your child by the hand and look up at the sky,
Carson advised in the "Wonder" article. Listen to the wind. Feel the rain on
your face. Ponder the mystery of a growing seed. "Drink in the beauty, and
think and wonder at the meaning of what you see."[31] Savor the smell of low
tide, and the child, grown up, will smell the tide again and savor "the rush of

remembered delight."[32] And then Carson told of her plan to take her nephew into the garden in the fall. With flashlights, they would search for the crickets and katydids that play their music in the damp grass, and seek out the fairy bell ringer, an insect Carson had never found, no matter how many times she had followed the chimes of a tiny silver bell.

In reading Carson's list of titles for chapters in the planned book version of *The Sense of Wonder*, I was surprised to find, almost at the end, "The Miracle of Life." Carson was not a person to use words carelessly, so it was surely no oversight that the words "the miracle of life" appear here, but never appeared in the "Wonder" essay that was to be the basis of the book. I'd always thought that for Carson the true miracle of life is that it's no miracle at all—no divine violation of physical processes—but rather the working out of physical processes in all their beautiful and mysterious variety. Puzzled, I looked up 'miracle' in the dictionary. There I found what Carson had probably known all along: Miracle, n. from *miraculum*, from *mirari*, to wonder at.

Perhaps the human being's sense of wonder is itself one of those miracles—that the universe somehow evolved in such a way that it might wonder at its own marvelous workings, and by that means, come to honor and protect them.

BEAUTY IN NATURE: CONCLUSIONS

When I return late at night to the parking lot at the coast, my headlights sweep over twisted cypress and clumps of beach grass, unmoving now the wind has died. I pull on a jacket and follow my bobbing flashlight down the dunes trail to the beach. The fog has cleared and stars scatter over sea-waves that lift and lengthen the stars' reflected light. It's a long, low tide, the slosh of waves faint and far away. A flock of resting shorebirds startles from sleep. They rise in a great rush of air and fly off, their little cries falling like confetti. I play my light over the crusted rocks and shiny slabs of kelp, the strange land that appears and disappears with the phases of the moon. Finding a dry place to sit among the barnacles, I turn off the light and sit uneasily in the dark.

At first, I don't hear much. The sea itself, the soft breathing in, the asthmatic breathing out. A single peep, maybe a shorebird lost in the rush. A thread of sand sifting down the cliff behind. Then gradually, spaces between the rocks begin to tick and pop. Seaweed squeaks in the rise and fall. I force myself to be still while the animals get used to my presence, then I switch on the flashlight and peer into a tidal pool. In the narrow beam, a green anemone sways over a pink crust of coralline algae, and periwinkles inch along their little paths. I lean close to a patch of barnacles and finally I see them: the fluttery legs emerge thin as dotted lines from the barest crack between the barnacles' plates. The legs wave like ephemeral beckoning hands, each movement helping to sustain the life of the little spark that lies on its head inside the shell.

What truth is expressed by the legions of the barnacles, whitening the rocks, or the "sea lace, existing for some reason inscrutable to us, a reason that demands its presence by the trillion amid the rocks and weeds of the shore?" Rachel Carson's answer is the last line from *The Edge of the Sea*, the sentence she asked to have read at her funeral after she died with so much work left to be done. "The meaning haunts and ever eludes us," she wrote, but "in its very pursuit we approach the ultimate mystery of Life itself."[33]

There is moral significance in the search for meaning, and virtue in the life of one who seeks—like Carson, attentive and grateful, careful with science and open to mystery, humble and respectful, rejoicing in the fact of things, willing to be surprised. I don't know if humans are the only beings who wonder. But I do know that we have a great capacity to wonder at the world that ticks and sighs around us, and it may be that we will find the fulfillment of our potential as human beings in our awareness of the astonishing world, our care, and our thanksgiving.[34]

NOTES

1. Rachel Carson, *The Edge of the Sea* (Boston: Mariner Books, 1998 [1955]), 250.

2. Rachel Carson to Dorothy Freeman, Letter, Nov. 1963, in Rachel Carson, *Always, Rachel: The Letters of Rachel Carson and Dorothy Freeman, 1952–1964*, ed. Martha Freeman (Boston: Beacon Press, 1995), 490.

3. Rachel Carson, *The Sense of Wonder* (New York: HarperCollins, 1998 [1965]), 15.

4. Ibid.

5. René Descartes, *The Passions of the Soul* (Indianapolis: Hackett, 1989), 52.

6. Crispin Sartwell, *Obscenity, Anarchy, Reality* (Albany: State University of New York Press, 1996), 7–8.

7. Marguerite La Caze, "The Encounter between Wonder and Generosity," *Hypatia* 17 (2002): 1–19, 5; making reference to Luce Irigaray, *An Ethics of Sexual Difference*, trans. Carolyn Burke and Gillian Gill (Ithaca, N.Y.: Cornell University Press, 1993), 13, 75.

8. Eric Grey, personal communication, March 30, 2004.

9. Carson, *The Sense of Wonder*, 68–69.

10. Ibid., 67.

11. Abraham Heschel, "Radical Amazement," in his *Man Is Not Alone: A Philosophy of Religion* (New York: Farrar, Straus and Giroux, 1951), 12, 13, 15.

12. Ronald W. Hepburn, "Wonder," in his *"Wonder" and Other Essays: Eight Studies in Aesthetics and Neighboring Fields* (Edinburgh: Edinburgh University Press, 1984), 134; quoted in La Caze, "The Encounter between Wonder and Generosity," 5.

13. John Dewey, *Art As Experience* (New York: Capricorn Books, 1958), 325. Quoted in Yuriko Saito, "Appreciating Nature on Its Own Terms," *Environmental Ethics* 20 (1998): 135–49.

14. Dewey, *Art As Experience*, 333.

15. Saito, "Appreciating Nature on Its Own Terms," 142.

16. Carson, *The Edge of the Sea*, 5, 7.

17. Carson, *The Sense of Wonder*, 100.

18. Ibid., 101.

19. Philip Cafaro, "Thoreau, Leopold, and Carson: Toward an Environmental Virtue Ethics," *Environmental Ethics* 23 (2001): 3–17.

29. Ibid., 10, n.26.

21. Carson, *The Sense of Wonder*, 54.

22. Rachel Carson, "Design for Nature Writing," Acceptance Speech for the John Burroughs Medal, Apr. 7, 1952, in *Lost Woods*, 94.

23. Rachel Carson, *Silent Spring* (Boston: Houghton Mifflin, 1994 [1962]), 64.

24. Carson, "Design for Nature Writing," in *Lost Woods*, 94.

25. Ibid.

26. Ibid., 95.

27. Linda Lear, introduction to *Lost Woods*, xii.

28. Carson, *The Sense of Wonder*, 56.

29. It is important to pause here to notice how brave this was. When she insisted on the importance of feelings to the growth of knowledge, and when in her own writing, she combined emotion with science, Carson stood against the stiff wind of the Enlightenment and the scientists and ethicists who are its heirs. "For the Enlightenment, whatever does not conform to the rule of computation and utility is suspect," Max Horkheimer and Theodor Adorno warned in their *Dialectic of Enlightenment* (New York: Continuum International Publishing Group, 1972), 6. To defend the significance of feelings was courageous and to do so as a woman was especially brave; some of the response (to this "hysterical female") was predictably vile.

30. Carson, *The Sense of Wonder*, 55.

31. Ibid., 69.

32. Ibid., 83.

33. Carson, *The Edge of the Sea*, 250.

Contributors

ELYSSA BACK is a 2005 graduate of the Yale School of Management and lives in Boston, Massachusetts.

SUSAN POWER BRATTON is the Chair of the Department of Environmental Studies at Baylor University in Waco, Texas.

PHILIP CAFARO is an Associate Professor in the Department of Philosophy at Colorado State University in Fort Collins, Colorado.

J. BAIRD CALLICOTT is a Professor in the Department of Philosophy and Religion Studies at the University of North Texas in Denton, Texas.

MARIL HAZLETT is an independent scholar who lives in rural northeastern Kansas.

GARY KROLL is an Assistant Professor in the History Department at State University of New York Plattsburgh, in Plattsburgh, New York.

PETER C. LIST is an Emeritus Professor in the Department of Philosophy at Oregon State University in Corvallis, Oregon.

JANE LUBCHENCO is the Wayne and Gladys Valley Professor of Marine Biology and Distinguished Professor of Zoology in the Department of Zoology at Oregon State University in Corvallis, Oregon.

STEVE MAGUIRE is an Associate Professor in the Desautels Faculty of Management at McGill University in Montreal, Quebec.

CHRISTOPHER MERRILL is a Professor in the Department of English and the Director of the International Writing Program at the University of Iowa in Iowa City, Iowa.

KATHLEEN DEAN MOORE is Distinguished Professor of Philosophy at Oregon State University in Corvallis, Oregon, and Director of the Spring Creek Project for Ideas, Nature, and the Written Word.

VERA NORWOOD is a Professor in the Department of American Studies at the University of New Mexico in Albuquerque, New Mexico.

DAVID PIMENTEL is an Emeritus Professor in the Department of Entomology at Cornell University in Ithaca, New York.

LISA H. SIDERIS is an Assistant Professor in the Department of Religious Studies at Indiana University in Bloomington, Indiana.

MICHAEL SMITH is an Assistant Professor in the Department of History at Ithaca College in Ithaca, New York.

SANDRA STEINGRABER is a Distinguished Visiting Scholar in the Department of Environmental Studies at Ithaca College in Ithaca, New York.

TERRY TEMPEST WILLIAMS is the Annie Clark Tanner Scholar in Environmental Humanities at the University of Utah in Salt Lake City, Utah.

Index

Advocacy, 54, 73, 244; and scientists, 44-48, 50-54, 251-252
Albert Schweitzer Medal, 242
Aldo Leopold Leadership Program, 33
Aldrin, 18
Allen, Irwin, 127
American Medical Association, 148n54
Animal welfare, 73-74, 102, 105, 106, 243
Anthropocentrism, 64, 67-69, 71, 73, 89, 94-96, 106, 234
Atlantic Monthly, 196
Atrazine, 23

Bacillus thuringiensis, 148n53
Bacon, Francis, 173, 179, 180
Bailey, Liberty Hyde, 235, 236-237, 243, 244
Baldwin, I. L., 174
Bardach, John, 126
Barnacles, 267-268, 277-278
Barton, Bruce, 123
Beck, Ulrich, 209
Beebe, William, 119, 120, 122, 125, 126
Benchley, Peter, 31
Benson, Ezra Taft, 21
Berg, Peter, 109
Bergmann, Werner, 126
Beston, Henry, 108-109, 110, 111, 120
Bioregionalism, 109
Birch, Charles, 105
Birds, 191-192, 204-205, 238-239
Bookchin, Murray, 178-179
Bratton, Susan Power, 96-97, 100-101, 107, 109
Brooks, Paul, 19, 65, 137, 145n2, 161, 218
Buell, Lawrence, 261, 265n40
Burroughs, John, 151, 153, 160

Cafaro, Philip, 94-96, 109, 273
California Ocean Protection Act, 36
Callicott, J. Baird, 79-80
Calvinism, 233-235, 237, 244, 245
Cancer/carcinogens, 1, 8, 10, 24, 72, 138, 140, 144-145, 162, 191, 205, 222-223, 225, 226, 246, 260-262
Carolina Estuarine Reserve Foundation, 215
Carson, Maria McLean, 150, 151, 233, 235, 239, 253
Carson, Rachel, childhood, 151-159, 233-239; and children, 175, 185n35, 244, 253, 270, 273-274, 276-277; education, 19, 151-152, 170, 239-240; health, 8, 10, 24, 72, 138, 140, 144-145, 246; marital status, 21, 176; religious beliefs, 65-66, 70, 76n25, 160, 176, 232, 277 (*see also* Calvinism; Presbyterianism; Spirituality); as writer, 120-121, 154-156, 157-159, 161-162, 221-227, 254-255
Carson, Robert (brother), 246
Carson, Robert (father), 233
Chavez, Cesar, 251
Chemicals, 18, 198, 223, 226-227, 251, 256-257, 260-262. See also Dichlorodiphenyltrichlorethane; Pesticides
Chesapeake Bay, 83
Chlordane, 18, 198
Christie, Roger, 244
Cobb, John, 105
Coker, Robert Ervin, 119, 121
Cold War, 7, 123-124, 144, 169, 171, 220. *See also* War
Cole, LaMont C., 174
Comstock, Anna Botsford, 235, 236, 244

Control of nature, 66–67, 73, 125,
  143–145, 173, 179–180
Crile, George, 141–142
cummings, e. e., 239

Darby, William, 172–173, 174
Darwin, Charles, 98, 110
Darwinism, 6, 84, 101–104, 110
Dasman, Raymond, 109
DDT. *See* dichlorodiphenyltrichloroethane
Democracy, 4, 17, 18; and citizens' rights,
  138–142, 202–208, 251, 260–262
Descartes, René, 269
Descent of Man, The (Darwin), 6, 98–100,
  101, 103, 104, 110–111
Dewey, John, 271
Diamond, Edwin, 176
Dichlorodiphenyltrichlorethane (DDT), 1,
  9, 10, 18, 21, 36, 63, 142, 190–192,
  194–210, 241; banning of, 199–200,
  238; in breast milk, 206; and cancer,
  205; Carson's concern with, 197–198,
  201–208; and Dutch elm disease, 202,
  205; and gypsy moth, 202; and malaria,
  200–201, 203, 206, 208; media attention to, 202; properties of, 200, 203,
  204–205; risks and benefits, 208–209;
  symbolic meaning of, 195–196,
  199–209; in war, 195–197
Dieldren, 18, 61, 198
Douglas, William O., 258, 259
Dubos, René, 109

Earle, Sylvia, 88
Ecofeminism, 72–73, 96, 142–143,
  170–171, 178, 183n11
Economic values, 66, 88, 174, 178, 180,
  181, 207
Edge of the Sea, The (Carson), 1, 30, 65, 71,
  81–82, 160–161, 215, 216, 218, 223–224,
  246, 254–255, 267–268, 278
Egler, Frank, 259–260
Eiseley, Loren, 21
Eisenhower, Dwight D., 21
Endrin, 18, 198
Environmental Defense Fund, 22, 36, 199

Environmental ethics, 94–96, 98, 105–107,
  125, 269 (*see also* Ethics; Sea ethics);
  and ecotheology, 105
Environmental justice, 11, 178, 252–253,
  260–261
Environmental Protection Agency (EPA),
  22, 180, 199
Ethics, 5–6, 34, 50–54, 97, 103; and evolution, 98–100, 100–104, 124, 242–244.
  See also Environmental ethics; Sea
  ethics.

Fitzgerald, F. Scott, 239
Forbes, Stephen, A., 103–104, 110, 111
Fortune, 196
Freeman, Dorothy, 24, 120, 138–139, 141,
  145, 155, 246, 253–254, 255, 262, 276
Future generations, 180, 206–207, 208,
  209

Garb, Yaakov, 178–179
Garden Club of America, 22, 260
Gender, 7, 8, 149, 151–152, 158–159, 162,
  169–182
Genetic engineering, 180
Gibbs, Lois, 23, 251
Goodpaster, Kenneth, 105, 107

Halle, Louis, 121, 122
Haraway, Donna, 152
Harding, Sandra G., 169, 181
Harrison, Ruth, 65, 244
Health (human), 61–62, 63, 64, 140–141,
  162, 178, 190–191, 193, 195, 196, 204,
  205, 207, 226–227, 251
"Help Your Child to Wonder" (Carson),
  244–246, 268, 269. See also *Sense of
  Wonder, The*
Hepburn, R. W., 271
Heptachlor, 18, 198
Heschel, Abraham, 271
Huckins, Olga Owens, 20, 21

Insects, 62–63, 144–145. *See also* Pesticides
Interconnectedness (ecological), 3, 4, 9, 18,
  67, 89, 141, 156, 180, 207, 255, 257
Intergovernmental Panel on Climate
  Change, 34

Irigaray, Luce, 105, 107, 109
Iselin, Columbus, 127

Jeffries, Richard, 81, 120
John Burroughs Medal, 71, 122, 159, 275
Johns Hopkins University, The, 19, 70,
    151–152, 170
Jukes, Thomas H., 174
Jungle, The (Sinclair), 177–178

Kant, Immanuel, 97, 104–105
Keats, John, 252–253
Keller, Evelyn Fox, 169
Kennedy, John F., 22, 176, 199
King, C. G., 177
Krebiozen, 141–142, 145
Kristeva, Julia, 105
Kropotkin, Petr, 101

Land ethic, 79–80, 84, 88–89, 94, 96,
    97–100, 118. See also Leopold, Aldo
Lane, Ferdinand, 121
Lear, Linda, 22, 32, 42–43, 60, 65, 73, 81,
    87, 102, 155, 235, 240, 276
Leopold, Aldo, 6, 8, 54, 79, 86, 88–89, 94,
    96, 100–103, 105, 118, 125. See also
    Land ethic
Leopold, Ellen, 146n24
Levinas, Emmanual, 106–107, 109, 111
Life Magazine, 176
Llewelyn, John, 106–107, 109, 111
Love Canal, 23

Marx, Wesley, 128
McFague, Sallie, 105, 143
Merchant, Carolyn, 8, 143, 170, 179,
    186n42
Merriman, Daniel, 126–127
Michigan State University, 41
Millennium Ecosystem Assessment, 34–36
Minteer, Ben A., 95–96
Moltmann, Jürgen, 105
Monsanto Chemical Company, 21, 171
Monterey Bay Aquarium, 29–30, 37
Moore, Kathleen Dean, 111
Muller, Paul, 195
Murdoch, Iris, 105

National Agricultural Chemicals
    Association, 21
National Review, 175
Nature study, 11, 150, 235–239, 243,
    244–245
Nelles, Maurice, 126
New England Journal of Medicine, 225
New England Wildflower Preservation
    Society, 22, 260
New Republic, 196
New York Times, 20, 23, 24, 136, 140,
    174, 202
New York Times Magazine, 199
New Yorker, 22, 168–169, 171, 175, 197,
    199, 201
Newsweek, 175–176
Norton, Bryan G., 95

O'Brien, Mary, 23
Ocean-centrism, 6, 119–120, 121–123, 125,
    128
Ocean ecosystems, 20, 27, 34–36, 84–85,
    86, 90–92, 103–104, 110, 118 156–157,
    255; harvesting of, 125–128; resiliency
    of, 125–129
Origin of Species, The (Darwin), 6, 101,
    110–111, 168, 220
Our Stolen Future, 181

Pennsylvania College for Women, 19,
    239–240, 253
Peperzak, Adriaan, 106
Persistent Organic Pollutants (POPs), 200,
    207, 208
Pesticide Action Network, 23
Pesticides, 9, 18, 61, 95, 162, 171, 172, 174,
    175, 176, 177, 178, 180–181, 190–193,
    198–199, 202, 221; and resistance, 192,
    204; and wildlife, 191–193, 197, 202,
    204. See also Chemicals; Dichlor-
    odiphenyltrichlorethane
Pew Oceans Commission, 36, 118
Plankton, 126–127
Plants, 252–263; management of;
    257–260; as weeds, 256–258, 262

Predation, 31-32, 84-86, 88, 105, 106,
    115n44
Presbyterianism, 11, 233
President's Science Advisory Committee,
    22, 199

Quammen, David, 31

Rachel Carson National Wildlife Refuge,
    24, 262
Rampton, Sheldon, 171
Regan, Tom, 105
Reuther, Rosemary Radford, 105
Riley, Gordon, 127
Risk, 209-210, 221
Rodell, Marie, 124, 137
Rolston, Holmes, III, 105
Rossiter, Margaret, 169-170
Ruckelshaus, William D., 200
Russell, Edmund, 144

Safina, Carl, 118
Sale, Kirkpatrick, 109
Salmon, 44-46
Sartwell, Crispin, 269
Schweitzer, Albert, 5, 10, 54, 65, 169, 171,
    203, 232-246
Science, 43-54, 71, 91, 124, 141, 143,
    150-154, 169-170, 181, 182, 239; femi-
    nist critiques of, 169-171, 181-182 (see
    also Ecofeminism); and religion,
    149-162, 233-237, 239-240; and senti-
    ment/emotion, 150-151, 153, 157,
    159-160, 173-178, 235-237, 279; spe-
    cialization of, 142-143; and wonder, 141,
    235-237, 242-243, 272, 276
Scott, Ruth, 260
Sea Around Us, The (Carson), 1, 6, 20, 30,
    33, 69-70, 81, 108, 118-129, 154, 156,
    240, 246, 254, 255-256; omitted chap-
    ter of, 119, 127
Sea ethics, 6, 7, 30, 79-92, 96, 100-110,
    118-119, 124-125; compared with land
    ethic, 84-89, 110-111; and otherness,
    104-109, 118

Sense of Wonder, The (Carson), 1, 244-246,
    253, 268, 269-271. See also "Help Your
    Child to Wonder" (Carson)
Shepard, Paul, 62
Shrader-Frechette, Kristin, 48-49
Sideris, Lisa, 105
Silent Spring (Carson), 1, 2, 5, 7, 9, 17, 18,
    21, 33, 36, 43, 54, 137-145, 168-182,
    190, 194-210, 220, 221-223, 241-242,
    244, 256-260, 261, 268-269; and emo-
    tionalism, 70, 149, 171-176; and envi-
    ronmental ethics, 60-67, 72-73, 94-96;
    "Fable for Tomorrow," 179, 181, 197,
    203, 253, 256
Singer, Peter, 105
Skinker, Mary Scott, 253
Smith, Mick, 109, 111
Smith, Walton, 126
Snake River, 44-46
Spirituality, 10-11, 26, 65-66, 70,
    149-162, 232-246
Sports Illustrated, 176-177
Sputnik, 145, 241
St. Nicholas Magazine, 19, 238-239
Stare, Frederick, 173
Stauber, John, 171
Steelhead, 44-46
Steingraber, Sandra, 138, 261-262
Stratton-Porter, Gene, 238-239, 243, 244

Taylor, Paul, 85, 105, 106
Teale, Edwin Way, 121-122
Time Magazine, 21, 175, 196
Tomlinson, Henry, 120
Topfer, Klaus, 200
Tuan, Yi-Fu, 109

Uncle Tom's Cabin, 22, 168
Under the Sea-Wind (Carson), 1, 20, 30,
    68-69, 81, 82-92, 101-102, 107, 108,
    154-156, 216
"Undersea" (Carson), 120
U.S. Department of Agriculture (USDA),
    196, 197

U.S. Fish and Wildlife Service, 17, 19, 60, 70, 73, 120, 125, 153, 170, 196–197, 240

Vogt, William, 126

Walker, Alice, 252, 260–261
Wallace, George J., 41, 42–44, 54
War, 17, 118, 120, 121–122, 155, 196, 206, 221; and nature, 66–67, 137–138, 144–145, 173–174, 179–180, 204. See also Cold War

White, E. B., 239
White sharks, 31–32
White-Stevens, Robert, 21, 177
Williamson, Henry, 120
Wonder, 11, 12, 120, 157, 159, 236, 237, 241, 243, 244–245, 268–278; and ethics, 273–278; and natural beauty, 252, 258–259, 270–271
World Health Organization (WHO), 201

Ziedler, Othman, 195
Zwinger, Ann, 33